THE ILLUSION OF NEUTRALITY

THE ILLUSION OF NEUTRALITY

Robert A. Divine

THE UNIVERSITY OF CHICAGO PRESS

Library of Congress Catalog Card Number: 62-10993

THE UNIVERSITY OF CHICAGO PRESS, CHICAGO & LONDON
The University of Toronto Press, Toronto 5, Canada

Published 1962. Composed and printed by THE UNIVERSITY OF CHICAGO PRESS, *Chicago, Illinois, U.S.A.*

To Doug, Lisa, and Rick

PREFACE

In historical writing on the 1930's, the New Deal has acted as a magnet, attracting the eye of the historian and blinding him to the other vital events and trends of this period. The tragedy and suffering of the depression, which challenged the traditional American dream of the onward rush of the nation toward perpetual abundance, and the multi-sided efforts of the administration of Franklin D. Roosevelt to overcome the economic decline and reinvigorate American society, provide the outline of a great saga. Intent on telling this story, writers have relegated the area of foreign policy to a secondary position. Only when the world crisis brought on by Japan and Nazi Germany began to reach a climax toward the end of the decade, did historians shift their attention to the international realm. Yet throughout the 1930's, vital developments were taking place in American foreign policy. At the very height of the New Deal in 1935, Congress began passing neutrality legislation designed to keep the United States out of future wars. This quest for neutrality, which had its origins in the previous decade, gradually became the touchstone of American foreign policy in the 1930's. Long before the Second World War broke out in Europe, the American people and their leaders engaged in an intense national debate over the role the United States would play in that conflict.

The neutrality legislation marks the high tide of American isolationism in the twentieth century. In the 1920's, despite the Senate rejection of the League of Nations, the United States played an active role on the world scene. Though the nation refused to commit itself to the defense of the Versailles settlement, Americans did not retreat from the world. Businessmen actively engaged in international economic life, extending their markets into new areas and investing capital throughout the world, and American diplomats participated in the major international conferences of the decade. Both the Washington Conference and the Kellogg-Briand Pact resulted from American initiative, and they stand as testimony to the continuing, though cautious, activity of the United States in the world arena. But with the advent of the depression, a new mood gripped the nation. The economic catastrophe gave a powerful impetus to isolationist tendencies. The breakdown of world trade and the intense concern with domestic recovery turned the eyes of the American people inward. Then the rapid deterioration of world peace, beginning with the Japanese thrust into Manchuria and spreading to Europe with the rise of Hitler, intensified the isolationist mood. As the people realized the increasing likelihood of war in Europe and Asia, they responded by demanding American immunity from the disease of war. Frightened by the complex forces threatening the peace of the world, Americans sought to escape them by taking refuge in ironclad neutrality.

My purpose is to trace the history of the neutrality legislation of the 1930's. In pursuing this theme, I have delved back into the 1920's to examine the origins of the legislation, and I have carried the narrative down to the fall of 1939, when the legislation underwent major revision. Though the neutrality act continued in remnant form until the United States entered the war in 1941, I have not dealt with this phase, which properly is part of the story of American entry into World War II. My focus is on the debate between isolationists and internationalists on how best to prevent American involvement in a future conflict prior to the beginning of hostilities. I have used the term "internationalists" for want of a better antithesis to isolationists, and by it I mean those individuals who believed that national security depended on American cooperation with other nations to preserve a stable world order.

It is my hope that this study will restore a better sense of balance to the history of the United States in the 1930's. The New Deal was the major focus of national energy in the depression decade, but that fact should not obscure the vital significance of developments in American foreign policy prior to the coming of the Second World War. In the neutrality legislation, the American people attempted to escape from the reality of the world scene. The failure of this retreat had a significant bearing on the subsequent reorientation of American diplomacy. Today the neutrality legislation stands as a monument on the path from isolation to active participation in world affairs.

In the writing of this book, I have incurred many debts. I wish to thank Buford Rowland and Watson Caudill of the National Archives, Herman Kahn and his courteous assistants at the Franklin D. Roosevelt Library, E. Taylor Parks of the Historical Division of the Department of State, and the gracious staff of the Houghton Library at Harvard University. I am especially indebted to Lilla Lévitt for permission to use the diary of her late husband, J. Pierrepont Moffat. I deeply appreciate the co-operation of the overburdened personnel at the library of the University of Texas, where I conducted the bulk of my research.

Joseph C. Green read the entire manuscript and shared with me his remarkable memory of many of the events which I have treated. I am grateful for his many helpful suggestions. Two fellow historians, David D. Van Tassel and George F. Scheer, lent me their support and advice, and I am deeply indebted to them. My wife, Barbara Renick Divine, contributed sustaining interest, constant encouragement, and thoughtful criticism which made this book in many ways a joint enterprise.

Financial assistance from the American Philosophical Society and the Research Institute of the University of Texas made it possible for me to complete this work.

CONTENTS

CHAPTER ONE

THE NEW NEUTRALITY

War between nations was renounced by the signatories of the Briand-Kellogg Pact. This means that it has become illegal throughout practically the entire world.

HENRY L. STIMSON, August, 1932

"Neutrality is no longer feasible or desirable where the peace of the world is involved," declared Woodrow Wilson in his war message on April 2, 1917.[1] With this statement Wilson hoped to reverse one of the oldest traditions of American foreign policy. Since 1793, when President George Washington had inaugurated a policy of neutrality toward the wars of the French Revolution, the United States had tried to avoid entanglement in European conflicts, while profiting from expanded trade with belligerents. The contradiction in this policy, combining as it did economic participation with political aloofness, had led to a breakdown of neutrality and eventual American involvement in major European wars in 1812 and 1917. Wilson, having failed in his effort to defend neutrality from 1914 to 1917, put forward the new concept of collective security. In the future that Wilson envisioned, the nations of the world would band together to settle all disputes by peaceful means. If any nation resorted to armed attack, the United States

[1] Ray Stannard Baker and William E. Dodd (eds.), *The Public Papers of Woodrow Wilson* (6 vols.; New York, 1925–27), VI, 381.

could not remain neutral—it would be obligated to join with other countries to halt the aggression.

At Versailles, Wilson saw the fulfillment of his hopes in the Covenant of the League of Nations. Article X contained a mutual guaranty for the territorial integrity and political independence of League members, while Article XVI provided for economic and military sanctions against any nation violating this pledge. These provisions denied the possibility of neutrality for members of the League. In the future, the nations of the world would judge all wars and participate against the aggressive country.

When the Treaty of Versailles reached the Senate, the opponents of collective security concentrated their attack on Article X. The "irreconcilables," led by Senator William E. Borah of Idaho, ridiculed the concept of maintaining peace by force, claiming that the League Covenant would mean endless war in defense of the status quo. The reservationists, ranging from intense nationalists such as Henry Cabot Lodge to mild internationalists like Elihu Root, objected to the rigid commitment of Article X. They demanded freedom of action for the United States, advocating a series of reservations including one that would allow Congress to decide whether the United States would join in collective measures against aggressors. This position implied that if Congress disagreed with the League Council in judging the outbreak of hostilities, America would remain neutral. Wilson, determined to commit the United States to the policy of unconditional collective security, refused to accept the reservation on Article X and the treaty was defeated. Though a complex combination of conflicting ideas, emotions, and personalities was involved in this American rejection of the League of Nations, the Senate vote signified the denial of Wilson's effort to revise the traditional neutrality of the United States.

The American refusal to enter the League greatly hampered efforts at collective security in the 1920's. The member nations realized the great difficulties that would arise if they attempted to employ the weapon of economic sanctions against an aggressor and America refused to co-operate. The United States, by asserting its traditional neutral rights, could furnish the outlawed country with the supplies and trade denied by the League members. The British, whose naval strength would make them the prime enforcers of any League blockade, were aware that sanctions might lead to a dangerous clash with the United States. In 1925, David Mitrany, an English writer, suggested that the United States should pledge itself not to interfere with any League efforts to enforce peace by economic measures. Mitrany urged this be done by a presidential message to Congress to the effect that any Americans trading with a nation judged an aggressor by the League did so at their own risk. Two years later, Wickham Steed, a well-known British editor, made a similar suggestion, asking that the United States assure the world it would "never weaken the hands of other nations which may band themselves together for the purpose of deterring an aggressor."[2]

Though the American government ignored these British proposals, there was a small but influential group of men in the United States who worked unceasingly for American co-operation with the League of Nations. James T. Shotwell, a professor of history at Columbia University, was one of the most active of the League supporters. In 1923, he formed a small study group composed of scholars and former diplomats including General Tasker Bliss, one of the five American delegates to the Versailles conference, and David Hunter Miller, who had done much of the actual drafting of the League Covenant. In 1924, this group drew up a Draft Treaty of Disarmament and Security which they presented to the League of Nations at Geneva. This plan provided for the outlawing of aggressive war and for gradual disarmament. To prevent acts of aggression, the Shotwell group suggested a form of negative sanctions—the aggressor would be denied any protection for his property under international law and any nation could enforce whatever economic sanctions it chose to employ. This scheme, designed to appeal to American opinion by allowing the

[2] David Mitrany, *The Problem of International Sanctions* (London, 1925), pp. 75–88; H. Wickham Steed, "A Proposal for an American Doctrine of World Peace," *Current History*, XXVII (December, 1927), 347–49.

United States to co-operate against aggression yet retain complete freedom of action, was rejected. Instead the League Council adopted the Geneva Protocol, which called for ironclad co-operation on sanctions, only to have it turned down by the League members themselves.[3]

While advocates of collective security met with frustration in the 1920's, other Americans worked for world peace through disarmament. Many of the peace societies in the United States, either hostile to the League or despairing of American entry into it, saw the fundamental cause of war in the large armies and navies of the major powers. When the United States took the lead in naval limitation at the Washington Conference by negotiating the Five-Power Treaty, pacifist groups hailed it as a great step forward. Efforts at land disarmament were less successful, and it was not until the 1930's that a general disarmament conference began its meetings at Geneva. Meanwhile, there was a movement under way to limit the traffic in arms between nations. In 1919 the United States had joined with the Allies in signing the Saint-Germain Treaty, which restricted the export of arms to those countries signing the treaty. However, the Harding administration, claiming that the pact operated unfairly against countries which were not signatories, refused to accept the agreement. The League of Nations continued to work on the problem, and in 1925 it held the International Conference for the Supervision of the International Trade in Arms and Munitions at Geneva. The United States sent two delegates, Representative Theodore E. Burton of Ohio and Hugh S. Gibson, the American minister to Switzerland. At the conference, the American delegates, objecting to any control over the manufacture of armaments, finally agreed to a treaty which provided for a system of licensing the export of arms and munitions to foreign governments. This Geneva convention did not place any restrictions on the arms trade, but was designed merely to publicize munitions shipments. Each government was to issue quarterly reports on all arms exported, but even this provision ap-

[3] James T. Shotwell, *On the Rim of the Abyss* (New York, 1936), pp. 14–19.

plied only in time of peace. The Senate Foreign Relations Committee held a hearing on the Geneva Convention in 1926, but there was little enthusiasm for even this very mild form of supervision in the United States and the Senate took no action on it until the 1930's.[4]

With the failure of efforts at collective security and disarmament, Americans turned to a third approach to peace in the 1920's —the idea of renouncing war. In 1921, Salmon O. Levinson, a Chicago lawyer, formed the American Committee for the Outlawry of War and began an intensive propaganda campaign to have war declared illegal under international law. Levinson's efforts created a strong sentiment in favor of outlawing war, but he failed to achieve any immediate action. Then in March, 1927, James T. Shotwell, in Europe as a visiting lecturer, arranged an interview with Aristide Briand, the French Foreign Minister. During the conversation, Shotwell suggested that Briand invite the United States to sign a treaty renouncing war as an instrument of national policy. Briand quickly agreed, and on April 6 he made this proposal in the form of an open letter to the American people. In the United States, the peace societies played up Briand's invitation, putting heavy pressure on the State Department to enter into a treaty.[5]

Secretary of State Frank B. Kellogg reacted strongly against the proposed antiwar treaty. He realized that Briand's motive was to strengthen French security. France had recently signed a series of security treaties with the smaller powers of Europe, and Briand was hoping to involve the United States indirectly in the French treaty structure by the antiwar pact. Faced with mounting pressure at home, Kellogg decided to outmaneuver Briand by suggesting that the treaty renouncing war be open to all the countries in the world that wished to sign it. Briand was neatly trapped, and in

[4] Benjamin H. Williams, *American Diplomacy* (New York, 1936), pp. 374–79; "Supervision of International Trade in Arms," *Hearings before the Senate Committee on Foreign Relations*, 69th Cong., 1st sess. (Washington, 1934), pp. 3–4.

[5] Robert H. Ferrell, *Peace in Their Time* (New Haven, 1952), pp. 67–70.

1928 negotiations got under way that culminated in the signing of the Kellogg-Briand Pact in Paris on August 27. Fourteen nations agreed to renounce war as an instrument of national policy and to settle all disputes by peaceful means. Eventually nearly all the countries in the world signed the treaty.

When Secretary Kellogg returned from Paris to secure ratification of the treaty, he met with little difficulty. Senator Borah, now chairman of the Senate Foreign Relations Committee, was a supporter of the outlawry movement and his advocacy of the treaty virtually assured Senate approval. The Foreign Relations Committee held brief hearings during which the senators questioned Kellogg on the significance of the treaty. After the Secretary assured the committee that it contained no sanctions or commitments for enforcement, the treaty was reported to the Senate, which approved it with only one dissenting vote.[6]

The Kellogg-Briand Pact, hailed by contemporaries as the beginning of a new era of peace, was scarcely more than an empty gesture. Without any provisions for enforcement, it contributed little to the stability of the world in the 1920's. Yet it opened up new possibilities of American co-operation for collective security and the Wilsonian dream of ending neutrality. Though there was nothing committing the United States to take action against any nation resorting to war, the pact did create a moral obligation not to aid an aggressor. In the future, if a nation violated the treaty, American opinion would be against trading with the belligerent that began hostilities and would favor some measure of co-operation toward League efforts to embargo the violator. Realistic supporters of collective security, aware of the limitations of the Kellogg-Briand Pact, nevertheless saw it as a constructive step and they began to consider ways in which the treaty could be made meaningful. Out of their efforts came the seeds of the neutrality legislation of the 1930's.

[6] "The General Pact for the Renunciation of War," *Hearings before the Senate Committee on Foreign Relations*, 70th Cong., 2d sess. (Washington, 1928), pp. 3–4, 14.

I

On November 18, 1927, Representative Theodore E. Burton, chairman of the American delegation to the 1925 Geneva conference on the arms trade and president of the American Peace Society, announced that he intended to introduce a resolution in Congress to embargo the export of arms to aggressor nations. In the resolution, which he introduced on December 5, Burton defined an aggressor as a nation which resorted to war in violation of a treaty pledging it to settle disputes by peaceful means. "It is perfectly clear," Burton stated, "that any nation violating such a pledge or treaty is guilty of an offense against the family of nations. There would be hesitancy in waging war if the United States, with the facilities for furnishing arms and munitions, should establish a policy of refusal to aid an aggressor nation."[7] Thus, nine months before the signing of the Kellogg-Briand Pact, a movement was under way to alter the traditional neutrality of the United States toward foreign wars.

The Burton resolution projected a radical change in the historic policy of the United States. Since the 1790's, American neutrality had been based on impartiality—treating all belligerents on an equal, non-discriminatory basis. Moreover, the nation had traditionally defended the right of its citizens to engage in trade in contraband materials with nations at war. Thomas Jefferson had asserted this right in 1793 when the British protested against the shipment of arms to France by American citizens, and the principle had gone unchallenged until World War I. In 1915, some sentiment developed in Congress to embargo arms shipments to belligerents, but both Secretary of State William Jennings Bryan and his successor, Robert Lansing, had upheld the right of Americans to trade in arms. The only exceptions dealt with civil wars in certain areas of the world. In 1912 Congress had authorized President Taft to embargo arms to Latin American countries where "conditions of domestic violence" existed. Ten years later Congress amended this law to allow embargoes on civil disturbances

[7] *New York Times*, November 19, 1927, p. 2.

in countries where the United States exercised extraterritorial jurisdiction, primarily China.[8] The Burton resolution, involving the broad issue of trade in arms in general wars, far transcended these limited regional embargoes.

Peace societies quickly supported Burton's proposal. The League of Nations Non-Partisan Association adopted a resolution, sponsored by Professor Shotwell, urging the immediate passage of the arms embargo. The National Conference on the Cause and Cure of War, representing eleven national women's groups, also endorsed the Burton resolution. In January, 1928, an avalanche of letters, petitions, and memorials from local chapters of women's societies and peace groups descended on the House Foreign Affairs Committee. A typical letter, from the American Friends Service Committee, praised the arms embargo proposal as a "great deterrent to war."[9] But in official quarters there was a noticeable lack of enthusiasm. In a press conference on November 25, 1927, President Coolidge pointed out the difficulty in determining when a nation had committed an act of aggression.[10] Members of the House Foreign Affairs Committee shared this doubt, and finally, to overcome the objections, Burton revised his resolution to make the arms embargo apply impartially toward all belligerents upon the outbreak of war. A last vestige of his original proposal remained in a clause reserving to Congress the right to make exceptions in the blanket embargo.[11]

On January 30, 1928, the Foreign Affairs Committee unanimously reported out the revised arms embargo resolution. Representative Burton, author of the committee report, described the

[8] Elton Atwater, *American Regulation of Arms Exports* (Washington, 1941), pp. 23–25, 51, 126; Williams, *American Diplomacy*, pp. 382–86.

[9] *New York Times*, January 4, 1928, p. 29; *Report of the Third Conference on the Cause and Cure of War* (Washington, 1928), p. 225; House Foreign Affairs Committee Papers, 70th Cong., 1st sess., File 70A-D9, National Archives, Record Group 233. Hereafter cited as "HCP."

[10] *New York Times*, November 26, 1927, p. 2.

[11] *Congressional Record*, January 25, 1928, p. 2045; Joseph P. Chamberlain, "The Embargo Resolutions and Neutrality," *International Conciliation*, No. 251 (June, 1929), p. 333.

measure as "a notably advanced step for the prevention of war and the promotion of universal peace." Yet actually Burton had retreated from his far more radical position of November. In explaining the purpose of the bill, he made no mention of any intent to curb aggression, stressing instead the way in which the resolution would prevent American munitions manufacturers from gaining profits from foreign wars.[12]

The original purpose of the Burton resolution—to align the United States against aggressor nations—now became obscured as the impartial arms embargo threatened the interests of American munitions makers. In Washington, Colonel Aiken Simons, representative of the Du Pont Company, called on members of the War Department in late January to point out the dangers of an arms embargo. His arguments evidently impressed army officials. A few weeks later the head of the army's chemical warfare section was describing the Burton resolution as "exceedingly bad" in a letter to the Du Pont Company. Irénée du Pont noted on this letter, "It seems to me that this is a very grave question, and the passage of the resolution should be opposed and defeated."[13] Colonel Simons continued to work quietly to secure this objective. On February 22 he wrote to a representative of the arms manufacturing industry suggesting that appeals be made to Secretary of Commerce Herbert Hoover "requesting protection for American industry." H. F. Beebe, sales manager for Winchester Arms, agreed with Simons on the need for joint efforts. On March 5, Beebe wrote to Secretary Hoover, pointing out the adverse effect the Burton resolution would have on the munitions industry and asking the Department of Commerce to hold a special conference of arms manufacturers. A few days later one of Hoover's assistants politely rejected this suggestion.[14] But Simons was not discour-

[12] "To Prohibit the Exportation of Arms, Munitions, or Implements of War to Belligerent Nations," *House Report No. 492*, 70th Cong., 1st sess. (Washington, 1928), pp. 1–3.

[13] "Investigation of the Munitions Industry," *Hearings before the Special Senate Committee Investigating the Munitions Industry*, 73d and 74th Cong. (Washington, 1934–36), Part 12, pp. 2726, 2729–30.

[14] *Ibid.*, pp. 2732–37.

aged. On March 15 he told Beebe that there was little to worry about because the War, Navy, Commerce, and State Departments were against the arms embargo resolution. "Since the four most powerful departments are opposed to the bill," he concluded, "I believe we can rest our case."[15]

The American Legion joined the munitions industry in lobbying against the Burton resolution. On March 3 the Legion's legislative committee requested local posts to begin applying pressure on their congressmen against the arms embargo. The next day telegrams from local Legion posts began to arrive in Congress.[16] The Legion's national defense committee discussed the Burton resolution on March 10 and finally decided it was "inimical to the public interest." Colonel John Thomas Taylor, chief lobbyist for the veterans group, then sent letters to every member of Congress pointing out the Legion's opposition to the arms embargo and urging its defeat.[17] This pressure had immediate results. Members of the House Military and Naval Affairs Committees asked the Foreign Affairs Committee to hold public hearings on the Burton resolution. Although this was an unusual procedure, since hearings are usually held only before a committee acts on a bill, the Foreign Affairs Committee acquiesced.[18]

Opponents of the arms embargo dominated the hearings, which began on March 15 and lasted for a week.[19] The leading witnesses, Secretary of War Dwight F. Davis and Secretary of the Navy Curtis D. Wilbur, attacked the Burton resolution for weakening national defense. They were strongly supported by members of the

[15] *Ibid.*, p. 2842.

[16] "Proceedings of the Tenth National Convention of the American Legion," *House Document* No. 388, 70th Cong., 2d sess. (Washington, 1929), p. 155; HCP, File 70A-D9.

[17] "Proceedings of the American Legion," *House Document* No. 388, 70th Cong. 2d sess., pp. 155–56.

[18] *Congressional Record*, March 13, 1928, p. 4646; Albert C. F. Westphal, *The House Committee on Foreign Affairs* (New York, 1942), p. 180.

[19] "Exportation of Arms, Munitions, or Implements of War to Belligerent Nations," *Hearings before the House Committee on Foreign Affairs*, 70th Cong., 1st sess. (Washington, 1929).

Military and Naval Affairs Committees. The only industrial witness to testify was an adviser to the Chemical Foundation. The munitions industry evidently heeded the advice of Colonel Simons who warned that any testimony by arms manufacturers "would enable the pacifist and seditious elements to claim that munitions manufacturers encourage war."[20] More surprising was the failure of any of the peace societies to send spokesmen. The one-sided testimony left the case for the arms embargo to the members of the Foreign Affairs Committee, who vigorously challenged all attacks on the Burton resolution.

Secretaries Davis and Wilbur presented a forceful argument against the arms embargo. Pointing out that the United States relied on private industry for the supplies and weapons vital to national defense, they claimed that while the United States was at peace the munitions manufacturers could stay in business only through an extensive international trade. If an arms embargo were adopted, foreign governments would place their orders in other nations in order to be assured of continued trade in wartime. Thus, an embargo would weaken American security by crippling the munitions industry. In developing this argument, the secretaries cited the period from 1914 to 1917, explaining that heavy exports of munitions to the Allies helped prepare the nation for war by greatly increasing the productive capacity of the arms industry. The secretaries also questioned the international effect of an arms embargo. They claimed that such a policy favored the aggressive nation that prepared for war and penalized the peaceful country unready for sudden attack.[21]

In countering these arguments, members of the committee revealed that their primary concern was to restrict the activities and profits of the munitions industry. Labeling the arms-makers "merchants of death," the advocates of the Burton resolution claimed it was "morally, fundamentally wrong" to furnish war supplies to

20 "Investigation of the Munitions Industry," Special Senate *Hearings*, 73d and 74th Cong., Part 12, p. 2842.

21 "Exportation of Arms," House *Hearings*, 70th Cong., 1st sess., pp. 7–17, 43–8.

belligerents. "There are men in America today," claimed Representative Henry Cooper of Wisconsin, "who would deliberately sacrifice lives if it would tend to gorge their respective pocketbooks."[22] Others took a less emotional position, asserting that limitation of the arms trade would tend to prevent war by denying belligerents the weapons of destruction. Representative R. Walton Moore of Virginia praised the Burton resolution as "the very first legislation that has been proposed since the armistice in the direction of trying to reduce the possibility and horrors of war."[23] Representative Hamilton Fish of New York offered a quite different defense of the arms embargo by asserting that it would keep the United States out of foreign wars. Charging that the export of arms to the Allies was the principal cause of American entry into World War I, Fish proclaimed, "... this resolution has a tendency to stop us from being dragged into every foreign war by shipping munitions." Other members of the committee immediately attacked this argument, and Fish seems to have been alone at this time in viewing the arms embargo as a means of isolating the United States from foreign wars.[24]

During the hearings, there was considerable discussion of the attitude of the State Department. Secretary of the Navy Wilbur claimed that when the arms embargo was discussed in a cabinet meeting, Secretary of State Kellogg opposed it.[25] The chairman of the House Foreign Affairs Committee then wrote Kellogg requesting his views on the Burton resolution and the Secretary sent a noncommittal answer, merely noting that as long as the embargo applied impartially to all belligerents, it "would not violate the obligations of neutrality." He warned that if Congress acted to lift the embargo after war began, it would have to do so for all belligerents.[26] Thus Kellogg did not oppose the impartial arms embargo reported by the committee, but he did reveal his opposition to Burton's original proposal for discrimination against aggressors.

[22] *Ibid.*, pp. 5–6, 17, 132.

[23] *Ibid.*, pp. 42, 132.

[24] *Ibid.*, pp. 12, 68, 96–97.

[25] *Ibid.*, pp. 116–17.

[26] *Ibid.*, pp. 78–79.

When the hearings closed, the Burton resolution died a quiet death. It remained on the House calendar, but it was never brought up for passage. The strong opposition from the military and naval leaders, together with the effective lobbying by the munitions industry and the American Legion, created insurmountable obstacles. Yet the abortive resolution began a debate that would smolder on until it flared up into a major issue in the 1930's. Most of all, the Burton resolution revealed in embryo form the major ideas that would influence the future fight on neutrality—the concept of embargoes on aggressors, the emotional bias against munitions manufacturers, and the isolationist belief that the shipment of arms entangled the United States in European wars.

II

On February 11, 1929, Senator Arthur Capper of Kansas dramatically reopened the debate on American neutrality when he introduced a new resolution in Congress. Coming four weeks after the Senate had approved the Kellogg-Briand Pact, the Capper resolution proposed that whenever the President determined that a nation violated the antiwar treaty, he would be authorized to embargo the export of "arms, munitions, implements of war, or other articles for use in war" to the aggressor country. In addition, the resolution stated that the American government would not protect the trade of its citizens with a violator of the Kellogg pact.[27] In a public statement explaining the purpose of this proposal, Capper declared, "I believe the adoption and effectuation of this resolution will tend to make the peace pact effective. It will in a measure underwrite the peace pact without compelling us to police the world." Capper added that he did not expect the adoption of his resolution during the current session of Congress, but rather he hoped to provoke discussion that would lead to action in the future.[28]

If widespread publicity was Capper's objective, he was quickly

[27] *New York Times,* February 11, 1929, p. 1.

[28] *Ibid.,* p. 2.

rewarded, and perhaps embarrassed, by the vigorous support he received from League advocates in the United States and Europe. The French Foreign Office enthusiastically praised his proposal as "a logical step" to complete the Kellogg-Briand Pact. In Geneva, according to the *New York Times,* officials of the League of Nations welcomed the Capper plan "with as much joy as scientists would have at the discovery of 'the missing link.' "[29] Prominent Americans, ranging from Governor Franklin D. Roosevelt of New York to President James Angell of Yale University, endorsed the proposal in public statements, while Professor Shotwell wrote, ". . . the Capper Resolution constitutes a new step in advance, for, as the Kellogg-Briand Treaty renounces war as an instrument of national policy, the Capper Resolution proposed to renounce neutrality. . . ."[30] Congressman Franklin F. Korrell of Oregon, author of a similar resolution in the House, agreed with Shotwell's analysis, stating, "Neutrality is inconsistent with the covenants of the treaty."[31]

Newspaper and periodical opinion was less enthusiastic. Though a few leading papers, including the *New York Times,* praised the Capper resolution, most of the nation's editors warned against possible entanglements in League affairs. Many newspapers, while affirming the need to strengthen the Kellogg-Briand Pact, warned that the Capper plan would give the President a dangerous power in determining when a nation had violated the antiwar treaty.[32] The editors of the *Nation* suggested that an international conference should decide when an act of aggression took place; *Commonweal* preferred to see this power vested in Congress.[33] A few news-

[29] *Ibid.,* pp. 1, 2.

[30] *Ibid.,* p. 1; James T. Shotwell, "Neutrality and National Policy," *Outlook,* CLI (April 17, 1929), 620.

[31] *Congressional Record,* February 22, 1929, p. 4009. Korrell's resolution provided for an arms embargo, but it did not include Capper's plan for suspension of governmental protection for trade with aggressors.

[32] *New York Times,* February 12, 1929, p. 21; "To Keep Guns from Warring Nations," *Literary Digest,* C (February 23, 1929), 10–11.

[33] "Teeth for the Kellogg Treaty," *Nation,* CXXVIII (February 27, 1929), 246; "Teeth in the Kellogg Pact," *Commonweal,* IX (February 27, 1929), 474–75.

papers voiced a deeper fear. "The Capper idea rejects the non-coercive principle of the Kellogg pact," the *Philadelphia Bulletin* charged, "and returns to the old thought of punitive sanctions. It implies entanglements and involvements against which the American people have decided."[34]

The wide discussion of the Capper resolution by the nation's press found little response in Congress. Most congressmen avoided comment on the proposal and those who did speak out were hostile. Senator Borah announced his opposition as soon as the resolution was made public, stating that the Kellogg-Briand Pact required no sanctions. Senator Walter E. Edge of New Jersey was more blunt. "The Capper resolution," he declared, "strikes me as a proposal that would quite likely put the United States into war while trying to avert it."[35] Members of the House, with the exception of Korrell and, surprisingly, Hamilton Fish, who introduced a resolution identical to Capper's, were equally opposed. "The Capper resolution is a dangerous suggestion," asserted Representative Melvin J. Maas of Minnesota. "It would make the multilateral treaty an instrument for war rather than for peace."[36]

The reactions to the Capper resolution revealed quite clearly the continuing hostility of the American people to measures of collective security. Capper had offered a negative sanction for the Kellogg-Briand Pact—one that did not involve any military action by the United States but only the withholding of American arms and trade from an aggressor. Yet even this mild form of co-operation for peace pleased only the small minority of internationalists in the nation. The overwhelming majority of Americans so deeply distrusted the League of Nations and the concept of collective security that they rejected any suggestion for effective co-operation against aggressors.

The controversy over the Capper plan tended to obscure another

[34] *Literary Digest*, C, 11.

[35] *New York Times*, February 12, 1929, p. 21; *ibid.*, February 13, 1929, p. 4.

[36] *Ibid.*, February 12, 1929, p. 21. In introducing his resolution Fish indicated his purpose was not to make the Kellogg pact more effective, but rather to place a curb on the munitions industry.

arms embargo resolution which had a very different purpose. On February 11, 1929, Representative Stephen Porter, chairman of the House Foreign Affairs Committee, put forward a resolution empowering the President to embargo arms to any country in the world where "conditions of domestic violence or of international conflict exist or are threatened."[37] This resolution, which in effect made universal the 1922 arms embargo powers for Latin America and China, reflected a desire to curb the munitions trade rather than halt aggression. In a press release, Porter stated, "This resolution is intended to put the control of the munitions traffic in the hands of the President, who is fully informed as to conditions in foreign countries and can exercise this power with all the facts before him. . . ."[38] Yet the resolution gave the President such wide discretionary power that he would be able to use it to embargo aggressors in case of war, or even before war actually developed.

The House Foreign Affairs Committee held a brief hearing on the Porter resolution at which Secretary of State Kellogg was the only witness. Despite the fact that Porter had previously announced Kellogg's endorsement of his resolution, the Secretary was very noncommittal. When asked directly if he approved the Porter resolution, Kellogg said, "I see no objection to it. The question of policy is for Congress."[39] In discussing the effect of an arms embargo on preventing war, Kellogg maintained that unilateral action by the United States would be ineffective unless all the other arms-producing nations adopted a similar policy. Kellogg's most forceful statement dealt with the question of applying the embargo against an aggressor. "I know of no way," he said, "by which the President could place an embargo on arms to one country party to an international conflict and not apply it to the other party or parties without committing an unneutral act."[40] It was clear that Kellogg still

[37] *Ibid.*, February 12, 1929, p. 1.

[38] *Ibid.*, p. 21.

[39] "Prohibiting the Exportation of Arms or Munitions of War from the United States to Certain Countries," *Hearing before the House Committee on Foreign Affairs*, 70th Cong., 2d sess. (Washington, 1929), p. 5.

[40] *Ibid.*, p. 3.

believed in the traditional concept of neutrality and opposed any revision of American policy in the direction of collective security.

Following the hearing, the House committee, dividing evenly on the question of reporting out Porter's resolution, decided to table it. When a new Congress assembled in April, 1929, another series of arms embargo resolutions were introduced. Though Senator Capper renewed his proposal for action against violators of the Kellogg pact, the resolutions offered in the House reflected Kellogg's insistence on impartial embargoes. Representative Porter changed his resolution to make it apply to all belligerents, and Hamilton Fish, who had earlier supported the Capper plan, also sponsored an impartial arms embargo.[41] Stating that the process of determining an aggressor was "difficult and dangerous," Fish declared, "The whole theory of aggression is a mere cover for sanctions which, stripped of its holy setting, means war. Putting 'teeth' into the Kellogg pact means putting war into it."[42] Though neither Fish nor Porter was successful in getting action on his measure, their opposition to the Capper plan blocked this proposal. The conflict between advocates of partial and impartial arms embargoes, reflecting the incompatible objectives of enforcing the Kellogg pact and controlling the munitions industry, ended any chance for a reversal in neutrality policy at this time.

III

Although the Burton and Capper resolutions failed to win widespread support in Congress, they did serve to revive interest in the question of neutrality among the experts in international law. Beginning in 1929, lawyers and political scientists began to debate the role of neutrality in American foreign policy. At the annual meetings of the American Society of International Law and in the pages of scholarly journals, advocates of collective security advanced the concept that the creation of the League of Nations and the signing of the Kellogg-Briand Pact had destroyed neutrality. They

41 Chamberlain, "Embargo Resolutions," pp. 334–35, 339.

42 *New York Times*, April 15, 1929, p. 1.

were vigorously challenged by defenders of traditional neutrality, who asserted that the old policy remained unaltered by the attempts to create world organization and to outlaw war. Though this debate was confined to a small group of specialists, it produced conflicting theories that would shape the later congressional discussion of neutrality in the 1930's.

The Kellogg-Briand Pact provided the basic point of departure for the advocates of the "new neutrality." Maintaining that the antiwar treaty revolutionized international relations, they claimed that no nation signing the pact could remain indifferent when violations occurred. Senator Capper, speaking before the American Academy of Political and Social Science in 1929, charged that any country that embarked on aggressive war was "guilty of an international crime and an offense against the United States. . . . In such a case," Capper continued, "the old equality of treatment given by the eighteenth-century rule of neutrality no longer applies."[43] Specialists in international law agreed with Capper. At the annual meeting of the American Society of International Law in 1930, Quincy Wright of the University of Chicago and Clyde Eagleton of New York University delivered papers on the effect of the Kellogg pact on neutrality. Both men argued that the antiwar treaty made the concept of neutral rights obsolete. If war broke out, the United States would be obligated to follow a policy of partiality, joining with the League of Nations against the aggressor. "If we want peace, as we have said in the Pact of Paris, we must support peace when the Pact is broken," concluded Eagleton. "We must consult and co-operate with other states to that end."[44]

The "new neutrality" provoked intense controversy among the specialists in international law in the early 1930's. Many experts agreed on the desirability of American co-operation with the

[43] Arthur Capper, "Making the Peace Pact Effective," *Annals of the American Academy of Political and Social Science*, CXLIV (July, 1929), 40–48.

[44] Quincy Wright, "Neutrality and Neutral Rights Following the Pact of Paris for the Renunciation of War," *Proceedings of the American Society of International Law, 1930* (Washington, 1930), pp. 79–87; Clyde Eagleton, "Neutrality and Neutral Rights Following the Pact of Paris for the Renunciation of War," *ibid.*, pp. 87–95.

League against aggressors, but they questioned the assertion that the Kellogg pact had in fact doomed neutrality. They pointed out that under the pact defensive wars were still permitted and that in many cases it was difficult, if not impossible, to determine which nation was guilty of breaking the peace. Manley O. Hudson of Harvard, a leading advocate of international co-operation, argued that the world was in a state of transition and that until all nations fully accepted the principle of collective security, neutrality would remain a meaningful and valid policy.[45] Thus even those who sympathized with the "new neutrality" saw it as a future possibility rather than as an established rule of international law.

While the experts argued over the status of neutrality, Secretary of State Henry L. Stimson, who succeeded Kellogg when Herbert Hoover became President in 1929, gave a powerful boost to the advocates of collective security. In a speech before the Council on Foreign Relations in August, 1932, Stimson discussed the effect of the Kellogg pact on American foreign policy.[46] Warning that modern war could lead to the destruction of civilization, Stimson declared that the League of Nations and the Kellogg pact signified "a revolution in human thought." He then asserted:

> War between nations was renounced by the signatories of the Briand-Kellogg Pact. This means that it has become illegal throughout practically the entire world. It is no longer to be the source and subject of rights. It is no longer to be the principle around which the duties, the conduct, and the rights of nations revolve. It is an illegal thing. Hereafter when two nations engage in armed conflict either one or both of them must be wrongdoers—violators of the general treaty. We no longer draw a circle about them and treat them with the punctilios of the duelist's code. Instead we denounce them as lawbreakers.[47]

This was a forceful denial of traditional neutrality. However, Stimson greatly weakened the impact by stating that the only weapon

[45] *Ibid.*, pp. 95–100, 141; *Proceedings of the American Society of International Law*, 1933, pp. 171–72.

[46] Henry L. Stimson, "The Pact of Paris: Three Years of Development," *Foreign Affairs*, XI (Special Supplement, October, 1932), i–ix.

[47] *Ibid.*, p. iv.

that could be used against aggressors was the moral sanction of public opinion.[48]

Other supporters of the "new neutrality" came forward with more specific proposals for achieving their objective. In 1932 a committee on economic sanctions, appointed by the Twentieth Century Fund and headed by President Nicholas Murray Butler of Columbia University, developed a new plan to strengthen the Kellogg pact. In its report, the committee, claiming that the Kellogg treaty had killed off "old-fashioned neutrality," urged that the United States call an international conference to negotiate a treaty whereby all signatories of the antiwar pact would agree to join in economic sanctions against any nation guilty of aggression. The committee report specifically called for an automatic arms embargo on aggressors and then proposed that additional embargoes on trade be imposed by joint agreement.[49] John B. Whitton of Princeton University offered a less rigid plan. He suggested a multilateral treaty permitting nations to take whatever measures against aggressors they desired. Whitton argued that his proposal would in effect abolish neutrality without compelling nations to engage in a policy of sanctions.[50]

The advocates of the "new neutrality," divided as they were, formed a majority in the ranks of the experts on international law, but a stubborn and articulate minority constantly reasserted the historic concept of neutrality. These traditionalists, led by Edwin Borchard of the Yale Law School, held that neutrality was a humane and progressive idea which limited the extent of war. "Neutrality," Borchard maintained, "is a peace-preserving institution—one of the beneficent achievements of a long struggle

[48] *Ibid.*, p. v. Stimson personally favored a stronger policy, and in the original draft of his speech he advocated American co-operation with other countries in applying economic sanctions against aggressors. However, President Hoover, who censored the speech beforehand, asked Stimson to drop out all references to embargoes and economic sanctions. Richard Current, *Secretary Stimson: A Study in Statecraft* (New Brunswick, N.J., 1954), p. 108.

[49] Evans Clark (ed.), *Boycotts and Peace* (New York, 1932), pp. 3–5.

[50] John B. Whitton, "What Follows the Pact of Paris?" *International Conciliation*, No. 276 (January, 1932), pp. 5–48.

with barbarism. Its abandonment, in the name of a supposed universal 'peace,' would be likely to spell universal chaos."[51] The most effective defense came from John Bassett Moore, for many years a professor at Columbia University and generally acknowledged to be the most distinguished American authority on international law. Stressing the need to confine the spread of war, Moore denied that neutrality expressed moral indifference toward foreign conflicts. He argued that the nation could always enter a war if it felt its interests involved. "The law of neutrality merely applies the rule of common honesty," Moore contended. "Parties to an armed conflict are entitled to know who are in it and who are not."[52]

The upholders of neutrality attacked the alternative of collective security with biting scorn. They reiterated the difficulty in determining when a nation committed an act of aggression. "Our very pacific friends . . . organize embargoes against 'aggressors' whom they could pick at once," remarked Borchard, "whereas historians take decades to establish such an alleged fact and then do not agree."[53] The traditionalists were bitterly critical of economic sanctions, claiming that attempts to enforce peace could only lead to perpetual war. Throughout the debate, the defenders of neutrality linked their stand with isolationism by asserting that only an impartial attitude toward foreign wars would enable the United States to keep clear of entanglement.[54] Most of all, the traditionalists were pessimists who believed that war was inevitable and that the most an enlightened nation could do was to stand aloof through an impartial policy. Professor Moore expressed the prevailing attitude when he wrote:

[51] *Proceedings of the American Society of International Law, 1933* (Washington, 1933), pp. 160–62; Edwin Borchard, "The 'Enforcement' of Peace by 'Sanctions,'" *American Journal of International Law*, XXVII (July, 1933), 523.

[52] John Bassett Moore, "An Appeal to Reason," *Foreign Affairs*, XI (July, 1933), 563.

[53] *Proceedings of the American Society of International Law, 1933*, p. 63.

[54] *Ibid.*, pp. 61–62; Borchard, "Enforcement of Peace," p. 523.

The struggle for existence still continues and it will go on. As one long and intimately acquainted with men of arms, I may say that they do not share the new view that peace and tranquillity on earth may be promoted and stabilized by boycotts, by playing fast and loose with the laws of neutrality, and by the extension of the area of wars.[55]

The debate over neutrality, engendered by the Kellogg-Briand Pact and the Burton and Capper resolutions, led to no specific conclusions or results. Like most academic controversies, it revealed only a theoretical dispute between groups far removed from positions of power or responsibility. If most of the experts in international law were sympathetic to the "new neutrality," this was hardly significant in terms of American foreign policy, for the majority of the American people remained firm in their opposition to any action on the part of the United States that tended to align the country with the League of Nations. But the debate was significant in that it marked the beginning of an interest in neutrality that would soon spread beyond the confines of academic and legislative circles and reach the center of national concern as the peace of the world began to disintegrate in the 1930's. The final irony would come when the nation began to demand a form of neutrality radically different from that advocated by either the traditionalists or the supporters of collective security.

[55] Moore, "Appeal to Reason," p. 587.

CHAPTER TWO

THE DEFEAT OF COLLECTIVE SECURITY, 1932–33

I regard neutrality as the greatest gift that God has put in the hands of the American people.

EDWIN BORCHARD, March 28, 1933

On the evening of September 18, 1931, Japan announced that a group of Chinese soldiers had exploded a bomb on the South Manchurian Railway a few miles north of Mukden. The Japanese army quickly began to occupy the line of the railway and then gradually spread out into the remainder of Manchuria. Though at first foreign observers believed this was only another in a series of minor skirmishes between Japan and China in Manchuria, the Mukden incident soon developed into the most serious international crisis since World War I, challenging the fragile structure of collective security embodied in the League of Nations and the Kellogg-Briand Pact.[1]

For the United States, the abstract question of American neutrality toward aggression became a real and pressing issue. President Herbert Hoover, deeply concerned about the depression which had steadily worsened since 1929, quickly made his decision —facing catastrophe at home, the nation must avoid any risk of entanglement in foreign war. But Secretary of State Stimson, a

[1] Robert H. Ferrell, *American Diplomacy in the Great Depression* (New Haven, 1957), pp. 122–24.

dedicated advocate of collective security, was equally determined to use American influence and prestige to curb Japan's aggression in Manchuria. Throughout the remainder of the Hoover administration, these two leaders disagreed on the role the United States should play in the Far Eastern crisis, and though they finally compromised on the principle of non-recognition, this moralistic formula only disguised their fundamental divergence on American policy toward aggression overseas.[2]

I

In the fall of 1931, before the extent of the Manchurian crisis became known, the United States followed a very cautious policy. Stimson, believing that moderate elements in the Japanese government could restrain the army, refrained from sending strong protests to Japan. In October, the United States did begin to cooperate with the League, dispatching Prentiss Gilbert, an American consular officer at Geneva, and later Charles G. Dawes, the ambassador to Britain, to attend meetings of the League Council. Stimson realized that economic sanctions would be the only effective action the League could undertake against Japan, and in late October he suggested to Hoover that the United States should cooperate with the League by refusing to interfere with any economic measures directed against a violator of the Kellogg pact. Though Hoover firmly denounced military and economic sanctions as "roads to war," on November 19 Stimson informed Dawes that while the United States could not participate in any embargo of Japan, "we would not probably in any way interfere through our fleet with any embargo by anybody else."[3] This suggestion of a limited surrender of traditional neutral rights evidently had little

[2] Richard Current, *Secretary Stimson: A Study in Statecraft* (New Brunswick, N.J., 1954), p. 113.

[3] Henry L. Stimson and McGeorge Bundy, *On Active Service in Peace and War* (New York, 1947), p. 233; Current, *Secretary Stimson*, pp. 80–81; *Papers Relating to the Foreign Relations of the United States: 1931* (Washington, 1946), III, 496. Hereafter cited as "*FR.*"

effect, for the League Council rejected the use of sanctions and instead created the Lytton Commission to investigate the Manchurian situation.

While the United States and the League dallied, the Japanese army continued its invasion of Manchuria, moving into Chinchow, on the border of China proper, on January 2, 1932. Stimson, infuriated by this evidence that Japan planned to occupy all Manchuria, responded on January 7 by notifying Japan that the United States refused to recognize as legal the Japanese seizure of any portion of Manchuria. This policy of non-recognition, originally suggested by Hoover in early November, sought to apply a moral sanction against Japanese aggression, but Japan calmly ignored the American caveat and continued to consolidate its position in Manchuria. On January 28, Japan went even further, moving troops into Shanghai to end a Chinese boycott. Stimson began to consider the use of economic sanctions, but again President Hoover vetoed this suggestion. Stimson finally contented himself with a restatement of the non-recognition principle in the form of an open letter to Senator Borah, chairman of the Senate Foreign Relations Committee. The Borah letter marked the culmination of Stimson's policy toward the Manchurian crisis. With Hoover consistently ruling out the possibility of an embargo, American policy was limited to the moral sanction of non-recognition.[4]

The Manchurian crisis had a deep impact on the American people. In the nineteenth century, Americans had developed a romantic view of China, visualizing it as a vast potential market for American goods, American culture, and American democracy. The Open Door policy, announced by John Hay in 1899, reinforced this feeling of a special bond between the United States and China. When the Japanese began to invade Manchuria, American sympathies lay overwhelmingly on the side of China, and though the nation was deeply preoccupied with the depression, a significant number of people criticized the weak policy the administration had adopted toward Japan. This resentment was strong in

[4] Stimson and Bundy, *On Active Service*, p. 244; Current, *Secretary Stimson*, pp. 99–100.

Congress, and it quickly led to attempts to force a bolder policy upon the State Department.

The first effort came in December, 1931, when Representative Morton Hull of Illinois introduced a resolution to embargo all trade to any nation violating the Kellogg-Briand Pact. The House Foreign Affairs Committee began considering Hull's resolution in January, and on the twenty-eighth the chairman, Representative J. Charles Linthicum of Maryland, asked Stimson for his opinion of the proposal, stating that he felt it was "essential." On February 2, Stimson replied that he considered the Hull resolution inadvisable. "I am sure," he stated, "you will understand, for example, the unfortunate elements that might be introduced into an already delicate international situation by a debate in Congress on such a matter at this time."[5] Representative Hull then withdrew his resolution, but in March he introduced a bill to forbid loans to a nation guilty of aggression, pointing out that such a measure would enable the United States to bring powerful financial pressure to bear on Japan. While Stimson did not oppose this resolution, no action was taken by the House committee.[6] A final attempt at a discriminatory embargo came in the Senate in April when Senator Capper again introduced his proposal for a ban on the export of munitions to a violator of the Kellogg pact, only to have it die in committee.[7]

While sympathizers with China failed in their efforts to enact an embargo against Japan, another group in Congress saw the Manchurian crisis as an opportunity to curb the munitions trade. In December, 1931, Representative Hamilton Fish again introduced his resolution to embargo arms to all belligerents in time of war, and the following month Senator Clarence C. Dill of Washington sponsored a bill to ban the export of munitions to both

[5] Linthicum to Stimson, January 28, 1932, 811.113/153, State Department Files, National Archives, Record Group 59; Stimson to Linthicum, February 2, 1932, 811.113/153. Hereafter all citations followed by file numbers refer to the State Department files.

[6] *Congressional Record,* March 9, 1932, p. 5587; Stimson to Linthicum, March 17, 1932, HCP, File 72A-D8.

[7] *Congressional Record,* April 21, 1932, pp. 8560–61.

China and Japan. Arguing that the United States should not become "the slaughterhouse of the world" by furnishing "fuel for the flames of war," both men bitterly denounced the munitions industry.[8] On February 3 the Senate Foreign Relations Committee discussed Dill's resolution and finally rejected it on the grounds that it would hurt China, which imported its munitions, far more than Japan, which possessed its own arms industry. Fish's resolution, however, met with strong approval in the House Foreign Affairs Committee, and it quickly became an embarrassing issue for the State Department.[9]

In late January, Chairman Linthicum asked Stimson for his views on the Fish resolution. In his reply, the Secretary indicated he had no serious objections to it, but suggested that it be redrafted in the form of an amendment to the 1922 law authorizing the President to embargo arms to Latin America and China.[10] Fish immediately changed the resolution to satisfy Stimson, and the House Foreign Affairs Committee scheduled a hearing on the measure for February 9, inviting the Secretary of State to testify.[11] Stimson, deeply concerned about the Japanese attack on Shanghai, began to doubt the wisdom of any congressional discussion of arms embargoes at this time. On Sunday, February 7, he met with Hoover to discuss the Fish resolution, and they finally decided that since the hearing would probably attract little attention, it could be held, but Stimson would not attend.[12]

When the committee met on the morning of February 9, the hearing room was packed with a large crowd that overflowed into the corridor. Fish had previously secured the support of Dorothy Detzer, lobbyist for the Women's International League for Peace

[8] *Ibid.*, January 28, 1932, p. 2861; *ibid.*, January 29, 1932, pp. 2948–49.

[9] *New York Times*, February 4, 1932, p. 13.

[10] Linthicum to Stimson, January 28, 1932, 811.113/153; Stimson to Linthicum, February 2, 1932, 811.113/153.

[11] Hamilton Fish to James Grafton Rogers, February 4, 1932, 811.113/155½; Robert A. Beer to Stimson, February 5, 1932, 811.113/154.

[12] Drew Pearson and Constantine Brown, *The American Diplomatic Game* (New York, 1935), p. 370.

and Freedom, and Miss Detzer had not only arranged for thirty-two witnesses to testify in behalf of the Fish resolution, but she had also publicized the hearing among pacifist groups in the Washington area. Chairman Linthicum, taken completely by surprise, immediately had the room cleared, announcing that the committee would first hold a five-minute executive session. Linthicum then telephoned Assistant Secretary of State James Grafton Rogers and informed him of the situation. Following a hurried conference with Stimson, Rogers asked Linthicum to cancel the meeting, and after an angry debate, the committee agreed by a one-vote margin. When the doors opened again, Linthicum announced the cancellation, telling Miss Detzer, "the Fish bill is dynamite." As reporters eagerly interviewed the committee members, Linthicum explained, "We are afraid the Japanese would be offended by the idea that we didn't want to sell them munitions."[13]

The State Department's maladroit handling of the hearing served only to intensify the efforts of Hamilton Fish and Miss Detzer to get the issue out into the open. Local branches of the Women's International League for Peace and Freedom deluged the House Foreign Affairs Committee with protests, demanding that an arms embargo be placed on Japan immediately. Fish adopted a more subtle tactic. On the afternoon of February 9 he introduced a resolution to instruct the American delegates to the General Disarmament Conference, then meeting in Geneva, to propose a multilateral treaty banning the export of arms and munitions to any foreign nation. In this resolution, Fish cleverly suggested that since the Kellogg pact banned war, it was only logical to end the international arms trade. This proposal, innocuous enough to prevent State Department interference yet liberal enough to attract the supporters of collective security, was a parliamentary work of art.[14]

When Linthicum wrote the State Department for its views on the new Fish resolution, Assistant Secretary Rogers replied favor-

[13] *Ibid.*, pp. 269–70; Dorothy Detzer, *Appointment on the Hill* (New York, 1948), pp. 142–47.

[14] HCP, File 72A-D8.

ably, and the House Foreign Affairs Committee scheduled a hearing for March 8. However, when Fish personally requested that the State Department send a representative to testify, Rogers refused.[15] Meanwhile, in a speech on the floor of the House, Fish revealed his motive in sponsoring arms embargo legislation. After an impassioned attack on the munitions makers, he stated, "The surest way to become involved in war, anywhere in the world, is to ship munitions of war. That is the first step toward war, because it causes the hatred of the country that does not get the munitions."[16] For Hamilton Fish, an arms embargo was essential for the preservation of American isolation.

When the hearings were held in March, Miss Detzer presented a series of witnesses representing peace societies ranging from the internationalist League of Nations Association to the isolationist National Council for the Prevention of War. The testimony shed little light on the question of arms embargoes. Most of the witnesses began with a blast at the munitions industry (one compared the traffic in arms to the opium trade) and then urged adoption of the resolution as a way of implementing the Kellogg pact.[17]

On March 30 the House Foreign Affairs Committee reported favorably on the Fish resolution. The majority report, written by Fish, repeated the arguments brought out in the hearings, with special emphasis on the evils of the arms trade. "If we must have war in the future," Fish wrote, "let it be in defense of our country, but not in defense of our munitions makers."[18] A minority report, submitted by Representative Melvin J. Maas of Minnesota, was more interesting. Maas, a marine aviator in World War I who had business contacts with the aviation industry, warned that

[15] Rogers to Linthicum, February 18, 1932, 811.113/156A; Rogers to Harvey H. Bundy, March 7, 1932, 811.113/158.

[16] *Congressional Record*, February 24, 1932, p. 4654.

[17] Typescript of unpublished hearings before the House Committee on Foreign Affairs, March 8 and 15, 1932, HCP, File 72A-D8.

[18] "Agreement Renouncing Sale or Export of Arms, Munitions, or Implements of War to Any Foreign Nations," *House Report No. 941*, 72d Cong., 1st sess. (Washington, 1932), Part 1, pp. 1–3.

the outlawing of the munitions trade would intensify the arms race, since every small country would then have to stockpile a large supply of munitions in peacetime. Calling the Fish resolution a sentimental gesture, he said it would be as meaningless as the Kellogg treaty.[19]

The munitions makers evidently disagreed with Maas's evaluation of the significance of the Fish resolution. In early March, before the hearings began, Representative Augustine Lonergan of Connecticut, acting in behalf of several munitions companies, called at the State Department to discover the department's attitude toward arms embargoes.[20] After the House committee reported favorably on the Fish resolution, Colonel Aiken Simons, the Washington representative for the Du Pont Company, visited the War and Navy Departments and enlisted the help of several officers. In a report to his superior, Simons stated, "Captain Cage will take appropriate action to have the bill opposed on the floor of the House."[21] This oposition by the military, coupled with the coolness of the State Department, evidently was effective, for the Fish resolution died in Congress.

Thus, while the Manchurian crisis raised the question of American neutrality toward aggression overseas, no decisive answer emerged. Stimson personally favored redefining neutrality, at least to the extent of non-interference with League sanctions, but the determination of President Hoover to avoid American entanglement prevented the Secretary from aligning the United States with the League in restraining Japan. Stimson was placed in the uncomfortable position of quashing all embargo proposals in Congress, even those which were aimed at halting Japanese aggression. The issue was further confused by the conflicting motives which lay behind the embargo movement in Congress. Ardent pacifists believed that an arms embargo, by crippling the munitions indus-

[19] *Ibid.*, Part 2, pp. 1–3.

[20] Memorandum of conversations between Lonergan and Harvey H. Bundy, March 7, 1932, 811.113/161.

[21] "Munitions Investigation," Special Senate *Hearings*, 73d Cong., Part 12, pp. 2721–22.

try, would automatically further world peace; isolationists like Hamilton Fish were convinced that an impartial embargo would end the risk of American involvement in foreign wars; advocates of collective security saw in a discriminatory embargo a way for the United States to co-operate with the League of Nations. With this wide divergence in objectives, it is not surprising that the embargo proposals failed to win support from a majority in Congress.

II

As the Manchurian crisis simmered throughout the remainder of 1932, it became increasingly evident that Japan had succeeded in its aggression. In March, 1932, the Japanese created the puppet state of Manchukuo and in May they withdrew their troops from Shanghai. The Lytton Commission carried out an extremely thorough investigation and in September finally submitted its findings to the League. The Lytton report found the Japanese guilty of aggression, stated that Manchukuo was only a subterfuge for Japanese dominion, and recommended that Manchuria be reorganized under Chinese sovereignty but with proper protection for Japanese economic rights. When the League began considering the report in November, Japan indicated it would refuse to accept any League recommendations. The United States remained silent on the Far Eastern problem, waiting for the League to act on the Lytton report.[22]

In the summer of 1932 another undeclared war broke out, this time in South America between Bolivia and Paraguay. For over a century, both countries had laid claim to the Chaco Boreal, the northern part of the Gran Chaco that lies between the Paraguay River and the Andes. In June, 1932, Bolivia, cut off from ocean ports since the 1880's, began hostilities in the Chaco in an effort to gain access to the sea by way of the Paraguay River. Paraguay quickly counterattacked, and though neither side declared war, both countries continued to skirmish in the Chaco. The United

[22] Walter Lippmann, *The United States in World Affairs, 1932* (New York, 1933), pp. 210–26.

States co-operated with other American countries by participating in a Neutral Commission which endeavored to end the fighting by negotiation, but these attempts proved fruitless.[23]

Meanwhile, Secretary Stimson persisted in his efforts to reshape American policy in the direction of effective co-operation for world peace. In August he delivered his address to the Council on Foreign Relations in which he proclaimed the passing of traditional neutrality.[24] Though Hoover's opposition had prevented Stimson from effecting any actual changes in American policy, the Chaco War provided a new opportunity. Despite the efforts of the United States to end the conflict, American manufacturers were selling arms and munitions to both belligerents. Concerned over this development, and still hoping to secure a major shift in American policy toward collective security, Stimson sent Hoover a message on December 15 recommending that the administration ask Congress for authority to embargo arms to countries where hostilities existed or were threatened.[25] This proposal, drafted in the form of an amendment to the 1922 embargo act, implied a far-reaching change in American policy. The legislation Stimson requested would permit the United States to embargo arms to any nation, even before the outbreak of war, and would allow the President discretion to act against an aggressor.

Hoover considered Stimson's proposal for several days, and finally, on December 21, he gave reluctant approval, suggesting that the message to Congress be redrafted in the form of a request by Stimson, with a short covering letter by the President.[26] Undersecretary of State William R. Castle wrote Stimson the same day opposing the arms embargo measure. Warning that the munitions industry would strongly object to any embargo, Castle added, "It would merely introduce another controversial issue which might cause the administration a lot of trouble."[27] Meanwhile, news of

[23] *Ibid.*, pp. 62–69

[24] See above, p. 19.

[25] Stimson to Hoover, December 15, 1932, 811.113/189A.

[26] Hoover to Stimson, December 21, 1932, 811.113/194.

[27] Castle to Stimson, December 21, 1932, 500.A14/608½.

the proposed action had leaked to the press, and the arms industry quickly applied pressure on the administration. Representative Lonergan of Connecticut called at the State Department on December 21 to register complaints from several companies, and the next day the New Haven Chamber of Commerce wired Hoover, "Diverting such of the [munitions] business as comes to this country to others would merely aggravate our unemployment problem." The Remington Arms Company, which was doing a brisk business with Bolivia and Paraguay, contacted high officials in Washington, including Secretary of War Patrick J. Hurley, in an attempt to sway President Hoover.[28] These protests had an immediate effect—by December 23 Hoover had definitely decided against sending the message to Congress. Lawrence Richey, the President's correspondence secretary, told a State Department officer that "the rumor that the Duponts had protested was all wrong; it was not the Duponts who had intervened, but the Colts, Remingtons and Winchesters!"[29]

Stimson, however, did not surrender. He brought up the proposal again on January 4, 1933, now supported by Undersecretary Castle, who feared the reversal would lead to charges that the Hoover administration was under the influence of the munitions industry. Hoover finally suggested a compromise—Stimson was to redraft the message, requesting the Senate to ratify the 1925 Geneva convention for control of the arms trade, and then proposing the arms embargo as an alternative. On January 6, Stimson took the revised proposal to a cabinet meeting, and though the entire cabinet opposed the measure as injurious to American industry, he finally secured Hoover's approval. On January 10, the President sent the new version of Stimson's proposal to Congress.[30]

[28] Memorandum by Joseph C. Green, December 21, 1932, 811.113/196; New Haven Chamber of Commerce to Hoover, December 22, 1932, 811.113/200; "Munitions Investigation," Special Senate *Hearings*, 73d Cong., Part 10, pp. 2357, 2393; Pearson and Brown, *American Diplomatic Game*, pp. 371–72.

[29] Nancy Harvison Hooker (ed.), *The Moffat Papers* (Cambridge, Mass., 1956), p. 79.

[30] *Ibid.*, pp. 80–81.

The message of January 10 was a curious document. In a brief covering letter, Hoover stressed "the urgent need of more authority to the Executive in control of the shipment of arms from the United States" in order to lessen the danger of war. He then urged ratification of the 1925 Geneva convention, which offered no authority beyond publicizing arms exports in peacetime. Hoover finally recommended, as an alternative, the passage of an arms embargo resolution limited to "cases where special undertakings of co-operation can be secured with the principal arms manufacturing nations."[31] In other words, Hoover preferred mild international supervision without control, and he only consented to control if all other arms-producing nations acted in unison.

The main body of the message consisted of a letter from Stimson to President Hoover which was far bolder. Discussing the need to control the international arms trade, Stimson emphasized the importance of arms embargo authority in preserving world peace. Though he did not mention any specific countries, he urged that "the proposed legislation should be made to apply to the whole world." "The day is gone when the spread of a conflagration is easily confined to any continent or hemisphere," he continued. "The taking by the United States of this additional step in its domestic policy will tend to give encouragement and momentum to the struggle for world peace and against the use of force . . . [in] this unsettled period in international relationships."[32] Stimson clearly had more in mind than just restraining the export of arms to the Chaco conflict—he was striving to achieve a new kind of sanction to implement his policy of resisting aggression in the world.

The public reaction to the arms embargo proposal was largely favorable. Most newspapers interpreted it as a move toward shutting off the flow of munitions to the Chaco War, and endorsed it on this basis. A few editors were more skeptical, fearing that the embargo power would be used against Japan. The *New York*

[31] "Shipment of Arms for Military Purposes," *Senate Document No. 169*, 72d Cong., 2d sess. (Washington, 1933), p. 1.

[32] *Ibid.*, pp. 2–4.

Evening Post complained, "Congress should hold on to the war-making power. We are opposed to turning over any of it to a State Department that has been making Japan angry. . . ."[33] A more significant reaction came from President-elect Franklin D. Roosevelt, who had been informed of the proposal by Stimson at a conference between the two men on January 9. Though Roosevelt refused to comment directly on Hoover's message, he stated, "I have long been in favor of the use of embargoes on arms to belligerent nations, especially to nations guilty of making an attack on other nations—that is, against aggressor nations."[34]

Congress acted quickly on the arms embargo. On January 10, Senator Borah invited Undersecretary Castle to attend an executive session of the Senate Foreign Relations Committee. The next day Castle, accompanied by Francis White, Assistant Secretary for Latin American affairs, and Joseph C. Green, who had prepared the Hoover message, appeared before the Senate committee with a draft arms embargo resolution. After a brief discussion in which the State Department officers indicated that the embargo was aimed solely at the Chaco War, the committee agreed to report out the administration bill without further consideration. The resolution, formally sponsored by Senator Borah, empowered the President to lay an embargo on the shipment of arms or munitions of war to any country he might designate, provided that he secured the cooperation of other arms-producing nations.[35]

Senator Borah brought his resolution before the Senate on January 19, and he succeeded in gaining unanimous consent for its passage without any debate. However, the following day Senator Hiram Bingham of Connecticut, who was absent when the Senate passed the Borah bill, blocked final passage by moving for reconsideration of the measure. Under the rules of the Senate, Bingham's action prevented adoption of the resolution without a full-

[33] "Mr. Hoover Takes a Punch at Mars," *Literary Digest*, CXV (January 28, 1933), 9.

[34] *Ibid.*, p. 9; Current, *Secretary Stimson*, pp. 117–18.

[35] Jay Pierrepont Moffat Diary, January 10, 11, 1933 (Houghton Library, Harvard University); *Congressional Record*, January 11, 1933, p. 1551; *ibid.*, February 8, 1933, p. 3590.

scale debate. On February 8, Borah asked Bingham to drop his objections to the arms embargo resolution, but Bingham refused, stating, "the passage of such legislation would get us into serious difficulty and might lead to war."[36]

It is very probable that Bingham's opposition stemmed from his concern for the munitions industry, which centered in Connecticut. In addition Bingham was intimately connected with the aviation industry, serving as president of the National Aeronautic Association. The arms manufacturers, after their failure to prevent Hoover from issuing his message to Congress, continued to work against embargoes. On January 9, Samuel Beebe of Winchester Arms wired the War, Navy, and Commerce Departments that an arms embargo would have a disastrous effect on the munitions companies, and thus on national defense. A few days later the ubiquitous Colonel Simons of Du Pont was calling at both the War and Navy Departments to stir up opposition.[37] These tactics were highly effective. In February, Senator Borah was complaining that War Department pressure was swaying many senators against his resolution. Stimson finally had to ask Secretary of War Hurley to end the lobbying by his subordinates in the War Department.[38]

Support from peace societies helped offset opposition to the resolution. When newspapers first revealed the proposed arms embargo plan, pacifist groups wrote to both Hoover and the State Department expressing their approval. As early as December 20, Dorothy Detzer sent a letter to Hoover pledging her support for an embargo, and a week later John Nevin Sayre of the Fellowship of Reconciliation praised Hoover for plans "to put a stop to the nefarious munitions traffic."[39] After the message to Congress in

[36] *Ibid.*, January 19, 1933, p. 2096; *ibid.*, January 20, 1933, pp. 2134–35; *ibid.*, February 8, 1933, pp. 3589–90.

[37] "Munitions Investigation," Special Senate *Hearings*, 73d Cong., Part 12, pp. 2722, 2748.

[38] Memorandum of conversation between Dorothy Detzer and Joseph C. Green, February 14, 1933, 811.113/230; Moffat Diary, February 15, 1933.

[39] Dorothy Detzer to Hoover, December 20, 1932, 811.113/201; John Nevin Sayre to Hoover, December 27, 1932, 811.43 Fellowship of Reconciliation/75.

January, nearly every major peace organization in the country went on record in favor of arms embargo legislation. The House Foreign Affairs Committee received a large volume of letters, telegrams, and petitions from pacifist groups, all urging adoption of the Borah resolution as a means of implementing the Kellogg pact. Miss Detzer lobbied constantly in Congress and kept the State Department fully informed of the situation in the Senate.[40]

Despite this pressure, Hiram Bingham's opposition still blocked action in the Senate. Threatening a filibuster, which could interfere with important domestic legislation, Bingham was able to gain enough support to prevent Borah from bringing up his resolution for adoption. In late January the State Department decided to shift its attention to the House. On the twenty-seventh Undersecretary William Castle conferred with Representative Sam D. McReynolds of Tennessee, chairman of the House Foreign Affairs Committee, and after a lengthy discussion in which Castle stated that the embargo was intended only for the Chaco War, McReynolds agreed to co-operate. Three days later he introduced a resolution in the House similar to Borah's.[41]

The House Foreign Affairs Committee began week-long hearings on the arms embargo resolution on February 7. Representatives of peace societies and industrial concerns offered most of the testimony. Dorothy Detzer, Jeannette Rankin, who had voted against war as a congresswoman in 1917, and Helen Hoy Greeley, a representative at the Geneva Disarmament Conference for a number of women's peace societies, argued vigorously for the resolution as a measure furthering American co-operation to prevent war.[42] Most of the other witnesses represented the aviation industry. Stating that one-third of all airplanes produced in the United States were sold overseas, they claimed that the embargo would cause other

[40] HCP, File 72A-D8; memorandum of conversation between Dorothy Detzer and Joseph C. Green, February 14, 1933, 811.113/230.

[41] *FR: 1933*, I, 358–59; *New York Times*, January 31, 1933, p. 2.

[42] "Exportation of Arms or Munitions of War," *Hearings before the House Committee on Foreign Affairs*, 72d Cong., 2d sess. (Washington, 1933), pp. 7–8, 10, 17–18, 19.

nations, especially the small Latin American countries, to go elsewhere for the purchase of war planes. They reiterated the charge that the embargo legislation would hamper the nation's security. "The aircraft industry is a vital factor in the national defense of this country," asserted the president of the Aeronautical Chamber of Commerce. "The industry must therefore be maintained on a scale which renders it possible of effective emergency use." Representatives of the Colt, Winchester, and Remington arms companies offered similar arguments, contending that the proposed legislation would serve only to divert the American arms export trade to other nations.[43]

The State Department also expressed its views at the hearings. On the first day, Joseph C. Green presented the arguments for an arms embargo, stressing the need to prevent war by cutting off supplies. Green then underwent a fierce cross-examination by Representatives Maas and Fish, who charged that the administration planned to invoke an embargo against Japan which could well lead to war.[44] Stimson was incensed at this attack, and when the committee invited him to testify, he told an associate he would not go up "to that beer garden" for any public hearing.[45] However, Stimson finally agreed to appear at an executive session and though his testimony was to be secret, a member of the committee gave the press a copy of a memorandum the Secretary had left behind. In this summary, Stimson argued that neutrality was no longer valid in the modern world. "Today nearly all of the world except the United States and Russia are members of the League of Nations and so closely bound by agreements in the Covenant and other treaties that real neutrality in a large-scale war is almost impossible." Stimson stated that the United States would only employ an embargo when all other major powers agreed to cooperate. If the other nations of the world designated an aggressor, he continued, "the participation of the United States in a general arms embargo would be not merely practical and sound, but

[43] *Ibid.*, pp. 25–29, 31–33, 41–42, 51, 59–69.

[44] *Ibid.*, pp. 1–7.

[45] Moffat Diary, February 7, 1933.

practically necessary to preserve our national dignity and standing as a peaceful nation."[46] Though J. Pierrepont Moffat, the chief of the Division of Western European Affairs, felt that Stimson had "silenced Ham Fish with one or two effective blows," the Secretary's testimony actually served to confirm isolationist fears that he was leading the United States directly into the orbit of the League of Nations.[47]

When the House Foreign Affairs Committee met on February 15 to consider the arms embargo resolution, the Far Eastern situation had again become critical. In January the Japanese had advanced into Shanhaikwan in North China and had begun preparations to invade the province of Jehol. Then, on February 14, the League's Committee of Nineteen, to which the Lytton findings had been referred, issued a report condemning Japan for aggression in Manchuria.[48] Hamilton Fish now became more convinced than ever that the embargo legislation was aimed at Japan. According to Chairman McReynolds, he told the committee that if Congress passed the resolution, "we would be at war with Japan in less than a month." Fish then threatened to attach a series of crippling amendments to the proposal, and if they were rejected, he announced he would join with Maas in signing a minority report. McReynolds finally worked out a compromise, whereby he would accept an amendment limiting the arms embargo to the Western Hemisphere if Fish and Maas would sign the committee report and refrain from opposing the resolution in the House. In justifying his action to the State Department, McReynolds stated that opposition by Fish and Maas would kill all chances for action before the end of the session in early March.[49]

[46] *FR: 1933*, I, 361–62. The memorandum, which was written by James Grafton Rogers, was deliberately left behind by Stimson. Letter from Joseph C. Green to author, November 19, 1960.

[47] Moffat Diary, February 9, 1933.

[48] Walter Lippmann and William O. Scroggs, *The United States in World Affairs, 1933* (New York, 1934), pp. 35–37.

[49] Memorandum of conversation between Hamilton Fish and Joseph C. Green, February 14, 1933, 811.113/229; Moffat Diary, February 15, 1933; Joseph C. Green to Stimson, February 16, 1933, 811.113/231.

The House committee reported favorably on the amended arms embargo resolution on February 15. In his majority report, Representative McReynolds reprinted the original message from Hoover asking for legislation, and pointed out that the amendment limiting the embargo to the Western Hemisphere marked a retreat from the administration's request.[50] Much to McReynolds' indignation, Maas submitted a minority report in which he called the resolution "a direct violation of neutrality under existing international law" and claimed it was likely to lead to war.[51] Though President Hoover subsequently sent an additional message to Congress urging passage of the resolution, Congress failed to take any action. On March 1, Stimson cabled the American delegate to the Geneva Disarmament Conference, "There would appear to be no *repeat no* likelihood of the passage of the arms embargo resolution during the present session of Congress."[52]

Henry Stimson was bitterly disappointed by the failure of Congress to act on the arms embargo. When he learned of the Western Hemisphere limitation, he told J. Pierrepont Moffat that it would break up the solid front he had been building against Japan.[53] Though Stimson had allowed his subordinates to present the embargo as primarily aimed at the Chaco War, he himself had had wider applications in mind. Encouraged by Franklin Roosevelt's expressed willingness to support an active American policy against aggression, Stimson hoped that at last the United States was ready to accept responsibility for world peace by abandoning its traditional neutrality. The re-emergence of the Manchurian crisis had proved fatal to Stimson's plans. Fearful of war with Japan, isolationist elements led by Hamilton Fish had joined with the powerful munitions lobby to kill the embargo resolution. Once again

[50] "Prohibit the Exportation of Arms or Munitions of War from the United States under Certain Circumstances," *House Report No. 2040*, 72d Cong., 2d sess. (Washington, 1933), Part 1, pp. 1–3.

[51] *Ibid.*, Part 2, pp. 1–2.

[52] *Congressional Record*, February 20, 1933, p. 4553; Stimson to Hugh Wilson, March 1, 1933, 811.113/222.

[53] Moffat Diary, February 15, 1933.

the split in the embargo ranks between discriminatory and impartial measures had led to defeat.

III

On March 4, 1933, a new era in American history began with the inauguration of Franklin D. Roosevelt. For three and a half years the nation's economy had steadily deteriorated under the impact of the depression—factories that had once throbbed with activity stood silent; lines of bewildered and defeated men queued up before employment offices; desperate farmers ambushed trucks carrying crops to glutted markets in a futile effort to halt the decline in prices. And the slow process of economic erosion had reached a sudden crisis as the banks of the country, undermined by a loss of public confidence, closed their doors. Jaunty and optimistic, Roosevelt appeared unshaken by the magnitude of the disaster as he told the nation it had nothing to fear but fear itself. Attracting a host of young, ambitious men, drawn from college faculties, law offices, and social agencies, Roosevelt proceeded to fight the depression with a series of bold, experimental programs. The feverish excitement of the "one hundred days" marked the first real attempt to overcome the economic catastrophe, and the nation slowly began to regain hope.

Though the New Deal domestic reforms overshadowed foreign affairs, the Roosevelt administration gave promise of a sweeping change in America's role in the world. The party of Woodrow Wilson returned to power after twelve years of Republican rule, and those who had kept alive the dream of collective security since 1920 became optimistic. Their chief hope lay in the President himself. Born into the eastern aristocracy, educated at Groton and Harvard, and widely traveled in Europe, Roosevelt was completely lacking in the narrow provincialism that characterized the isolationists. His political career, marked by an early enthusiasm for his cousin Theodore's imperialism and a devotion to Wilsonian principles that grew out of his experience as Assistant Secretary of the Navy and as a vice-presidential candidate in 1920, stamped him as an internationalist. Though he had grown cool toward the League of Nations in the 1920's, and had publicly opposed American entry in 1932 in order to please William Randolph Hearst, these actions could be interpreted as the realistic maneuvers of a shrewd politician. In the presidential campaign, Roosevelt largely ignored issues of foreign policy, but after his election he embraced the policies of Henry Stimson, especially the principle of nonrecognition of aggression. By the time of his inauguration, he gave the impression of being a cautious advocate of collective security.

In the State Department, the re-emergence of the Wilsonian tradition was even more apparent. Secretary of State Cordell Hull, a gaunt, sorrowful-looking Tennesseean, had served in Congress under Wilson and had become firmly attached to the ideals of free trade and international co-operation for peace. Aloof and dignified, but possessed of a fiery temper, Hull was determined to translate his lofty principles into a revitalized American foreign policy. In the early years of the New Deal, his closest associate was Norman H. Davis, who held the unique rank of ambassador-at-large. Davis, also from Tennessee, had made a fortune in Cuban banking as a young man. With American entry into World War I, he had entered government service working first in the Treasury Department and then becoming chief financial adviser to Wilson at the Versailles Conference. After a brief period as Undersecretary of State after the war, he had returned to private banking. In 1931 he became one of the American delegates to the Geneva Disarmament Conference, and after seriously considering him for the post of Secretary of State, Roosevelt asked Davis to become chairman of the American delegation at Geneva with the rank of ambassador. Soft-spoken and even-tempered, Davis was an excellent negotiator who quickly won the respect of European diplomats. A trustee of the Woodrow Wilson Foundation, he shared with Hull the belief that the United States had to play an active and constructive role in world affairs.[54]

In the first few days after Roosevelt's inauguration, Hull and Davis discussed the arms embargo proposal that Stimson had

[54] *New York Times,* May 28, 1933, VI, 15; *ibid.,* July 2, 1944, p. 20.

originated. They found considerable disagreement among the State Department experts. Stanley K. Hornbeck, who was chief of the Far Eastern Division, advised against raising the issue at that time, warning that it would serve only to antagonize Japan. Joseph C. Green argued, however, that to drop the arms embargo resolution "would undoubtedly be construed in many quarters as a backward step taken at the behest of American arms manufacturers and in fear of offending Japan." Hull and Davis finally conferred with Stimson, now in private life, and then urged Roosevelt to adopt the arms embargo policy. On March 10 the President agreed. The State Department sent letters reccommending passage of an arms embargo resolution to the chairmen of the House and Senate committees, Representative McReynolds and Senator Key Pittman of Nevada, and on March 16 McReynolds introduced a resolution identical to the one he had sponsored in the previous Congress.[55]

The orderly progress toward securing an arms embargo law from Congress suddenly halted in mid-March. Hornbeck, still very concerned over the possible Japanese reaction, convinced Undersecretary of State William Phillips that the administration should adopt a completely aloof attitude toward the arms embargo legislation. Phillips then went to McReynolds and Pittman, took back the letters requesting legislation, and destroyed the copies in the department's files. McReynolds was very angry, claiming that "he was to be left to hold the bag." Those opposing the arms embargo, especially Hamilton Fish, were delighted by the confusion in the State Department and demanded public hearings on the resolution. McReynolds had no choice but to agree.[56]

The House Foreign Affairs Committee held a one-day hearing on March 28.[57] The three witnesses—Edwin Borchard, Edward A. Harriman, a lawyer and lecturer on international law, and Major

[55] Memorandum by Stanley Hornbeck, March 7, 1933, 893.113/1467; memorandum by Joseph C. Green, March 9, 1933, 811.113/264; Moffat Diary, March 9, 10, 11, and 13, 1933.

[56] *Ibid.*, March 20 and 27, 1933.

[57] "Exportation of Arms or Munitions of War," *Hearing before the House Committee on Foreign Affairs*, 73d Cong., 1st sess. (Washington, 1933).

General Amos A. Fries, retired head of the army's Chemical Warfare Service—all opposed the resolution. Borchard was the most effective witness. In a memorandum which he read to the committee, Borchard argued that a discriminatory arms embargo was a flagrant breach of neutrality. "The discrimination is an unfriendly and hostile act of greatest significance," he stated, "and against a strong power might very readily be a prelude to war. It is, indeed, a warlike act, if not itself an act of war." Under questioning by Fish and Representative George H. Tinkham of Massachusetts, Borchard claimed that if such an embargo were applied to Japan, it would lead to immediate hostilities. Borchard closed by saying, "I regard neutrality as the greatest gift that God has put in the hands of the American people."[58]

Though the State Department did not send any representative to testify at the hearing, it worked quietly behind the scenes. J. Pierrepont Moffat, learning that Fish planned to call former Secretary of War Patrick J. Hurley to testify against the resolution, went to Henry Stimson, who helped persuade Hurley to decline the invitation.[59] McReynolds, hoping to end the hearings quickly, did not invite any witnesses to testify in favor of his measure, but in order to refute Borchard's statement, he read a memorandum prepared by Joseph Chamberlain of Columbia University. Stating that the President had long possessed limited embargo powers, Chamberlain pointed out that the new authority would only be used in co-operation with other nations. "Undoubtedly, a country acting alone would run some risk of war," he wrote, "but is it likely that any country would make war on all the important powers of the world because of an embargo on arms?"[60]

At the end of the hearing, the committee went into executive session and approved the McReynolds resolution by a vote of 15 to 6, with all the negative votes coming from the Republican minority.[61] In the majority report, McReynolds stated that the

[58] *Ibid.*, pp. 14–17, 22.

[59] Moffat Diary, March 27, 1933.

[60] "Exportation of Arms," House *Hearing*, 73d Cong., 1st sess., pp. 31–32.

[61] *New York Times*, March 29, 1933, p. 1.

administration strongly favored his proposal, and then, in an effort to make the issue bipartisan, added Hoover's original request for such legislation.[62] Representative Fish wrote a lengthy minority report which was signed by the Republican members of the committee. Repeating the arguments advanced by Borchard, Fish claimed that the embargo "constitutes the avowed abandonment of the American principle of neutrality and involves the menace of war." He also included the memorandum presented by Borchard at the hearing, together with a letter from John Bassett Moore which argued that the embargo resolution was unconstitutional because it would enable the President to usurp the war-making power from Congress.[63]

The favorable action by the House Foreign Affairs Committee finally dispelled the lingering doubts inside the State Department. On April 5, Secretary Hull wrote to McReynolds strongly supporting the enactment of the arms embargo resolution without any amendments. In the letter, Hull stressed the need for flexible authority which would enable the President to deal with different situations as they developed. Hull concluded by stating:

> In justice to the firm convictions of the American people and to its own dignity, the Government should no longer be left in the position of being unable to join the other governments of the world in preventing the supply of arms and munitions for use in an international conflict when it is exercising its diplomacy and the whole weight of our national influence and prestige to prevent or put an end to that conflict. The enactment of this legislation would strengthen the position of this Government in its international relations and would enable us to co-operate more efficiently in efforts to maintain the peace of the world.[64]

This strong support by the administration led to prompt action in Congress. The Rules Committee brought the McReynolds reso-

[62] "Prohibit the Exportation of Arms or Munitions of War from the United States under Certain Conditions," *House Report No.* 22, 73d Cong., 1st sess. (Washington, 1933), Part 1, pp. 1–4.

[63] *Ibid.*, Part 2, pp. 1–9.

[64] *FR: 1933*, I, 364–65.

lution to the floor of the House on April 13 and a bitter, partisan debate ensued. The supporters of the resolution, using arguments prepared by the State Department and by Manley O. Hudson of Harvard,[65] described the measure as one necessary for the preservation of peace. "The enactment of this resolution," asserted Representative John A. Martin of Colorado, "is but a single item on the world program for international peace, for which all civilized peoples are earnestly striving." Claiming that the President would only use the embargo in co-operation with other nations, proponents of the resolution expressed complete confidence in Roosevelt's ability to use discretionary power wisely. They denied that the administration planned to levy an embargo against Japan, pointing out that Japan produced its own munitions. A few speakers claimed that anyone opposing the arms embargo was influenced by the munitions lobby. Thus Representative Luther A. Johnson of Texas asserted, "the cause of peace and the prevention of war is of more importance to America than the profits of any group."[66]

The small but vocal Republican minority lashed out vigorously against the embargo resolution. Hamilton Fish led the assault. "As far as I know," he charged, "there is just one reason, and that is to go in with the League of Nations, to declare an embargo against Japan, as the aggressor nation in the Far East, and have the United States declare that embargo, with those European nations, against Japan." Other speakers elaborated on these themes, declaring that the resolution would involve the United States in "the Oriental maelstrom," force the nation "into the back door and the trapdoor of the League of Nations," and "cause in time, the sands and soil of the United States to be stained with thousands of barrels of blood from the hearts of the young men of America." Still others resented the granting of additional power

[65] Hudson wrote to McReynolds on March 29 offering his services to counter the arguments advanced by Borchard. McReynolds accepted his help, and in a letter of April 15, McReynolds told Hudson that several members of the committee used his arguments word-for-word in the debate on the floor of Congress. HCP, File 73A-D10.

[66] *Congressional Record*, April 13, 1933, pp. 1683, 1695, 1700; *ibid.*, April 14, 1933, pp. 1751, 1757–58, 1762, 1773–74.

to the President. "It is one more abdication of power on the part of Congress, one more instance of the surrender of its rights and the shirking of its responsibilities; for the Constitution lays upon Congress, and upon Congress alone, sole responsibility for making war," proclaimed a Connecticut congressman. Nearly all the opponents of the McReynolds resolution spoke out in favor of an impartial arms embargo, objecting only to allowing the President to discriminate against aggressors.[67]

The debate ended in an overwhelming vote in favor of the arms embargo resolution. On April 17, after rejecting an amendment by Hamilton Fish to make the embargo apply impartially, the House voted 254 to 109 in favor of McReynolds' measure.[68] The ballot showed a strong partisan division, with only nine Republicans supporting the resolution and twenty-three Democrats opposing it. A sectional analysis of the vote reflects little more than the party alignment, but it is significant that two-thirds of the Democrats who voted against the measure came from the Middle and Far West, while six of the nine Republicans favoring it were from the Northeast.[69] Party loyalty was obviously the main consideration for most congressmen, but the West revealed a stronger pull toward isolationism than did the South or Northeast. In any case, the new administration had scored an impressive triumph in its first major struggle in the field of diplomacy.

IV

While the House was passing the McReynolds resolution, Roosevelt and Hull were about to reach a vital decision that elevated the arms embargo into a major issue for American foreign policy

[67] *Ibid.*, April 13, 1933, pp. 1683, 1697–98; *ibid.*, April 14, 1933, pp. 1748, 1753, 1761, 1768.

[68] *Ibid.*, April 17, 1933, p. 1850.

[69] The sectional breakdown on the vote is as follows:

Section	*Yes*	*No*
Northeast	50	50
South	94	3
Middle West	87	39
Far West	23	17

When he took office in March, Roosevelt showed deep concern over the failure of the Geneva conference to achieve any progress on the problem of disarmament. By the spring of 1933 the conference had reached a critical point. France, possessing the largest armed forces in Europe, flatly refused to disarm until the major powers, especially England and the United States, would offer guaranties of assistance in case of German attack. The rise of Hitler to power in 1933 intensified the French fear of Germany. Great Britain was sympathetic to the French security problem but refused to give the assurances France desired without some form of support from the United States. In March the British tried to break the deadlock. Prime Minister Ramsay MacDonald offered a new, comprehensive plan of disarmament which provided for consultation among the European powers in case of any aggression. At the same time, Arthur Henderson of Great Britain, chairman of the Geneva conference, approached the American delegates with a new proposal for American participation in collective security. The essence of this plan was for the United States to agree to consult with the major powers when aggression occurred in Europe, and if agreement was reached on the identity of the aggressor, the United States would refrain from supplying the guilty party with arms or other war supplies and would refuse to protect its citizens engaging in such trade. In short, the United States would abandon neutrality and passively co-operate in the use of sanctions against a European aggressor.[70]

Details of the Henderson proposal reached Washington in early March. Norman H. Davis, the new chairman of the American delegation to the Geneva conference, discussed the suggestion with Hull and Roosevelt in a series of conferences, but no decision was reached.[71] In late March, Davis sailed for Europe, stopping off in London to confer with British diplomats, and then moving on to Paris for discussions with the French. On April 16, Davis made

[70] Hugh Gibson to Hull, March 8, 1933, *FR: 1933*, I, 26; Gibson to Hull, March 12, 1933, *ibid.*, p. 32.

[71] Davis to Roosevelt, undated memorandum, Norman H. Davis Papers, Box 43, Library of Congress.

up his mind. In a cable to Secretary Hull, he strongly urged that the United States agree to the plan outlined by Henderson. Warning that unless the United States accepted some degree of responsibility for European security the conference would fail, Davis argued that it was America's "moral duty" as a signatory of the Kellogg-Briand Pact to refrain from taking any action that would aid a violator. "Such an agreement for us," he wrote, "would merely codify the implications of the Kellogg Peace Pact and the precedents established under it." In a second cable, sent an hour later, Davis stressed the negative nature of the proposed American pledge to surrender its neutral rights. "While we may under certain conditions forego our rights we are also freed from corresponding obligations. These former rights of neutrality which are becoming somewhat obsolete are now merely rights to get into trouble as the world has evolved today." Davis closed with a plea for a prompt decision on his proposals.[72]

Hull immediately forwarded Davis' suggestions to Roosevelt, but for several days the President was too busy with domestic affairs to consider them. Meanwhile, the State Department studied them carefully. J. Pierrepont Moffat, at the suggestion of Undersecretary Phillips, sought the advice of Henry Stimson. The former Secretary of State strongly endorsed the new plan but suggested that Roosevelt should announce the surrender of neutral rights in a formal statement rather than through a treaty which the Senate might reject. Phillips forwarded this suggestion to the President, who was now preparing to receive Ramsay MacDonald and Edouard Herriot, former Premier of France, who were coming to Washington to confer personally with Roosevelt on the issues of war debts, the forthcoming London World Economic Conference, and disarmament.[73]

While Davis waited impatiently for a decision from Washington, the President met with Prime Minister MacDonald. On April

[72] Davis to Hull, April 16, 1933, *FR: 1933*, I, 89–92, 96–97.

[73] Moffat Diary, April 17, 1933; Moffat to Phillips, April 19, 1933, Franklin D. Roosevelt Papers, PSF, Box 30, Roosevelt Library, Hyde Park, New York.

23, when the two leaders turned to the issue of disarmament, Roosevelt told MacDonald that if the European powers agreed on disarmament, he was willing to co-operate against aggressors by refraining from exercising traditional American neutrality. Pointing out that the Senate would probably object to a treaty commitment, Roosevelt read a draft declaration of American policy which stated that if the United States concurred in determining the aggressor, "we would undertake to refrain from any action and to withhold protection from our citizens if engaged in activities which would tend to defeat the collective effort which the States in consultation might have decided upon against the aggressor." Three days later Roosevelt made a similar statement to M. Herriot.[74]

On April 25, Secretary Hull belatedly informed Davis of the President's decision to abandon neutrality in cases of collective action against aggressors. Hull pointed out to Davis that the new policy transcended his original suggestion—it would apply to aggression anywhere in the world, not just in Europe.[75] Though the administration did not make these commitments to MacDonald and Herriot public, in the course of questioning by the press Herriot revealed Roosevelt's willingness to alter traditional American neutrality.[76] Considerable speculation over the exact agreement which had been reached continued until May 22, when Davis revealed the new American policy in the course of a speech to the Geneva conference. Stating that American action was dependent on the signing of a genuine disarmament agreement, Davis pledged:

> . . . we are willing to consult the other states in case of a threat to peace, with a view to averting the conflict. Further than that, in

[74] Memorandum of conversation between Roosevelt and MacDonald by Sir Robert Vansittart, April 23, 1933, *FR: 1933*, I, 103–4; memorandum of conversation between Roosevelt and Herriot by William Phillips, April 26, 1933, *ibid.*, pp. 109–10.

[75] *Ibid.*, pp. 106–7.

[76] *New York Times*, April 27, 1933, p. 1; Pearson and Brown, *American Diplomatic Game*, p. 375.

the event that the states, in conference, determine that a state has been guilty of a breach of the peace in violation of its international obligations and takes measures against the violator, then, if we concur in the judgment rendered as to the responsible and guilty party, we will refrain from any action tending to defeat such collective effort which these states may thus make to restore peace.[77]

The new policy, outlined by Roosevelt to MacDonald and Herriot and confirmed publicly by Davis, marked a vital change in America's relationship to collective security. Though hedged about with qualifications, particularly in regard to the prior reaching of a disarmament agreement and the freedom of the United States in determining the aggressor, the pledge signified an American willingness to assume a degree of responsibility for world peace for the first time since the Senate had rejected the League of Nations. The futile efforts of Shotwell, Burton, Capper, and Stimson had finally led to a reversal in American policy toward collective security. Most important, the arms embargo resolution, already passed by the House, now assumed a far wider significance. If the Senate passed this measure, the United States would be able to carry out the pledge made by Roosevelt and Davis and thus assure the European powers of assistance in time of crisis.

V

The arms embargo resolution now lay in the Senate Foreign Relations Committee, headed by Senator Key Pittman. A southerner by birth, Pittman had taken part in the Klondike gold rush, and though he failed as a miner, he became a successful prosecuting attorney in Nome. He followed the lure of gold to Nevada, where he settled down to a law practice. Elected to the Senate in 1912, Pittman's main concern was in furthering the silver interests of the West. He had no strong views on world affairs, but he felt strongly that Congress should have an independent voice in the formulation of foreign policy. Tall and sinewy, Pittman was a

[77] Department of State, *Peace and War: United States Foreign Policy, 1931–1941* (Washington, 1943), pp. 188–89.

brusque, short-tempered man who was fond of his liquor, swore constantly, and took orders from no one.[78] Though Pittman was formally in charge of the committee, his control was frequently challenged by the two senior Republican members, William E. Borah of Idaho and Hiram Johnson of California. These two men, who had led the fight against the League of Nations in 1919, were intense nationalists who demanded that the United States pursue a totally independent course of action in international affairs.

The Senate committee began considering the arms embargo resolution on May 10, 1933. Though Borah, who had sponsored a similar resolution for the Hoover administration, continued to favor the legislation, Johnson strongly opposed it.[79] After the committee discussed the proposal thoroughly, Senator Pittman wrote to Hull expressing the serious doubts that members of the committee had raised. Pittman stated that the committee feared that if the President applied an embargo against an aggressor, it "would have a strong tendency to involve the United States to such an extent that a condition of war might arise," and in particular he stressed the anxiety that the administration planned to employ an embargo against Japan in co-operation with the League. Warning that a number of amendments had been proposed, the senator suggested that Hull appear before the committee to answer the questions that had been raised.[80]

The State Department reacted swiftly to this new threat. On May 15, Hull replied to Pittman, declining to appear personally before the committee but agreeing to send Joseph C. Green with a written statement of the department's views. He asked Pittman to read the committee the last sentence of his letter, which urged favorable action on the resolution without any amendments.[81] On the same day, Green sent Pittman two lengthy memorandums prepared by Manley O. Hudson and David Hunter Miller, Historical

[78] *New York Times*, May 21, 1939, VIII, 12, 22.

[79] *Ibid.*, March 23, 1933, p. 7; *Congressional Record*, April 22, 1933, pp. 2141–42.

[80] *FR: 1933*, I, 365–66.

[81] Hull to Pittman, May 15, 1933, 811.113/297.

Adviser of the State Department, to use in arguing against amendments by the committee.[82] Then, on May 17, Green appeared before the committee, meeting in executive session, to read a statement signed by Hull. This lengthy document reiterated the peaceful intent of the arms embargo resolution. The arms embargo power, Hull wrote, "would be exercised by any Chief Magistrate of the United States to the sole end of maintaining the peace of the world and with a due and prudent regard for our national policies and national interests." Hull stressed that the authority would only be used in co-operation with other nations. The Secretary made no mention of the administration's plan to abandon neutrality toward aggressors, but he did state that it was "conceivable" that the United States would levy an embargo against a nation violating the Kellogg-Briand Pact. Hull stated that the administration planned to ban the export of arms to both Paraguay and Bolivia, but he emphatically denied any intention of using the embargo power against Japan, pointing out that the Japanese were self-sufficient in the production of munitions. In an effort to ease the isolationists' fears over involvement in the Far East, Hull promised, "this Government does not expect to take any action of this nature [against Japan]; if any action is taken it will certainly be taken with a due and prudent regard for American interests and in particular with our paramount interest of remaining free from any entanglements which would involve this country in a foreign war."[83]

After hearing Hull's defense of the arms embargo resolution, the Senate committee postponed final action on the legislation for a week. When the committee met again on May 24, Hiram Johnson offered an amendment which stipulated that any embargo levied by the President had to apply impartially to all belligerents.[84] The Johnson amendment radically altered the nature of the arms em-

[82] Green to Pittman, May 15, 1933, Senate Foreign Relations Committee Papers, File 73A-F10, National Archives, Record Group 46. Hereafter cited as SCP.

[83] *FR: 1933*, I, 369–78.

[84] *New York Times*, May 25, 1933, p. 12; *ibid.*, May 26, 1933, p. 3.

bargo resolution, proposing to transform a method of co-operating with collective security measures into an isolationist effort to avoid involvement in foreign wars, and thereby threatening to destroy the new policy announced by Davis on May 22. Pittman conferred with Hull about this critical development on May 25, and then went to Roosevelt and flatly stated that his committee would not accept the resolution without the Johnson amendment. Without consulting Hull, the President approved the amendment.[85] When the committee met on May 27, it unanimously adopted the amendment and then reported favorably on the arms embargo resolution.[86]

Cordell Hull was stunned when he learned of the President's decision. In a note to Roosevelt on May 27, he warned that since the amendment was "in direct conflict with our position at Geneva as expressed by Norman Davis, it would be well for the government to deal with the matter in the light of this situation." Hull then suggested that it would be better for the administration to stand by its original position, even if it meant failure in Congress, in order to force the isolationist senators to assume full responsibility for blocking a vital effort for world peace.[87] Though Hull was unable to get Roosevelt to reverse his stand, the President, who had already asked McReynolds to get House approval for the revised resolution, now agreed to drop the whole embargo issue. In a news conference on May 29, 1933, Hull expressed his disappointment over the Senate committee's action but stated that the administration would fight for its original proposal at the next session of Congress. Under questioning by reporters, Hull confessed that the Johnson amendment in effect nullified the administration's plan to co-operate against aggressors.[88]

[85] *Ibid.*, May 26, 1933, p. 3; Moffat Diary, January 2, 1934; *The Memoirs of Cordell Hull* (2 vols.; New York, 1948), I, 229.

[86] *Congressional Record*, June 5, 1933, p. 4967; "Prohibiting the Exportation of Arms or Munitions of War," *Senate Report No. 101*, 73d Cong., 1st sess. (Washington, 1933).

[87] *Hull Memoirs*, I, 229–30.

[88] McReynolds to Sol Bloom, May 27, 1933, HCP, File 73A-D10; *New York Times*, May 30, 1933, p. 4.

In April, J. Pierrepont Moffat had written in his diary, ". . . to such a degree our foreign affairs centralize with the President that no one here really knows what is going on."[89] Roosevelt's action on the arms embargo resolution proved the validity of Moffat's observation. Acting solely on his own discretion, the President had undercut the efforts of Hull and Davis to reorient American foreign policy away from the isolationism of the 1920's. Since the President did not have to justify his action to anyone, there is little direct evidence of the reasons that shaped his decision. Undoubtedly the major consideration was his intense concern for carrying through his domestic reforms. The hundred days were drawing to a close by May, but major legislation, notably the National Recovery Act and the Glass-Steagall banking reform, was still being considered by Congress. A full-scale debate on foreign policy would have jeopardized these measures and created tensions that might have undermined the solid support Roosevelt was gaining from Congress. Another important factor was the isolationist cast of the early New Deal. Struggling to resurrect the American economy from the ashes of the depression, Roosevelt was committed to a program of national planning at home that deliberately excluded international economic co-operation. Raymond Moley, holding the official rank of Assistant Secretary of State and still Roosevelt's most intimate adviser, represented this aspect of the New Deal. Moley opposed the idea of co-operation with European powers for collective security, and it was Moley who informed a number of Democratic senators that Roosevelt had no objections to the Johnson amendment.[90] The ultimate explanation lies hidden in the inner recesses of Roosevelt's thought, and it is possible that the President, talked into abandoning neutrality by Hull and Davis, was expressing his own convictions when he reversed the earlier policy.

The effect of Roosevelt's action is equally difficult to determine. For Hull and Davis, it seemed a blatant step backward which prevented the United States from exercising a responsible role in

[89] Moffat Diary, April 17, 1933.

[90] Edwin Borchard to McReynolds, June 18, 1934, HCP, File 73A-D10.

world affairs. Davis, in a letter to Walter Lippmann on May 31, wrote that a repudiation of the new policy of consultation and surrender of neutral rights would in effect annul the Kellogg-Briand Pact.[91] Yet both Hull and Davis were overly optimistic in believing that their policy would lead to a new era of world peace. The Davis pledge was a purely negative statement whereby the United States would co-operate only on a passive basis, and even this commitment was dependent upon the signing of an effective disarmament agreement. Although the British were pleased by the American proposal, the French felt it was a "timid" step which failed to give France adequate protection against German aggression.[92] The subsequent history of the Geneva Disarmament Conference, ending in total failure in 1934, indicates that even if Roosevelt and Congress had approved the arms embargo, the necessary conditions for fulfillment of the Davis pledge would never have been achieved.

The real significance of the failure of the arms embargo resolution is that even a small step in the direction of a more active American policy toward the world proved unattainable in 1933. The strength of the Wilsonian tradition, embodied in the sincere efforts of men like Hull and Davis, could not dissolve the grip of isolation on the people, the Congress, and the President.

[91] Davis to Lippmann, May 31, 1933, Davis Papers, Box 43.

[92] Lord Tyrrell to Sir John Simon, May 24, 1933, in E. L. Woodward and Rohan Butler (eds.), *Documents on British Foreign Policy, 1919–1939* (London, 1956), Ser. 2, V, 274.

CHAPTER THREE

THE DRIFT TOWARD ISOLATION 1933–35

May the neutrality of the future be based upon the impartiality of justice and humanity, and not upon the impartiality of profits wrung indifferently from the warring peoples.

JAMES BROWN SCOTT, April, 1935

The arms embargo resolution of 1933, intended as a springboard for American participation in collective security, became instead the last stand of the internationalists. In the next two years, other groups began to take over the arms embargo concept and turn it to quite different uses. Peace societies, long concerned over the evils of the international arms trade, suddenly began to find widespread support for their campaign against the munitions industry which culminated in the appointment of the Nye investigating committee in 1934. The subsequent revelations helped stimulate a vociferous demand for the absolute prohibition of arms exports to all belligerents as a way of curbing "the merchants of death." At the same time, international lawyers began to reconsider the traditional concept of neutrality in light of the experience of World War I. Arguing that nations at war no longer respected the rights of neutrals, they contended that only a restrictive neutrality policy which minimized trade and financial contact with belligerents could keep the United States out of future wars. This new concept of neutrality was quickly reinforced by historians, who now claimed that the economic ties between the United States and the Allies had led directly to American entry into World War I. These various groups, beginning from different premises, all arrived at the same conclusion—the United States, instead of cooperating to prevent the outbreak of war, as the internationalists contended, should adopt a stern policy of neutrality designed to insulate the nation from the wars of the future. And above all else, they advocated an impartial arms embargo which would deny the munitions makers their sordid profits and at the same time avoid American economic involvement in foreign conflicts.

I

When Congress convened in January, 1934, the Roosevelt administration had to decide what action to recommend on the arms embargo resolution. There were three alternatives, each backed by members of the State Department. Joseph C. Green, a strong advocate of collective security, urged that the administration press for passage of the original resolution without the Johnson amendment. Citing the strong pressure from the peace societies for arms embargo legislation, Green argued that the end of the Manchurian crisis had removed the danger of antagonizing Japan. Norman H. Davis, still attending the disarmament conference at Geneva, supported Green's position. In a letter to Roosevelt in January, 1934, Davis reminded the President of the necessity for arms embargo legislation to implement the new neutrality policy announced in 1933.[1] A new member of the department, Assistant Secretary of State R. Walton Moore, spoke out in favor of an impartial arms embargo as embodied in the Johnson amendment. Warning that it was very difficult to determine the aggressor, Moore argued that it was dangerous to give the President discrim-

[1] Green to Phillips, November 29, 1933, 811.113/355½; undated memorandum by Joseph C. Green, Davis Papers, Box 2; Davis to Roosevelt, January 25, 1934, 711.00111/54.

inatory authority.[2] J. Pierrepont Moffat offered a more moderate view. In a memorandum to Hull, he advised the Secretary to have the Senate leaders drop the embargo resolution. Moffat believed that any attempt to pass the legislation without the Johnson amendment would lead to a serious controversy in Congress, which at the very least would jeopardize the passage of other administration bills, and which might well lead to an outright defeat. Moffat warned that if Congress did reject the arms embargo resolution, the new policy of neutrality announced by Davis would be completely discredited.[3]

After considering these conflicting viewpoints, President Roosevelt decided to follow the moderate course suggested by Moffat. On February 16 he told William Phillips that "he felt it was wiser to let the arms embargo resolution remain dormant for the present."[4] The State Department informed Senator Pittman of this decision, but Pittman took no action to remove the legislation from the Senate calendar, and on February 28 the Senate unanimously adopted the impartial arms embargo resolution that had been reported by the Senate committee the previous May.[5] Hull, furious at what he felt was an underhanded move by Pittman, cabled Davis in Geneva for advice. Pointing out that it was unlikely that the Senate would accept the resolution without the Johnson amendment, the Secretary asked Davis whether it would be better to accept an impartial embargo or to have the House kill the resolution. On March 3, Davis replied in favor of dropping the whole embargo issue. An impartial embargo, Davis wrote, "would be construed as a repudiation by Congress of the statement made in my speech before the General Commission of the

[2] Moore to Phillips, December 20, 1933, 811.113/377. Moore, a former congressman from Virginia, entered the State Department in the summer of 1933 as a replacement for Raymond Moley.

[3] Moffat to Hull, January 23, 1934, 811.113/378; Moffat Diary, January 23, 1934.

[4] Memorandum by Phillips, February 16, 1934, 811.113/380.

[5] Moffat Diary, February 28, 1934; *Congressional Record*, February 28, 1934, p. 3390.

Disarmament Conference on May 22, 1933."[6] Hull agreed with Davis, and, on March 5, Green secured a promise from Representative McReynolds to block any action on the impartial arms embargo in the House.[7]

The State Department found the issue increasingly difficult in the spring of 1934. Trying to preserve the policy of passive co-operation against aggressors announced by Davis in 1933, the department succeeded in stalling the impartial arms embargo in Congress. But the continuing warfare in the Chaco created an increasing demand to halt the flow of American munitions to Bolivia and Paraguay. The League of Nations had been investigating the Chaco dispute since 1933, and by April, 1934, several members of the League were pressing for an arms embargo against both belligerents.[8] Desiring to co-operate with the League, Hull asked three of his subordinates, Green, Moffat, and Edwin C. Wilson, to study the whole arms embargo question. The three men agreed that a general impartial embargo was unwise, since it "would invariably favor the strong and weaken the weak." In a report to Hull, they suggested instead that the administration should ask Congress for an impartial arms embargo limited exclusively to the Chaco War.[9] In this way, the United States could co-operate with the League in choking off munitions to Bolivia and Paraguay while avoiding the adoption of an impartial arms embargo policy for all situations.

In early May the League committee which had been investigating the Chaco War recommended an embargo on arms to both Bolivia and Paraguay. Great Britain, realizing that American co-operation was essential, sounded out the State Department on the possibility of joint action by the United States. On May 15, Hull

[6] Hull to Davis, March 1, 1934, 811.113/381A; Davis to Hull, March 3, 1934, 811.113/382.

[7] Green to Hull, March 5, 1934, 811.113/383.

[8] Whitney H. Shepardson and William O. Scroggs, *The United States in World Affairs, 1934–1935* (New York, 1935), pp. 131–32.

[9] Moffat Diary, April 3, 4, 1934; memorandum by Joseph C. Green, April 5, 1934, 811.113/411.

conferred with his advisers, and after a lengthy discussion they agreed to seek special embargo powers from Congress to deal with the Chaco War.[10] Though Hull began to have doubts about the wisdom of *ad hoc* legislation, on May 18 he authorized Green to take draft resolutions calling for a Chaco arms embargo to Pittman and McReynolds. Both congressional leaders indicated they preferred to pass the impartial arms embargo measure already before Congress, but they both finally agreed to support the new legislation.[11]

Senator Pittman introduced the State Department resolution on May 18, 1934, and three days later McReynolds sponsored an identical measure in the House. The two resolutions authorized the President to prohibit the sale of arms to both Paraguay and Bolivia, if, in his judgment, such action would contribute to the restoration of peace between the two nations.[12] In letters to Pittman and McReynolds on May 22, Hull strongly urged the adoption of the Chaco legislation. "War in any part of the world," Hull wrote, "is a matter of concern to this Government. But war between two American republics is of special and vital concern, which neither our humanitarian sentiment nor our feeling of American solidarity will permit us to ignore." When McReynolds read this letter to the House Committee on Foreign Affairs, one member asked why the administration did not simply adopt the impartial arms embargo resolution still pending in the House. Green explained the State Department's desire not to nullify the Davis pledge of May 22, 1933, and after some discussion the House

[10] Shepardson and Scroggs, *U.S. in World Affairs, 1934–35*, p. 132; Moffat Diary, May 15, 1934.

[11] Moffat Diary, May 17 and 18, 1934.

[12] "Prohibit Sale of Arms or Munitions of War in the United States under Certain Conditions," *House Report No. 1727*, 73d Cong., 2d sess. (Washington, 1934), p. 1. The embargo applied to the *sale* rather than the *export* of arms to Paraguay and Bolivia because the United States had commercial treaties with those countries which could be interpreted as prohibiting an export embargo. Elton Atwater, *American Regulation of Arms Exports* (Washington, 1941), p. 193.

committee agreed to report out the Chaco embargo resolution.[13] The Senate Foreign Relations Committee also acted favorably, and the measure passed Congress on May 24, 1934, without opposition.[14] On May 28, President Roosevelt signed the Chaco resolution and issued a proclamation banning the sale of arms and munitions of war to both Bolivia and Paraguay. Though the League of Nations never officially adopted an embargo against the Chaco belligerents, eventually twenty-seven other nations embargoed arms to the two Latin American countries.[15]

On the surface, the Chaco embargo appeared to be a step toward American participation in collective security. For the first time in history, the United States employed an arms embargo for the avowed purpose of ending hostilities between two nations. Moreover, this action was taken in order to parallel similar measures by members of the League of Nations. Yet at the same time, it marked a retreat from the policy of a discriminatory embargo that the Roosevelt administration had advocated the year before. The ambiguous position taken by Roosevelt in 1933 continued to hamper the administration's handling of the arms embargo resolution. Desiring a policy which would permit the United States to act co-operatively against an aggressor, but fearing a possible setback in the Senate, the administration lost the initiative and finally had to settle for a limited embargo which left the larger issue of American policy toward aggression in the world unresolved. Though the State Department was still clinging to the Davis pledge of 1933, the retreat from collective security was under way.

II

While the State Department faltered, leadership in the movement for an arms embargo began to pass to the peace societies.

13 *House Report No. 1727*, 73d Cong., 2d sess., pp. 1–2; Green to Hull, May 22, 1934, 724.3415/3722.

14 "Prohibit the Sale of Munitions of War," *Senate Report No. 1153*, 73d Cong., 2d sess. (Washington, 1934); *Congressional Record*, May 23, 1934, p. 9433.

15 *New York Times*, May 29, 1934, p. 1; Atwater, *American Regulation of Arms Exports*, p. 194.

Since the end of World War I, the peace movement in the United States had flourished. Old, conservative organizations such as the American Peace Society and the World Peace Foundation continued to grow, but they were overshadowed by a large number of new groups that emerged during and right after the war. The older societies, using educational techniques to inform the people of international problems, tended to favor co-operation with the League of Nations, but the newer organizations, impelled by an emotional reaction against World War I, were more concerned with isolating the United States from future wars than in international co-operation for peace. Such societies as the National Council for the Prevention of War (NCPW) and the Women's International League for Peace and Freedom (WIL) sought to employ every means of modern public relations to arouse the people against war. Intensive lobbying in Congress, mass rallies with overtones of Protestant evangelism, mammoth petitions bearing thousands of signatures—these and other techniques were skillfully used by the small group of professional workers who directed these societies.[16] In their need for simple, clear-cut issues to present to the public, they focused upon disarmament as a major objective. Operating on the premise that armaments themselves breed wars, leaders such as Frederick J. Libby of the NCPW and Dorothy Detzer of the WIL set out to convince the American people that disarmament was the surest road to world peace.

Until 1933, the peace societies hoped to achieve this goal through international agreement. Encouraged by the limited success of naval reduction in the 1920's, they had looked forward to the Geneva Disarmament Conference with great optimism. They were quickly disillusioned by the futile negotiations at Geneva, and they began to shift their attention to the international arms trade. In the summer of 1933, Dorothy Detzer, convinced that the munitions industry had sabotaged the arms embargo resolution in Congress, renewed a crusade she had begun in 1932 to secure a congressional investigation of American arms companies. Winning support from a number of major peace societies, Miss Detzer ap-

[16] Robert H. Ferrell, "The Peace Movement," in Alexander De Conde (ed.), *Isolation and Security* (Durham, N.C., 1957), pp. 82–83, 99–103.

proached Senator George W. Norris of Nebraska for help in finding a sponsor for the proposed investigation. Together they went down the roster of the Senate, crossing out virtually every name that appeared, until finally they were left with one man—Senator Gerald P. Nye of North Dakota. Norris heartily endorsed Nye, and after considerable persuasion by Miss Detzer, the North Dakota senator agreed to champion the investigation.[17]

Nye, a lean man with a sharp nose and alert, pale-blue eyes, was well suited for his new assignment. Born in Wisconsin, he had become an admirer of Robert M. La Follette, who believed that wars were caused by the same groups responsible for domestic ills —bankers and industrialists. During World War I, Nye moved to North Dakota and became editor of the Cooperstown *Sentinel-Courier*. At this time the Non-Partisan League, a radical political movement that combined the wheat farmers' grievances against eastern financiers and manufacturers with the bitter German-American opposition to American entry into World War I, controlled North Dakota politics. Nye supported the Non-Partisan League in his editorials, and he participated in their strong denunciation of the war as a plot by bankers and munitions makers. Though he was not active in politics, in 1925 he was appointed to the Senate to fill a vacancy. Not quite thirty-three, Nye soon established a reputation as a champion of the common people. He showed a flair for exposing wealth and corruption, participating in the latter stages of the Teapot Dome investigation and heading a committee which probed into election frauds in 1930. Nye was a tense, determined man, sincere but humorless, who was essentially emotional rather than intellectual. Though he had little knowledge of either the munitions industry or the disarmament problem, from his midwestern progressive background he had inherited a set of prejudices which would guide his proposed investigation.[18]

In January, 1934, Nye asked Joseph C. Green, the State Depart-

[17] *Congressional Record*, August 5, 1935, pp. 12464–65; Dorothy Detzer, *Appointment on the Hill* (Washington, 1948), pp. 151–57.

[18] Beverly Smith, "A Voice from the Bleachers," *American Magazine*, CXIX (May, 1935), 47, 116–18; E. Francis Brown, "The Crusading Mr. Nye,"

ment expert on arms control, to draft a resolution calling for an investigation of the munitions industry. Green complied, and on February 8 Nye introduced his resolution in Congress. It was promptly referred to the Senate Foreign Relations Committee. Senator Pittman, hostile to the proposed investigation, then had the resolution transferred to the Military Affairs Committee, where the chances for favorable consideration appeared to be remote.[19]

The Nye resolution might well have remained buried in a Senate committee if it had not been for a sudden outpouring of books and articles on the international arms trade that profoundly influenced the American public. Most significant were two books, *Merchants of Death* by H. C. Engelbrecht and F. C. Hanighen and *Iron, Blood and Profits* by George Seldes, and an anonymous article, "Arms and the Men," published in *Fortune* in March, 1934. These publications, though differing in scope, in tone, and in conclusions, all shared a common premise—the belief that the armsmakers conspired to foment war and disrupt the peace of the world. Referring to them variously as "the blood brotherhood," "merchants of death," and "sinister conspirators," these authors presented case after case where munitions makers had artificially created war scares, had armed their own country's rival, and had sold arms to enemy nations in time of war. The *Fortune* article presented the axiom of the industry, "when there are wars, prolong them; when there is peace, disturb it"; Seldes described the armsmakers as "organized into the greatest and most profitable secret international of our time—the international of bloodshed for profits."[20] Engelbrecht and Hanighen were less emotional in their account, tending to place responsibility on an international order which permitted the munitions industry to thrive, but still they

---

Current History, XLI (February, 1935), 521–27; Samuel Lubell, *The Future of American Politics* (New York, 1951), pp. 136–41.

[19] Memorandum of conversation with Senator Nye by Joseph C. Green, January 18, 1934, 811.113 Senate Investigation/1; Detzer, *Appointment on the Hill*, pp. 157–59.

[20] "Arms and the Men," *Fortune*, IX (March, 1934), 120; George Seldes, *Iron, Blood and Profits* (New York, 1934), p. 13.

described the arms-maker as "one of the most dangerous factors in world affairs—a hindrance to peace, a promoter of war."[21]

These publications, creating the stereotype of the evil munitions maker greedily fomenting war, won nationwide support for the Nye resolution. The peace societies, capitalizing on this publicity, began an all-out effort to win Senate approval. Letters, telegrams, and petitions poured into Congress in March and April pleading for action. Miss Detzer, realizing that administration approval was vital, held a long interview with Cordell Hull, and on March 19, 1934, the Secretary publicly endorsed an investigation of the munitions industry.[22] Finally, on April 12, Nye, by clever parliamentary maneuvering, succeeded in gaining acceptance for his resolution.

A few days later Vice-President John Nance Garner announced the membership of the special Senate committee which would conduct the investigation of the munitions industry. To Hull's astonishment, Nye was made chairman. Ordinarily, Key Pittman, as chairman of the Foreign Relations Committee, would head such an investigation, but Pittman told Garner that he preferred to see Nye conduct the inquiry.[23] Three other members of the committee, Senators Bennett C. Clark of Missouri, Arthur H. Vandenberg of Michigan, and Homer T. Bone of Washington, shared Nye's isolationist viewpoint; W. Warren Barbour of New Jersey and Walter F. George of Georgia held moderate views; only James P. Pope of Idaho was a firm advocate of collective security. The committee quickly chose Stephen Raushenbush, a crusading lawyer who was sponsored by Dorothy Detzer, as chief investigator. In the summer of 1934, Raushenbush, along with his assistant, Alger Hiss, began searching through the files of the major muni-

[21] H. C. Engelbrecht and F. C. Hanighen, *Merchants of Death* (New York, 1934), p. 9.

[22] *Congressional Record*, August 5, 1935, pp. 12464–65; Detzer, *Appointment on the Hill*, pp. 159–61; National Council for the Prevention of War, *News Bulletin*, XIII (April, 1934), 3, 5.

[23] Detzer, *Appointment on the Hill*, pp. 161–63; *The Memoirs of Cordell Hull* (2 vols.; New York, 1948), I, 398.

tions companies for the evidence to present at the public hearings, scheduled to begin in September.[24]

The new committee created a serious dilemma for the Roosevelt administration. Dominated by isolationists, the Nye group was out to prove that the munitions trade, unless curbed by the government, was likely to involve the United States in foreign wars. Though the administration held a different view, believing that the arms problem could only be dealt with through international co-operation, the immense popular support for the Nye investigation made it politically unwise for Roosevelt to voice his opposition. On May 18, 1934, the President attempted a compromise. In a message to Congress, he warmly endorsed the munitions investigation and urged the Senate to appropriate enough money to allow the committee to carry out its task with a "thoroughness commensurate with the high importance of the questions at stake." But then the President recommended that the Senate also approve the 1925 Geneva Arms Convention, stating, "The enlightened opinion of the world has long realized that this is a field in which international action is necessary."[25] Thus Roosevelt supported the Nye committee while championing the ideal of multilateral agreement as the proper solution to the arms problem. It was a skillful political maneuver, but it left the administration in a highly ambiguous position, supporting two incompatible courses of action.

The Senate responded to Roosevelt's plea by approving the Geneva Arms Convention on June 15, 1934. However, Senator William H. King of Utah succeeded in attaching a technical reservation relating to Persia that was unacceptable to the other signatories and thus blocked American adherence to the convention. Though later in the year the United States submitted a new draft treaty for the supervision of the arms trade to the Geneva Disar-

[24] Detzer, *Appointment on the Hill*, pp. 164–68.

[25] "Control of Arms and Munitions Traffic," *Senate Document No. 180*, 73d Cong., 2d sess. (Washington, 1934), p. 1.

mament Conference, this plan never proceeded beyond the discussion stage.[26] The administration's efforts to achieve a solution to the arms problem through international agreement failed, leaving only the alternative of unilateral action favored by the Nye committee.

III

The retreat from collective security, evident in both the Chaco embargo and the creation of the Nye committee, was reinforced by a new interpretation of neutrality that won wide acceptance in 1934. The author was Charles Warren, a distinguished international lawyer who had served as Assistant Attorney-General prior to American entry into World War I. Warren first voiced his views on neutrality at the annual meeting of the American Society of International Law in the spring of 1933. In the midst of a debate between traditionalists, who upheld the historic policy of neutrality, and the advocates of collective security, who favored one-sided action against aggressors, Warren suggested that the only wise course was to curtail trade severely in wartime to avoid involvement in the conflict. In developing this argument, Warren said that neutrality had become a meaningless concept; in World War I both sides consistently violated the neutral rights claimed by the United States. In future wars, Warren suggested, it would be better to abandon all rights and secure whatever trade concessions either belligerent would be willing to permit.[27]

Warren's ideas created great interest, and in January, 1934, the Council on Foreign Relations invited Warren and a number of prominent experts in international affairs, including Borchard, Moffat, Stimson, and Davis, to hold a round-table discussion on neutrality. Warren read the group a paper entitled "How To Try

[26] *Congressional Record*, June 15, 1934, p. 11601; *Hull Memoirs*, I, 231–33.

[27] Charles Warren, "What Are the Rights of Neutrals Now, in Practice?" *Proceedings of the American Society of International Law, 1933* (Washington, 1933), pp. 128–33.

To Keep Out of War," which led to a heated discussion.[28] Two months later, the Council on Foreign Relations published the Warren paper as an article in its periodical *Foreign Affairs* under the title "Troubles of a Neutral." In the introduction, Warren stated that he personally favored a policy of co-operation with other nations to resist aggression abroad, but since most Americans preferred to remain neutral, he was writing to demonstrate how difficult genuine neutrality would be. "There is no magic in the word 'neutrality' as a protection to us against war," Warren declared. "In fact, the very condition of neutrality engenders frictions which nowadays are likely eventually to implicate a powerful neutral in any war in which the Great Powers may be engaged."[29]

In this article, Warren advocated the adoption of a strict neutrality code which would insulate the United States from commercial and financial contact with foreign wars. Among other things, Warren suggested an impartial arms embargo on all belligerents, a ban on loans to warring governments, and a declaration by the United States warning all citizens that they traded with belligerents at their own risk. He drew upon the experience of the First World War to prove the necessity for these restrictions, and he continually emphasized that this type of neutrality required a willingness to sacrifice the profits of neutral trade. Aware that many would find the price of neutrality too high, Warren asserted, "It is better that our citizens should run the risk of commercial loss than the country should be involved in a war to protect their alleged commercial rights."[30]

In the next issue of *Foreign Affairs*, Allen W. Dulles, who had served as Davis' aide at the Geneva conference, replied to Warren in an article entitled "The Cost of Peace."[31] Dulles agreed with

[28] Edwin Borchard to William Borah, December 23, 1933, William E. Borah Papers, File 345, Library of Congress; Moffat Diary, January 10, 1934.

[29] Charles Warren, "Troubles of a Neutral," *Foreign Affairs*, XII (April, 1934), 377.

[30] *Ibid.*, pp. 378–91.

[31] Allen W. Dulles, "The Cost of Peace," *Foreign Affairs*, XII (July, 1934), 567–78.

Warren's view that traditional American neutrality, as practiced from 1914 to 1917, would inevitably lead to American involvement in any major war. However, he challenged the assertion that limitations on trade would be effective. Dulles argued that only a complete surrender of all foreign trade and investment could successfully insulate the United States from a major war, and he predicted that "the American people would never be willing to do anything of the kind." Dulles then asserted that the only practical policy was one of benevolent neutrality, whereby the United States would join with other nations to embargo all trade with the aggressor. Such a policy would serve to keep the United States out of war by preventing conflicts from ever developing. "We are inextricably and inevitably tied in to world affairs," Dulles concluded. "We should not delude ourselves that like Perseus of mythology we can put on a neutrality as a helmet and render ourselves invisible and immune to a world in conflict around us."[32]

Dulles had provided a penetrating criticism of Warren's thesis, but the nation was not in the mood to accept a policy of collective security in 1934. Even the State Department, despite its earlier agreement with Dulles' views, was impressed by Warren's article. On April 17, 1934, Hull asked Moffat, William Phillips, R. Walton Moore, and Green H. Hackworth, the legal adviser, to begin a study of possible neutrality legislation "with a view to keeping us out of further trouble." The four State Department officers, finding that they were too busy to devote time to the neutrality problem, decided to ask Warren to prepare a study for them. On June 7, Warren agreed to undertake the project.[33]

In early August, Warren submitted a 210-page memorandum which presented in detail the program he had outlined in his article in *Foreign Affairs*.[34] The principal recommendation was an impartial arms embargo to be invoked upon the outbreak of any

[32] *Ibid.*, p. 578.

[33] Moffat Diary, April 17, May 31, June 1 and 7, 1934.

[34] A Memorandum on Some Problems on the Maintenance and Enforcement of the Neutrality of the United States, by Charles Warren, August, 1934, 811.04418/28.

foreign war. Calling this measure "imperative," Warren also urged that arms shipments to other neutrals in wartime should be limited to prewar levels in order to prevent transshipment to the belligerents. To avoid any unneutral aid to a warring nation, Warren proposed that the government should prohibit the entry of belligerent armed merchant ships, submarines, and aircraft into American ports or airfields. Recalling the friction created by Americans traveling on belligerent ships prior to American entry into World War I, Warren suggested that the President be empowered to ban American travel on such vessels. The most far-reaching change that Warren advocated dealt with trade in contraband materials other than arms. Pointing out that this commerce had created the most serious problems in the period from 1914 to 1917, he proposed limiting all trade with belligerents to the prewar average. He claimed this could be accomplished by a quota system for all goods on the belligerents' contraband lists—as each additional item appeared on these lists, the United States would automatically set export quotas on that material based on the average for the five years preceding the outbreak of war. In justifying this departure from tradition, Warren asserted, "Under modern conditions, there is no reason why the United States Government should run the risk of becoming involved in a war simply to preserve and protect such excessive profits to be made out of wartrading by some of its citizens."[35]

The Warren memorandum proposed a radical change in American neutrality policy. From a thorough study of the violations of neutral rights that had contributed to American entry into World War I, Warren had devised a neutrality code designed to minimize the danger of American involvement in future wars. This was a pessimistic program which implied that war was inevitable. It denied both the traditional concept of protecting American neutral trade and the newer belief in American co-operation to prevent the outbreak of war. Most of all, it was an isolationist scheme which offered a way to escape entanglement in war and thus fitted perfectly into the national mood of the 1930's.

[35] Warren Memorandum, 811.04418/28, p. 167.

In late August the State Department sent the Warren memorandum to the President. A month later, Roosevelt wrote to Hull expressing a strong interest in the proposals and asking the State Department to prepare draft legislation for possible action by Congress.[36] Hull's original neutrality committee then began studying the Warren program and by November they had agreed upon a tentative neutrality bill. This legislation, drawn up by Green H. Hackworth, followed Warren's suggestions closely. It included an impartial arms embargo, a prohibition on American travel on belligerent ships, and a ban on the entry of belligerent armed merchantmen, submarines, and aircraft into American territory. However, in order to preserve some degree of flexibility, the State Department draft gave the President discretion on whether or not to apply these provisions. Thus the President would not have to invoke an arms embargo or other restrictions unless he felt there was a genuine risk of American involvement in a foreign war. In addition to this change from Warren's proposals, the State Department committee omitted the suggestion of quotas on trade in contraband materials other than arms.[37]

Having reached apparent agreement on a program, the neutrality committee then submitted its proposals to the Justice, War, and Navy Departments for their approval. In a letter to the Attorney-General, William Phillips stated that the purpose of the proposed legislation was "keeping us out of future wars," and he added that if the other departments did not object, it would be sent to the President for submission to Congress.[38] The Justice and War Departments found the proposals acceptable, but the Navy Department raised strong objections. After a conference on December 14, J. Pierrepont Moffat recorded, ". . . the Navy [was] not only obstructive but entirely satisfied with things as they are and entirely prepared to 'wage neutrality.' They opposed any self-

[36] R. Walton Moore to Roosevelt, August 27, 1934, 811.04418/28; Roosevelt to Hull, September 25, 1934, 811.04418/29.

[37] Moffat Diary, September 24, October 12 and 22, 1934; memorandum by Green Hackworth, November 26, 1934, 811.04418/8.

[38] Phillips to Homer Cummings, December 3, 1934, 811.04418/8.

denying ordinances on our part. . . ."[39] In particular, high-ranking naval officers expressed fear that such legislation would give other countries strong grounds for refusing to export strategic materials to the United States in time of war. Admiral C. C. Bloch, the Judge Advocate General, summarized the objections in a letter to Secretary of the Navy Claude A. Swanson. "It would seem," he wrote, "that the proper way to protect the interests of the United States as a neutral would be by international agreement, and not by the enactment of the proposed legislation, which surrenders some of our sovereign rights, in theory at least, and to which no other nation has agreed."[40]

The Navy's opposition created an embarrassing situation for the Roosevelt administration. Early in December, the President had informed reporters that the State Department was preparing neutrality legislation, but he asked them to refrain from making this development public until the administration sent the proposals to Congress. However, the *Washington Post* went ahead and published a report on the neutrality legislation, and on December 16 other newspapers around the country followed suit. These press reports were vague, stating only that the administration planned to ask Congress to pass legislation that would restrict American commerce in time of foreign war.[41] With the Navy now strongly objecting to the proposed legislation, the administration hesitated to make any recommendations to Congress. When the new session began in January, 1935, Senator King of Utah introduced an impartial arms embargo resolution which Senator Pittman referred to the State Department. Assistant Secretary Moore replied that the department was still considering the issue of neutrality and had not yet reached any final conclusions.[42]

[39] Moffat Diary, December 14, 1934.

[40] Claude Swanson to Hull, December 15, 1934, 811.04418/9; C. C. Bloch to Swanson, December 7, 1934, 811.04418/9.

[41] *New York Times*, December 16, 1934, p. 1; Moffat Diary, December 16 and 17, 1934.

[42] R. Walton Moore to Walter Lamb, clerk of the Senate Foreign Relations Committee, January 25, 1935, 811.113/556.

The situation inside the State Department became further confused in mid-January. Norman H. Davis, asked by Hull to comment on the draft legislation prepared by Hackworth, strongly criticized the impartial arms embargo proposal. Warning that in many cases an impartial embargo would favor an aggressor, Davis stated, "I think the President should be given authority to decide whether an embargo on arms should be applied to any one belligerent rather than necessarily to all." Then Davis pointed out that unless the President was given the power to levy a discriminatory embargo, the neutrality legislation would be construed as a repudiation of the pledge to co-operate against aggressors that he had made in 1933.[43]

Davis had raised the central issue—whether the United States should adopt a discriminatory or an impartial arms embargo. Many officials in the State Department, influenced by Warren's persuasive arguments and by Roosevelt's ambiguous stand, had abandoned the attempt to align the United States against aggressors and were now willing to embrace an isolationist policy. Davis, who still believed that American co-operation was essential for European stability, fought desperately to halt the reversal inside the State Department. His arguments evidently impressed his colleagues, for in February the neutrality committee was meeting again and several members of the department were urging Hull to withhold any action until further study could be undertaken.[44] But if Davis had succeeded in temporarily postponing the decision on neutrality policy, it was clear that the administration's faith in the discriminatory arms embargo and the concept of collective security had been seriously undermined.

IV

While the State Department hesitated over Warren's neutrality program, the Nye committee began its investigation of the muni-

[43] Davis to Hull, January 18, 1935, Davis Papers, Box 43.

[44] Moore to Hull, February 8, 1935, 811.04418/30.

tions industry. In the summer of 1934, a score of investigators searched through the files of the major armament companies. Using the Senate's power of subpoena, they carried away thousands of letters, secret agreements, and legal memorandums to provide the evidence for the committee's inquiry. When the public hearings opened in September, 1934, the senators called a succession of witnesses from the shipbuilding, aircraft, powder, armament, and chemical industries.[45] Using the material gathered by its staff, the committee proceeded to expose the practices of the munitions industry. Representatives of the companies tried to defend and explain their actions, but the senators sought confessions, not explanations. Badgering witnesses and insisting on their own interpretation of the endless exhibits, the members of the committee turned the investigation into an inquisition designed to prove the thesis that armament makers were directly responsible for war. Ranging over the two decades prior to 1934, they did reveal many shocking facts. They established a close connection between the munitions makers and the War and Navy Departments; they exposed the extensive lobbying efforts in behalf of military and naval appropriation bills; they demonstrated the arms-makers' dependence on foreign wars for peacetime prosperity; they showed the huge profits earned by munitions companies during World War I; and they brought to light an endless catalogue of dubious business techniques. Though the hearings were published, their greatest impact on the people came through the press. Newspapers followed the proceedings closely, selecting the most dramatic revelations and presenting them with blazing headlines. Senator Nye, who was relatively circumspect in his statements at the hearings, used the press as a vehicle for his more controversial accusations. In statements to reporters and in numerous speeches, Nye made charges that went far beyond the record presented at the hearings.

[45] "Investigation of the Munitions Industry," *Hearings before the Special Senate Committee Investigating the Munitions Industry*, 73d and 74th Cong. (Washington, 1934–36), Parts 1–39. Hearings were held September 4–21, 1934; December 4–20, 1934; January 21–April 26, 1935; and January 7–February 20, 1936.

As a result, the nation received a distorted view of the investigation, learning only of the most sensational evidence and the most extreme interpretations.

In the course of the inquiry, the committee members showed a strong interest in the relationship of the munitions industry to American entry into World War I. Though the committee did not turn its full attention to this subject until 1936, during the September hearings Senator Bone revealed that the Du Pont Company earnings rose from $5 million in 1914 to $82 million in 1916 and that in the latter year the company paid dividends equal to the par value of its stock. Pointing out that this sudden wealth was due to the shipment of exports to the Allies, Bone asked, "Do you suppose we would have had any trouble with Germany if it had not been for our insistence on the exportation of munitions during the war?"[46] The question was rhetorical, but in December, 1934, Senator Clark returned to this subject while questioning Irénée du Pont.

SENATOR CLARK. Of course, Mr. du Pont, you approach the matter of war from an entirely different viewpoint from that held by a good many others.

MR. IRÉNÉE DU PONT. Yes; perhaps. You were not in the game, or you might have a different viewpoint from that held by a good many others.

SENATOR CLARK. I was in the game, though, when it came to putting on a uniform.

MR. IRÉNÉE DU PONT. That is quite true.

SENATOR CLARK. In other words, you approach the subject of war from a viewpoint that regards war as a situation out of which there may be made two or three hundred million dollars of profits and come out with a whole hide. . . . But as far as coming back to the question of the financial relations with the Allies, I think it is of very great importance, because a great many people in this country, including myself, as I said the other day, believed that the insistence of the United States in shipping munitions to one series of combatants ultimately led us into the war. . . .[47]

[46] *Ibid.*, Part 5, pp. 1040–44.

[47] *Ibid.*, Part 12, pp. 2709–10.

When the first half of the Nye hearings closed in the spring of 1935, the American people had become conscious of the evils of the munitions trade and aware that munitions makers helped bring on war. This idea was soon reinforced with the publication of *Road to War: America, 1914–1917*, a book which questioned the wisdom of American entry into World War I.[48] The author was Walter Millis, an editorial writer for the *New York Herald Tribune* who had already published a cynical, debunking account of the Spanish-American War. While he avoided any simple theory of causation, Millis implied that American participation in the war was due to British propaganda, unwise American decisions on neutral rights, and a completely unneutral economic alliance between the United States and the Allies. Millis challenged the view that the United States had any vital interest in the outcome of the war, referring to the conflict as the product of "the ceaseless, intricate, and insane game of European diplomacy."[49] He paid particular attention to the development of the munitions trade with the Allies. Pointing out that the American economy was in a slump at the outbreak of the war, he argued that the "golden stream of prosperity" which began in 1915 was due primarily to the shipment of arms and raw materials to the Allies; ". . . the mighty stream of supplies flowed out and the corresponding stream of prosperity flowed in," he wrote, "and the United States was more deeply enmeshed than ever in the cause of Allied victory."[50]

The most effective portions of the book dealt with the American decisions on neutrality. Millis carefully traced the development of Wilson's stand on neutral rights, showing how the United States acquiesced in the British interruption of American trade to Germany while firmly opposing German submarine attacks on Allied shipping. This differential neutrality, Millis asserted, made the United States "a silent partner of the Entente," thus destroying

[48] Walter Millis, *Road to War: America, 1914–1917* (Boston, 1935).

[49] *Ibid.*, p. 21.

[50] *Ibid.*, pp. 331, 336.

any chance for true impartiality in American policy. The heroes of the book were William Jennings Bryan, who resigned as Secretary of State when Wilson insisted on opposing German submarine warfare, and the pacifist groups, who unsuccessfully tried to enact an impartial embargo on the export of arms. Though Millis refrained from drawing any explicit conclusions, he suggested that an arms embargo would have achieved a practical, as opposed to a formal, neutrality and thus might have prevented American involvement in the war.[51]

Millis' book had a profound impact on the American people. Though a few writers in the 1920's had advanced the same thesis, they had been almost completely ignored. Now the public, aroused by the Nye investigation, eagerly embraced the revisionist interpretation. *Road to War* became a Book-of-the-Month Club selection and eventually sold over 20,000 copies.[52] Vividly written, the book appealed to a generation that was repelled by the horrors of war and was searching frantically for policies that could guarantee American abstention from future conflicts. The growing feeling that American entry into the war had been a tragic mistake now had a historical sanction, and increasingly Americans came to believe that by learning from the errors of the past, they could secure immunity from the contagion of war.

The new concern for American neutrality policy found expression at the annual meeting of the American Society of International Law in April, 1935. The old dispute between advocates of traditional neutrality and supporters of co-operation against aggressors disappeared; Edwin Borchard was the only speaker to defend the historic concept of upholding neutral rights. In its place there arose a new controversy between the co-operationists and a large body of international lawyers who supported the views originally

[51] *Ibid.*, pp. 89, 100–101.

[52] Richard Leopold, "The Problem of American Intervention, 1917: An Historical Retrospect," *World Politics*, II (April, 1950), 408–12. Earlier revisionist accounts include John Kenneth Turner, *Shall It Be Again?* (New York, 1922), and C. Hartley Grattan, *Why We Fought* (New York, 1929), which sold less than 1,000 copies.

advanced by Warren. Henry L. Stimson, Quincy Wright, and Clyde Eagleton continued to preach the new neutrality, stressing the need to co-operate against aggressors in order to prevent the outbreak of war.[53] But they were seriously challenged by those who argued that war was inevitable and that the only safe policy was to curb American contact with the belligerents.

James Brown Scott, who had served as chairman of the State-War-Navy Neutrality Board from 1914 to 1917, opened the meeting with a vigorous attack on traditional neutrality. Asking, "Are we to be dragged into foreign wars by a continuation of a policy of neutrality?" he proceeded to condemn the course the United States had followed during the First World War. He charged that neutral rights served only to protect "the profits of death," and he then recommended that the government end the arms trade and require that all other commerce with belligerents be at the shipper's own risk. "May the neutrality of the future," he concluded, "be based upon the impartiality of justice and humanity, and not upon the impartiality of profits wrung indifferently from the warring peoples."[54] Other speakers elaborated on this theme, stating that traditional neutrality encompassed the incompatible objectives of staying clear of war and at the same time gaining the profits of trade with the belligerents. Only by sacrificing the economic advantages of neutral trade could the nation achieve the higher goal of avoiding involvement in war. "It is high time neutrals decided whether neutrality means peace or profits," asserted one speaker. "It seems doubtful that it can longer mean both."[55]

The meeting adjourned without coming to any conclusion, but it was evident that the overwhelming majority of international lawyers had abandoned the traditional concept of neutrality. As with the State Department, there was a sharp division between those who wished to replace the historic policy with measures

[53] *Proceedings of the American Society of International Law, 1935* (Washington, 1935), pp. 25, 90, 121–27, 130–33.

[54] James Brown Scott, "The Neutrality of the Good Neighbor," *ibid.*, pp. 6–11.

[55] *Ibid.*, pp. 56–58, 66–67, 83–85.

tending toward isolation and those who preferred to substitute a program of collective security. This was a vital disagreement, but it masked the significant fact that both groups agreed on the need for a radical change in the nation's neutrality policy. It meant that the pressures for neutrality legislation were becoming intense, and that the question was no longer whether the nation should redefine its policy but rather what the character of the new program should be. And by the spring of 1935, the trend was clearly toward an isolationist policy. The supporters of collective security, who had originally urged a change in American neutrality, found their proposals gradually being turned against them. The wavering attitude of the Roosevelt administration, the coherent program set forth by Charles Warren, the sensational disclosures of the Nye committee, the historical interpretation advanced by Millis—all these factors were transforming the impulse for neutrality revision into a rigid program of isolation.

CHAPTER FOUR

THE TRIUMPH OF ISOLATION, 1935

Congress is in a state of hysteria. The Administration is silent.

JOSEPH C. GREEN, August 21, 1935

In the spring of 1935, the debate on American neutrality moved toward a climax. For seven years international lawyers, interested congressmen and senators, and State Department officers had wrestled with the problem of American policy toward foreign aggression. Yet the people, caught up in the turmoil of the depression, had paid little attention to the controversy. As long as the world remained at peace, neutrality seemed only to be an abstract and theoretical issue. But by the early months of 1935, the public, already aroused by the Nye investigation, was becoming deeply concerned over an increasingly serious European crisis and its possible effect on American security. As Germany and Italy began to threaten the status quo, Americans sought desperately for a way to insulate themselves from the possibility of war.

Many American observers had been aware of this threat as early as the autumn of 1933, when Germany withdrew from the Geneva Disarmament Conference and severed its connection with the League of Nations. The Geneva conference resumed its sessions in the spring of 1934, but it began a slow and lingering death in June when the plenary session adjourned and left the vital problems of security, armament, and the munitions trade in the hands of committees. Meanwhile, an arms race was under way. The world expenditure on military weapons rose rapidly between 1933 and 1935, and even the United States, removed from the immediate rivalries of Europe, adopted its largest peacetime military budget in 1935. The most alarming development came on March 16, 1935, when Adolf Hitler announced that Germany was inaugurating a policy of universal military conscription designed to raise an army of 500,000 men. Great Britain and France protested against this open violation of the Treaty of Versailles, and though the League Council formally condemned Germany's rearmament, Britain tacitly condoned it by signing a treaty with Germany in June allowing Hitler to build a navy one-third the size of England's. The growth of armaments, reminiscent of the years before 1914, was accompanied by a return to power politics which ignored the collective ideal of the League of Nations. In the spring of 1935, France and the Soviet Union signed a treaty of mutual assistance which reflected their growing fear of Germany, while England, holding herself aloof from this alliance, attempted to achieve a balance of power in Europe by continually shifting her support from one nation to another.[1]

The first overt act occurred in December, 1934, when a small Italian force clashed with Ethiopian troops at the desert oasis of Walwal on the undefined border between Abyssinia and the Italian Somaliland. Italian reinforcements finally drove the Ethiopians back, but only after sporadic fighting had led to several hundred casualties. Border clashes were common in this area, but when Haile Selassie, the emperor of Ethiopia, rejected Italian demands for an apology and an indemnity of $100,000, Benito Mussolini sent large numbers of troops into Italian East Africa. In January, Italy finally withdrew her demands and agreed to arbitration of the Walwal incident, but the tension continued as Mussolini delayed selecting arbitrators and continued to pour troops and military supplies

[1] Arnold J. Toynbee and V. M. Boulter, *Survey of International Affairs, 1935* (2 vols.; London, 1936), I, 33–58; Whitney H. Shepardson and William D. Scroggs, *The United States in World Affairs, 1934–35* (New York, 1935), pp. 213, 231–37.

into his African colonies. England and France, deeply concerned about Germany's resurgence under Hitler, moved cautiously, trying to moderate Mussolini's policy without creating an open break with Italy. By May, the arbitration had not yet begun, and the danger of war in Africa had increased. For a generation which vividly remembered the obscure incidents leading to the outbreak of hostilities in 1914, the Ethiopian crisis was a dangerous affair that threatened the peace of the entire world.[2]

These events abroad intensified the prevailing mood of isolationism in the United States. In January the Roosevelt administration, in an effort to redeem a campaign promise, decided to ask the Senate to approve American adherence to the World Court. Although created by the League of Nations, it was an independent organization open to all nations of the world. In 1926 the Senate had voted in favor of American membership on the Court, but a reservation sponsored by isolationists had proved unacceptable to the other members. In 1929, Elihu Root had formulated an acceptable compromise, but opponents, charging that it was subservient to the League, were able to delay Senate consideration until 1935. On January 9, the Senate Foreign Relations Committee recommended American participation in the World Court, and a few days later an intense debate began on the Senate floor. At first, observers predicted an easy victory, but in the last week in January an avalanche of letters, petitions, and telegrams, stimulated by the Hearst press and the Detroit radio priest, Father Coughlin, arrived in Washington opposing the Court as a backdoor entrance to the League of Nations. Roosevelt, though he had earlier sent a brief message to the Senate urging a favorable vote, refused to commit himself further on the issue, and when the final vote was taken on January 29, the protocol for American membership on the Court fell seven votes short of the required two-thirds majority. While this action did not necessarily mirror the sentiments of the American people, it was clear proof that a sizable and vocal

[2] *Ibid.*, pp. 238–42; Toynbee and Boulter, *Survey of International Affairs, 1935*, II, 133–38.

section violently opposed any form of international commitment, however innocuous, by the United States.[3]

This deepening isolationism of the American people in the mid-1930's was accompanied by a strong surge of pacifism among college students. Impressed by their elders' disillusion with the First World War, college youth began to question the validity of military service. In the spring of 1933, the Brown University campus newspaper, reacting against newsreels that glorified military and naval preparedness, conducted a poll of college opinion on war. Over twenty thousand students in sixty-five colleges participated, and of this number, 72 per cent voted against serving in the armed forces in wartime, with nearly half stating that they would not bear arms even if the United States were invaded.[4] The following year, left-wing student organizations sponsored a nationwide strike against war. On April 13, 1934, an estimated 25,000 students left their classes to attend antiwar demonstrations where students and faculty members gave impassioned speeches denouncing military service and urging the youth to pledge themselves never "to support the Government of the United States in any war it might conduct."[5] In 1935 even bigger demonstrations were held under the sponsorship of Communist, Socialist, and religious youth organizations. On April 12, a reported 60,000 students participated in the antiwar strike. In New York City, 10,000 youths paraded on campuses, carrying placards that read, "Life Is Short Enough," "Build Schools—Not Battleships," and "Abolish the R.O.T.C."[6] Though representing only a tiny fraction of the nation's youth, the college pacifists reflected the distaste for war which underlay the dominant isolationism of the American people.

[3] Shepardson and Scroggs, *United States in World Affairs, 1934–35*, pp. 222–26; Dexter Perkins, *The New Age of Franklin Roosevelt* (Chicago, 1957), pp. 97–98.

[4] Harold Seidman, "The Colleges Renounce War," *Nation*, CXXXVI (May 17, 1933), 554–55; *ibid.*, CXXXVI (May 24, 1933), 571.

[5] *New York Times*, April 14, 1934, p. 1.

[6] *Literary Digest*, CXIX (March 23, 1935), 17; *New York Times*, April 13, 1935, pp. 1, 3.

It was against this backdrop—impending war in Africa, the resurgence of an armed Germany, deepening isolationism and pacifism in the United States—that the neutrality debate emerged as a significant issue for the American people. The theoretical arguments about American co-operation against aggressors and the disputes over arms embargoes became important to the average American for the first time. The advocates of rigid neutrality now sought to capitalize upon the public concern to achieve a legislative program that would guarantee American abstention from European war. The result was a flight from reality, fed by fear and insecurity, which culminated in the passage of the first neutrality act in August, 1935.

I

When Congress convened in January, 1935, the Roosevelt administration found itself in a difficult position. The State Department had already prepared draft neutrality legislation, but the disagreement inside the department over whether the arms embargo should be discriminatory or impartial, coupled with the Navy's opposition to any renunciation of traditional neutral rights, caused the President to postpone making any recommendations to Congress on this subject. However, the armament issue could not be so easily put aside. The Nye committee had stimulated such intense national interest in the munitions trade that some form of action by Congress was almost inevitable. The State Department preferred to work along the lines of international agreement, hoping for either unqualified Senate approval of the 1925 Geneva Arms Convention or negotiation of a new international treaty similar to the one submitted by the United States to the Geneva Disarmament Conference in November, 1934. In an effort to implement this approach, Joseph C. Green suggested to Senator Nye that he introduce a munitions control bill which would allow the United States to license and supervise the export of arms and munitions. In February, Nye agreed to this proposal, but at the same time he indicated that he also favored legislation to abolish the private manufacture of arms and place this industry under an absolute government monopoly.[7]

On March 14, Secretary of State Hull, in reply to a request by Roosevelt for advice, sent the President a long memorandum on the arms issue. Warning that the Nye committee planned to issue a preliminary report to the Senate on April 1, Hull urged Roosevelt to refrain from making any recommendations to Congress on arms legislation before that date. Discussing the various alternatives, Hull advised against a government monopoly and instead suggested that Roosevelt meet with the investigating committee to urge their acceptance of a draft munitions control bill being prepared under Green's supervision. Pointing out that this measure would enable the United States to co-operate with other nations in regulating the arms trade, Hull stressed the need to direct the Nye committee toward an international solution to the munitions problem. The Secretary specifically requested the President to ask the Nye committee to support the American plan for a new international arms control treaty, and if this proved too difficult to negotiate, to assist in gaining Senate approval for the 1925 Geneva Arms Convention.[8]

When the President met with the Nye committee on March 19, he completely disregarded Hull's memorandum. After discussing the possibilities of taking the profit out of war by levying high taxes on industry, he turned to the issue of neutrality legislation. Stating that he now believed that Secretary of State Bryan had been absolutely right in 1915, Roosevelt told the senators that he was preparing to recommend legislation prohibiting American ships and American citizens from traveling to belligerent nations in time of war. The President then urged the committee to begin studying the whole issue of neutrality and to prepare appropriate legislation. When the astonished senators readily agreed, Roosevelt asked them to submit their proposals to him before introducing them in Congress. The meeting ended with only an incidental

[7] February 20, 1935, *FR: 1935*, I, 316; Joseph C. Green to author, November 19, 1960.

[8] *Ibid.*, I, 318–21.

reference to the question of control of the international arms traffic.[9]

Roosevelt's suggestion that the Nye committee prepare neutrality legislation, described by the *New York Times* as a "casual remark," had a profound influence on subsequent developments.[10] The committee, which up to that time had not considered making any legislative proposals on neutrality, now felt it held a mandate from the President to act on this subject. In late March, Stephen Raushenbush told Green that the committee "was 'hot on the trail' of this neutrality matter." When Green replied that the problem was very complex and suggested that the senators should hold off for a while, Raushenbush told him, "the committee was now so interested in the subject of neutrality and so anxious to get ahead with the drafting of legislation, that he doubted very much whether it would be willing to delay."[11]

Roosevelt's motive in directing the Nye committee into the neutrality issue is difficult to determine, but it seems highly improbable that he did so accidentally. He may have hoped to divert the investigators from their sensational inquiry into the munitions industry, for the administration was already embarrassed by Nye's publication of confidential diplomatic correspondence. Even more likely, the President may have become dissatisfied with the State Department's procrastination on the matter of neutrality legislation. Though he had asked the department to prepare recommendations in September, the bitter disagreement among the officers of the department had prevented the emergence of any clear-cut proposals. Impatient with this delay, he could well have been using the Nye committee as a way of forcing the State De-

[9] Memorandum of conversation with Senators Nye and Pope by Joseph C. Green, March 20, 1935, *ibid.*, I, 363–64; John T. Flynn, *The Roosevelt Myth* (New York, 1948), pp. 168–69; memorandum of conversation with Stephen Raushenbush by Joseph C. Green, March 27, 1935, 811.113 Sen. Invest./242.

[10] *New York Times*, March 27, 1935, p. 21.

[11] Memorandum of conversation with Stephen Raushenbush by Joseph C. Green, March 27, 1935, 811.113 Sen. Invest./242.

partment to act.[12] In any case, whether Roosevelt was acting casually or with deliberate shrewdness, his conference with the senators was the catalyst that precipitated action on neutrality legislation. The Nye committee, given free rein by the President, was now determined to achieve a program that would keep the United States out of the next war.

The new concern of the Nye committee with neutrality legislation soon became apparent. On March 28, while questioning Bernard M. Baruch, Senator Homer T. Bone stated that in case of foreign war the United States should forbid "the movement of both commodities and human beings into the war zone," claiming that such a policy would have averted American entry into the First World War.[13] Two days later, in a speech at Lexington, Kentucky, Senator Nye told his audience that President Roosevelt had suggested that the investigating committee study the neutrality problem and that the President "has voiced a determination to keep America out of another war at all costs." Then Nye spelled out his formula for avoiding involvement in future conflicts by advocating an embargo on arms and loans to belligerents and a ban on American travel on belligerent ships.[14]

In late March, members of the Senate Foreign Relations Committee became angry when they heard rumors that the Nye committee was planning to recommend neutrality legislation to the Senate. Senator Pittman protested vigorously to Hull, who instructed Green to inform Nye that neutrality was solely within the province of the Foreign Relations Committee. Though Stephen Raushenbush replied that the investigating committee was acting "at the specific request of the President," the protest was effective.[15] When Senator Nye presented the preliminary re-

[12] Ernest K. Lindley, *Half Way with Roosevelt* (New York, 1937), p. 310.

[13] "Munitions Investigation," Special Senate *Hearings*, 74th Cong., 1st sess., Part 22, 6344–45.

[14] *New York Times*, March 31, 1935, p. 26.

[15] Memorandum by Joseph C. Green, March 30, 1935, *FR: 1935*, I, 324–25; Stephen Raushenbush to Senator Nye, March 30, 1935, Papers of the Special Senate Committee Investigating the Munitions Industry, Box 20, National Archives, Record Group 46.

port of his committee on April 1, he stated that his group had agreed on the need to regulate the export of arms but that other aspects of the neutrality problem were beyond the investigating committee's jurisdiction.[16] On the same day, Nye asked his group to approve a letter to Roosevelt stating that the neutrality proposals would be left to the Senate Foreign Relations Committee.[17]

Though Senator Nye was willing to placate Pittman, he had no intention of abandoning the neutrality issue. On April 9, Nye and Bennett C. Clark, acting as individual senators rather than as members of the investigating committee, introduced two neutrality resolutions in Congress.[18] The first proposed to grant the President power to "withhold the issuance of passports to citizens of the United States travelling in war zones or travelling on any vessel of any belligerent power except under such rules as the President may prescribe."[19] The companion measure forbade the issuance of loans or the extension of credit for the purchase of contraband goods to any belligerent government. This ban was to be applied automatically upon the outbreak of war, and in case of a conflict other than a declared war, the President could apply it at his discretion.[20] These two resolutions, embodying some of the most important features of Warren's neutrality program, were acceptable to Senator Pittman, since they were to be referred to the Foreign Relations Committee for consideration.[21]

Even before Nye and Clark introduced their proposals, two congressmen, influenced by the munitions committee's concern over neutrality, sponsored sweeping legislation in the House. Maury Maverick of Texas, a fiery and outspoken freshman Representative, introduced a resolution embodying an embargo on

16 *Congressional Record*, April 1, 1935, p. 4726.

17 Minutes of committee meeting, April 1, 1935, Munitions Committee Papers, Box 157.

18 Memorandum by Joseph C. Green, April 10, 1935, *FR: 1935*, I, 329.

19 Text of Senate Joint Resolution 99, SCP, File 74A-E2.

20 "Prohibit the Extension of Credits and Issuance of Loans," *Senate Report No.* 988, 74th Cong., 1st sess. (Washington, 1935), p. 1.

21 Pittman to Wallace Murray, April 11, 1935, *FR: 1935*, I, 330.

arms and contraband materials to all belligerents and a ban on travel on belligerent ships, while Representative Frank Kloeb of Ohio put forward a bill prohibiting loans similar to the Nye-Clark measure in the Senate.[22] Thus, three weeks after Roosevelt's conference with the Nye committee, a wide range of neutrality proposals was before the two houses of Congress.

Secretary of State Hull, unprepared for Roosevelt's sudden interest in neutrality and the resulting legislative proposals, tried to resolve the continuing dispute inside the State Department. On April 10 departmental officers drafted a memorandum to be sent to the President over Hull's signature outlining a comprehensive plan of legislation. The draft proposals were identical to those prepared by Green H. Hackworth in the fall of 1934—an impartial arms embargo, a travel ban, and a prohibition on the entry of submarines into American ports. The memorandum stressed the need "to lessen the chances of our being drawn into any future war," and in the section on the arms embargo, the authors emphasized the impartial feature, stating, "this being necessary in order to preserve our neutrality."[23] When Joseph C. Green saw this draft, he raised vigorous objections which finally led Hull to veto the memorandum.[24] Instead the Secretary met personally with the President on April 10 to explain the lack of agreement on neutrality legislation. In a press conference held after this meeting, Hull stated that the State Department was still studying the problem and was not yet ready to submit any final recommendations to the President. Though Hull admitted that Roosevelt was concerned about neutrality legislation because of the danger of war in Europe, he indicated that the administration wished to avoid a long, protracted debate which would interfere with pressing domestic legislation in Congress.[25]

[22] *Congressional Record*, April 6, 1935, pp. 5184–85; *ibid.* (March 29, 1935), p. 4719.

[23] Draft of memorandum from Hull to Roosevelt, April 10, 1935, 811.-04418/42½.

[24] Green to Moffat, April 10, 1935, 811.04418/42½.

[25] *New York Times*, April 11, 1935, p. 3.

The next day Hull sent the President a memorandum in which he reiterated the statements he had made to the press on April 10. After reviewing the Nye committee's action following the conference with Roosevelt, Hull emphasized the complexity of the neutrality problem and "the great diversity of opinion" among the President's advisers. Though Hull offered to send along the latest State Department proposals, he added, "I am not prepared to advocate this or any other specific program for legislation on this subject at this time."[26] In his *Memoirs*, Hull bluntly states that he was firmly opposed to any legislation on neutrality, and that he particularly objected to the strict measures advocated by Nye which Hull felt would shackle American foreign policy and thus prevent the United States from playing a constructive and moderating role in the developing world crisis.[27] Though Hull was probably speaking from hindsight when he expressed these views, there is no doubt that he was opposed to isolationist neutrality in 1935. However, the strong movement in Congress, together with Roosevelt's support for new legislation, forced him to move cautiously in attempting to prevent passage of a rigid neutrality program. His most effective tactics were delay and procrastination, and he used them constantly in the spring of 1935 in an effort to kill the neutrality proposals without publicly opposing them.

Hull's task was difficult, for the neutrality enthusiasts in Congress, spurred on by ominous news from Europe, pressed hard to overcome the State Department's inactivity. In a letter on April 10, Maury Maverick urged Hull to support his resolution, warning that the imminence of war made delay dangerous. The Secretary called the Texas congressman in for a conference and explained the complexity of the neutrality problem and the need for continued study.[28] When McReynolds asked him for advice on the Kloeb bill, Hull instructed Joseph C. Green to explain that "until the question could be more thoroughly studied and some definite

[26] *FR: 1935*, I, 331–32.

[27] *The Memoirs of Cordell Hull* (2 vols.; New York, 1948), I, 406–10.

[28] Maverick to Hull, April 10, 1935, 811.04418/37; Hull to Maverick, April 16, 1935, 811.04418/37.

line of action decided upon, it would be unwise for the Secretary to express his opinion on any bill, such as H.R. 7125, dealing with one phase of the subject."[29] These tactics did not end the drive for legislation, but they did help dampen the ardor of the neutrality bloc in Congress. On April 12, Green, after attending an executive session of the munitions committee, reported that Senator Nye "wished that the committee could wash its hands of the whole question of neutrality legislation; that the committee had never contemplated dealing with such legislation until 'the President had laid it on our doorstep.' "[30]

While Hull attempted to delay the neutrality movement in Congress, the debate over American policy attracted considerable attention from groups concerned with foreign affairs. In early April the *Nation* attacked the Nye-Clark resolutions, asserting that the United States could not cut off all contact with the world in case of war. "Any great war would ultimately affect interests which we are incapable of denying," the editors wrote. "The genuine guarantee of peace for ourselves is peace for the world at large."[31] Later in the month, speakers at a dinner of the Foreign Policy Association were equally critical. Senator James Pope, a member of the Nye committee, charged that a strict neutrality program would signify a policy of "hiding and ducking," while Congressman Frederic R. Coudert exclaimed, "you can't turn the American eagle into a turtle." Walter Millis was the only speaker to defend the Nye-Clark resolutions, stating that they would tend to keep the nation out of war by establishing a genuine neutrality.[32]

The reaction of peace societies was more friendly. The National Council for the Prevention of War, which in October of 1934 had adopted a resolution opposing neutrality in favor of co-operating

[29] McReynolds to Hull, April 8, 1935, 800.51 Kloeb Bill/1; Green to Hull, April 12, 1935, 800.51 Kloeb Bill/1.

[30] *FR: 1935*, I, 340.

[31] "The Problem of Neutrality," *Nation*, CXL (April 10, 1935), 404.

[32] *New York Times*, April 23, 1935, p. 5.

with other nations to prevent war, suddenly changed its position. In May, Frederick J. Libby, the editor of *Peace Action*, official monthly magazine of the NCPW, urged his readers to support the neutrality resolutions sponsored by Nye, Clark, and Maverick. Libby justified his sudden shift by explaining that the danger of war in Europe, coupled with the continuing reluctance of the American people to support collective security measures, made strict neutrality the only expedient method for insuring American abstention from a European conflict. "We support this legislation," he wrote, "while at the same time we cherish no illusions that efforts to keep out of general war are any substitute for the prevention of war through the World Court and a revised League of Nations."[33] Libby was facing a dilemma that soon divided the entire peace movement on the issue of neutrality legislation. Many pacifist organizations, torn between a belief in collective security and the desire to avoid American involvement in war, abandoned the Wilsonian ideal for the immediate goal of rigid neutrality.

Encouraged by increasing support from pacifist groups, Senators Nye and Clark introduced a third resolution on May 7 which proposed an embargo on the shipment of arms to all belligerents. In addition, their measure stated that the government would not protect or defend the export of goods declared to be contraband by any belligerent—such shipments would be at the risk of the exporter.[34] The impartial arms embargo was a logical and an expected addition to the Nye-Clark program, but the contraband goods clause was an innovation that revealed the complexity of any effort to minimize commercial contacts with nations at war. In an undated memorandum to Stephen Raushenbush, probably written in the spring of 1935, Senator Nye confessed, "My own belief is that a complete embargo on all trade is the only absolute insurance against the United States being drawn into another prolonged major war between great powers. I am convinced that

[33] *Peace Action*, I (November, 1934), 10; *ibid.*, I (May, 1935), 1, 9.

[34] Text of Senate Joint Resolution 120, May 7, 1935, SCP, File 74A-E2.

drastic legislation to accomplish this could not be passed even in time of peace."[35] Thus Nye, believing that only a total embargo would guarantee American abstention from a world war, sought a feasible compromise by banning all arms exports and discouraging the shipment of contraband raw materials.

The threefold neutrality program offered by Nye and Clark led to an intensive appeal by peace societies to end the administration's procrastination. On May 27 the National Peace Conference, a committee representing twenty-eight different pacifist groups, held a mass meeting in Carnegie Hall in New York City. Under the slogan, "How To Keep America Out of War," Senators Nye and Clark, along with Representative Maverick, delivered fiery speeches to an enthusiastic audience. Denouncing bankers, industrialists, and munitions makers as instigators of war, they appealed for adoption of a strict policy of neutrality. They repeatedly stressed the need for urgency—war was approaching in Europe and the United States must be prepared to avoid the costly mistakes of 1917. Senator Clark summed up their views when he declared that neutrality legislation, while not an "automatic safeguard, does lessen some of the most important dangers as revealed by our World War experience."[36]

A week later the National Peace Conference adopted its statement of principles. In regard to neutrality, the declaration stated that the policy of the United States "should be revised in order that the risk of entanglement in foreign wars may be reduced and in order that the United States may not obstruct the world community in its efforts to maintain peace."[37] This ambiguous statement reflected the continuing dilemma of the pacifist groups. Having campaigned for years for a discriminatory arms embargo aimed at aggressors, they were loath to abandon completely their collective security orientation. Yet their goals were now incompatible—the rigid neutrality that they advocated was the very

[35] Munitions Committee Papers, Box 149.

[36] *Peace Action,* I (June, 1935), 6; *New York Times,* May 28, 1935, p. 27.

[37] *Peace Action,* II (August, 1935), 8.

antithesis of the policy of co-operation for peace. This same problem faced the religious groups which now rallied to the support of neutrality legislation. In June the Federal Council of Churches adopted a resolution which stated, "We believe that the United States should withhold aid from all belligerents in any conflict that might arise in the future." Yet at the same time this body went on record in support of the World Court and a policy of international co-operation for peace.[38]

Despite their own internal doubts, the peace societies began to apply mounting pressure on Congress in behalf of neutrality legislation. In June and July of 1935, telegrams and letters began arriving in Washington from local branches of the Women's International League urging passage of the Maverick resolution. The writers referred to the policy of neutral rights that led to American entry into World War I and appealed for a new program before war came again in Europe. Letter after letter mentioned the tense Ethiopian situation, describing it as the prelude to a great war.[39] At the same time, the NCPW began a series of radio broadcasts over eight eastern stations. Each week prominent congressmen spoke out in favor of rigid neutrality legislation.[40] By the beginning of summer, the nation was becoming fully aware of the pending neutrality legislation.

In Congress, Representative Maverick became the most vocal advocate of rigid neutrality. In a speech in late May, he pleaded for action on his resolution. "How are we going to stay out of a war if one starts?" he asked. "The answer is: by maintaining neutrality from the very beginning and not meddling in affairs that do not concern us."[41] Maverick's pressure, coupled with the effective lobbying by the peace societies, finally forced Representative McReynolds to schedule hearings before the House Foreign Af-

[38] Federal Council of Churches of Christ in America, *Annual Report, 1935* (New York, 1936), p. 91.

[39] HCP, File 74A-D14.

[40] Gilbert D. Stinger, "Tune in the NCPW," *Peace Action*, II (August, 1935), 7.

[41] *Congressional Record*, May 29, 1935, p. 8413.

fairs Committee on the Kloeb and Maverick bills in mid-June.[42] The authors of the two measures were the chief witnesses, and they reiterated the now-familiar arguments for neutrality legislation. Representative Kloeb, pleading for his proposed ban on loans, denied that he was an isolationist. His motive was "the preservation of white civilization," he announced, and then he asserted that governments would hesitate to engage in war if they knew beforehand that American financial resources would be closed to them.[43] Maverick was less altruistic. Acknowledging that the United States had some responsibility for world peace, he nevertheless asserted, ". . . I think the best way that we can discharge that obligation to humanity at this stage of history is by staying out of war ourselves; it seems perfectly apparent that we cannot stop that war; so the best way is to stay out of it ourselves at least."[44] The only other witness to appear was Phillip Bradley, a professor of social science at Amherst College who spoke for the National Peace Conference. Bradley urged adoption of a four-point program designed to keep American arms, contraband goods, money, and travelers away from belligerent countries. There were no witnesses to testify against the neutrality bills, but several members of the committee, especially Chairman McReynolds and Luther Johnson of Texas, revealed their opposition during intense cross-examination of Kloeb, Maverick, and Bradley.[45]

When the hearings closed, the committee took no action on the pending legislation. Thus McReynolds was able to carry through a promise he had made earlier to Secretary Hull not to report out any neutrality measures without prior State Department approval.[46] But the hearings did serve to stimulate still further the growing national demand for action on American neutrality.

[42] "American Neutrality Policy," *Hearings before the House Committee on Foreign Affairs*, 74th Cong., 1st sess. (Washington, 1935).

[43] *Ibid.*, pp. 1–7.

[44] *Ibid.*, pp. 42–54.

[45] *Ibid.*, pp. 12–14, 19, 25, 34, 37–38.

[46] Joseph C. Green to Norman H. Davis, July 8, 1935, Davis Papers, Box 26.

II

While the administration was trying to stall the neutrality legislation, the State Department renewed its efforts toward international control of the arms trade. Though Hull had urged Roosevelt to get the Nye committee to support a bill to create a munitions control board to regulate arms exports, the President neglected to mention this subject to the members of the committee when he met with them in March. At a second conference with the Nye group in April, Roosevelt again avoided bringing up the State Department proposal. Green, who ardently believed that such a measure was vital if the United States was to co-operate with other nations to control the munitions traffic, learned from Raushenbush in early May that the committee had gained the impression that the President was not interested in the proposal and thus they had dropped it.[47] Green then prevailed upon Hull to urge the President to reconsider, and when Roosevelt met with the investigating committee a third time on May 13, he asked the group to sponsor legislation empowering the administration to supervise the arms trade.[48] With this support, Green was able to persuade Senator Pope to introduce a munitions control bill. On June 20 the Senate Foreign Relations Committee reported favorably on the Pope bill, which proposed to establish a National Munitions Control Board to license all arms shipments and publish the export totals annually.[49]

At the same time, Hull pressed for unqualified Senate approval of the 1925 Geneva Arms Convention. On June 6, Senator Pittman brought this treaty before the Senate and requested approval as a step toward international control of the munitions traffic. After rejecting a reservation that had blocked ratification of the convention the year before, the Senate quickly gave its consent.[50]

[47] Green to Hull, May 7, 1935, 811.113/608.

[48] Hull to Roosevelt, May 8, 1935, 811.113/608; R. Walton Moore to Hugh Wilson, June 3, 1935, 811.113/613.

[49] "Trade in Arms, Ammunition, and Implements of War," *Senate Report No. 915*, 74th Cong., 1st sess. (Washington, 1935), pp. 1–4.

[50] *Congressional Record*, June 6, 1935, pp. 8790–99.

Thus, by mid-June, the administration had finally succeeded in achieving an international approach to the arms problem which offered an alternative to the isolationist efforts to abolish the private manufacture of arms. Though this program did not lessen the growing demand for neutrality legislation, it gave some hope to those who still believed that American security rested fundamentally on policies of international co-operation.

The administration had little time to enjoy this small victory. On June 26, without warning, the Senate Foreign Relations Committee agreed to report out the Nye-Clark resolutions restricting travel and loans in time of war.[51] The committee also planned to act favorably on the third Nye-Clark measure, the impartial embargo on arms, but this was postponed until their next meeting when time ran short. Hull, who believed he had an informal understanding with Pittman not to act on any of the neutrality bills, was astonished.[52] After consulting the President, Hull sent Norman H. Davis to persuade Senator Pittman to have the Foreign Relations Committee reconsider its action. Davis spent several hours with Pittman on the evening of June 27, and the next morning he reported that Pittman was now willing to "stifle" the legislation. However, Davis suggested that both Hull and Roosevelt talk to Pittman personally to prevent him from wavering again. Davis stressed the need for confidential meetings, warning that it would be unwise for the administration to oppose the neutrality legislation openly.[53]

Davis was overly optimistic; the President met with Pittman on June 29, but he was unable to reach a satisfactory agreement.[54] Then on July 3, the House Foreign Affairs Committee, thinking that the administration no longer objected to neutrality measures,

[51] "Passports to American Citizens in Time of War," *Senate Report No.* 987, 74th Cong., 1st sess. (Washington, 1935); *Senate Report No.* 988, 74th Cong., 1st sess.

[52] Memorandum by Joseph C. Green, June 27, 1935, 138/3427; *Hull Memoirs*, I, 410.

[53] William Phillips to Hull, June 28, 1935, 811.04418/55.

[54] Memorandum by Phillips, June 29, 1935, 811.04418/55.

reported out the Kloeb bill to ban loans to belligerents.[55] Hull immediately telephoned McReynolds, explained his opposition to all neutrality legislation, and secured a promise that regardless of what action the Senate took, McReynolds would prevent any neutrality bills from coming to a vote in the House.[56] Hull could count on McReynolds' discretion, but Pittman's willingness to follow administration desires was highly questionable. In a cabinet meeting on July 6, Hull raised the whole issue, and President Roosevelt finally agreed to meet with Pittman again. Failing to win Pittman's support, the President then asked Hull to confer with the Nevada senator. On Sunday, July 8, Hull met with Pittman and the two men finally reached a compromise. The Secretary would attend the next meeting of the Senate Foreign Relations Committee, scheduled for July 10, and though he would not directly oppose the neutrality bills, he would ask that they be recalled for further study.[57]

In order to be well informed on the Nye-Clark neutrality program, Hull asked Green to prepare a memorandum on the various proposals. In his analysis, Green argued that a rigid neutrality program was unwise because it would deprive the President of all control over a vital area of the nation's policy. He particularly singled out the impartial arms embargo advocated by Nye and Clark, pointing out that it directly contradicted the position taken by the Roosevelt administration in 1933.[58] At the same time, Senators Nye and Clark prepared a memorandum of their own to present to the Senate Foreign Relations Committee in support of their impartial arms embargo resolution. Stating that "the only way we can maintain our neutral rights is to fight the whole world," Nye and Clark insisted that only an absolute em-

[55] "Prohibit the Making of Loans," *House Report No. 1558*, 74th Cong., 1st sess. (Washington, 1935).

[56] Joseph C. Green to Norman H. Davis, July 8, 1935, Davis Papers, Box 26.

[57] Green to Davis, July 8, 1935, Davis Papers, Box 26.

[58] Memorandum by Green, July 9, 1935, Davis Papers, Box 26.

bargo on arms and a withdrawal of protection for trade in war materials could keep the nation out of future conflicts.[59]

Secretary Hull, accompanied by R. Walton Moore, met with the Senate Foreign Relations Committee in executive session on July 10. The news that morning was ominous. Headlines proclaimed that Italy had abandoned the arbitration proceedings and was intensifying its preparations for war against Ethiopia.[60] Hull opened the meeting by making some general comments about the complexity of the neutrality problem, stressing the need for caution and careful study. Then Moore delivered a more detailed critique of the Nye-Clark proposals. These remarks antagonized several senators, who angrily questioned any delay in view of the increasingly critical world situation, but the committee finally agreed to recall the Nye-Clark resolutions and appoint a subcommittee to work with the State Department in formulating a comprehensive neutrality program.[61] Hull, who would have preferred to see the whole subject postponed until the next session of Congress, had nevertheless succeeded in delaying action temporarily.[62]

The next day Pittman received permission from the Senate to recall the Nye-Clark resolutions for further study by the Foreign Relations Committee.[63] After securing a promise from Pittman that the Foreign Relations Committee would reconsider the neutrality resolutions at a meeting on July 17, Senator Nye began to lay plans for a concerted drive in Congress designed to force the administration's hand. Beginning on July 18, a small band of senators, composed of Nye, Clark, and Bone from the munitions

[59] In late June, Raushenbush wired Charles Warren, asking him to appear at the July 10 meeting to bolster the argument for an impartial arms embargo. Warren politely declined the invitation, saying that he would be out of town at that time. Munitions Committee Papers, Box 149.

[60] Shepardson and Scroggs, *U.S. in World Affairs, 1934–35*, p. 242; *New York Times*, July 11, 1935, pp. 1, 14.

[61] William Phillips to Roosevelt, July 16, 1935, *FR: 1935*, I, 342; Green to Davis, July 19, 1935, Davis Papers, Box 26.

[62] *Hull Memoirs*, I, 410.

[63] *Congressional Record*, July 11, 1935, pp. 10997–98.

committee and including such outstanding Progressives as Robert M. La Follette, Jr., and George W. Norris, would speak for at least an hour each day in behalf of rigid neutrality legislation. Nye hoped that a two-week campaign would stir up enough support to compel the Foreign Relations Committee to send the Nye-Clark resolutions to the Senate floor.[64] Worried by this threat, the Foreign Relations Committee voted on July 17 to appoint a subcommittee, composed of Senators Pittman, Borah, Johnson, Robinson, and Connally, to proceed immediately to draft a comprehensive neutrality resolution in co-operation with the State Department. Pleased by this decision, Nye agreed to refrain from debating the issue in the Senate as long as the subcommittee made progress.[65]

The decision of the Foreign Relations Committee to work for immediate neutrality legislation compelled the State Department to end its months of delay and indecision. The central issue now had to be faced—would the department recommend a discriminatory or an impartial arms embargo? Undersecretary William Phillips and Joseph C. Green insisted on a discriminatory embargo, arguing that the President should have the power to act against aggressors. R. Walton Moore, Green H. Hackworth, and J. Pierrepont Moffat clung to the concept of an impartial embargo. In a memorandum to Phillips, Moffat wrote, "The status of international law involves, I think, no very doubtful question. . . . Our government, in order to comply with its duties under international law, must be impartial."[66] Secretary Hull sided with Phillips and Green, but at this critical moment he was away from Washington on a vacation. Realizing that the President would have to make the final decision, Phillips, on July 18, wired Norman H. Davis, who was vacationing at his summer home in Stock-

[64] Stephen Raushenbush to William Stone, July 11, 1935, July 12, 1935, and July 16, 1935, Munitions Committee Papers, Boxes 149, 150.

[65] Memorandum by Stephen Raushenbush, undated, Munitions Committee Papers, Box 150; Green to Davis, July 19, 1935, Davis Papers, Box 26.

[66] Green to Davis, July 19, 1935, Davis Papers, Box 26; Moffat to Phillips, July 18, 1935, 811.04418/57.

bridge, Massachusetts. "I am sending you this telegram," Phillips wrote, "in order to let you know that the issue involved in the Johnson amendment may be definitely decided one way or another very shortly and thus give you an opportunity to express your views to the President or elsewhere."[67]

Hoping for Davis' support, Phillips, who was serving as Acting Secretary of State in Hull's absence, decided to put the issue before the President on July 21, 1935. Green prepared a new draft of the State Department's neutrality plan, making one vital change—the arms embargo was to be levied at the discretion of the President. In a supporting memorandum prepared for Phillips' conference with Roosevelt, Green admitted that "there is no unanimity of opinion among the President's principal advisers as to the form which this legislation should take," but he went on to argue for an arms embargo against any country the President might designate. Referring to the Davis pledge of May 22, 1933, Green concluded, "The decision of the President as to whether the policy of the Administration is to be maintained or abandoned will have important effects in respect both to domestic politics and international politics."[68]

Phillips met with the President at the White House on July 21, and Roosevelt agreed to support a discriminatory arms embargo.[69] The long struggle inside the State Department which began with the Warren study had reached an end. The efforts of Davis, assisted by Green and Phillips, had finally led to a return to the policy of 1933. Roosevelt had decided to stand again behind a program of neutrality which would allow him to co-operate with other nations to stop aggression overseas. Yet this was only one phase of the struggle—the administration now faced the larger problem of persuading an isolationist Congress to adopt the program of discriminatory neutrality.

[67] Green to Davis, July 19, 1935, Davis Papers, Box 26; Phillips to Davis, July 18, 1933, 811.04418/58.

[68] Green to Phillips, July 20, 1935, 811.04418/69.

[69] *Hull Memoirs*, I, 410–11.

Roosevelt, fully aware of the difficulties he faced in Congress, followed a skillfully noncommittal policy. When a reporter asked him his attitude at a press conference on July 24, he said, "We do want and ought to have some additional neutrality legislation but we are faced with a legislative situation at the end of the session." The President then repeated a statement he had made to Phillips that morning: "I am perfectly willing if we can get an agreement on neutrality legislation, so long as it does not block the adjournment of Congress. . . . but no protracted debate on it—we do not want to even suggest that Congress stay for that reason." Despite repeated questions as to what type of measures he advocated, the President refused to reveal his decision in favor of a discriminatory arms embargo.[70]

Roosevelt had replied in a similar vein the day before in a letter to Congressman Fred J. Sisson of New York, who had written urging the President to sponsor neutrality legislation. "If such legislation can still be passed before adjournment, without interminable debate," Roosevelt wrote, "it would be very satisfactory to you, to me and to the whole country. But can that be done, especially in the Senate?"[71] Roosevelt, having decided to press for discretionary neutrality, must have known that it could not be done. The Nye group was determined to enact a rigid policy, and the bitter attack they had made against any hint of discretion for the President was a firm warning that they would oppose, even to the extent of a filibuster, any effort to adopt a discriminatory arms embargo. Roosevelt, who undoubtedly remembered the Senate's refusal to accept such a measure in 1933 when Europe was relatively peaceful, could not have believed that Congress would approve a program of collective security with war threatening to break out at any moment in Ethiopia. It is impossible to penetrate behind his bland mask of affability, but it seems likely that Roosevelt, once again pressured into supporting an internationalist pol-

[70] Typescript of Press Conference No. 222, July 24, 1935, PPF 1-P, VI, 45, FDR Papers; *New York Times*, July 25, 1935, p. 1.

[71] Sisson to Roosevelt, July 18, 1935; Roosevelt to Sisson, July 23, 1935, 811.04418/74.

icy, was still prepared to accept the rigid neutrality the nation apparently desired.

On July 25 the meetings between the State Department and the subcommittee appointed by the Senate Foreign Relations Committee began. Norman H. Davis, the firmest advocate of a discriminatory arms embargo, came down from Stockbridge to join Phillips and Moore in presenting the administration's proposals.[72] After the first preliminary session, the conferees met again on July 30 to hear Phillips read a memorandum in which he reviewed the long interest of the State Department in neutrality legislation. Stressing the complexity of the subject, Phillips made a plea for flexible, rather than rigid, legislation: ". . . there should be enough flexibility in whatever legislation is enacted to enable our Government to deal with changing conditions and shape its course according to the varying and unforeseen situations with which, as time goes on, it will doubtless be confronted." He then reminded the senators of the administration's efforts to achieve international control over the arms trade. He appealed for favorable action on the Pope bill to create a National Munitions Control Board, pointing out that this measure would enable the United States to carry out its adherence to the Geneva Arms Convention as well as provide a technique for administering any embargo Congress enacted. He closed by promising delivery of the State Department's draft neutrality legislation in a few hours time.[73]

The next day Phillips sent the draft to Senators Pittman and Nye and to Chairman McReynolds of the House Foreign Affairs Committee. The draft followed closely the earlier proposals of the State Department, but there were two significant changes. The arms embargo was made discretionary—the President could designate the nation or nations to be embargoed. In addition, Congress was expressly given the power to revoke any embargo the President levied. The other major change was embodied in a new section

[72] *New York Times*, July 26, 1935, p. 11.

[73] *FR: 1935*, I, 343–44.

banning loans to belligerent governments. The President could, when he felt it necessary for the public interest, prohibit loans impartially to all nations engaged in war. Other sections allowed the President to deny the use of American ports as bases of supply for belligerent ships, to close American ports to submarines, to prohibit American ships from carrying munitions to belligerents, to deny belligerents who misused the American flag the right to enter American harbors, and to proclaim that Americans traveling on belligerent vessels did so at their own risk.[74] All in all, the draft was flexible, leaving each prohibition to the discretion of the President, and thus was completely contrary to the concept of rigid neutrality championed by the Nye group.

As soon as Senator Nye learned of the neutrality proposals of the State Department, he began a parliamentary tactic suggested earlier by William T. Stone of the Foreign Policy Association. Knowing that the State Department eagerly sought the passage of the Pope munitions control bill, Nye planned to block action on that measure, and if he found the Senate Foreign Relations Committee unwilling to sponsor rigid neutrality measures, he would then attach the three Nye-Clark resolutions to it as amendments.[75] This maneuver began on July 30, when Senator King of Utah, at the request of Nye and Clark, objected to unanimous consent for the passage of the Pope bill without debate.[76] This action had the desired effect on the State Department—on August 2, Green wrote Norman Davis that the opposition to the Pope bill made it "imperative" that the Foreign Relations Committee report out neutrality legislation "without unnecessary delay."[77]

[74] *Ibid.*, I, 345–50; Phillips to McReynolds, July 31, 1935, 811. 04418/68B; memorandum by Stephen Raushenbush, August 2, 1935, Munitions Committee Papers, Box 149.

[75] William Stone to Stephen Raushenbush, July 18, 1935, Munitions Committee Papers, Box 150; Green to Davis, August 2, 1935, Davis Papers, Box 26. Stone, a friend of Raushenbush who strongly favored neutrality legislation, had close contacts with a number of State Department officers, and he kept the Nye committee informed of the developments inside the department.

[76] *Congressional Record*, July 30, 1935, p. 11963.

[77] Davis Papers, Box 26.

The meetings between the State Department officers and the Senate subcommittee continued through the first week in August without any result. Finally, on August 7, the subcommittee flatly rejected the State Department draft and promised Senator Nye that the following week they would recommend rigid neutrality legislation to the full Foreign Relations Committee. According to Stephen Raushenbush, the senators were alarmed by Nye's threat to attach neutrality amendments to the Pope bill, and they gave him "every assurance, as the phrase goes, that something would be reported out."[78] By August 9, the subcommittee had prepared its own draft which combined the State Department suggestions with the mandatory provisions of the Nye-Clark resolutions. The result was a rigid bill which contained an impartial arms embargo, a ban on travel, and a prohibition on loans to belligerents, all of which would go automatically into effect upon the outbreak of any war.[79] As a result, on August 10, Nye told Green that he no longer had any objection to the Pope bill and that he would not try to load it with neutrality amendments.[80] However, when Senator Pope asked unanimous consent for the passage of his bill on August 13, Hiram Johnson objected, telling Pope that the measure should only be considered "as part of a general program of neutrality legislation."[81]

Nye's hopes for quick action by the Senate Foreign Relations Committee were shattered on August 14. Though the subcommittee recommended a mandatory bill, the full committee was split between adherents of rigid and of flexible neutrality. Unable to reconcile these conflicting viewpoints, the members finally agreed to instruct the subcommittee to attempt a compromise bill and report

[78] *Hull Memoirs*, I, 411; Raushenbush to Stone, August 9, 1935, Munitions Committee Papers, Box 150.

[79] Memorandum by Raushenbush, August 9, 1935, Munitions Committee Papers, Box 150.

[80] Green to Davis, August 10, 1935, Davis Papers, Box 26.

[81] *Congressional Record*, August 13, 1935, p. 12923; Green to Davis, August 14, 1935, Davis Papers, Box 26.

back on August 21. Informing Davis of this development, Green commented, "This delay definitely puts an end to any hope for the passage of neutrality legislation this session."[82]

While the Senate Foreign Relations Committee deadlocked, James T. Shotwell and Clark Eichelberger, Executive Secretary of the League of Nations Association, arrived in Washington to represent the views of the internationalist wing of the peace movement. Claiming that many of the peace groups favored discretionary neutrality legislation, Shotwell and Eichelberger urged the State Department to make public its draft bill as a rallying point for pubic opinion. When Green told them there was no chance for passage of any comprehensive legislation, Shotwell suggested that the administration limit its program to a discriminatory arms embargo resolution which could be applied to the impending war between Italy and Ethiopia.[83] Green, impressed by this suggestion, consulted Secretary Hull and then prepared a draft bill which would give the President the authority to apply an arms embargo against any country he might designate, to be effective only until Congress reassembled the following January. This legislation, prepared on the morning of August 15, was quickly approved by President Roosevelt.[84]

That afternoon, Secretary Hull asked R. Walton Moore to take the new bill to Senator Pittman and request him to introduce it in Congress immediately. Before calling on Pittman, however, Moore went to the White House and asked the President what he should do if Pittman insisted that the embargo be made impartial. The President told Moore to accept such a change. Then Moore conferred with Pittman, who demanded that the bill be redrafted to apply impartially to all belligerents. Moore returned to the State Department and was in the process of revising the legislation when Roosevelt called and told Moore to drop the matter entirely. Green, who described this incident in a letter to

[82] Green to Davis, August 14, 1935, Davis Papers, Box 26.

[83] Green to Davis, August 13, 1935, Davis Papers, Box 26.

[84] Green to Davis, August 15, 1935, Davis Papers, Box 26.

Norman Davis, was deeply shaken. He realized its implications—the President was not fully committed to discretionary neutrality, and in the future, he might again agree to a mandatory bill. "Can you suggest anything," Green asked Davis, "which might be done to ensure against such a calamity?"[85]

By mid-August it appeared that there was no chance for passage of neutrality legislation before Congress adjourned at the end of the month. However, the Nye group, exasperated at the procrastination of the State Department and the Foreign Relations Committee, was preparing a final effort to force action. Beginning the week of August 19, the neutrality bloc in the Senate planned to filibuster, threatening to block important domestic legislation until the Senate acted on neutrality.[86] Meanwhile, Senator Pittman had decided to introduce a comprehensive neutrality bill with an impartial arms embargo designed to placate public opinion. Pittman, according to Clark Eichelberger, did not expect the Senate to act on it at this session.[87] When the State Department learned of Pittman's maneuver, it asked Representative McReynolds to sponsor the State Department draft in the House. On Saturday, August 17, McReynolds complied, introducing a bill which represented a flexible program—a discriminatory arms embargo and presidential authority to prohibit loans to belligerents and discourage travel on belligerent ships. In a public statement, McReynolds announced that his measure represented the administration's concept of neutrality legislation, but that he would not press for its adoption until the next session of Congress.[88]

On Monday morning, August 19, newspapers printed a statement by Senators Nye and Clark. Warning that war was likely to occur at any moment in Africa, they urged the Senate to act im-

[85] Green to Davis, August 16, 1935, Davis Papers, Box 26; Raushenbush to Stone, August 15, 1935, Munitions Committee Papers, Box 150.

[86] Gerald P. Nye to Fred Sisson, August 16, 1935, Munitions Committee Papers, Box 149.

[87] Memorandum of telephone conversation with Clark Eichelberger by Green, August 16, 1935, 811.04418/80.

[88] *New York Times*, August 18, 1935, p. 7.

mediately on neutrality legislation in order to guarantee American abstention. Headlines announcing Mussolini's rejection of final British and French efforts at a peaceful settlement of the Ethiopian crisis lent authority to the senators' prediction.[89] At ten o'clock, the members of the Foreign Relations Committee filed into their ornate meeting room in the south wing of the Capitol. After a long discussion, Senator J. Hamilton Lewis of Illinois, speaking for the administration, moved that the committee drop all neutrality legislation at this session. The committee rejected the proposal by a vote of 10 to 3. At noon, after a motion to recess until Wednesday was defeated, the members agreed, 11 to 3, to report out legislation the next day for a mandatory arms embargo, a ban on the carrying of munitions on American ships, and a prohibition of travel on belligerent vessels. Then the committee adjourned to allow Senator Pittman to draft the new bill.[90]

The same morning, Davis called Green from Stockbridge to suggest another attempt at a discriminatory arms embargo bill. Green proceeded to draft two letters. The first was from Hull to Roosevelt, requesting the President to ask Senator Pittman to introduce a new bill granting the President power to embargo arms to any nation he selected in case war broke out between Italy and Ethiopia while Congress was not in session. Enclosed was a second letter, from the President to Pittman, enclosing the draft bill and urging Pittman to sponsor it. In his note to the President, Hull stated, "I venture to suggest that if you send this letter, you may wish to release it to the press. Public knowledge of the position of the Administration in regard to this matter would, I believe, serve a useful purpose at this time."[91]

The Secretary took the two letters to the White House at one

[89] *Ibid.*, August 19, 1935, pp. 1, 9; Shepardson and Scroggs, *U.S. in World Affairs, 1934–35*, p. 245.

[90] Unsigned memorandum, August 19, 1935, Munitions Committee Papers, Box 149.

[91] Green to Davis, August 19, 1935, Davis Papers, Box 26; Hull to Roosevelt, August 19, 1935, FDR Papers, PPF 745; Roosevelt to Pittman, August 19, 1935, FDR Papers, PPF 745.

in the afternoon, and the President promptly signed the letter to Pittman and agreed to send it at once.[92] Stephen Early, Roosevelt's press secretary, fearful that an administration effort at flexible neutrality legislation would doom several New Deal measures pending in Congress, called Senator Pittman on the telephone before the letter was sent. Early informed Pittman of Roosevelt's decision, and the Nevada senator heatedly replied:

> ". . . I tell you Steve, the President is riding for a fall if he insists . . . on designating the aggressor in accordance with the wishes of the League of Nations. He had better have nothing than to get licked, and I assure you that is what he is facing. . . . I told R. Walton Moore the other day that I would introduce the resolution on behalf of the Administration without commitment personally. And so if he wants this done, I will introduce it, if he wants to take the licking. I will introduce it on behalf of the administration without comment, but he will be licked sure as hell."[93]

A few hours later, Pittman repeated this advice in a letter to Roosevelt. Informing the President that the Senate Foreign Relations Committee had agreed to support an impartial arms embargo bill, he warned that any effort to enact a discriminatory embargo would meet with a defeat in the Senate which would "do great harm in our foreign policy."[94] After learning of Pittman's attitude, the President withdrew the letter Hull had prepared.[95] Roosevelt had decided not to fight for a discriminatory arms embargo.

Hull was bitterly disappointed, but the next day he made a final effort. Acting on the advice of Norman Davis, he prepared a new

[92] Green to Davis, August 19, 1935, Davis Papers, Box 26; Green to Moffat, October 12, 1935, Moffat Papers.

[93] Memorandum of telephone conversation with Stephen Early by Key Pittman, August 19, 1935, FDR Papers, PPF 745. In a note accompanying this memorandum, Pittman explained his reason for sending Early a transcript of the conversation. "I have taken these precautions," Pittman wrote, "because I consider this the most vitally important matter in connection with foreign relations that has happened this session." Pittman to Early, August 19, 1935, FDR Papers, PPF 745.

[94] Pittman to Roosevelt, August 19, 1935, FDR Papers, PPF 745.

[95] *Hull Memoirs*, I, 412; Green to Moffat, October 12, 1935, Moffat Papers.

letter for the President to send to Representative McReynolds requesting him to introduce in the House the measure Pittman had rejected the previous day.[96] The Secretary went to the White House on August 20, but the President refused to send the letter to McReynolds. Hull returned to the State Department in defeat. "The Secretary was deeply hurt," Green wrote Davis, "that in a matter of this kind Steve Early's advice should be taken instead of his." The gloom in the old War-State-Navy building deepened in the late afternoon when word came in that the neutrality bloc had begun its filibuster in the Senate. "Congress is in a state of hysteria," wrote Green. "The administration is silent."[97]

III

At three o'clock on the afternoon of August 20, Senator Bone rose in the Senate to demand immediate consideration of neutrality legislation. Announcing that he was prepared to see Congress remain in session until January if necessary, Bone emphasized the danger of a major war growing out of the Ethiopian crisis and engulfing all Europe. Bone said that any further delay by Congress would be "a high crime against humanity" and then launched a bitter tirade against the concept of traditional neutral rights. "For the sake of profits, for dollars to protect the loans of certain commercial interests in this country," he declared, "50,000 boys now lie buried in France."[98] Senators Clark, Nye, and Vandenberg joined Bone in calling for passage of neutrality legislation. "From the date of the sailing of the first munitions ship in 1914, the United States was helpless to prevent entry into the war," Senator Clark proclaimed, and then he pleaded with his colleagues to adopt a policy of rigid neutrality to prevent American entanglement in the war that was coming.[99]

The filibuster had been in progress for less than three hours

[96] Green to Davis, August 20, 1935, Davis Papers, Box 26; Roosevelt to McReynolds, August 20, 1935, FDR Papers, PPF 5236.

[97] Green to Davis, August 21, 1935, Davis Papers, Box 26.

[98] *Congressional Record*, August 20, 1935, pp. 13775–79.

[99] *Ibid.*, pp. 13783, 13787.

when Senator Pittman arrived on the floor of the Senate with the neutrality bill approved by the Foreign Relations Committee the day before. After reading the measure, which contained an impartial arms embargo, a ban on the shipment of munitions on American ships, a prohibition of travel by American citizens on vessels of warring nations, and the main features of the Pope bill creating a National Munitions Control Board, Pittman described it as a compromise proposal designed to harmonize the conflict between advocates of flexible and mandatory neutrality. He explained the absence of any provision barring loans, stating that this was a complex subject which required further study. Pittman asked the senators to examine the measure overnight so that they could act on it the next day.[100] The Senate then adjourned for the day with the neutrality bloc triumphant. It was undoubtedly the shortest, and possibly the most successful, filibuster the Senate had ever witnessed.

Soon after the Senate assembled at noon on August 21, Senator Pittman asked for unanimous consent to consider the neutrality bill. There was no objection, and, virtually without debate, the Senate proceeded to pass the measure and send it on to the House.[101] When news of the Senate's action reached the State Department, Hull called a conference of his principal advisers. For over three hours they discussed the problem. Hull, Moore, and Green all agreed it would be better to have no legislation than the mandatory bill passed by the Senate and they finally decided to ask the President to urge Representative McReynolds to kill the Pittman resolution in the House.[102] At nine that evening,

[100] *Ibid.*, August 20, 1935, pp. 13795–97. According to Joseph C. Green, when the filibuster began, Senator Pittman, instead of preparing the bill, was quietly getting drunk. Several senators finally took him back to his office, sobered him up, and helped him draft the legislation. Green to Moffat, October 12, 1935, Moffat Papers.

[101] *Congressional Record*, August 21, 1935, pp. 13951–56. Joseph C. Green recalls that many of the senators he spoke to at the time never even read the Pittman bill. They told Green that all they knew was that they had voted to keep the United States out of war. Green to author, November 19, 1960.

[102] Green to Davis, August 21, 1935, Davis Papers, Box 26; Green to Moffat, October 12, 1935, Moffat Papers.

Hull, Moore, and McReynolds went to the White House to confer with the President. Worried over the possibility that the neutrality group would block action on several important domestic bills pending in Congress, Roosevelt refused to have the Pittman resolution buried in the House. Finally, the President jotted down a memorandum for McReynolds. He would accept the Pittman measure provided that the arms embargo was limited to six months and that certain technical changes were made in the section creating a munitions control board.[103]

The President had made a far-reaching decision. That morning, when a group of representatives led by Maury Maverick had asked him to accept the Pittman resolution, Roosevelt had firmly announced his complete opposition to mandatory neutrality.[104] But during the day, he had changed his mind. There was an excellent chance that the administration leaders in the House could beat back all efforts to pass the neutrality bill, but the President hesitated to risk his prestige and leadership in foreign policy on this issue.[105] And even if he were successful in the House, the Nye group could gain revenge by killing the Guffey coal act and other domestic legislation of vital concern to Roosevelt. There was still another consideration—in the approaching African war, an impartial arms embargo would hurt Italy, with the money and shipping to purchase arms in the United States, while it would not affect Ethiopia, which could not secure munitions from the United States regardless of an embargo. Always the pragmatist, Roosevelt looked to the immediate situation and decided that as long as the embargo was limited to a six-month period, it would not affect the course of American foreign policy. But the Presi-

[103] Green to Moffat, October 12, 1935, Moffat Papers; memorandum by Roosevelt, undated, HCP, File 74A-D14; *Hull Memoirs*, I, 412; *New York Times*, August 22, 1935, p. 1.

[104] Warren D. Mullins, "The Neutrality Victory," *Peace Action*, II (September, 1935), 6–7; telegram from Raushenbush to Stone, August 21, 1935, Munitions Committee Papers, Box 150.

[105] In a letter to Raushenbush on August 23, William Stone expressed fear that if Roosevelt held out against the Pittman resolution, the House would not approve it. Munitions Committee Papers, Box 150.

dent failed to realize that he was establishing a precedent that would prove nearly impossible to overcome.

On the morning of August 22, the House Foreign Affairs Committee met to consider the Pittman neutrality resolution. A three-cornered fight quickly developed. Republican George H. Tinkham of Massachusetts, a confirmed isolationist, favored approving the Senate measure without any changes; McReynolds insisted on the compromise amendments ordered by Roosevelt; and a small group of Democrats, led by Luther A. Johnson of Texas, held out for the discriminatory arms embargo. Finally, after rejecting a motion by Tinkham to report out the Senate bill unchanged, the committee appointed a subcommittee to amend the measure along the lines the President desired. In the early afternoon, Senator Pittman, who had just lunched with Roosevelt, came to the House committee room and announced that the President had sent him to redraft the bill. When Pittman rejected all proposed amendments except the time limitation on the arms embargo section, a violent argument ensued. Finally, the House committee agreed to report out the bill with the six-month limit and a few technical changes in the munitions control board section. Both McReynolds and Johnson, who had been working closely with the State Department, expressed to Green their deep distress at the administration's policy.[106]

The House passed the compromise neutrality resolution on August 23, and the next day the Senate accepted the House amendments with only two dissenting votes.[107] The debate was brief in both chambers, with the supporters of rigid neutrality reluctantly agreeing to Roosevelt's time limitation but announcing that they would fight for permanent legislation at the next session of Congress. A few speakers objected to the inflexible features of

106 Green to Davis, August 23, 1935, Davis Papers, Box 26; *New York Times*, August 23, 1935, pp. 1, 11; I. R. Barnes, clerk of the House Foreign Affairs Committee, to Rodney Dutcher, August 31, 1935, HCP, File 74A-D14.

107 *Congressional Record*, August 23, 1935, p. 14370; *ibid.*, August 24, 1935, p. 14434. Two Democrats, Senators Peter G. Gerry of Rhode Island and John H. Bankhead II of Alabama, voted against the resolution.

the resolution. Representative James W. Wadsworth, a New York Republican, called the measure "an open invitation to the great and powerful to attack the weak," while in the Senate Tom Connally of Texas declared, "I cannot subscribe to the doctrine that no matter where the contest, no matter what the issue, America in advance promises that she will exert no influence, will do no act either to bring peace or to prevent the outrage of the weak and the defenseless by the strong and by the aggressor."[108] Senator Hiram Johnson of California made the most interesting commentary on the neutrality resolution. Though he did not oppose its passage, he warned that neutrality legislation was no guaranty against involvement in war. Johnson argued that only the firm determination of the American people to isolate themselves from Europe could insure peace for the future. Yet Johnson hailed the Pittman resolution as a symbol of that determination. "The joint resolution makes plain the policy of the United States of America to keep out of European controversies, European wars, and European difficulties," he declared. "So today is the triumph of the so-called isolationists and today marks the downfall, although we may not know it, of the internationalist. . . ."[109]

The neutrality act finally passed by Congress provided that "upon the outbreak or during the progress of war between, or among, two or more foreign states, the President shall proclaim such fact, and it shall thereafter be unlawful to export arms, ammunition, or implements of war . . . to any port of such belligerent states. . . ." This mandatory embargo feature, which expired on February 29, 1936, allowed the President discretion in defining arms, ammunition and implements of war and in applying this embargo to other states when they entered a war already in progress. The act created a National Munitions Control Board, headed by the Secretary of State, to license and supervise all arms shipments and it prohibited the carrying of munitions in American ships either to belligerents or to neutrals for transshipment to bel-

[108] *Ibid.*, August 23, 1935, p. 14358; *ibid.*, August 24, 1935, p. 14433.

[109] *Ibid.*, August 24, 1935, pp. 14430–32.

ligerents. Additional sections gave the President discretionary power to prevent any vessel from carrying supplies from an American port to a warship of a belligerent nation, to ban the entry of submarines of nations at war into American territorial waters, and to proclaim that American citizens traveling on belligerent ships do so at their own risk.[110] In essence, the act was a compromise which combined the mandatory arms embargo advocated by the Nye group with the discretionary features suggested by the State Department.

When Congress ended its session on August 26, there was little doubt that the President would sign the neutrality resolution. In a press conference on August 28, Roosevelt told reporters, "As a matter of fact, on the neutrality bill I suppose the easiest way of putting it is this: that it is entirely satisfactory. . . . The question of embargoes as against two belligerents meets the need of the existing situation. What more can one ask? And, by the time the situation changes, Congress will be back with us, so we are all right."[111] The President, realizing that the impartial arms embargo would operate against Italy in a war with Ethiopia, accepted the neutrality resolution in the belief that the next Congress would adopt a more flexible policy.

In the last week of August, Secretary Hull and his advisers debated whether or not to submit a critical statement for the President to release when he signed the neutrality resolution. Hull, stung by Roosevelt's repeated disregard for his advice, finally decided to risk one more rebuff.[112] On August 29 the Secretary sent Roosevelt his views on the neutrality legislation. Although Hull reluctantly stated that he could not advise a veto, he strongly criticized the impartial arms embargo. Calling it "an invasion of the constitutional and traditional power of the Executive," he warned, "this provision would tend to deprive this Government of a great

[110] Department of State, *Peace and War: United States Foreign Policy, 1931–1941* (Washington, 1943), pp. 266–71.

[111] Press conference No. 233, August 28, 1935, FDR Papers, PPF 1-P, VI, 114.

[112] Green to Davis, August 24 and September 4, 1935, Davis Papers, Box 26.

measure of its influence in promoting and preserving peace." Hull also enclosed a draft statement for the President to release which questioned the inflexible provisions of the Pittman resolution.[113]

Roosevelt signed the neutrality act on August 31, 1935. Much to the surprise of the State Department, he revised and strengthened the draft statement before releasing it to the press. Praising the objective of keeping out of war, Roosevelt nevertheless urged further consideration of the impartial arms embargo. He then stated:

> It is the policy of this Government to avoid being drawn into wars between other nations, but it is a fact that no Congress and no Executive can foresee all possible future situations. History is filled with unforeseeable situations that call for some flexibility of action. It is conceivable that situations may arise in which the wholly inflexible provision of Section I of this act might have exactly the opposite effect from that which was intended. In other words, the inflexible provisions might drag us into war instead of keeping us out.[114]

The last sentence, added by Roosevelt himself, revealed the President's own misgivings over a policy which he felt forced to accept.

IV

Nationwide reaction to the neutrality act is difficult to gauge. Public opinion polls had not yet come into widespread use, and newspaper and periodical editorials revealed the editors' bias far more than the attitude of the public. Thus the *New York Times*, which favored collective security, argued that the neutrality act hampered American efforts to prevent war, and its Washington columnist, Arthur Krock, labeled the legislation "one of the most dangerous measures of foreign policy ever written."[115] The *Nation* and *Collier's* published similar evaluations, pleading for a policy

[113] *FR: 1935*, I, 350–51.

[114] *Peace and War, 1931–1941*, p. 272.

[115] *New York Times*, August 22, 1934, p. 14; *ibid.*, August 24, 1935, p. 14.

which would allow the President discretion to co-operate with other nations against aggression.[116] However, the *New Republic*, which followed an isolationist line, generally approved of the new act, though its editors felt it did not go far enough. In particular, they wished to see an embargo on all war supplies, including raw materials, in order to insulate the United States completely from a European war.[117]

Business opinion was evenly divided on the neutrality issue. Business journals agreed on the need for the United States to stay out of war, but many editors criticized the neutrality act as a surrender of traditional American rights on the high seas.[118] In a poll conducted by *Business Week* half of the industrial leaders interviewed supported the neutrality act, but nearly all opposed any extension of the embargo to cover raw materials or manufactured goods other than arms. Most businessmen, thoroughly alienated by the New Deal domestic reforms, distrusted Roosevelt's leadership in foreign affairs and opposed any presidential discretion in the neutrality legislation.[119] In general, business groups were willing to accept the arms embargo but violently objected to any further restrictions on American trade. The one exception was the *Magazine of Wall Street*, which advocated abandoning wartime commerce. "Whatever comes the United States must stay out of armed conflict," wrote the editors. "There must be no yielding even though business be prostrated for a time and the depression continued."[120]

116 "Must We Fight in the Next War?" *Nation*, CXLI (August 28, 1935), 228–29; "Sanctions or War?" *ibid.*, CXLI (September 4, 1935), 256–57; "The Hard Task of Staying Neutral," *Collier's*, XCVI (November 23, 1935), 78.

117 George Soule, "Will We Stay Out of the Next War?" *New Republic*, LXXXIV (August 21, 1935), 38–41; "Neutrality or Shadow-Boxing," *ibid.* (October 2, 1935), 202–3.

118 Roland N. Stromberg, "American Business and the Approach to War, 1935–1941," *Journal of Economic History*, XIII (Winter, 1953), 64; "Keep Us Out of War," *Business Week*, August 31, 1935, p. 32; "The Imperative Duty of Keeping Out of War," *Commercial and Financial Chronicle*, CXLI (August 24, 1935), 1151–53.

119 "A Plan for Neutrality," *Business Week*, December 28, 1935, p. 14.

120 "War?" *Magazine of Wall Street*, LVI (September 28, 1935), 573.

The greatest praise for the neutrality act came from the pacifist and religious groups that had worked so hard for its adoption. Claiming that the legislation "sets a precedent of vast historic importance," *Christian Century* declared, "no cost which protects peace is too high."[121] Yet many of the peace advocates denied that the neutrality act was an isolationist measure. The Federal Council of Churches stated, "The churches, in supporting neutrality, are not to be understood as endorsing an isolationist policy," while Frederick J. Libby argued in *Peace Action* that the arms embargo aided collective security by preventing the United States from shipping munitions to an aggressor.[122] Leaders of the major peace societies, however, realizing that the neutrality legislation tended to heighten isolationism in the United States, sent a telegram to Roosevelt on August 27 urging the President to declare that the neutrality legislation would not alter American determination to uphold the Kellogg-Briand Pact.[123] Pacifists, though they still subscribed to the ideal of collective security, were driven by their fear of war into supporting an isolationist policy.

Though these varying responses to the neutrality act revealed a broad range of views, there can be little question that the great majority of the American people accepted the legislation as a necessary step to protect the nation from involvement in war. Certainly President Roosevelt, always sensitive to the shifting moods of the people, was convinced that the public ardently favored the legislation. In his own mind, doubts still lingered. In a letter to Colonel House in September he complained of "the very large and perhaps increasing school of thought which holds that we can and should withdraw wholly within ourselves and cut off all but the most perfunctory relationships with other nations. They imagine that if the civilization of Europe is about to destroy itself through internal strife, it might just as well go ahead and do it

[121] "Peace before Profits," *Christian Century*, LII (September 4, 1935), 1099.

[122] "Neutrality Is Not Isolation," *Federal Council Bulletin*, XVIII (October, 1935), 5; *Peace Action*, II (September, 1935), 1.

[123] Clark Eichelberger *et al.* to Roosevelt, August 27, 1935, 811.04418/83.

and that the United States can stand idly by."[124] Yet Roosevelt, despite this implied criticism, was willing to support such a policy. In December he told William Dodd, the American ambassador to Germany, that the neutrality act was not "an unmitigated evil," and he added, "I hope that next January I can get an even stronger law, leaving, however, some authority to the President."[125]

Though Roosevelt's attitude toward neutrality legislation appears contradictory, there was a thread of consistency running through all his actions. Unlike Hull, he was skeptical of the degree to which the United States could co-operate to prevent war. From the time he first learned of the State Department's neutrality study in September, 1934, Roosevelt favored the adoption of a policy that would enable him to prevent the United States from drifting into war. When he told the Nye committee in March that he desired neutrality legislation, he was expressing a firm conviction that restraints were needed to avoid a repetition of the incidents that had led to American entry into the First World War. And when he finally acquiesced to the rigid neutrality resolution demanded by the Nye group, he did so only partly out of political expediency. His ultimate consideration was to control the future course of American foreign policy. He realized that the United States might eventually enter a European conflict, but he wanted to insure that such a decision would be made on the basis of a careful weighing of national interests rather than in a vain effort to protect the profits of neutral trade.

Roosevelt was not an isolationist—he was a realist. He did not share the belief that the United States could withdraw from the world, but he did believe that the nation could control its future policy. Above all, he wished to avoid Wilson's dilemma over neutral rights. If the President had the power to restrain American trade and travel in time of foreign war, he could make the decision between war and peace free from the emotional demands of

[124] Elliott Roosevelt (ed.), *F.D.R.: His Personal Letters, 1928–1945* (2 vols.; New York, 1950), I, 506.

[125] *Ibid.*, pp. 530–31.

national honor and the pressure of economic interests. Thus Roosevelt desired neutrality legislation which permitted him to exercise a large degree of executive leadership. His real compromise in 1935 was not in accepting neutrality legislation but in accepting the mandatory features that the Nye group forced upon him. Roosevelt desired a flexible policy which would leave him free, not necessarily to co-operate against aggressors as the State Department advocated, but to decide in each situation the most effective course of action for the nation to pursue.

CHAPTER FIVE

THE NEUTRALITY FIASCO, 1936

The good judgment of the Foreign Relations Committee of the Senate has probably saved this country from a most tragic mistake.
HIRAM JOHNSON, February 12, 1936

At dawn on October 3, 1935, Italy launched its long-expected invasion of Ethiopia. Without formally declaring war, Mussolini sent columns of motorized troops into Ethiopian territory, where they faced only light resistance. When the news of the fighting reached the United States, President Roosevelt was cruising off the coast of Lower California aboard the U.S.S. "Houston." The day before, the President had witnessed a huge naval maneuver involving over one hundred American warships and fifty thousand seamen, and then the "Houston" had dropped anchor off Magdalena Bay, where the President and his party listened to the World Series while they fished. The somber news from Africa destroyed the gay atmosphere of the President's vacation. Roosevelt was quickly put in telegraphic contact with the State Department, and he began to grapple with the critical problems raised by the Italian aggression.[1] The first major European war since 1920 posed a critical test for the new American neutrality policy.

In Washington, a series of hasty conferences got under way in the State Department. Before leaving the capital in September,

[1] Arnold J. Toynbee and V. M. Boulter, *Survey of International Affairs, 1935* (2 vols.; London, 1936), II, 382; *Time*, XXVI (October 14, 1935), 13.

Roosevelt had signed a neutrality proclamation for Hull to issue if war broke out in Africa in his absence. The Secretary sent urgent dispatches on October 3 to the American embassies in London and Rome, requesting information on whether or not the fighting signified the outbreak of full-scale war.[2] On October 4, Roosevelt wired Hull that in his opinion any reports of battles and casualties inside the borders of Ethiopia, even though war had not been declared, would necessitate a proclamation of American neutrality. Roosevelt then suggested that in addition to invoking an arms embargo against both belligerents, Hull should issue a public statement announcing that the government planned to publish the names of all American citizens traveling on belligerent ships and to publicize the export of all essential raw materials to Italy and Ethiopia.[3]

This telegram indicated that Roosevelt was prepared to pursue a bold neutrality policy aimed at discouraging American trade with Italy. Though his measures would be technically impartial, since they applied to both belligerents, any attempt to reduce trade in essential raw materials would not affect Ethiopia, which had neither ships nor ocean ports, but it would seriously injure the Italian war economy, which was heavily dependent on imports of oil, cotton, iron ore, and other strategic supplies. Secretary Hull was sympathetic to Roosevelt's proposals, but other advisers urged a more cautious policy. Hugh Wilson, the American minister at Geneva, telephoned Hull on Saturday, October 5, and advised the Secretary to wait for the League of Nations to act before recognizing the existence of a state of war. Officials in Washington, especially R. Walton Moore, agreed on the necessity for proclaiming neutrality, but they warned that any additional steps to discourage trade might be viewed by isolationist congressmen as unwarranted interference designed to injure Italy.[4]

[2] Herbert Feis, *Seen from E. A.* (New York, 1947), pp. 234–35; *FR: 1935*, I, 790, 791–94.

[3] *Ibid.*, I, 794.

[4] *Ibid.*, pp. 798; Feis, *Seen from E. A.*, pp. 234–35.

Hull finally decided on a middle course. In a long cable to the President on October 5, he agreed on the need to invoke the arms embargo, but suggested it be delayed until after the League Council met on October 7. In an attempt to find a compromise on the trade issue, Hull advised Roosevelt to issue a statement warning Americans that if they engaged in commerce with either belligerent, they did so at their own risk. The Secretary advised against a blacklist of exporters as too drastic. He urged Roosevelt to wait, and if abnormal trade in strategic raw materials developed, then he could issue further warnings and as a last resort publish the names of those engaging in such commerce. Hull also objected to a proclamation warning American citizens to refrain from traveling on belligerent ships, pointing out that since there was no danger to Americans on Italian ships, such a proclamation would be taken by Italy "as a gratuitous affront in the nature of sanctions."[5]

The President was only partially persuaded by Hull's arguments. In a cable received in Washington at 4:45 on the afternoon of October 5, Roosevelt directed Hull to issue the arms embargo proclamation at once, and in a later message he insisted that American citizens be warned not to take passage on belligerent ships. However, the President did accede to Hull's plan to limit action on trade restrictions to a simple statement informing shippers that if they exported goods to either Italy or Ethiopia, they did so at their own risk.[6] As a result, shortly before midnight on October 5, the State Department released two proclamations, one invoking the arms embargo, the other warning against travel on belligerent ships. In addition, Hull issued a public statement in Roosevelt's name which declared that the United States was "compelled to recognize the simple and indisputable fact that Ethiopian and Italian armed forces are engaged in combat, thus creating a state of war. . . ." "In these specific circumstances," the statement continued, "I desire it to be understood that any of our

[5] *FR: 1935*, I, 798–800.

[6] *Ibid.*, pp. 797–98, 800.

people who voluntarily engage in transactions of any character with either of the belligerents do so at their own risk."[7]

The policy hammered out between Roosevelt and Hull was a novel attempt to transcend the inflexible limitations of the 1935 neutrality act. Forced to act impartially, the administration went beyond the letter of the law to urge Americans to refrain from aiding Italy. The travel warning, designed by legislators to prevent the loss of American lives on the high seas, was now being used to deprive Italy of American passenger revenues. The trade warning was far more significant. As Charles Warren had pointed out repeatedly, the crucial problem was neither arms nor passenger travel—the real issue of neutrality was trade in contraband materials which were vital to modern warfare. By invoking what Hull was to call a "moral embargo" on this category of trade, the United States was in effect declaring its disapproval of Italian aggression in Africa. The ultimate importance of the administration's policy lay in its relationship to the possible punitive sanctions the League of Nations might adopt. By recognizing the war in Italy before the League acted, the administration avoided the charge that it was following in the League's footsteps. And by discouraging trade in raw materials before the League employed sanctions, the administration was attempting to insure the success of any economic measures that were invoked against Italy. While the administration's action did not guarantee that American merchants would refrain from trading with Italy, at least it gave the members of the League prompt notice that the Roosevelt administration, so far as an isolationist public would allow, passively supported measures of collective security against Italy.[8]

On Monday, October 7, the Council of the League of Nations formally declared that the Italian attack on Ethiopia violated the Covenant. This verdict was ominous in its implications, for it meant that the member nations could now undertake economic

[7] Department of State, *Press Releases*, XIII (October 5, 1935), 251–57; Department of State, *Peace and War: United States Foreign Policy, 1931–1941* (Washington, 1943), p. 283.

[8] *The Memoirs of Cordell Hull* (2 vols.; New York, 1948), I, 429–31.

sanctions to restrain Italy's aggression. Acting with surprising speed, on October 10 the League established a Co-ordination Committee to consider what economic measures to pursue.[9] The attention of the world now centered on Geneva—for a moment, at least, it seemed that new life had been breathed into the dying concept of collective security.

For the State Department, this action was welcome, but dangerous. Hull now had to avoid any overt co-operation with the League while at the same time he tried to pursue policies that would prevent American merchants and exporters from undermining the sanctions invoked against Italy. On October 9, the Secretary instructed the American diplomats at Geneva to ask the League not to invite the United States to participate in any proposed sanctions. Warning that such an invitation would be not only unnecessary but "inadvisable," Hull stated, "we regard it advisable in every respect for the League to understand that definite measures have already been taken by the United States in accordance with our own limitations and policies; that these measures include long steps in restricting commercial and financial transactions with the belligerents; and that we desire to follow our course independently according as circumstances develop."[10] The League officials, realizing the delicacy of Hull's position, carefully refrained from embarrassing the United States with any open request for co-operative action.

Hull's second goal, preventing American merchants from trading with Italy, proved much more difficult to achieve. On October 10, the Secretary admitted that there was no legal ban on commerce with the belligerents in materials other than arms, but he strongly urged American businessmen to co-operate with the administration's policy. Hull carefully chose his words to avoid any suggestion that the administration was acting against Italy. He emphasized that the sole objective was "keeping this country out of war—keeping it from being drawn into war."[11] The next

[9] F. P. Walters, *A History of the League of Nations* (2 vols.; London, 1952), II, 654–55, 658–59.

[10] *Peace and War, 1931–1941,* pp. 283–84.

[11] *FR: 1935,* I, 803–4.

day, Roosevelt, who had doubts as to the effectiveness of the warning he and Hull had issued, asked the Secretary if it would be possible to add such raw materials as processed copper and steel to the list of embargoed items. The President also brought up again the idea of publishing the names of exporters who engaged in trade at their own risk with Italy. Hull quickly informed Roosevelt that the 1935 neutrality act clearly limited the arms embargo to actual weapons and munitions of war. The Secretary also urged Roosevelt not to publish the names of shippers trading with Italy, at least not until the effectiveness of the administration's requests could be judged.[12] The President reluctantly accepted Hull's advice on both points and used his arguments in replying to letters from correspondents who pleaded for a more active policy.[13]

By mid-October, the League's Co-ordination Committee had agreed on a fourfold policy of sanctions. Moving cautiously, the committee had put into effect an arms embargo and a ban on loans and credit to Italy. On October 21 the committee recommended that League members refrain from importing Italian goods. These measures, especially the latter two, would severely injure the Italian economy over a long period of time, but the vital issue remained the question of embargoing the export of strategic raw materials to Italy. On October 19 the Co-ordination Committee approved a plan to embargo, beginning November 18, the export of certain materials whose supply was controlled largely by League members. No action was taken, however, on such materials as oil, coal, cotton, and scrap iron which were available for export from nations outside the League. Oil was by far the most important item that Italy imported, and an effective embargo on petroleum products would have crippled the Italian war effort within a few weeks. France, more fearful of Germany than ever, refused to support a sanction on oil, and Great Britain would not

[12] Roosevelt to Hull, October 11, 1935, Hull to Roosevelt, October 11, 1935, FDR Papers, OF 200, Box 93.

[13] Roosevelt to W. Russell Bowie, October 30, 1935, in Elliott Roosevelt (ed.), *F.D.R.: His Personal Letters, 1928–1945* (2 vols.; New York, 1950), I, 514; Roosevelt to David Stern, December 11, 1935, FDR Papers, PPF 1039.

take this serious step without French support. Though several of the smaller League nations were willing to embargo oil, they could not act without the co-operation of England and France. Thus the League sanctions, formulated and partially in effect by October 21, were strong enough to antagonize Italy but not effective enough to check Mussolini's African adventure.[14]

The United States carefully watched the League develop its economic measures, but the administration refused to commit itself to any co-operative action. When the chairman of the Coordination Committee informed Hull of the steps that had been taken, the Secretary sent a piously noncommittal reply. After summarizing the measures the United States had adopted, Hull stated that the nation would continue to pursue an "independent and affirmative policy." The United States, Hull continued, "views with sympathetic interest the individual and concerted efforts of other nations to preserve peace or to localize and shorten the duration of the war."[15] At the end of the month both Roosevelt and Hull reaffirmed the administration's stand and issued stronger pleas for American exporters to desist from trading with the belligerents. In a public statement on October 30 the President declared, "I do not believe that the American people will wish for abnormally increased profits that temporarily might be secured by greatly extending our trade in such materials; nor would they wish the struggles on the battlefield to be prolonged because of profits accruing to a comparatively small number of American citizens." In a similar announcement the same day, Hull warned that the government was closely observing the statistics on trade with the belligerents and pleaded for co-operation from American shippers.[16]

Despite these statements, American trade with Italy in essential raw materials increased sharply in October, 1935. The most alarming rise came in oil exports, which were double the usual

[14] Toynbee and Boulter, *Survey of International Affairs, 1935*, II, 223–31, 272–77; Walters, *History of the League*, II, 659–63.

[15] *Press Releases*, XIII (November 2, 1935), 336–38.

[16] *FR: 1935*, I, 812–13.

level for the month.[17] This flouting of the administration's moral embargo worried Hull, for it meant that American commerce would seriously weaken the League's limited export sanctions, due to go into effect on November 18. In an effort to curb this rising trade, Hull issued a further statement on November 15. After reviewing the government's policy, the Secretary announced that despite previous warnings, there had been large increases in the export of oil, copper, trucks, tractors, scrap iron, and scrap steel. "This class of trade," Hull declared, "is directly contrary to the policy of this Government as announced in official statements of the President and Secretary of State, as it is also contrary to the general spirit of the recent neutrality act." Hull closed by stating that the government was compiling detailed lists of these exports, thus hinting at the possible disclosure of the names of the exporters who were disregarding the government's warnings.[18]

The administration did not rely on verbal statements alone in its efforts to discourage trade with Italy. As early as October 9, the Export-Import Bank, controlled by the government, had announced it would not extend loans or credits for trade with belligerents.[19] The United States Shipping Board, under the jurisdiction of the Department of Commerce, took a more stringent step by informing maritime companies that it could not permit ships on which the government held mortgages to engage in trade with Italy or Ethiopia. In the case of one ship, the tanker "Ulysses," scheduled to carry a cargo of oil to Italy, the Shipping Board actually threatened to foreclose on the mortgage unless the owners complied with government policy. The boldest statement came on November 21, when Harold L. Ickes, Secretary of the Interior and Petroleum Administrator, urged American producers to "keep the spirit and letter" of the neutrality act by refusing to sell oil to Italy. Since the neutrality act did not forbid such shipments, Ickes

[17] Feis, *Seen from E. A.*, p. 307.

[18] *FR: 1935*, I, 819; *Hull Memoirs*, I, 435.

[19] Toynbee and Boulter, *Survey of International Affairs, 1935*, II, 242.

eventually had to retract his statement.[20] Yet despite these actions, American exports to Italy continued to mount. A number of large concerns co-operated with the government, but small companies eager to develop new markets greatly expanded their trade with Italy. Thus oil exports in November reached a value of $1,184,000, three times the normal peacetime level and 50 per cent greater than the October figure.[21] The moral embargo, despite Hull's exhortations and the government's administrative edicts, failed to curb the new trade opportunities opened up by the Ethiopian war. It seemed as if American businessmen were intent on proving Nye's thesis that they favored profits above peace.

The reaction of the American people to the government's neutrality policy was generally favorable. In October the State Department received over 3,000 letters endorsing the moral embargo. Most of the writers viewed the steps taken as insurance against American involvement in the war, but a significant minority praised the administration for its tacit co-operation with the League of Nations.[22] This support from advocates of both rigid neutrality and collective security was characteristic of congressional and journalistic opinion. Senators Nye and Borah both endorsed the moral embargo as a measure of isolation from the European conflict, while the *Nation*, which strongly favored co-operation with the League, hailed the attempt to reduce trade with Italy as a blow against aggression.[23] However, a few neutrality enthusiasts were more concerned over the one-sided impact of the administration's policy against Italy. Thus Raymond Moley, editor

[20] Whitney H. Shepardson and William O. Scroggs, *The United States in World Affairs, 1936* (New York, 1937), pp. 20–21.

[21] Feis, *Seen from E. A.*, pp. 307–8. Notable among the companies complying with the government's policy was the Ford Motor Company, which discontinued the export of trucks to Italy upon the outbreak of hostilities. Toynbee and Boulter, *Survey of International Affairs, 1935*, II, 243.

[22] Memorandum from Charles W. Yost to Joseph C. Green, December 21, 1935, 811.04418/92½.

[23] *New York Times*, October 17, 1935, p. 5; *ibid.*, November 29, 1935, p. 10; *Nation*, CXLI (October 16, 1935), 425.

of *Today*, attacked the President for co-operating with the League, stating, "I cannot say with too much seriousness that taking sides in this fashion will almost automatically make us a party to the wider war that might easily develop out of the present war."[24]

Business groups were highly critical of the moral embargo. Soon after the trade-at-your-own-risk policy was announced, a group of New York exporters attacked it as a "hasty and ill-advised" concept that threatened to destroy American commerce.[25] By November the discontent in export circles was building up dangerously. Charles Sherrill, president of the New York State Chamber of Commerce, warned Roosevelt of this feeling in a letter on November 9 and went on to note that "exporters and merchants on our eastern seaboard are now more interested in the freedom of the seas for American ships than at any time since the World War."[26] Business journals took a more moderate position, admitting that the national concern for peace probably justified the trade restrictions. Several editors argued, however, that the administration had gone far beyond the actual terms of the neutrality act in an effort to punish Italy. Claiming that this type of favoritism violated the spirit of neutrality, *Business Week* declared, "We must sell to all belligerents in all wars or we must sell to none."[27]

The most strenuous objections to the administration's policy came from the Italian government and influential groups of Italian-Americans inside the United States. On October 16, 1935, Augusto Rosso, the Italian ambassador in Washington, complained to William Phillips that the moral embargo, however im-

[24] Raymond Moley, "Toward War," *Today*, V (December 7, 1935), 12–13.

[25] "State Department vs. Export Trade," *Literary Digest*, CXX (October 19, 1935), 6.

[26] Sherrill to Roosevelt, November 7, 1935, FDR Papers, OF 176.

[27] "Impartial Neutrality," *Barron's*, XV (October 14, 1935), 1; "What Price Neutrality," *Magazine of Wall Street*, LVII (October 26, 1935), 6; "Neutrality," *Export Trade and Shipper*, XXXII (November 25, 1935), 6; "Neutrality," *American Exporter*, CXVIII (January, 1936), 40–41; "For Honest Neutrality, Not Favoritism," *Business Week*, November 30, 1935, p. 40.

partial in theory, operated solely against Italy. Rosso then charged that the United States was aligning itself with Great Britain and the League of Nations in an effort to cripple the Italian war effort.[28] A month later Rosso repeated these charges to Secretary Hull and went on to assert that the moral embargo violated the Treaty of 1871 between the United States and Italy which guaranteed "complete freedom of commerce and navigation."[29] Italian-American groups strongly supported the protests of the Italian government. Italian-language newspapers denounced the neutrality policy of the United States and suggested that British influence in Washington was paramount. By December an organized campaign of letter-writing was under way. In ten days the State Department received 2,500 form letters from Italian-Americans attacking the administration's moral embargo.[30] Since the great majority of Italians were members of the Democratic party, these protests had considerable political weight.

While the administration firmly resisted pressures from business and Italian groups, it suddenly found its policy undermined from an unexpected source—the League of Nations. On December 10 the world was startled to learn that Sir Samuel Hoare, British Foreign Secretary, and Pierre Laval, Premier of France, had sent a special peace offer to Italy and Ethiopia. The Hoare-Laval plan proposed an exchange of territory in Africa with Italy taking 60,000 square miles of Ethiopian land and giving up only 3,000 in return. In addition, Italy was to gain exclusive economic

[28] Memorandum of conversation with Rosso by Phillips, October 16, 1935, *FR: 1935*, I, 807–10.

[29] Memorandum of conversation with Rosso by Hull, November 22, 1935, *ibid.*, pp. 826–32. Rosso's protests angered Hull, who replied with a ringing denunciation of Italian bad faith ranging from the non-payment of war debts to the violation of the Kellogg-Briand Pact in attacking Ethiopia.

[30] John Norman, "Influence of Pro-Fascist Propaganda on American Neutrality, 1935–1936," in Dwight E. Lee and George E. McReynolds (eds.), *Essays in History and International Relations* (Worcester, Mass., 1949), pp. 195–97; memorandum from Yost to Green, December 21, 1935, 811.04418/92½.

rights over the southern, and most fertile, half of Ethiopia.[31] Though this proposal was quickly withdrawn after a wave of protest swept England and other League countries, it left serious doubts about the willingness and ability of the League to carry through effective measures of collective security. In the United States, isolationists eagerly seized upon the Hoare-Laval agreement as proof of European duplicity, while government leaders sorrowfully realized that there was now little chance for effective American co-operation with League sanctions. Though the moral embargo continued, the administration relaxed its efforts to restrict trade with Italy. The hopes for co-ordinated, though separate, economic restraint of Italian aggression collapsed. Collective security had failed its most serious test.

The Ethiopian War continued for several more months, but in the summer of 1936 Italy completed its conquest. For Roosevelt, the episode was a disillusioning experience. Despite the inflexible provisions of the neutrality act and the continuing isolationist sentiment of the American people, he had skillfully framed a policy which enabled the United States to co-operate passively with the League of Nations. Publicly proclaiming that his objective was to keep the nation out of war, he had tried to insure the success of League sanctions by restraining American commerce with Italy. The policy had not been completely effective, but it had held American exports, except for oil, reasonably close to normal levels.[32] Yet despite these efforts, England and France, fearful of a war with Italy that would give Germany a free hand in Central Europe, had sabotaged the effort to prove the effectiveness of collective security against aggression.

The most significant result of the Ethiopian War for the United States was the way in which it underlined the basic prob-

[31] Walters, *History of the League*, II, 668–69; Toynbee and Boulter, *Survey of International Affairs, 1935*, II, 295–96.

[32] American trade with Italy for the last three months of 1935 was slightly less than 20 per cent greater than the corresponding period in 1934. Feis, *Seen from E. A.*, p. 304.

lems of neutrality. In their innocence, the American people had believed that arms and munitions were the only dangerous exports in time of war. The Ethiopian conflict made people realize the importance of all trade, and especially strategic raw materials. Both isolationists and internationalists now understood the need for broader legislation to include controls on all categories of exports. For those who demanded abstention from war, it became imperative to embargo raw materials as well as arms, while for advocates of collective security, the necessity of withholding oil, cotton, and minerals from aggressors was now apparent. Thus both sides in the neutrality debate began preparing new and more complex neutrality programs which became the focus of congressional controversy in 1936.

I

The passage of the 1935 act had not resolved the neutrality debate—it only postponed a final decision. Since the vital arms embargo feature was due to expire on February 29, 1936, it was certain that permanent neutrality legislation would be a major issue when Congress reconvened in January. On October 1, 1935, two days before the outbreak of the Ethiopian War, Cordell Hull met with Charles Warren and a number of State Department officials to begin preparing a neutrality program to recommend to Congress. By November, Joseph C. Green, who was now chief of the Office of Arms and Munitions Control, R. Walton Moore, and Green H. Hackworth were busily engaged in drafting the administration's bill.[33] At the outset, Hull had decided to accept the mandatory arms embargo feature in the realization that there was no possibility that Congress would approve a discriminatory policy. Roosevelt concurred in this decision, but he urged Hull to frame a program that would give him discretionary power to limit trade with belligerents in essential raw materials.[34]

[33] *Hull Memoirs,* I, 460; Green to Wilbur Carr, November 5, 1935, 811.04418/90; Green to Moffat, November 25, 1935, Moffat Papers.

[34] *Hull Memoirs,* I, 461–62; *The Secret Diary of Harold Ickes* (3 vols.; New York, 1953–54), I, 483.

The State Department committee worked for six weeks to find what Green called "the impossible compromise between what the administration wants and what we can presumably get through the Senate." On December 14, Green finally submitted a draft bill which, in addition to an impartial arms embargo, granted the President complete discretion in placing whatever restrictions he felt necessary on other items of trade as long as they applied equally to all belligerents. Hull, however, rejected Green's draft, fearing that its broad discretionary features would be objectionable to the isolationist bloc in the Senate, and he then asked Moore and Hackworth to prepare a more restricted plan.[35]

While the State Department struggled to find a satisfactory neutrality formula, the peace societies, aroused by the war in Ethiopia, clamored for more stringent legislation. During the fall of 1935, both the National Council for the Prevention of War and the Federal Council of Churches adopted resolutions calling for a ban on loans to belligerents and the extension of the arms embargo to include essential raw materials.[36] Then, in December, a special committee of the National Peace Conference put forward a sweeping draft neutrality bill for congressional consideration. Though this committee was headed by James T. Shotwell, its members were divided over the issue of whether American policy should be aimed at isolating the nation from war or discouraging the outbreak of aggression. They finally compromised by recommending the continuation of the arms embargo, a ban on loans to belligerents, and a discretionary embargo on raw materials whereby the President could prohibit the export of strategic items which he considered essential to any war in progress. The embargoes were to apply impartially to all belligerents, but if the President found that any nation went to war in violation of the Kellogg-Briand Pact, with the consent of Congress he could lift

[35] Green to Moffat, November 25, 1935, Moffat Papers; Green to Davis, December 14, 1935, Davis Papers, Box 43; Green to Moffat, January 9, 1936, Moffat Papers.

[36] *Peace Action*, II (November, 1935), 3; *Federal Council Bulletin*, XVIII (November-December, 1935), 3–4.

all embargoes on the countries that had been attacked. This last provision, written into the draft bill by advocates of collective security, stirred up considerable controversy among the peace societies, with many opposing any suggestion that the United States take sides in any way toward a foreign conflict.[37]

When the National Peace Conference released its committee's draft legislation on December 26, 1935, the administration had not yet completed its own program. On December 28, the State Department requested the American ambassadors in the major European capitals to comment on neutrality legislation. The replies all stressed the need for a flexible policy which would permit the President to act in response to the different situations that might arise. In regard to trade, most of the American diplomats favored limiting the export of raw materials to normal peacetime levels instead of attempting to impose more drastic restrictions. The ambassadors all warned that the European countries were watching the development of American neutrality policy very closely and they urged moderation.[38]

The State Department completed its neutrality bill in late December and presented it to Senator Pittman and Representative McReynolds at a White House meeting on the last day of the year. The bill, drafted by Moore and Hackworth, was an attempt to strike a balance between the discretionary policy advocated by American diplomats abroad and the mandatory neutrality that the Senate desired.[39] The measure contained an impartial arms embargo, a mandatory ban on loans, and a novel quota system which permitted the President to limit the export of raw materials he selected, except for food and medicine, to the normal prewar average. In addition, the President was authorized to exempt short-term commercial credits from the ban on loans and to declare that all commerce with belligerents would be at the trader's own risk.

[37] *New York Times*, December 26, 1935, p. 1; "A Study of Neutrality Legislation," *International Conciliation*, No. 316 (January, 1936), pp. 1–61.

[38] *FR: 1936*, I, 165–73.

[39] Green to Moffat, January 9, 1936, Moffat Papers; Moore to Roosevelt, December 31, 1935, 811.04418/98A; *New York Times*, January 1, 1936, p. 1.

On the whole, the bill went far toward pleasing the advocates of mandatory neutrality. The ban on loans, the continued arms embargo, and a clause stipulating that trade quotas must apply impartially to all belligerents reflected concessions to the neutrality bloc in the Senate.[40] The discretion embodied in the trade quotas, in the trade-at-your-own-risk feature, and in the short-term credit provision gave the President some degree of flexibility in administering the law. In a war where the aggressor controlled the sea, the President could severely restrict American trade; yet in a case in which the victim of aggression had access to American markets, the President could permit supplies of raw materials to flow without interruption. It was undoubtedly this feature that led Roosevelt to agree to the numerous mandatory provisions considered essential to placate isolationist opinion in Congress and in the country at large.

After a discussion lasting an hour and a half, the congressional leaders agreed to introduce the bill when Congress reconvened on January 3. Senator Pittman, hoping to avoid a fight with the Nye group, was pleased with the proposal, but McReynolds was very disappointed, feeling that the bill was a surrender of principle by the administration.[41] Unquestionably the legislation marked a retreat on the part of the State Department, yet it was one dictated by political realities. In an election year, Roosevelt hoped to avoid a long and bitter struggle over neutrality that would create serious divisions inside his own party. By offering a compromise proposal at the outset, he hoped to insure prompt and harmonious action by Congress. Once again, considerations of domestic politics were playing a dominant role in the framing of American foreign policy.

On January 3, Roosevelt stated his views on neutrality in the

[40] The text of the bill is printed in "American Neutrality Policy," *Hearings before the House Committee on Foreign Affairs*, 74th Cong., 2d sess. (Washington, 1936), pp. 1–6. The legislation stated that all embargoes and restrictions would be applied equally to all belligerents unless Congress, with the President's approval, decided otherwise. This clause had little meaning, since Congress always possessed the power to amend legislation that it had approved earlier.

[41] Green to Moffat, January 9, 1936, Moffat Papers.

course of his annual message to Congress. Breaking precedent by delivering his speech in the evening in order to reach as many people as possible over a national radio network, the President dealt at length with world affairs. Warning that the increase in armaments and aggression overseas was leading toward "the tragedy of general war," Roosevelt announced his determination to follow a "twofold neutrality" policy to prevent American involvement. "First," he declared, "we decline to encourage the prosecution of war by permitting belligerents to obtain arms, ammunition, or implements of war from the United States; second, we seek to discourage the use by belligerent nations of any and all American products calculated to facilitate the prosecution of a war in quantities over and above our normal exports to them in time of peace."[42] The full details of this program were revealed the same day when Pittman and McReynolds introduced identical neutrality resolutions in Congress incorporating the administration's policy.[43]

The neutrality bloc, fearing that the administration was planning to sponsor discriminatory neutrality legislation, had prepared its own mandatory proposal which was introduced on January 3 by Senators Nye and Clark and Representative Maverick. All three men expressed their surprise at the strictness of the administration's measure, and they announced that they would accept its general outlines but fight to make it absolutely mandatory.[44] The Nye-Clark-Maverick bill followed closely the basic features of the administration's proposal, but it differed by denying the President any discretionary power. Under its terms, the President would automatically declare trade quotas for essential raw materials upon the outbreak of war, he would have to prohibit absolutely American passenger travel on belligerent ships, and he would not be allowed to exempt short-term commercial credits from the loan ban. In addition, the Nye bill included a cash-and-carry feature first suggested by Bernard Baruch in November, 1935. Instead of

[42] *Congressional Record*, January 3, 1936, p. 28.

[43] *New York Times*, January 4, 1936, p. 1.

[44] *Ibid.*, January 5, 1936, p. 34; *Congressional Record*, January 6, 1936, pp. 87–89.

permitting American exporters to trade at their own risk, the cash-and-carry clause required that all trade with belligerents had to be conducted in foreign ships and that American merchants had to transfer title to all such exports before the goods left the United States.[45]

Though there were important differences between the two bills, their many common features—the impartial arms embargo, the trade quota system, the ban on loans—gave promise of a compromise between the administration and the neutrality bloc in Congress. Representative Louis Ludlow of Indiana did introduce a bill to place an absolute embargo on all trade with belligerents, but only a few extreme isolationists supported this drastic measure.[46] There were no bills introduced in Congress advocating a discriminatory arms embargo—this issue had been resolved in 1935. Thus the controversy narrowed down to the degree of flexibility and discretion to be granted the President. Roosevelt, having made broad concessions in advance to the neutrality enthusiasts in Congress, was determined to retain enough authority to control the course of American neutrality in the unforseeable situations that might arise in the future. Yet the Nye group insisted upon a neutrality program that would bind the President to a rigid policy determined in advance by Congress. In essence, it was a question of who would control American foreign policy in case of war abroad—Congress or the President. Thus despite the outward similarities between the two major legislative programs, there was a profound divergence that produced an intense and vital debate in Congress.

II

Congressional discussion of neutrality legislation began immediately after the session opened in January, 1936, and reached its

[45] "American Neutrality Policy," House *Hearings*, 74th Cong., 2d sess., pp. 89–98; Bernard Baruch, "Cash and Carry," *Today*, V (November 2, 1935), 6–7.

[46] *Congressional Record*, January 8, 1936, pp. 163–64.

peak in early February. Facing a deadline with the expiration of the 1935 act on February 29, legislators realized the need for a prompt decision. Yet as the debate progressed, the seemingly clear-cut division between advocates of discretionary and mandatory neutrality grew increasingly blurred. The complexity of the neutrality problem soon became apparent as a wide variety of interests began to conflict. Advocates of freedom of the seas, Italian-Americans concerned over the impact of legislation on the Ethiopian War, businessmen, farmers, and miners who suddenly realized the possible impact of trade restrictions on their own economic security—these and other groups now entered into the debate, each advancing criticisms of both the Nye and the administration proposals and putting forth plans of their own. As a result, the discussion degenerated into a welter of conflicting and contradictory claims that bewildered the average American. "Local groups dedicated to the pursuit of peace, after hearing various proposals for neutrality legislation torn to pieces by critics from many camps," commented the *Christian Century*, "find themselves so confused that they are reduced to virtual impotence."[47] If nothing else, the verbal strife destroyed the illusion that there was a simple neutrality formula which would automatically safeguard the nation from the dangers of war.

The debate took place primarily in the hearings conducted by committees of both the House and the Senate. The House Committee on Foreign Affairs held a week-long session beginning on January 7, 1936. Some twenty witnesses, ranging from State Department experts to prominent Americans of Italian descent, filled over 300 pages with testimony on the various neutrality proposals.[48] The Senate hearings, held in executive session, were briefer. The chief witness was Secretary of State Hull, who tried to explain and defend the administration's program in the face of hostile questioning by Johnson and Borah. In addition, the senators heard from several eminent international lawyers who defended the tra-

[47] "Do We Want To Be Neutral?" *Christian Century*, LIII (February 5, 1936), 214.

[48] "American Neutrality Policy," House *Hearings*, 74th Cong., 2d sess.

ditional concept of freedom of the seas.[49] Though the public was not permitted to attend, the record of these proceedings was published at the insistence of Senator Johnson.[50] In addition, the nation learned of the various viewpoints from frequent speeches in the House and Senate, from a large number of periodical articles, and from numerous newspaper editorials. Meanwhile, behind the scenes, interested groups worked intensively to influence the final outcome in Congress. Lobbyists representing peace societies, Italian-American organizations, and such diverse economic interests as cotton, oil, and shipping, pressed their views on individual congressmen and senators.

From the complexity of the debate, there emerged one focal issue—the question of restricting trade in material other than arms. Though a few individuals expressed their disapproval of the impartial arms embargo, there was a general consensus for continuing this feature of the 1935 act. There was even greater agreement on the need for a ban on loans to belligerent governments. The Nye committee, at its final set of hearings held in January, revealed many of the hitherto secret details of American bankers' loans to the Allies in the years prior to 1917, and these disclosures convinced most Americans that loans to nations at war were incompatible with genuine neutrality. On the question of trade, however, there was no such harmony. The administration and the Nye group, though agreeing to the principle of limiting commerce in essential raw materials to normal peacetime levels, differed sharply on whether such restriction should be mandatory or at the discretion of the President. Even more important, advocates of traditional neutrality, motivated by nationalistic, economic, and ethnic considerations, objected to any restriction on American trade in time of war beyond the arms embargo. Though there was considerable shading and overlapping between these three viewpoints, they formed the principal outline of the controversy. An

[49] "Neutrality," *Hearings before the Senate Committee on Foreign Relations*, 74th Cong., 2d sess. (Washington, 1936).

[50] Memorandum of conversation with Key Pittman by R. Walton Moore, February 3, 1936, 811.04418/140.

analysis of these three positions reveals the major factors which influenced the eventual decision by Congress.

At the hearings Cordell Hull and R. Walton Moore presented the arguments for the administration's policy of flexible controls on trade. Both men declared that the State Department no longer advocated a discriminatory arms embargo. "We have interred the aggressor theory," Moore told the Senate Foreign Relations Committee.[51] But then he and Hull stressed the need for consistency in American policy, pointing out the contradiction in banning the export of arms to nations at war while permitting the shipment of scrap iron which was used to manufacture weapons and petroleum products that propelled tanks and planes. "If there is danger of our being drawn into war on account of exporting finished commodities," Hull asserted, "the danger is all the greater about being drawn in on account of exporting these [raw] materials in abnormal quantities."[52] Asserting that a total embargo on all exports to belligerents would be disastrous to the American economy, Hull defended the trade quota system as the only feasible plan to limit trade to normal levels. On the crucial point of allowing the President discretion in instituting the quotas, Hull drew a distinction between minor and major conflicts. In the case of a small war that carried no danger of American involvement, it would be foolish to require a curtailment of American trade. The President, Hull argued, should have the power to restrict trade so that he could apply it only in the case of a general war which threatened to involve the United States.[53] In the face of repeated questions by Senator Hiram Johnson, Hull denied that the administration wanted discretionary power over trade in order to co-operate with the League of Nations in sanctions against aggressors.[54]

[51] "Neutrality," Senate *Hearings*, 74th Cong., 2d sess., p. 100.

[52] *Ibid.*, p. 20; "American Neutrality Policy," House *Hearings*, 74th Cong., 2d sess. p. 15.

[53] "Neutrality," Senate *Hearings*, 74th Cong., 2d sess., pp. 70–71, 75.

[54] *Ibid.*, pp. 41, 73–74.

The Secretary and his associate made a poor showing at the hearings. The badgering questions from isolationists like Johnson, coupled with Hull's previous commitment to the policy of discriminatory embargoes, created the impression that the State Department was supporting the discretionary trade quota plan for ulterior motives. This suspicion was heightened by the support the administration received from individuals and groups that favored the policy of collective security. Representative William Richardson of Pennsylvania, who endorsed the administration's proposals at the hearings, later stated on the floor of Congress, "Peace for us in America can best be preserved by stressing our faith and belief in free institutions and by keeping the American Government free to take every possible action to protect and preserve those free institutions in the international field."[55] Another congressional supporter of discretionary neutrality, Representative Fred Sisson of New York, told the House Foreign Affairs Committee that isolation was impossible and urged a policy of co-operating with other nations against aggressors.[56] Such statements reminded many congressmen and senators of the way in which the State Department had applied its moral embargo against Italy and led them to conclude that the administration's request for discretionary power undercut the isolationist objectives of neutrality legislation.

Outside of Congress, there were many influential voices raised in support of the discretionary program. Charles Warren, respected by many as a sincere advocate of impartial neutrality, urged that the President be given "broad and elastic powers" so that he could cope with varying circumstances and conditions.[57] In a radio address on January 18, Walter Lippmann delivered a strong appeal for a flexible policy. "The only way to be prepared for an unpredictable emergency is to be able to move, to have your hands

[55] *Congressional Record*, January 31, 1936, pp. 1299–1300.

[56] "American Neutrality Policy," House *Hearings*, 74th Cong., 2d sess., pp. 162–63.

[57] Charles Warren, "Safeguards to Neutrality," *Foreign Affairs*, XIV (January, 1936), 199–200, 206.

free, to be alert, resourceful, powerful, and unentangled," Lippmann reasoned. "The simple truth is that we are not wise enough to tell a future Congress and a future President what they must do."[58] The most unexpected endorsement of the administration's program came from Walter Millis. In an article in the *Nation*, Millis warned that effective neutrality legislation must be flexible, containing broad discretionary powers for the President, and in a subsequent newspaper interview he stated, "We must not forget that legislation may work in a quite unforseeable fashion when an actual war arises."[59]

In contrast to the poor showing made by the administration's spokesmen, the advocates of mandatory neutrality argued forcefully and persuasively throughout the long debate. At the hearings and in congressional speeches, a coalition of prominent Republican and Democratic legislators emphasized the need for rigid legislation. "It is my opinion that Congress should state specifically the provisions of neutrality legislation," declared Representative John W. McCormack of Massachusetts, "and that the delegation of broad powers would be unwise," while Emanuel Celler of New York bluntly announced, "As little power as possible in this matter should be left to Presidential discretion."[60] Though this group agreed with the administration on the concept of trade quotas, they sharply challenged the discretionary provisions of the Pittman-McReynolds bill. Citing the World War I experience, when a heavy trade in essential raw materials helped undermine American neutrality, they demanded that trade quotas be applied automatically upon the outbreak of war. They also insisted on the

[58] Walter Lippmann, "Neutrality: The Immediate Problem," *Vital Speeches*, II (January 27, 1936), 263.

[59] Walter Millis, "The Last War and the Next: What Does Neutrality Mean?" *Nation*, CXLII (January 29, 1936), 125–27; "Peace Passion Cold," *Time*, XXVII (February 24, 1936), 16. Millis' statements amazed members of the Nye committee. Senator Bone commented, "It was upon what this man exposed so well in his book that I postulated my stand for a strong, mandatory neutrality program."

[60] *Congressional Record*, January 6, 1936, p. 115; "American Neutrality Policy," House *Hearings*, 74th Cong., 2d sess., p. 83.

adoption of the cash-and-carry feature of the Nye bill. While admitting that these steps might injure the American economy, they claimed that neutrality was worth any price. "Business will suffer by such a policy," Celler asserted. "But better that business suffer than that millions of men be drawn to the colors with consequent loss of thousands and thousands of lives."[61] Maury Maverick went even further. "I would just as soon close every port in the United States," he stated, "including Houston and Galveston, if it would save the life of one human being."[62]

Though the advocates of rigid neutrality concentrated on the issue of trade quotas, they also pressed for mandatory clauses in other areas. Representative George H. Tinkham, though he approved the loan ban, objected to giving the President power to exempt short-term commercial credits, and Maury Maverick urged an absolute prohibition on passenger travel on belligerent ships so that "globe-trotting individuals shall no longer have the right to involve any lives other than their own when they mingle their own fate with alien targets."[63] Even greater objections were raised to the opening sentence of the embargo section which authorized the President to invoke the arms ban "upon the outbreak of or during the progress of any war." Maverick and Tinkham, arguing that the President could wait until a war was nearly over before beginning the embargo, insisted on a more specific wording. In an effort to meet this criticism, Senator Pittman agreed to substitute for this clause one that read, "As soon as the President shall find that a state of war exists."[64]

In the public debate, a number of prominent Americans spoke out in behalf of a mandatory neutrality program. Charles A.

[61] *Ibid.*, pp. 84, 93, 101–2, 195, 230–31; "Neutrality," Senate *Hearings*, 74th Cong., 2d sess., pp. 151–53, 158; *Congressional Record*, January 7, 1936, pp. 124–25; *ibid.*, February 3, 1936, p. 1403.

[62] "American Neutrality Policy," House *Hearings*, 74th Cong., 2d sess., p. 99.

[63] *Ibid.*, pp. 29, 97.

[64] *Ibid.*, pp. 7–10, 12, 90; "Neutrality," Senate *Hearings*, 74th Cong., 2d sess., p. 90.

Beard, in a series of articles in the *New Republic,* reviewed the evidence presented by the Nye committee and concluded that the World War I experience proved that presidential discretion could lead to war. Pleading for a mandatory policy, Beard asserted, ". . . we nearly burnt our house down with one experiment; so it seems not wholly irrational to try another line."[65] An equally strong plea for rigid legislation came from Admiral William S. Sims, who had been in charge of Atlantic naval operations during World War I. Condemning neutral trade as "essentially an inhuman and bloodstained traffic," Sims urged a complete embargo on the export of all contraband goods. "We, as a people, must come to understand that peace is priceless; that it is worth any reasonable sacrifice of war profits; that a decent regard for humanity must be placed ahead of gold."[66] The bitterest attack on presidential discretion was delivered by Raymond Moley. Writing in *Today,* he charged that the trade quota section of the administration bill "would place in the hands of the Executive, unrestricted by Congress, the power to embargo such particular materials as would bring defeat to *one* side in a war."[67]

Though a few advocates of a mandatory policy, notably Louis Ludlow, held out for a total embargo on all trade with belligerents, there was general agreement between the Nye group and the administration on the trade quota plan as a feasible compromise.[68] Other critics of the administration bill objected to any limitations on commerce beyond the arms embargo. Led by Senator Hiram Johnson and Edwin Borchard of the Yale Law School, this group loudly championed the traditional concept of freedom of the seas. They considered the trade quota plan, the trade-at-your-own-risk

[65] Charles A. Beard, "Heat and Light on Neutrality," *New Republic,* LXXXVI (February 12, 1936), 8–9; Charles A. Beard, "In Time of Peace Prepare for War," ibid. (March 18, 1936), pp. 156–59.

[66] William S. Sims, "Freedom of the Seas," *Forum,* XCV (January, 1936), 5–7.

[67] Raymond Moley, "Out with Section 4," *Today,* V (January 25, 1936), 13.

[68] "American Neutrality Policy," House *Hearings,* 74th Cong., 2d sess., pp. 121, 144–47.

clause, and the cash-and-carry provision base surrenders of historic American rights which violated the dignity and integrity of the nation. They were joined in their criticisms by economic and ethnic interests which, while they subscribed to the lofty ideals proclaimed by Johnson and Borchard, had more selfish motives for their views. The result was a curious coalition of patriotic isolationists, irate exporters, and indignant Italian-Americans.

John Bassett Moore, in a memorandum read by Borchard to the Senate Foreign Relations Committee, gave the most eloquent argument for freedom of the seas. He recited the long history of American defense of neutral rights, stating that it would be "inconceivable" for the nation to abandon its historic position for "a gopher-like policy of seclusion."[69] Borchard and Johnson vigorously denied that an insistence on neutral rights led to American entry into war in 1917. They claimed, rather, that the failure to challenge British violations, because of what Borchard termed "executive incompetence," was the chief cause of American involvement. Borchard, advocating simply an extension of the 1935 act without any trade restrictions, maintained that such a policy would not endanger the nation. "When you know international law and how to assert it," he declared, "you can keep out of war."[70]

The proponents of traditional neutrality savagely attacked the administration bill. In his memorandum, Moore condemned the Pittman-McReynolds bill for conferring "practically unlimited discretionary powers as regards peace and war," while Borchard maintained that the measure "gives complete power to the President to be just as unneutral as he wishes to be."[71] The trade quota section drew the heaviest criticism. Both Johnson and Borchard repeatedly claimed that presidential discretion to limit trade in raw materials was a thinly disguised effort to permit cooperation with League sanctions. "When you give an absolute discretion to the President, he may select such articles as he de-

[69] "Neutrality," Senate *Hearings*, 74th Cong., 2d sess., p. 187.

[70] *Ibid.*, pp. 125–27; "American Neutrality Policy," House *Hearings*, 74th Cong., 2d sess., pp. 54, 58–61.

[71] *Ibid.*, p. 51; "Neutrality," Senate *Hearings*, 74th Cong., 2d sess., p. 173.

sires," Johnson charged, "and it gives him an opportunity, by the selection, to pick the aggressor, and to do as he sees fit in regard to the conflict."[72] Despite Hull's denials, Johnson insisted that the moral embargo in the Ethiopian War was directed at Italy and that in future conflicts Roosevelt would use his discretionary authority to co-operate with the League and thereby risk American involvement. Borchard summed up this objection when he asserted, "The Congress would be unwise to vest the Executive with discretion thus, under the guise of neutrality, to make the United States an aid to one side in a foreign war, with all the risks of entanglement and participation therein involved."[73]

When Johnson and Borchard extended their criticisms to the trade-at-your-own-risk provision, they were strongly supported by senators from cotton, oil, and mineral exporting states. Pointing out that under the trade quota plan the administration specifically sanctioned commerce within normal limits, Senator Borah maintained that it was absolutely contradictory to then state that the government would not protect this trade. "I only want protection for the American citizen in what we say in our law is a legitimate business," Borah declared. "I do not consider that neutrality is synonymous with cowardice."[74] Senator Tom Connally of Texas strongly seconded him. Warning that the trade-at-your-own-risk policy would encourage belligerent attacks on American commerce, Connally asserted, "We are advertising to the world that we are a bunch of white-livered people who will not protect our own citizens."[75] Encouraged by this unexpected support, Johnson concluded, ". . . we have either got to go forward with the protection of the rights of our own people, or we have got to abandon them."[76]

[72] *Ibid.*, pp. 142–43, 200–212.

[73] *Ibid.*, pp. 118, 123; "American Neutrality Policy," House *Hearings*, 74th Cong., 2d sess., pp. 54–56, 70–71.

[74] "Neutrality," Senate *Hearings*, 74th Cong., 2d sess., pp. 53, 78–81.

[75] *Ibid.*, pp. 27, 54, 144.

[76] *Ibid.*, p. 31.

While international lawyers and nationalistic senators defended traditional neutral rights, business groups expressed their disapproval of the proposed restriction on American trade. Exporters led the attack. The editors of *Export Trade and Shipper* referred to the various plans to limit commerce in raw materials as "political panaceas" and "individual fetishes"; the *American Exporter* was amazed at the "extraordinary complacency" of the American public toward the threatened abandonment of historic neutral rights.[77] The *Commercial and Financial Chronicle* took the most extreme stand, arguing that the "humiliating" legislation before Congress proposed "the denial of legitimate war profits to American business, industry, and finance, on the specious theory that war as such is morally wrong and no neutral should profit by it." The only proper course, the editors affirmed, "is a clear and unmistakable assertion of neutral rights, backed . . . with whatever use of force the circumstances may require."[78] The New York State Chamber of Commerce took a similar position, criticizing the Pittman-McReynolds bill as a "supine declaration" which "invites attack" by other countries.[79] In developing their arguments against the trade restrictions, business groups warned that the proposals would injure peacetime as well as wartime trade. Thus the Department of Commerce Business Advisory Council reported, "The effect of the proposed legislation would undoubtedly be to divert a large volume of normal peacetime trade in materials essential to the importing nation in time of war to other sources of supply."[80] A few exporting groups, realizing that some form of trade restriction was inevitable, indicated their willingness to accept a cash-and-carry policy which would permit trade to

[77] "Neutrality Legislation," *Export Trade and Shipper*, XXXII (February 3, 1936), 8; "Neutrality," *American Exporter*, CXVIII (March, 1936), 42.

[78] "Neutral Rights versus Neutral Policies," *Commercial and Financial Chronicle*, CXLII (January 18, 1936), 355.

[79] *New York Times*, February 2, 1936, III, 9; *ibid.*, February 7, 1936, p. 7.

[80] Report of the Committee on Neutrality of the Business Advisory Council, Department of Commerce, February 5, 1936, 811.04418/210.

continue without risking involvement in war.[81] But on the whole, the business community, already hard hit by the loss of foreign trade in the depression years, was hostile to any surrender of traditional neutral rights.

The most intense opposition to the administration's neutrality program came from Americans of Italian descent. Already aroused by the moral embargo policy, Italian-Americans became even more indignant when they learned the details of the trade quota provision in the Pittman-McReynolds bill. The American Friends of Italy inaugurated a chain-letter campaign designed to encourage the dispatch of hundreds of thousands of letters to members of Congress protesting against the administration's neutrality program. The form letters, which were received in huge quantities in Washington, stated, "I am strongly against any modification of the Neutrality Act which would give the President discretionary power." Other organizations, notably the Sons of Italy and the American-Italian Union, tried to win over American public opinion by sending speakers to club meetings, arranging radio addresses, and distributing pamphlets and circulars pleading the Italian case.[82] In December, Italians in New England formed the League for American Neutrality, which claimed to represent Americans of all national, racial, and religious backgrounds. To reinforce these group activities, prominent individuals journeyed to Washington to use whatever influence they possessed. Generoso Pope, publisher of *Il Progresso*, the largest Italian-language newspaper in the country, held conversations in late January with President Roosevelt, Secretary Hull, and a dozen congressional leaders, while Salvatore A. Cotillo, a justice of the New York Supreme Court, called on a number of congressmen and submitted a legal brief on neutrality to every member of the House and the Senate.[83] In

[81] "Neutrality Problems," *Business Week*, January 4, 1936, p. 34.

[82] Norman, "Influence of Pro-Fascist Propaganda," pp. 203–4.

[83] *Ibid.*, pp. 205–10; "American Neutrality Policy," House *Hearings*, 74th Cong., 2d sess., p. 192; "Neutrality," Senate *Hearings*, 74th Cong., 2d sess., pp. 259–83. In calling for a neutrality policy that would favor Italy, Cotillo declared that it would be "positively un-American" to grant the President discretionary powers. *Ibid.*, p. 283.

addition, congressmen from New England, where there was a heavy concentration of Italians in the population, entered numerous letters and resolutions from local societies in the *Congressional Record* calling for opposition to any ban on trade with Italy.[84]

The Italian-Americans presented their views in greatest detail at the hearings before the House Foreign Affairs Committee. Representatives of the Sons of Italy, the American-Italian Union, and the League for American Neutrality bitterly criticized the trade quota plan as a deliberate attempt to injure the Italian "colonial expedition" in Ethiopia. "We protest against a policy," stated a Massachusetts judge, "which radically changes the rules of neutrality to the disadvantage of one belligerent—Italy."[85] The Italian representatives repeatedly charged that the real intent of the legislation was to permit the United States to co-operate in League sanctions against Italy. Claiming that the British were waiting for American adoption of the trade quota plan before embargoing oil to Italy, one witness declared, "You may call it a neutrality resolution, but it is an insurance policy for the British Empire."[86] Under questioning by committee members, these witnesses expressed no objection to the arms embargo or the proposed ban on loans—their sole concern was with trade restrictions. Indeed, several Italian spokesmen stated that they did not object to trade quotas in principle, and they would accept their inclusion in neutrality legislation if the current Ethiopian War were specifically exempted.[87] In general, though they pleaded for a return to the

[84] *Congressional Record*, January 6, 1936, p. 46; *ibid.*, January 28, 1936, p. 1138; *ibid.*, February 12, 1936, p. 1944.

[85] "American Neutrality Policy," House *Hearings*, 74th Cong., 2d sess., pp. 171–72, 186, 206–7, 209.

[86] *Ibid.*, pp. 179, 200, 212.

[87] *Ibid.*, pp. 186–87, 190, 198–206, 211, 215. Though there was no Ethiopian group in the United States to counter the influence of Italian-Americans, the administration did consider the possibility of asking American Negroes to agitate for discriminatory embargoes against Italy. Nothing came of this idea, put forward by Senator Robert Wagner of New York and Assistant Secretary of State R. Walton Moore. There is no evidence of any activity

historic policy of freedom of the seas, the Italian groups were interested only in the impact of legislation on Italy's war effort.

By the time the hearings closed, any illusion of calm congressional deliberation had been shattered. Committee members grew increasingly short-tempered; charges and accusations of sinister motives were common. For the average American, viewing the three-cornered struggle between advocates of discretionary trade restrictions, mandatory limitations, and traditional neutrality, it was difficult to come to any clear conclusions on which policy best served the national interest. Members of Congress, faced not only with conflicting arguments but with the tug of economic and ethnic pressures, dreaded the prospect of making a final decision that would of necessity alienate some portion of their constituency. Unlike the arms embargo issue, which had been presented as a simple choice between isolation and collective security, the question of trade restriction had become a complex and politically dangerous subject. No longer was it a matter of restraining greedy industrialists and blood-stained merchants of death—the nation now had to decide how far it was willing to go toward sacrificing internal harmony and economic well-being in the hope of guaranteeing American isolation from future wars.

III

With the deadline of February 29 approaching rapidly, Congress had to choose between three alternative proposals which corresponded to the viewpoints expressed during the hearings and the public debate. The first two measures, the Pittman-McReynolds bill and the Nye-Clark-Maverick proposal, presented a choice between discretionary and mandatory trade restrictions. A third plan, introduced on January 16 by Senator Elbert D. Thomas of Utah, proposed an extension of the 1935 act until May 1, 1937, with the addition of a ban on loans to belligerents. In offering this

---

by Negro organizations during the debate. Moore to Roosevelt, January 23, 1936, FDR Papers, OF 1561, Box 1.

compromise, Thomas, who had long been active in the peace movement, stated that he feared that any attempt to legislate on trade quotas might jeopardize the arms embargo. He suggested that in another year the Ethiopian War would be over and then Congress could better resolve the difficult problems involved in limiting commerce in raw materials.[88] Though the State Department tried to persuade Thomas to withdraw his measure, it quickly won widespread backing from the groups which opposed restrictions on trade.[89]

The House Foreign Affairs Committee, which concluded its hearings on January 15, was the first congressional body to reach a decision on neutrality legislation. When the committee met to consider the McReynolds bill, its Republican members, led by George H. Tinkham, made a determined effort to amend the measure in order to deprive the President of all discretion. On January 23, Representative Walter Lambeth of North Carolina called the White House to report that several Democratic members of the committee were beginning to waver. Urging Roosevelt to speak to these men, Lambeth said that "the situation . . . got so bad this morning that McReynolds and I beat our fists on the table." Roosevelt refused to intervene, referring the matter to Hull.[90] The administration lines finally held firm—on January 23 the committee rejected Tinkham's motion to exclude Italy and Ethiopia from the terms of the legislation.[91] Then, on January 28, the committee reported out the McReynolds bill with only minor amendments. The first, which Senator Pittman had originally suggested, changed the opening clause of the arms embargo to read, "Whenever the President shall find that there exists a state of

[88] "Neutrality," Senate *Hearings*, 74th Cong., 2d sess., p. 91; *New York Times*, February 5, 1936, p. 12.

[89] Walton Moore to Roosevelt, January 23, 1936, FDR Papers, OF 1561, Box 1.

[90] Memorandum from Marvin McIntyre to Roosevelt, January 23, 1936, memorandum by H. M. Kannee, January 23, 1936, FDR Papers, OF 1561, Box 1.

[91] *New York Times*, January 24, 1936, p. 9.

war. . . ." Though this somewhat limited the discretion granted in the 1935 act, it still left the President some leeway in "finding" a state of war to exist.[92] The second amendment exempted countries in the Western Hemisphere from the terms of the legislation if they were at war with a nation outside the Americas. This addition was adopted at the request of Roosevelt, who feared that otherwise the United States would be unable to assist a Latin American nation in case of invasion by a European or Asian aggressor. This provision, which did not apply if the American country was allied with a non-American nation, created the interesting, if unlikely, possibility of the United States aiding a Latin American government in an aggressive war outside the hemisphere.[93]

In its report, the House Foreign Affairs Committee strongly endorsed the discretionary trade quota provision. "Our position," the members stated, "is that no belligerent country can complain so long as they are treated alike and are given their normal peacetime trade." The committee emphasized the impartial character of all features of the measure, stating, "There is no aggressor involved in this bill."[94] In their final summary, the members of the committee defended the granting of discretionary powers to the President:

> If you undertake to put our Chief Executive in a strait jacket in matters of this kind, you have to a great extent tied up our country so that it could not use its good offices for the prevention of wars. Our influence would be gone for world peace, when we ought to be in a position to use our influence to prevent wars, not, of course, becoming allied or connected politically with any foreign war. Oftentimes it is easier to aid in the prevention of wars than it would be at this time to keep out of war. . . .[95]

[92] "Neutrality Act of 1936," *House Report No. 1928*, 74th Cong., 2d sess. (Washington, 1936), p. 3.

[93] *Ibid.*, pp. 1–2; *Ickes Diary*, I, 514; Hull to Roosevelt, undated, FDR Papers, PSF, Box 33.

[94] *House Report No. 1928*, 74th Cong., 2d sess., pp. 3, 5.

[95] *Ibid.*, p. 9.

The favorable action by the House committee encouraged the administration, but by the end of January the outlook for the Pittman-McReynolds bill was becoming steadily worse. The Rules Committee, swayed by intense Italian-American pressure, delayed in arranging for consideration of the McReynolds bill on the floor of the House.[96] The greatest resistance came in the Senate Foreign Relations Committee, where Hiram Johnson, backed by Borah, threatened to filibuster against the administration's proposal.[97] Though Pittman, bolstered up by conferences with Roosevelt, continued to fight for his measure, by early February he was discouraged. In a letter to Raymond Moley on February 5, he wrote, "The necessity for foreign commerce is so great and political pressure at this particular time is so strong that possibly it is advisable to avoid weeks of acrimonious debate with probably no accomplishment, and simply extend the existing law for one year."[98] Always afraid of a showdown with Johnson and Borah, Pittman was undoubtedly relieved when McReynolds told him on February 7 that there was no chance for passage of their bill in the House. At a conference that afternoon with Roosevelt, Hull, and Moore, the two legislators recommended that the administration accept the Thomas extension resolution. Later in the afternoon Roosevelt brought the issue before the cabinet, and after an hour's discussion it was decided to accept this advice. The next day Senator Pittman, speaking on behalf of the administration, made public the decision to drop the trade quota bill and simply extend the 1935 act.[99]

On February 12 the Senate Foreign Relations Committee unanimously reported out the Thomas resolution with a few significant

[96] *New York Times*, February 5, 1936, p. 12.

[97] *Ibid.*, January 14, 1936, p. 4; *ibid.*, January 30, 1936, p. 13.

[98] Moore to Roosevelt, January 23, 1936, FDR Papers, OF 1561, Box 1; Pittman to Moley, February 5, 1936, SCP, File 75A-F9.1.

[99] Green to Moffat, April 22, 1936, Moffat Papers; *Ickes Diary*, I, 533; *New York Times*, February 9, 1936, p. 27. Pittman made clear his own relief in a letter to Moley on February 12. "Everybody seems happy," Pittman commented, "including myself." SCP, File 75A-F9.1.

changes. The senators adopted the two amendments incorporated into the earlier House committee report which exempted Western Hemisphere countries and altered the opening sentence of the arms embargo section. They also approved a ban on loans to belligerents, allowing the President to exempt short-term commercial credits. In addition, the Senate committee made one vital change in the wording of the 1935 act. Instead of allowing the President discretion in extending the arms embargo to other states that entered a war already in progress, the new bill required the President to do so.[100] This change meant that if members of the League became involved in war as a result of their efforts to punish an aggressor, they would automatically be denied the right to buy arms and munitions from the United States.

Congressional leaders now moved swiftly to pass the extension legislation. On February 14 the House committee reported out a bill identical to the Senate measure.[101] Three days later, both branches of Congress began debating the measure. Though the advocates of mandatory neutrality protested against what they termed a "makeshift" bill, the administration forces, now joined by the supporters of traditional neutrality, commanded an overwhelming majority. In the House, where debate was limited to forty minutes and no amendments were permitted, Louis Ludlow and Maury Maverick urged their colleagues to defeat the bill. However, most supporters of neutrality reluctantly acquiesced to the extension resolution when it was pointed out that if Congress rejected this measure, the arms embargo would expire on February 29.[102] Only one speaker, Representative Melvin J. Maas of Minnesota, opposed the fundamental concept of neutrality legislation. Warning that rigid neutrality aided aggressors, Maas prophesied:

[100] "Report Accompanying Senate Joint Resolution 198," *Senate Report No. 1557*, 74th Cong., 2d sess. (Washington, 1936), pp. 1–2; Minutes of Proceedings of the Senate Foreign Relations Committee, February 12, 1936, SCP, File 74A-E2.

[101] "Extending and Amending the Joint Resolution Approved August 31, 1935," *House Report No. 2001*, 74th Cong., 2d sess. (Washington, 1936).

[102] *Congressional Record*, February 17, 1936, pp. 2240–53.

While for a time we may escape involvement in foreign wars, the ultimate outcome will be that a few powerful, militaristic nations, unchecked by anything, will gradually create a situation of world-wide conquest, and the time will come when we alone will be left in the way of their complete world dominance. As surely as we take this attitude of smug indifference now, we ourselves will then become the object of attack and invasion.[103]

Despite this plea, the House passed the extension resolution by a vote of 353 to 27 on February 17. An analysis of the twenty-seven dissenting votes, cast by the extreme advocates of mandatory neutrality, shows an almost even division between the major parties, but more than half, including seven by the Progressive party, came from the Middle West.[104]

The Senate debate, though unhampered by time limitations, followed the pattern set by the House. The Nye group offered a series of amendments in an effort to salvage part of their program. They first proposed limiting the extension to three months in order to force a full debate on trade restrictions in the spring of 1936. After this motion was defeated by a vote of 61 to 16, they tried to incorporate the trade quota and the trade-at-your-own-risk provisions in the extension resolution. The Senate decisively rejected both trade amendments, however, and, on February 18, passed the Thomas bill by a voice vote. Though there was no roll call on the final passage, the voting patterns on the amendments corresponded to those in the House—ten of the eighteen senators who favored broader trade restrictions were from middle western states.[105]

[103] *Ibid.*, p. 2246.

[104] *Ibid.*, p. 2253. The negative votes were distributed as follows:

Region		*Party*	
Northeast	6	Republican	9
South	3	Democratic	11
Midwest	17	Progressive	7
Far West	1		

[105] *Ibid.*, February 18, 1936, pp. 2287–306. The only roll call vote on trade restrictions came on a proposal by Senator Bone to include a trade-at-

On February 29, 1936, President Roosevelt signed the extension resolution.[106] The new neutrality act continued the arms embargo and travel restrictions that had been adopted in 1935, and it added the prohibition on loans that had long been the goal of neutrality enthusiasts. The 1936 legislation further curtailed the President's freedom in the conduct of foreign policy in the event of war abroad. It denied him authority to restrict trade in raw materials, it limited his discretion in invoking the arms embargo, and it compelled him to extend the embargo to new belligerents entering a war already in progress. Though Roosevelt must have been keenly disappointed in the action of Congress, he did not criticize the legislation as he had in 1935. However, he did issue a statement upon signing the act announcing the continuation of the moral embargo on abnormal trade to Italy and Ethiopia. Stating his belief that excess commerce with belligerents "would serve to magnify the very evil of war which we seek to prevent," the President asked the American people "that they so conduct their trade with belligerent Nations that it cannot be said that they are seizing new opportunities for profit or that by changing their peace-time trade they give aid to the continuation of war."[107] Yet, despite the high moral tone of this statement, Roosevelt knew that his appeal was a poor substitute for the broad powers that Congress had denied him. Once again, the President had met with defeat on neutrality.

---

your-own-risk provision in the bill. This amendment was defeated 55 to 18, with the negative votes distributed as follows:

Region		*Party*	
Northeast	1	Republican	3
South	3	Democratic	13
Midwest	10	Progressive	1
Far West	4	Farmer-Labor	1

[106] *New York Times,* March 1, 1936, p. 1.

[107] *Ibid.,* p. 28.

IV

The complexity of the issues and the tangle of conflicting interests that were so evident in the debate in 1936 rule out any simple explanation of the outcome. Contemporary commentators singled out certain factors as determinants, but there was little agreement among them. Some cited the Italian-American pressure, others the intensive lobbying by oil, cotton, and shipping interests, still others the administration's concern for harmony in an election year.[108] The major credit, or blame, was assigned to Senator Hiram Johnson, whose threat of a filibuster in defense of freedom of the seas undoubtedly influenced the administration's decision to abandon the struggle for trade quotas. Johnson himself viewed the outcome as a personal triumph. When the Senate committee reported out the Thomas bill, he announced that this action "has probably saved this country from a most tragic mistake."[109] Yet if Johnson had not been aided by other groups who opposed the legislation for very different reasons, he could not have successfully carried out his threatened filibuster. The role of Italian-Americans, though difficult to gauge, was probably more significant. Their impact was greatest on the House of Representatives, which previously had supported the administration in neutrality struggles. A number of congressmen frankly told State Department officials that they faced certain defeat at the polls in the November election if they antagonized their Italian constituents by voting for the McReynolds bill. It was this factor which caused McReynolds to inform the administration that he could not carry his bill in the House.[110] And without the prospect of success in the House, there was no point in challenging Johnson to a showdown duel in the Senate.

[108] The most penetrating interpretations were made by Arthur Krock (*New York Times*, February 19, 1936, p. 18); Oswald Garrison Villard (*Nation*, CXLII [February 29, 1936], 239); Frederick Libby (*Peace Action*, II [March, 1936], 2); and the Washington correspondent of the *New Republic* (LXXXVI [February 19, 1936], 45).

[109] "Peace Passion Cold," *Time*, XXVII (February 24, 1936), 16.

[110] Green to Moffat, April 22, 1936, Moffat Papers.

The ultimate explanation, however, does not lie with any single factor. Despite the opposition of Italian-Americans, economic interests, and advocates of freedom of the seas, if the administration forces could have worked out a feasible compromise with the advocates of mandatory neutrality, they would have commanded solid majorities in both branches of Congress. In many ways the situation was parallel to the Senate debate over the League of Nations in 1919. In each case a great majority agreed on a basic policy but their disagreement on the way to achieve their common goal allowed the opposing minority to triumph. If this analysis is correct, then the disagreement over mandatory versus discretionary trade restrictions was the crucial obstacle that defeated the administration's program. The Nye group, fearing, with some reason, that Roosevelt wanted a discretionary policy allowing him to co-operate with the League in sanctions against aggressors, insisted on a rigid program of its own and thus split the potential majority for extending neutrality legislation to include restriction on essential raw materials. The real issue in 1936 differed little from that of 1935—it was isolation versus collective security. The administration, defeated on the arms embargo, still sought for ways to co-operate passively with the League in its efforts to restrain aggressors. The Nye group was equally determined to adopt a policy aimed solely at insulating the United States from contact with European wars. These objectives were incompatible, and the result was an impasse which simply postponed the issue for another year.

For President Roosevelt, the 1936 act was a serious setback. The year before, he had compromised in the face of an insistent demand for an impartial arms embargo knowing that it would deny aid to Italy in the approaching Ethiopian War. But when he found that raw materials were in many ways more vital than arms, he realized he needed authority to control the export of these goods. But the Nye group firmly denied him discretionary powers in restricting trade, and this time he could not compromise, for to accept rigid controls over the export of raw materials would be to surrender whatever hopes he had to use American influence and prestige to check the threat of aggression in Europe. His original advocacy of neutrality legislation, based on the belief he could substitute presidential discretion for a blind defense of neutral rights, now came back to haunt him. He had become the prisoner of his own policies.

CHAPTER SIX

THE CASH-AND-CARRY COMPROMISE, 1937

If we face the choice of profits or peace, the Nation will answer—must answer—"we choose peace."

FRANKLIN D. ROOSEVELT, August 14, 1936

After a year of intense controversy and discussion, the neutrality policy of the United States remained incomplete and uncertain. Believing that the defense of traditional neutral rights had directly led to American involvement in World War I, the American people had accepted limitations on the export of arms, on loans, and on passenger travel in time of foreign war. But on the wider issue of curtailing trade, there was little agreement. In 1937 the President, Congress, and the nation had to decide to what extent they were willing to forego the profits of neutral trade in order to avoid involvement in war. The problem was essentially economic, and it called into question the validity of the widely accepted thesis of the Nye committee that only stringent self-denial could preserve American neutrality. The American people had been eager to restrain financiers and munitions makers, but when they realized that further embargoes on foreign trade would have a devastating impact on the American economy and on their own individual fortunes, they began to voice their doubts. Faced with the apparent choice between peace and prosperity, they searched for a magic formula that would preserve both.

I

In the months that followed the adjournment of Congress in the spring of 1936, a number of individuals and groups spoke out on the economic implications of neutrality. The advocates of collective security, heartened by the failure of the Nye group to achieve its goals in Congress, pleaded again for a policy of co-operation to prevent war. At a meeting of the American Academy of Political and Social Science held in the spring, Allen Dulles and Felix Morley, editor of the *Washington Post*, denied the economic interpretation of war popularized by the Nye committee. Arguing that neither trade nor loans influenced the decision for war in 1917, they stressed the importance of the world balance of power. The nation's security, not its pocketbook, should be the basic consideration. "If either in Europe or Asia any nation became so powerful that it was completely dominant, the interests and possibly the safety of the United States might eventually be threatened," Dulles warned. Instead of adopting embargoes which would dangerously weaken the American economy, he contended, the United States should co-operate with other nations to halt aggression and thus create a secure world order.[1]

This plea for collective security had little impact upon President Roosevelt or his party. When the Democratic National Convention met in Philadelphia in June, the platform committee incorporated the Nye thesis into its plank on foreign policy. "We shall continue to observe a true neutrality in the disputes of others; . . . to work for peace and to take the profits out of war; to guard against being drawn, by political commitments, international banking, or private trading, into any war which may develop anywhere," the platform stated.[2] Cordell Hull, who was not consulted on this statement, was dumbfounded by such a blatant

[1] Allen W. Dulles, "Economic Implications of American Neutrality Policy," *Annals of the American Academy of Political and Social Science*, CLXXXVI (July, 1936), 41–47; Felix Morley, "Practical Implications of American Neutrality Policy," *ibid.*, pp. 48–54.

[2] *New York Times*, June 26, 1936, p. 13.

concession to isolationist opinion.[3] President Roosevelt pursued this same theme in his major campaign address on foreign policy, delivered at Chautauqua, New York, on August 14, 1936. Declaring, "We are not isolationists except insofar as we seek to isolate ourselves completely from war," the President vividly described his own horror of fighting. Turning to neutrality legislation, Roosevelt praised the "new weapons" which Congress had given him to preserve American peace, but he warned that if war broke out in the world, the lure of sudden wealth, which he called "fools' gold," would cause thousands of grasping Americans to attempt "to break down or evade our neutrality." "If we face the choice of profits or peace," the President declared, "the Nation will answer—must answer—'we choose peace.'" Yet after this strong endorsement of the Nye thesis, Roosevelt pleaded for a discretionary neutrality policy: ". . . we must remember that no laws can be provided to cover every contingency, for it is impossible to imagine how every future event may shape itself." "In spite of every possible forethought, international relations involve of necessity a vast uncharted area." Peace, he concluded, depends on the day-to-day decisions of the President and the Secretary of State.[4]

It would be easy to dismiss the Chautauqua address as a shrewd political maneuver to win isolationist votes. In part it was. Two weeks later, in a campaign speech attacking the Republicans for their failure to take a stand on neutrality, John Cudahy, the American ambassador to Poland, cited Roosevelt's address.[5] Yet Roosevelt's statements are in keeping with his early actions on neutrality legislation. He did believe in the Nye thesis, to the extent that he felt economic interests, if unrestrained in their quest

[3] *The Memoirs of Cordell Hull* (2 vols.; New York, 1948), I, 485–86. Hull had submitted suggestions on the platform to Roosevelt, but they were ignored.

[4] Department of State, *Peace and War: United States Foreign Policy, 1931–1941* (Washington, 1943), pp. 326–28.

[5] *New York Times*, August 30, 1936, p. 2. The Republican platform plank on foreign policy, written largely by Senator Borah, made no mention of neutrality legislation.

for the profits of neutral trade, could well force the nation into war. Disagreeing with the neutrality bloc's insistence on rigid legislation, the President was pleading for a discretionary policy that would allow him to restrict trade in order to prevent American entanglement in foreign conflicts. If he dramatically exploited the nation's fear of war, it was not merely to win votes but to convince the nation that he could be trusted to use discretionary powers wisely and safely. The President stood between the internationalist and the isolationist extremes—he wished to curtail traditional neutral rights without unduly endangering the nation's economic well-being and without committing the United States to a policy of collective security.

The President's plan of discretionary neutrality, while attractive to many experts in international relations, was too vague to win widespread public acceptance. The nation wanted a formula and it was Bernard Baruch who supplied it. In an article in *Current History* in June, 1936, Baruch forcefully restated the cash-and-carry plan he had suggested the previous November. Asserting that the overwhelming desire of the American people was to stay out of war, he warned that embargoes and limitations on trade would not achieve that end. Modern warfare, Baruch pointed out, "is a struggle to the death—not between armies alone, but between economic systems." Any interruption of trade with a belligerent country, even if applied impartially, would seriously injure that nation's war effort and could well cause it to retaliate against the United States. "Economic boycotts placed by us on [belligerent] nations . . . are a form of participation in war any way you look at it," Baruch contended. He therefore recommended that the sale of commodities for export, other than arms, be permitted without limitation. However, he did object to Americans financing or shipping goods purchased in the United States by a belligerent—these practices would inevitably lead to the destruction of American property and the loss of American lives on the high seas. To avoid this danger, Baruch put forward the cash-and-carry principle—"We will sell to any belligerent anything except lethal weapons, but the terms are '*cash on the barrel-head and come and get it.*' "[6]

Baruch's plan was an ingenious method of preserving the profits of neutral trade while minimizing the risk of involvement in a major war. It would avoid the incidents that had contributed to American entry into World War I; American bankers could not build up a stake in the economy of a belligerent nation and American ships would not be targets for submarine attacks. Yet it would not produce the "genuine neutrality" sought by the Nye group. As a State Department analysis of cash-and-carry pointed out, "It would amount, in fact, to a benevolent neutrality in favor of wealthy nations and against poor ones. Its possible outcome would be to make us eventually the Allies of the former."[7] Even more important, the Baruch plan would favor the nations with sea power and penalize their opponents. And the cash-and-carry proposal would not prevent the creation of the type of economic ties that the Nye committee so ardently deplored. Wealthy nations that controlled the sea could stimulate a war boom in the United States and thus create a powerful American interest in the outcome of any war in progress. Yet despite these drawbacks, the cash-and-carry plan offered an attractive alternative to a nation that wanted peace, but not at any price.

The cash-and-carry proposal appealed to the peace societies, who bitterly denounced the failure of Congress to adopt a sweeping mandatory neutrality bill in 1936. However, the pacifist organizations would apply it only to nonessential exports—their chief proposal was for an absolute embargo on all strategic commodities such as oil, scrap iron, and cotton. By the fall of 1936, the NCPW, the WIL, and the National Peace Conference had all adopted resolutions calling for the extension of the arms embargo to include "basic raw materials used for war."[8] They were joined

[6] Bernard Baruch, "Neutrality," *Current History*, XLIV (June, 1936), 32–44.

[7] Memorandum by Charles W. Yost, June 26, 1936, 811.04418/179½.

[8] *Peace Action*, II (May, 1936), 4; *ibid.*, III (November, 1936), 6; Dorothy Detzer to Key Pittman, May 28, 1936, SCP File 74A-E2.

by other organizations, notably the National Grange and the National Farmers Union, and by William Green, president of the AF of L.[9] Senator Arthur H. Vandenberg, a member of the Nye committee, best expressed the attitude of those favoring a rigid policy in a public statement in December, 1936. "In my view we want an American neutrality which quarantines us against the wars of others to the last possible practicable and realistic extent," he announced. "It cannot be done under the old rules which subordinate peace to commerce."[10]

By the end of 1936, there was still broad disagreement over the proper solution to the neutrality problem. Internationalists favored discriminatory embargoes aimed at aggressors; the President wanted discretionary power to limit commerce; Baruch proposed to ban the delivery and financing of exports to belligerents but not their sale; the neutrality bloc demanded an embargo on strategic raw materials and cash-and-carry for nonessential commodities. Though there were still powerful advocates of freedom of the seas in Congress, the choice appeared to be between these four alternatives, with little chance for adoption of the first. The peace societies were planning to hold 1,500 meetings in 500 cities around the nation in early 1937 to win support for their position, but the economic sacrifice implicit in even a limited trade embargo undercut their appeal.[11] The cash-and-carry plan had the best prospects for success, but the issue of presidential discretion remained in doubt. If Congress voted for the Baruch plan, it would still have to decide whether or not to invest the President with the permissive power which he wanted and which the Nye group feared. Regardless of the specific legislative device that was chosen, the real debate centered on the freedom and flexibility to be granted the President. Once again, Roosevelt would have to test his strength, enhanced by his impressive victory in the 1936 election, against the power of the mandatory neutrality bloc.

[9] *Peace Action*, III (December, 1936), 5; *New York Times*, September 24, 1936, p. 11.

[10] *Ibid.*, December 28, 1936, p. 7.

[11] *Peace Action*, III (December, 1936), 7.

II

The administration began developing its neutrality plans in December, 1936. Three days before Christmas, Roosevelt announced that he intended to ask Congress for permanent neutrality legislation when the new Congress convened in January.[12] Yet before the end of December, an emergency situation arose which forced both the President and Congress to postpone temporarily their consideration of comprehensive neutrality legislation.

When the Spanish Civil War broke out in mid-July, 1936, it appeared to have little relevance to American neutrality policy. The American legislation did not cover civil wars, since normally they would not threaten to involve the United States in a major conflict. The war in Spain, however, which began as an army coup against the Republican government, quickly assumed dangerous proportions. By August, Germany and Italy were offering aid to the Spanish Rebels, led by General Francisco Franco, while the Soviet Union rallied to the support of the Loyalists. The Civil War soon became an ideological conflict between fascism and communism which threatened the peace of Europe and, indeed, of the entire world. England and France, hoping to limit the fighting to Spain, took the lead in forming a Non-intervention Committee designed to prevent the dispatch of war materials to either side. Though the United States did not officially join in this collective effort, the administration was sympathetic to the efforts of the European democracies.[13] Unable to invoke the neutrality act, Secretary Hull again resorted to a moral embargo. On August 7 the State Department sent a circular telegram to American diplomatic and consular officers in Spain pointing out that although the arms embargo did not apply to the Civil War, the

[12] *New York Times*, December 23, 1936, p. 6.

[13] C. E. Black and E. C. Helmreich, *Twentieth Century Europe* (New York, 1950), pp. 616–18; Arnold Toynbee and V. M. Boulter, *Survey of International Affairs, 1937* (2 vols.; London, 1938), II, 1–23; *Hull Memoirs*, I, 475–77. F. Jay Taylor, *The United States and the Spanish Civil War* (New York, 1956) provides a thorough treatment of both American policy and American attitudes toward the Spanish conflict.

United States would "scrupulously refrain from any interference whatsoever in the unfortunate Spanish situation." "We believe that American citizens, both at home and abroad," the circular continued, "are patriotically observing this well-recognized policy."[14] Four days later, the State Department made this statement public. While it was not an official proclamation of neutrality, it did set forth the government's intention of discouraging trade in arms with either side in the Spanish Civil War.

The true intent of the administration's policy soon became apparent. On August 10, the Glenn L. Martin Company asked the State Department whether it would object to the sale of eight bombers to the Spanish government. After conferring by telephone with Roosevelt and Hull, who were both out of town, Acting Secretary of State William Phillips sent the Martin Company a copy of the circular telegram of August 7 and observed that the proposed sale of airplanes "would not follow the spirit of the Government's policy."[15] This statement, made public on August 22, was repeated to a number of other firms inquiring about the export of war material to Spain. It met with widespread approval. Isolationists applauded the moral embargo as a safeguard against American involvement in Spain; advocates of collective security praised it as a measure of co-operation with the British and French efforts to contain the Civil War.[16]

Throughout the fall of 1936, American manufacturers and exporters scrupulously observed the moral embargo. In late December, however, several individuals applied for permission to export airplanes to the Spanish government. Unable to withhold export licenses legally, the State Department announced on December 28 that it had granted permission to Robert Cuse, a New Jersey scrapdealer, to sell over $2 million worth of airplane parts and engines to the Loyalists. The Department had tried hard to dissuade Cuse, but he firmly demanded his rights. At a press conference the next

[14] *FR: 1936*, II, 471.

[15] *Ibid.*, pp. 475–76.

[16] *Hull Memoirs*, I, 478–79.

day, President Roosevelt denounced Cuse's action as legal but unpatriotic.[17]

This breach of the moral embargo led to a series of hasty conferences between Roosevelt, State Department officials, and congressional leaders. Roosevelt had originally intended to ask Congress to include discretionary power to embargo arms to civil wars when it tackled the general problem of neutrality revision. Now the President, fearing the shipment of war materials from the United States would undermine the efforts of the European Nonintervention Committee, decided to ask for immediate action by Congress on a civil war embargo when it convened on January 5.[18] At a meeting with Pittman, McReynolds, and R. Walton Moore on December 30, Roosevelt brought up this issue. Pittman favored a special amendment to the neutrality act covering all civil wars, but Assistant Secretary Moore suggested that in order to avoid lengthy debate Pittman and McReynolds should sponsor separate legislation that would apply specifically to the Spanish Civil War. At another conference on January 5, the congressional leaders finally agreed to this course.[19]

On January 6, Pittman introduced a joint resolution proposing an embargo on the shipment of arms, munitions, and implements of war to either side in the Spanish Civil War. In presenting this measure, he stressed the need for rapid action to avoid American involvement in what could well develop into a general European war.[20] Representative McReynolds introduced the resolution in the House at the same time. Pointing out that the State Department had already been forced to grant several licenses for the ex-

[17] *New York Times*, December 29, 1936, p. 1; *ibid.*, December 30, 1936, p. 1; R. Walton Moore to William C. Bullitt, December 29, 1936, *FR: 1936*, II, 618–19. Cuse, a naturalized citizen born in Latvia, represented the Vimalert Company, which acted as an agent of the Spanish government. Taylor, *U.S. and Spanish Civil War*, p. 95, n. 3.

[18] *New York Times*, December 23, 1936, p. 6.

[19] *Ibid.*, December 31, 1936, p. 1; Pittman to Roosevelt, December 30, 1936, SCP, File 75A-E2; Moore to Roosevelt, January 5, 1937, FDR Papers, PSF, Box 33.

[20] *Congressional Record*, January 5, 1937, pp. 73–74.

port of war material to Spain, McReynolds declared, "There is a race on between the Congress and the people who want to send these deadly instruments of warfare to Spain to help carry on this carnage."[21] Though no one in either House spoke against the Pittman resolution, members of the neutrality bloc criticized the way in which Spain was singled out for discriminatory treatment. Senators Nye, Clark, and Vandenberg and Representative Maverick all indicated they would prefer to enact a sweeping arms embargo that would apply to all civil wars. Several legislators, notably Nye and Maverick, suggested that the measure was unneutral in its effect, claiming that it would injure the Loyalists, who controlled the seaports, far more than Franco's Rebels.[22] The neutrality bloc did not press these objections, and the resolution was adopted unanimously in the Senate and with only one negative vote in the House. The lone dissenter was Representative John Toussaint Bernard, a Farmer-Laborite from Minnesota, who later claimed that the bill represented "pro-Fascist neutrality" aimed at injuring the democratic government of Spain.[23]

Though Congress acted with unprecedented speed, it was unable to prevent the export of war materials to Spain by Robert Cuse. While the congressional debate took place, Cuse loaded six airplanes and one engine on board the Spanish freighter "Mar Cantábrico" in New York harbor. The "Mar Cantábrico" then headed out to sea closely followed by a coast guard cutter and a patrol plane ready to stop the ship before it left American territorial waters upon orders from Washington. But a legal technicality prevented the resolution from going into effect until January 8, and the "Mar Cantábrico" went safely on its way only to fall eventually into the hands of the Spanish Rebels.[24]

[21] *Ibid.*, January 6, 1937, p. 86.

[22] *Ibid.*, pp. 74–79, 86–88, 92.

[23] *Ibid.*, January 7, 1937, pp. 80, 98; *ibid.*, January 21, 1937, Appendix, pp. 65–66.

[24] *New York Times*, January 7, 1937, p. 1; "Neutrality War," *Time*, XXIX (January 18, 1937), 15; Whitney H. Shepardson and William O. Scroggs, *The United States in World Affairs, 1937* (New York, 1938), p. 42.

Despite the unanimity in Congress, there was widespread agitation in the United States against the Spanish arms embargo. Socialist and Communist leaders, together with editors of liberal journals of opinion, condemned the embargo as a hostile act against an established government engaged in an unequal contest against fascism. For quite different reasons, business journals criticized the congressional action, claiming that it represented unwarranted governmental interference with foreign trade. At the same time, strong support was voiced for the embargo by representatives of the Catholic church and by isolationist groups in the United States. The *Christian Century* strongly endorsed the resolution as "an emphatic representation of the minds of the American people."[25] On the whole, these reactions reflected the growing divergence of opinion inside the nation toward the Spanish Civil War.

The Spanish arms embargo revealed many of the essential flaws in the policy of mandatory neutrality. As the *New York Times* observed, the episode showed the folly of attempting to cover every possible situation by rigid rules laid down in advance by Congress. If the President had possessed broad discretionary powers, he could have dealt with the problem swiftly and efficiently.[26] Even more significant, the embargo on Spain proved the impossibility of achieving a truly impartial neutrality policy. The ban tended to hurt the Loyalists, who normally could expect, as the established and recognized government of Spain, to import arms from abroad. Certainly it favored the Rebels. General Franco praised Roosevelt for a policy which he viewed as "a gesture we Nationalists will never forget."[27] For those who wished to see the United States use its influence to stem totalitarian aggression overseas, as well as for others who believed that neutrality should be synonymous with impartiality, the Spanish arms embargo was a bitter disappointment.

[25] Taylor, *U.S. and Spanish Civil War*, pp. 82–85.

[26] *New York Times*, December 30, 1936, p. 20.

[27] Taylor, *U.S. and Spanish Civil War*, p. 81.

III

The prompt congressional passage of the Spanish arms embargo resolution enabled the administration to resume its consideration of the over-all neutrality problem. In mid-January, Roosevelt and Hull decided not to put forward an administration bill but rather to allow Senator Pittman and Representative McReynolds to develop their own legislative programs. In part, this decision was based on Pittman's own desire to introduce an independent bill. The Nevada senator had frequently clashed with Hull and other State Department officials. Moreover, he had become convinced of the wisdom of the cash-and-carry plan, which he wished to include in his own legislation. The administration's failure the previous year to win congressional approval of the trade quota plan also influenced Roosevelt and Hull. By adopting a noncommittal attitude, yet working closely with McReynolds, who was always willing to co-operate, the administration leaders felt they could best achieve their basic objective—as broad discretionary authority for the President as Congress would grant.[28] Accordingly, on January 22, Senator Pittman introduced a comprehensive neutrality bill which continued the arms, loan, and travel bans and added a mandatory cash-and-carry feature. Three days later, McReynolds put forward his bill, which was nearly identical with the trade quota measure he had sponsored on behalf of the State Department the year before.[29]

The administration was now compelled to choose between the two alternatives of cash-and-carry and trade quotas. A series of meetings took place among State Department officers which culminated in a conference with Roosevelt at the White House on January 30 attended by Hull, R. Walton Moore, and Sumner Welles. In a memorandum to Roosevelt on the day of this meeting, Moore told the President that McReynolds was "perfectly

[28] *Hull Memoirs*, I, 506; Pittman to Roosevelt, December 30, 1936, SCP, File 75A-E2.

[29] *Congressional Record*, January 22, 1936, p. 337; *ibid.*, January 25, 1937, p. 406.

willing to go along with us."[30] Though no record of the conference is available, press reports during the next few days indicated that the administration had decided to accept the cash-and-carry plan as the basis for restrictions on general trade.[31] Two weeks later, when hearings opened on the two bills, State Department witnesses announced the administration's decision to substitute the cash-and-carry scheme for the trade quota plan, which they claimed was too complex to administer properly. At the same time, McReynolds stated that the Foreign Affairs Committee planned to redraft his bill in line with the State Department recommendations.[32]

Though a lack of evidence makes it difficult to generalize on Roosevelt's motives in accepting the cash-and-carry principle, two factors stand out clearly. First, the President was about to launch his plan to reorganize the Supreme Court. Aware of the controversy this would create, he undoubtedly was eager to avoid a showdown battle over neutrality. The great popularity of the cash-and-carry plan, both in Congress and among the people generally, made it expedient to choose this alternative.[33] Second, and probably more important, the President came to realize that the cash-and-carry proposal would favor Great Britain and France, with their control of the sea, if they became involved in war with Germany and Italy. The British had recently revealed their intense concern over the development of neutrality legislation. On January 19, Robert Bingham, the American ambassador to England, had reported Anthony Eden, the British Foreign Secretary, as saying that "this subject gave his Government considerable anxiety."[34] Three days later, Walter Runciman, president of the Brit-

[30] Moore to Roosevelt, January 30, 1937, FDR Papers, OF 1561, Box 1.

[31] *New York Times*, January 31, 1937, p. 28; *ibid*., February 3, 1937, p. 3.

[32] "American Neutrality Policy," *Hearings before the House Committee on Foreign Affairs*, 75th Cong., 1st sess. (Washington, 1937), pp. 6, 16, 23, 25, 30.

[33] Tom Connally and Alfred Steinberg, *My Name Is Tom Connally* (New York, 1954), p. 223.

[34] Memorandum of conversation with Anthony Eden by Robert Bingham, January 19, 1937, 852.00/4529.

ish Board of Trade, arrived in the United States to confer with Roosevelt and Hull on the possibility of negotiating a reciprocal trade treaty. In an interview before the talks began, Runciman said that neutrality legislation would be one of the major topics he would take up with President Roosevelt. The press interpreted this statement to mean that Britain would refuse to discuss a trade agreement unless it had some guaranty of being able to purchase goods in the United States in time of war.[35] Runciman undoubtedly pointed out to Roosevelt the advantages of cash-and-carry from the British standpoint. Thus considerations of international realities, as well as domestic politics, probably conditioned Roosevelt's decision to accept the cash-and-carry plan as embodied in the Pittman bill.

In early February, numerous other neutrality bills were introduced in Congress. Senators Nye, Clark, and Vandenberg put forward a comprehensive bill which included a rigid cash-and-carry clause. Though this bill had a great many additional mandatory features, it did not differ to any great degree from the Pittman measure.[36] Nye, who had privately indicated his willingness to join the administration in supporting permanent neutrality legislation, did not press for adoption of his measure, apparently accepting the Pittman resolution as reasonably satisfactory.[37] At the other extreme, Senator Elbert D. Thomas of Utah introduced a flexible bill giving the President broad power to embargo raw materials as well as arms, while Senator J. Hamilton Lewis offered a measure granting the President absolute discretionary authority to

[35] *New York Times*, January 23, 1937, p. 10; *ibid.*, January 24, 1937, p. 27. In an article in the *New York Times* on February 28, Edwin James suggested that the Runciman visit influenced the administration's shift to cash-and-carry. "The new neutrality plans indicate, in practice," James observed, "a co-operation between the United States and Great Britain which the most ardent Anglophiles in this country would not have dreamed possible a few short years ago." *Ibid.*, February 28, 1937, IV, 3.

[36] *Ibid.*, February 1, 1937, p. 1; *ibid.*, February 2, 1937, p. 12.

[37] Joseph C. Green to Hull, May 14, 1936, 711.00111/Armament Control/890.

impose arms, trade, travel, and loan restrictions as he saw fit.[38] These two bills, which had little chance for passage in Congress, received no support from the administration.

In mid-February, the two congressional committees held hearings on the neutrality issue.[39] The Senate session was very brief, limited to one witness, R. Walton Moore, who presented the State Department's views; the House hearings were much more extensive. Before both bodies, State Department officers stressed the need for presidential discretion. Moore told the Senate Foreign Relations Committee, ". . . the more legislation you put on the statute books which tends to tie the hands of the Government, the more definitely you advertise to war-minded nations what they can count upon when a war occurs."[40] Joseph C. Green and Green H. Hackworth made the same plea to the House Foreign Affairs Committee.[41] Though the State Department spokesmen did not endorse any specific legislation, Moore told the senators that the Pittman bill was "fairly satisfactory."[42] Green and Hackworth both strongly endorsed the cash-and-carry principle as the most effective way to limit trade. "If you are going to put restrictions on," Hackworth stated, "then the restrictions ought to be of such a character as not to interfere unnecessarily with American commerce; we should not bottle up our trade."[43] Hull declined invitations to appear before the two committees, but at a

[38] *Congressional Record*, February 10, 1937, pp. 1074–75.

[39] "American Neutrality Policy," House *Hearings*, 75th Cong., 1st sess.; "Neutrality," *Hearing before the Senate Committee on Foreign Relations*, 75th Cong., 1st sess. (Washington, 1937).

[40] *Ibid.*, p. 15.

[41] "American Neutrality Policy," House *Hearings*, 75th Cong., 1st sess., pp. 34–36.

[42] "Neutrality," Senate *Hearing*, 75th Cong., 1st sess., p. 17. In a letter to Roosevelt two days after his appearance at the hearings, Moore endorsed the Pittman resolution as "far less objectionable than any other measure carrying mandatory provisions." Moore to Roosevelt, February 15, 1937, FDR Papers, OF 1561, Box 1.

[43] "American Neutrality Policy," House *Hearings*, 75th Cong., 1st sess., pp. 17, 22, 25.

press conference on February 18 he expressed his preference for a bill that "might contain the smallest amount of purely mandatory and inflexible legislation."[44]

In addition to the State Department spokesmen, the House committee heard testimony from a variety of witnesses representing peace societies, veterans' organizations, and left-wing political parties. Spearheaded by the leaders of the NCPW, the pacifists who appeared pleaded for mandatory neutrality legislation. Their program, which was embodied in bills offered by Representatives Maury Maverick, Jerry Voorhis of California, and Herman Kopplemann of Connecticut, consisted of a total embargo on all essential war materials and a rigid cash-and-carry clause for all other exports. They repeatedly stressed the danger of presidential discretion. Mrs. Florence Brewer Boeckel, associate secretary of the NCPW, stated that it would be "a shirking of responsibility" for Congress to leave neutrality to the judgment of the President.[45] Representative Kopplemann went further, warning that "discretionary neutrality means that the United States will be ready, if not willing, to join the League of Nations in a policy of sanctions against an aggressor."[46] Others, including John Bassett Moore, Millard Rice, lobbyist for the Veterans of Foreign Wars, and Norman Thomas, Socialist leader, expressed the same fear that the President would use his authority to co-operate with other nations and thus risk American involvement in war.[47]

In addition to advocates of mandatory neutrality, witnesses expressing a wide variety of viewpoints appeared at the hearings. Quincy Wright, professor of international law at the University of Chicago, vigorously argued in behalf of discriminatory measures designed to punish aggressors. When Chairman McReynolds frankly told him that there was no chance for the passage of such

[44] *Hull Memoirs*, I, 509.

[45] "American Neutrality Policy," House *Hearings*, 75th Cong., 1st sess., pp. 53–58, 62–70, 89–93, 94–99.

[46] *Ibid.*, p. 65.

[47] *Ibid.*, pp. 47, 131–32, 154–55.

legislation, Wright pleaded for broad discretionary powers that would enable the President to use American influence to prevent the outbreak of war.[48] At the other extreme, Charles Weil, a New York exporter, attacked all proposed restrictions on American commerce, advocating instead a return to traditional neutral rights. In contrast to the 1936 hearings, Weil was the only witness to uphold freedom of the seas, though John Bassett Moore reiterated his views in a letter that Hamilton Fish read to the committee.[49] Finally, representatives of the Socialist party and the Communist-dominated American League against War and Fascism savagely criticized the Spanish arms embargo as being "anti-neutral and pro-Fascist." They also attacked a proposal, embodied in both the McReynolds and Pittman bills, to extend the arms embargo to all civil wars, warning that such a measure would encourage Fascists everywhere to rebel against established democratic governments.[50]

While the House hearings continued, the Senate Foreign Relations Committee met in executive session to consider the Pittman bill. After rejecting a number of changes in the direction of presidential discretion offered by Senator Thomas, the committee reported out this measure on February 20.[51] Pittman announced that the Nye group approved it; only Senators Johnson and Borah were opposed. Calling his legislation the "Peace Act of 1937," Pittman told reporters, "We are now cutting the cables by which we were dragged into the last war. . . ."[52] In its final form, the Pittman bill was a surprisingly rigid measure that severely limited the President's authority. It continued the mandatory arms embargo and the ban on loans, and it made travel on belligerent ships illegal, rather than at the risk of the passenger. The chief innovation was the cash-and-carry feature, which was put into two

48 *Ibid.*, pp. 121–27.

49 *Ibid.*, pp. 47–48, 103–5.

50 *Ibid.*, pp. 131–34, 139, 142–45, 150.

51 "Amendments to the Neutrality Act," *Senate Report No. 118*, 75th Cong., 1st sess. (Washington, 1937).

52 *New York Times*, February 18, 1937, p. 16; *ibid.*, February 21, 1937, pp. 1, 2.

separate sections. First, the Pittman bill allowed the President to select essential war materials which he could then ban from shipment on American vessels. This "carry" clause was thus discretionary. Second, the bill stated that whenever the arms embargo was invoked, no commodities could be exported by American citizens until the title to the goods was transferred to foreign purchasers. This mandatory "cash" section was designed to avoid the loss of American-owned property on the high seas. Other new features included the extension of the arms embargo, at the discretion of the President, to all civil wars, the grant of power to the President to exclude, at his discretion, armed belligerent merchantmen from American territorial waters, and a mandatory ban on the arming of American merchant ships trading with belligerent nations.[53] In effect, the Pittman measure, except for areas which obviously required flexibility, laid down prescribed rules which would automatically go into effect upon the outbreak of war anywhere in the world.

Five days later, the House Foreign Affairs Committee reported out a revised version of the McReynolds bill.[54] In many ways it was similar to the Pittman measure—it continued the arms and loan bans and it allowed the President to extend the arms embargo to civil wars and to bar armed belligerent merchantmen from American ports. The McReynolds bill also made travel on belligerent ships illegal, but the President was allowed to decide whether or not to invoke this cause. The principal difference between the two bills lay in the cash-and-carry section. The House measure gave the President discretion not only in the "carry" section but in the "cash" clause as well. Thus when war broke out, the President could either allow exports to continue on a normal basis or require that title be transferred on all sales to belligerent nations.[55] In the report, McReynolds stated that the com-

[53] *Senate Report No. 118*, 75th Cong., 1st sess., pp. 1–3.

[54] "Neutrality Act of 1937," *House Report No. 320*, 75th Cong., 1st sess. (Washington, 1937).

[55] *Ibid.*, Part 1, pp. 1–5.

mittee favored presidential discretion in order to avoid needless sacrifice of American trade in the case of minor wars.[56] Five Republican members, led by Hamilton Fish, issued a minority report in which they bitterly attacked the McReynolds bill for being "replete with discretionary power to the President, which might entangle us in foreign disputes and embroil us in war." They particularly challenged the cash-and-carry provisions, which they claimed would destroy the American merchant marine, and they suggested instead a complete embargo on all contraband goods.[57]

With the report of the two congressional committees in late February, the issue was clearly defined—Congress was presented with a choice between mandatory and discretionary cash-and-carry. The Pittman and McReynolds bills both reflected a trend toward sharply limiting the President's authority, with the chief difference being the greater degree of mandatory control in the Senate measure. Baruch's cash-and-carry concept had won the overwhelming support of the two committees. Both agreed on the need to allow the President to decide what goods to ban from American ships trading with belligerents—they disagreed only on the transfer of title provision. While this seemed to be a relatively minor discrepancy, it now assumed great symbolic importance in the continuing struggle between those who favored presidential discretion and those who feared it.

IV

Before examining congressional action on the Pittman and McReynolds bills, it is necessary to survey briefly the continuing public debate on neutrality legislation. By 1937 public opinion polls, which were just coming into widespread use, indicated a growing trend toward isolation. In March, 1937, the Gallup Poll asked whether American foreign policy should be directed toward preventing war abroad or toward keeping the United States out of

[56] *Ibid.*, p. 3.

[57] *Ibid.*, Part 2, pp. 1–4.

war. An overwhelming 94 per cent of those polled replied in favor of the latter policy.[58] On the more specific issue of mandatory versus discretionary neutrality legislation, 69 per cent of those questioned in January, 1937, believed Congress rather than the President should be responsible for American neutrality policy.[59] Though the American people showed themselves almost unanimously opposed to entry into another major war, they had considerable doubt whether neutrality legislation would avoid this possibility. In a poll taken soon after the passage of the 1936 act, nearly half of those replying believed the United States would be drawn into a general European conflict.[60] It seems evident from these limited surveys of popular thought that the great majority of Americans feared involvement in future wars and were willing to support mandatory neutrality measures in an effort to keep the nation at peace.

A sampling of national newspaper and periodical editorials reveals a greater degree of diversity. Prominent papers like the *New York Times,* widely read magazines such as the *Reader's Digest,* and liberal journals like the *Nation* struck out boldly for discretionary policies. In articles and editorials, writers in these publications labelled mandatory neutrality "irresponsible," "moral cowardice," and "pro-Fascist."[61] Louis Fischer, writing in the *Nation,* summarized this attitude with his slogan, "An ounce of war prevention is worth a pound of neutrality."[62] Yet at the same time a host of newspapers, led by the *Chicago Tribune,* and a broad spec-

[58] Hadley Cantril and Mildred Strunk (eds.), *Public Opinion, 1935–1946* (Princeton, 1951), p. 967.

[59] *Ibid.,* p. 966.

[60] In a Gallup poll taken in February, 1937, 95 per cent of the people interviewed believed that the United States should not take part in any future European war. *Ibid.*

[61] *New York Times,* February 10, 1937, p. 22; *ibid.,* February 23, 1937, p. 26; James Macalester, "The Cowardice of Fixed Neutrality," *Reader's Digest,* XXX (April, 1937), 37; "Pro-Fascist Neutrality," *Nation,* CXLIV (January 9, 1937), 33–34.

[62] Louis Fischer, "Keeping America Out of War," *Nation,* CXLIV (March 27, 1937), 349.

trum of periodicals, ranging from the *New Republic* to the *Saturday Evening Post,* staunchly supported the public's desire for rigid legislation.

Most of the peace societies, led by the NCPW and WIL, campaigned vigorously for mandatory legislation. In letters and telegrams to the President, the State Department, and individual legislators, they pleaded for the embargo of all war materials and rigid restraints on other trade.[63] Frederick J. Libby summed up their goal in *Peace Action.* "The object," he wrote, "is to restrict war, as one would a fire, to the smallest possible area. Neither one's sympathies nor one's sense of justice can justify making any war a world war."[64] A few pacifist groups which favored international co-operation actively worked for a very different policy. The League of Nations Association sent every congressman a pamphlet urging the adoption of discretionary legislation that would permit the President to embargo arms and raw materials to nations violating the Kellogg pact.[65] A number of women's organizations, including the National Conference on the Cause and Cure of War, the League of Women Voters, and the YWCA, also lobbied for discretionary neutrality.[66] These groups, however, represented a minority of the total peace movement.

American religious opinion was even more divided than the pacifist groups. The Federal Council of Churches maintained its earlier ambiguous stand, advocating both embargoes on raw materials and measures of international co-operation to prevent war.[67]

[63] Frederick J. Libby to Roosevelt, February 27, 1937, 811.04418/230; Dorothy Detzer to Pittman, February 27, 1937, SCP, File 75A-E2; Mrs. F. H. Finch to McReynolds, March 5, 1937, HCP, File 75A-D13.

[64] Frederick J. Libby, "Open Letter to Our Readers on Neutrality," *Peace Action,* III (March, 1937), 1.

[65] Clark Eichelberger to McReynolds, February 17, 1937, HCP, File 75A-D13.

[66] *New York Times,* January 30, 1937, p. 3; Theresa Paist, president of the YWCA, to Roosevelt and Hull, March 6, 1937, 811.04418/231; Gertrude Moffat, New York state chairman, League of Women Voters, to all New York congressmen, March 12, 1937, HCP, File 75A-D13.

[67] Federal Council of Churches, *Biennial Report, 1936* (New York, 1937), p. 200.

A number of Protestant writers questioned the moral soundness of neutrality legislation. W. Ellis Davis, in an article in the *Christian Register,* branded mandatory neutrality a "quack remedy" and declared, ". . . we have a moral obligation to exert our influence to the limit in protection of peoples in danger; we have an ethical responsibility to help preserve the peace of the world."[68] A contributor to the *Missionary Review of the World* emphatically proclaimed, "In the sphere of morals and religion, there is no proper place for neutrality when there is a clear issue between right and wrong."[69] In contrast, the editors of the *Christian Century* had no doubts about the morality of mandatory neutrality. In a series of editorials, they praised the Pittman bill, claiming that it would prevent unscrupulous bankers, manufacturers, and travelers from plunging the nation into war.[70] The Methodist Episcopal Church, meeting in general conference in February, took an equally strong stand for mandatory legislation.[71]

The business community, thoroughly absorbed in condemning Roosevelt's court-packing plan, paid less attention to neutrality legislation than it had the year before. Exporting groups, however, continued to object to any limitation on American trade. The New York Chamber of Commerce, the Business Advisory Council of the Commerce Department, and executives of such firms as Anderson, Clayton Company and General Motors warned that to surrender neutral rights would seriously injure the American economy. "We cannot, consistently, seek increased foreign trade," commented the Business Advisory Council, "while we impose or threaten to impose restrictions on exports to all coun-

[68] W. Ellis Davis, "Can America Become a Hermit Nation?" *Christian Register,* CXVI (March 11, 1937), 163.

[69] Arthur J. Brown, "Can Christians Be Neutral?" *Missionary Review of the World,* LX (April, 1937), 180.

[70] "Pittman Neutrality Law before Congress," *Christian Century,* LIV (March 3, 1937), 568; "Is Neutrality Moral?" *ibid.,* March 17, 1937, pp. 342–44.

[71] *New York Times,* February 19, 1937, p. 12.

tries."[72] Yet even among exporters, the desire for isolation had its impact. Franklin Johnson, editor of the *American Exporter*, expressed his amazement at constantly hearing export executives say that "they would rather see their trade stopped than to risk war."[73] The *Magazine of Wall Street*, admitting the need for some restrictions on neutral trade, favored a trade-at-your-own-risk policy, while *Business Week* endorsed the cash-and-carry plan.[74] Most businessmen, filled with distrust by Roosevelt's domestic policy, seemed to prefer mandatory to discretionary neutrality. "If there are to be embargoes," declared the editors of *Business Week*, "let Congress declare them when needed, after full discussion. Let us not get into war by clothing the President with the elastic authority to play God."[75]

The conflicting opinions expressed by these various groups suggest that the American people were far from unanimous in their support of neutrality legislation. Most people undoubtedly favored some degree of restraint on American commerce, but the crosscurrents created by advocates of both collective security and freedom of the seas prevented the development of any broad consensus. Moreover, the complexity and technical nature of neutrality legislation made it a difficult issue for the average American to comprehend. As a result, the cash-and-carry plan, with its apparent simplicity and its attractive appeal of preserving both trade and peace, won widespread support throughout the country. On

[72] Resolution adopted by the New York Chamber of Commerce, February 4, 1937, HCP, File 75A-D13; Recommendations of the Subcommittee on Neutrality of the Business Advisory Council, Department of Commerce, January 6, 1937, 811.04418/210; Lamar Fleming, Jr., to Representative Marvin Jones, March 8, 1937, HCP, File 75A-D13; James D. Mooney, "American Economic Policies for the Impending World War," *Annals of the American Academy of Political and Social Science*, CXCII (July, 1937), 89–92.

[73] Franklin Johnson, "Neutrality," *American Exporter*, CXX (February, 1937), 32.

[74] "Preparing for Neutrality," *Magazine of Wall Street*, XXIX (January 2, 1937), 332–33; "Power To Play God," *Business Week*, February 27, 1937, p. 64.

[75] *Ibid.*, p. 64.

the crucial issue of presidential discretion, the nation seemingly would accept the decision reached by its representatives in Congress.

V

Congressional consideration of permanent neutrality legislation began on March 1 when Key Pittman presented his resolution to the Senate for adoption. Stating that his measure embodied "an entire new peace policy" for the United States, Pittman claimed that its rigid features would prevent a repetition of the incidents that had led to war in 1917. "I sincerely believe," he declared, "that the enactment of this joint resolution will keep us out of the next great foreign war."[76] Members of the Nye committee strongly supported the Nevada senator, praising the mandatory features of the bill. Only on one point, the discretionary "carry" provision, did they balk. Senator Vandenberg warned that this section gave the President a double discretion—he could select the materials to be banned from American ships as well as decide whether to invoke this prohibition. Claiming that the President could use this authority to favor one belligerent over another, Vandenberg, with Nye's support, offered an amendment to strike out the "carry" section of the Pittman bill. After a brief debate, the Senate rejected this proposal by a vote of 48 to 24.[77]

Though the backing of the mandatory neutrality group insured Senate approval of the bill, Hiram Johnson and William E. Borah engaged in a two-man crusade against the whole concept of cash-and-carry. In a series of lengthy speeches, they branded cash-and-carry a cowardly and unpatriotic idea that would sacrifice both national pride and commerce in a questionable gamble for peace. "We seek to avoid all risks, all dangers," proclaimed Borah, "but we make certain to get all the profits." Senator Johnson asked, "What sort of government is this and what sort of men are we to accept a formula which will enable us to sell goods and then

[76] *Congressional Record*, March 1, 1937, pp. 1667–70.

[77] *Ibid.*, pp. 1674–75; *ibid.*, March 3, 1937, pp. 1798–1801.

hide?" Both men affirmed their belief in freedom of the seas. "I do not want peace at the price of every bit of honor our country may have," Johnson stated, while Borah declared, "I believe in fighting for the substantial rights which are essential to the preservation of the economic welfare of this Nation." Their most effective argument was to point out the consequences of cash-and-carry. Calling it a "British measure," they warned that it would inevitably favor sea powers like England and France in a major European war and thus fail to achieve a genuine neutrality. Moreover, Borah contended that in the Pacific it would be to the advantage of Japan in any war with China, and thus directly contradict the American commitment to the Open Door policy.[78]

These pleas had little effect on the Senate. Members of the neutrality bloc swept aside all criticism by asserting that trade rights could not be equated with human life. "I can't understand how anyone could weigh in the balance gold against blood," proclaimed Senator Josh Lee of Oklahoma.[79] Then, on March 3, the Senate voted 63 to 6 to accept the Pittman neutrality resolution. Four New Englanders, Henry Cabot Lodge, Jr. (Republican, Massachusetts), Peter G. Gerry (Democrat, Rhode Island), Warren Austin (Republican, Vermont), and Styles Bridges (Republican, New Hampshire), joined Borah and Johnson in opposing the bill.[80] Thus the Senate, with only these six advocates of freedom of the seas dissenting, finally agreed on permanent legislation embodying a mandatory cash-and-carry policy.

Unlike the Senate, the House engaged in a fiery and highly partisan debate over neutrality legislation that lasted for a week. The Foreign Affairs Committee substituted the McReynolds bill for the Pittman measure, and then the Rules Committee opened the way for free discussion by permitting ten hours of debate and no

[78] *Ibid.*, March 1, 1937, pp. 1677–83; *ibid.*, March 3, 1937, pp. 1778–79, 1806.

[79] *Ibid.*, March 3, 1937, pp. 1796–97.

[80] *Ibid.*, p. 1807.

limit on amendments.[81] This gave House members their first opportunity for protracted debate on neutrality, and they made the most of their opportunity. Republican congressmen led the assault, but they were eagerly supported by a number of Democrats who felt that the McReynolds bill did not provide adequate insurance against involvement in war. As in the Senate, the chief target was the cash-and-carry policy, but in the House the result was a free-for-all which nearly erupted into a full-scale rebellion against this compromise proposition.

The criticisms of cash-and-carry came from two quite different groups. First, the advocates of mandatory neutrality savagely condemned it as "an ingenious subterfuge" that sacrificed genuine neutrality for the profits of neutral trade. They repeatedly charged that there was no middle ground between rigid abstention from foreign wars and the inevitable involvement that stemmed from upholding traditional neutral rights. "We must make our choice between unlimited trade and peace," declared Jerry Voorhis of California. Several speakers cited the findings of the Nye committee to prove that cash-and-carry would not remove the greatest danger of all—the creation of a war boom in the American economy that would undermine neutrality. The only solution, many congressmen declared, was a total embargo on all trade in essential war supplies.[82] Others were willing to accept the general scheme of cash-and-carry, but they demanded that it be made absolutely mandatory. If the President had discretion, they warned, he could change the rules of neutrality after war broke out to favor one side and thus provoke reprisals by the other belligerent. A Nebraska congressman summed up this fear when he proclaimed, "Granting of wide discretionary powers places within the hands of one human being the possibilities of rendering one false deci-

[81] "Neutrality Act of 1937," *House Report No. 363*, 75th Cong., 1st sess. (Washington, 1937), p. 1; *Congressional Record*, March 12, 1937, pp. 2150–51.

[82] *Congressional Record*, March 12, 1937, p. 2173; *ibid.*, March 15, 1937, p. 2257; *ibid.*, March 16, 1937, pp. 2296, 2298–99; *ibid.*, March 18, 1937, pp. 2402–3.

sion that would not only wreck the spirit of neutrality but would plunge us into war."[83]

A second group of congressmen, composed of advocates of freedom of the seas and supporters of international co-operation, challenged the imposition of any restraints upon American commerce. Representatives from both industrial and farm states stressed the importance of foreign trade. Charles A. Eaton of New Jersey, claiming that the United States had its "economic roots struck deep in the world," argued that cash-and-carry would destroy the American shipping industry, while a Kentucky congressman asserted that any surrender of freedom of the seas would "lead to the injury of American commerce upon which the producers and workers in agriculture, industry and commerce depend for support."[84] The most vehement attacks came from men who feared the legislation would invite aggression overseas. Representative Eaton condemned the McReynolds bill as "a symptom of a moral sterilization of the American people in connection with our tremendous inescapable obligations to the rest of the world"; Congressman John T. Bernard of Minnesota charged that it lumped together "the robber and the robbed, the murderer and the murdered." Other speakers claimed that the legislation would favor the strong, militaristic nations and help usher in "the greatest period of aggressive warfare and of world conquest that history has ever seen."[85]

Though the critics of cash-and-carry dominated the debate, they were unable to shake the firm Democratic majority which supported the McReynolds bill. The gulf which divided those who favored greater restraints on trade and those who objected to all such limitations could not be bridged by their common opposition to a discretionary cash-and-carry policy. This fatal weakness became apparent as opponents of the bill attempted to amend it.

[83] *Ibid.*, March 2, 1937 pp. 2161–63; *ibid.*, March 15, 1937, pp. 2250, 2254; *ibid.*, March 16, 1937, pp. 2271, 2275.

[84] *Ibid.*, March 12, 1937, p. 2172; *ibid.*, March 16, 1937, pp. 2278, 2293.

[85] *Ibid.*, March 12, 1937, p. 2172; *ibid.*, March 16, 1937, pp. 2287, 2291; *ibid.*, March 18, 1937, p. 2384.

The neutrality bloc offered a series of amendments proposing the imposition of trade quotas, the removal of all presidential discretion in the cash section of the bill, and an embargo on all essential war material. All were defeated by decisive majorities. The House also rejected attempts to strike out the cash-and-carry provisions and adopt a trade-at-your-own-risk clause. The widespread discontent with cash-and-carry finally led McReynolds to agree to an amendment limiting this feature of his bill to a two-year trial period, a concession which pleased many critics of the bill.[86] When Hamilton Fish tried to unite the opposition by moving to send the McReynolds bill back to the Foreign Affairs Committee for revision, the House defeated his motion by a vote of 275 to 118. Then, on March 18, the McReynolds bill won final approval with only thirteen dissenting votes.[87]

An analysis of both roll call votes shows a clear partisan and sectional division. On the motion to recommit, two-thirds of the Republican members opposed the McReynolds bill, while over 80 per cent of the Democrats favored it. Sectionally, half of the votes for recommittal came from the Middle West.[88] Of the thirteen dissenting votes on the final passage of the bill, eight were cast by Republicans; six of the thirteen came from the Middle West. In both cases, some advocates of freedom of the seas and of collective security opposed the McReynolds bill, but the great majority of negative votes came from supporters of rigid neutrality. Though any generalization from these voting patterns is risky, it seems evident that the neutrality bloc in the House was composed primarily of Republicans from all sections allied with a small group of midwestern Democrats.

[86] *Ibid.*, March 18, 1937, pp. 2386–98.

[87] *Ibid.*, pp. 2409–10.

[88] The breakdown on the vote for recommittal of the McReynolds bill was as follows:

Party	*Yes*	*No*	*Section*	*Yes*	*No*
Republican	58	23	Northeast	32	82
Democratic	48	251	South	9	99
Progressive	7	1	Midwest	63	69
Farmer-Labor	5	0	Far West	14	25

The passage of the McReynolds bill marked a victory for the administration. Roosevelt and Hull had carefully refrained from taking any stand on the various bills, but they were known to favor the McReynolds resolution, which contained the greatest degree of discretionary power that Roosevelt could expect to receive from a suspicious Congress. Though the House bill contained many mandatory features which conflicted with Roosevelt's ideal of discretionary neutrality, it did permit the President to exercise his judgment in applying the cash-and-carry restriction on American commerce. Yet it was only a partial triumph, for the two branches of Congress still had to reconcile the important differences between the Pittman and McReynolds bills. The final battle between permissive and mandatory neutrality now had to be waged between the House and the Senate.

VI

On March 19, the day after the House passed the McReynolds bill, the Senate rejected it and asked for the appointment of a conference committee. Vice-President Garner appointed Pittman, Borah, and Joseph T. Robinson of Arkansas, Senate majority leader, as the Senate conferees.[89] Though Pittman was determined to stand firmly for his measure, both Robinson and Borah preferred the more discretionary House measure. The Nye group, which bitterly opposed the permissive features of the McReynolds bill, did not have a representative from the Senate on the conference committee. In the House, Speaker William Bankhead selected McReynolds, Luther Johnson, and Sol Bloom of New York, all Democrats who favored a discretionary policy, to serve with Republicans Hamilton Fish and Joseph W. Martin, Jr., on the conference committee. Though Fish strongly opposed the House bill, McReynolds felt confident that the majority of this group would support his measure faithfully.[90]

[89] *Congressional Record*, March 19, 1937, p. 2487.

[90] *Ibid.*, March 23, 1937, p. 2662; McReynolds to Sam McAllester, March 24, 1937, HCP, File 75A-D13.

The conference committee, which began meeting in late March, soon reached an impasse. Key Pittman, who had little respect for McReynolds, was completely unwilling to make any concessions. The major issue was whether to accept a discretionary or a mandatory transfer-of-title clause in the cash-and-carry section. In addition, Pittman held out for an automatic ban on travel upon the outbreak of war, a prohibition on the arming of American merchant ships, and a rigid definition of material to be included under the arms embargo. By mid-April no progress had been achieved, despite the fact that the 1936 act was due to expire on May 1. Unable to reason with Pittman, McReynolds finally asked Roosevelt to intervene.[91] On April 20 the President sent a brief note to Senator Robinson, asking him to "persuade Key [Pittman] to yield just as far as possible to the House bill." "I really believe a word from you to Key would help," Roosevelt continued. "You can use my name if you think it advisable."[92] Roosevelt's intercession evidently influenced Pittman, for on April 22 McReynolds informed the State Department that the conferees had reached "virtual agreement." McReynolds complained that he had felt obliged to back down on many points, but he refused to concede anything more to Pittman. On Saturday, April 26, the House conferees threatened to walk out of the committee, but Senator Robinson finally worked out a last-minute compromise which the conference committee accepted on Sunday.[93]

The conference report on neutrality legislation was presented to both Houses on April 29, less than forty-eight hours before the expiration of the 1936 act. On the principal issue, presidential discretion on invoking the transfer of title provision, the Senate conferees had given way and accepted the flexible version in the McReynolds bill. In return, the House conferees had agreed to a

[91] Memorandum of conversation with McReynolds by Joseph C. Green, April 22, 1937, 811.04418/262.

[92] Elliott Roosevelt (ed.), *F.D.R.: His Personal Letters, 1928–1945* (2 vols.; New York, 1950), I, 673.

[93] Green memorandum, April 22, 1937, 811.04418/262; memorandum by Green, April 26, 1937, 811.04418/267; *New York Times*, April 28, 1937, p. 1.

mandatory travel ban and prohibition on the arming of American merchant ships trading with belligerents. On the last point at issue, the definition of arms, a compromise had been reached—the President could include arms not previously embargoed but raw materials were specifically exempted.[94] In effect, the House had conceded the less important points in order to gain a completely discretionary cash-and-carry policy.

The House immediately accepted the conference report without controversy, but in the Senate, the Nye group raised bitter protests.[95] Despite Pittman's assurances that the President was "morally bound" to invoke the cash-and-carry provisions upon the outbreak of war, Senators Nye, Vandenberg, and Bone claimed that the compromise bill, by granting broad discretionary power, failed to achieve the rigid legislation that alone could prevent American involvement in war. "The neutrality resolution," Vandenberg charged, "transfers a substantial portion of the war-making power from the Congress to the Chief Executive." Nye was even blunter. "In many respects, no neutrality at all is better than a discretionary policy of neutrality," he declared. Yet despite these protests, the Senate proceeded to adopt the conference report by the margin of 41 to 15.[96] Senator Borah now voted for the bill, but other advocates of freedom of the seas joined with extreme supporters of mandatory neutrality in opposing it. As in the House, most of the opposition came from Republicans, but there was a different geographic pattern, with nearly half the dissenting votes coming from the maritime states of the Northeast.[97]

[94] "Amendments to the Neutrality Act," *House Report* No. 723, 75th Cong., 1st sess. (Washington, 1937), pp. 10–12.

[95] *Congressional Record*, April 29, 1939, p. 3978.

[96] *Ibid.*, pp. 3939–62.

[97] The negative votes were distributed as follows:

Party		*Section*	
Republican	10	Northeast	7
Democratic	5	South	0
		Midwest	5
		Far West	3

The adoption of the conference report by the House led to a dramatic race against time. On April 30 an airplane left Washington with a copy of the new legislation for the signature of the President, who was on a fishing cruise in the Gulf of Mexico. At Galveston, the document was transferred to a Navy seaplane, which flew out into the Gulf and landed next to the presidential yacht. At 6:30 on the morning of May 1, the day the old law expired, Roosevelt signed the new act.[98]

Roosevelt's signature completed the two-year effort to achieve permanent neutrality legislation. The result was a curious mixture of mandatory and permissive features designed to insulate the United States from contact with future wars. Whenever the President found the existence of a state of war between nations, or a civil war which endangered the peace of the United States, four major restrictions on the activities of American citizens automatically went into effect. These were the embargo on arms, ammunition, and implements of war, so defined as to exclude raw materials; the ban on loans, but exempting short-term commercial credits; the prohibition on travel on belligerent ships; and the ban on the arming of American merchant ships trading with belligerents. In addition, American vessels could not carry cargoes of arms to belligerents nor were representatives of belligerent governments or factions permitted to solicit funds or contributions from American citizens.[99] These were the mandatory restrictions, beyond the discretionary authority of the President, and as such they embodied the Nye thesis that munitions trade, loans, and travel had created incidents and situations which had caused American entry into World War I.

The most significant permissive feature of the neutrality act was

[98] *New York Times*, May 2, 1937, p. 37. The text of the act is printed in *Peace and War, 1931–1941*, pp. 355–65.

[99] This clause had been added in the McReynolds bill because of the large number of organizations that had been soliciting funds in behalf of the Spanish Loyalists. The law did permit the collection of funds by charitable groups to be used to furnish food and medicine to relieve human suffering. The 1937 act also continued the exemption for Western Hemisphere countries engaged in wars with non-American states.

the cash-and-carry plan, which was limited to a two-year trial period. After invoking the automatic restrictions, if the President believed that it was necessary for the security and peace of the United States, he could require that American citizens transfer title on all exports to belligerents before the goods left the United States. As a separate action, he could also ban the shipment of specified commodities on American vessels. Though Congress allowed the President to select the goods barred to American shipping, it was expected that he would include all material listed as contraband by belligerent countries.[100] The President also was granted discretionary authority to prevent American ports from being used as bases of supply by belligerent warships and to bar belligerent submarines and armed merchantmen from American territorial waters.

The legislation can best be described as a hybrid mixture reflecting the conflicting desires and ambitions of the American people. The automatic features satisfied the intense demand for abstention from war that characterized American sentiment in the 1930's. Yet at the same time, the discretionary cash-and-carry provisions revealed the unwillingness of the nation to accept the full implications of the Nye thesis. Having severely curbed munitions makers and bankers, Congress chose not to impair foreign trade by imposing drastic limitations on the export of contraband goods other than arms, despite the revelations of the Nye committee which indicated that general trade in wartime was far more likely to lead to involvement than the export of munitions. Congress was determined to follow the Nye thesis only where it was politically feasible—it did not wish to antagonize farmers, laborers, and manufacturers who all were dependent to some degree on foreign trade. Instead, the legislators decided to limit risks while preserving profits. By permitting the President to force merchants to surrender title to their exports and to ban the delivery of contraband goods in American ships, they hoped to avoid the provocative in-

[100] Shepardson and Scroggs, *U.S. in World Affairs, 1937*, p. 48.

cidents that had contributed to war in 1917, yet at the same time guarantee Americans the chance to benefit financially from any war that broke out.

This contradictory policy had a peculiar effect on America's role in the developing world crisis. The mandatory features, and especially the arms embargo, tended to aid nations with aggressive intentions. They would go to war fully armed, while their victims, if caught unprepared, would be denied the opportunity to purchase weapons and munitions from the United States. If other nations came to the aid of the country attacked, they too would automatically be barred from buying arms in America. The discretionary cash-and-carry policy, on the other hand, would tend to operate against the aggressors in a general European war. Nations such as Germany, Italy, and the Soviet Union were essentially land powers, and in any conflict with Britain and France, they would be unable to transport supplies across the Atlantic. Britain and France, however, with their naval strength and merchant marine capacity, could use the United States as a vast supply reservoir as long as their financial resources permitted. In the Pacific cash-and-carry would have the reverse effect, favoring Japan, with its control of the sea, in any further aggression undertaken against China.

Taken as a whole, it is difficult to see how the neutrality act of 1937 satisfied any single group. The advocates of rigid legislation, though pleased by the mandatory restrictions, were very unhappy over the discretionary cash-and-carry compromise. The isolationist press in general condemned the work of the conference committee and suggested that the administration had deliberately delayed the conference report in order to force congressional acquiescence to permissive trade controls. "The timing," claimed the editors of *Current History*, "was almost Machiavellian." They went on to point out the great weakness of the cash-and-carry plan from their standpoint. "There is no guarantee that there will not be a war-trade boom which could not be liquidated when the belligerents ran out of cash and which might eventually suck this nation into the vortex."[101]

Supporters of collective security reacted in just the opposite way—they applauded cash-and-carry while continuing to deplore the mandatory arms embargo. In an article in *Foreign Affairs*, Walter Lippmann analyzed the contradictions in the legislation, pointing out that while the neutrality advocates had tried to prevent a repetition of the events preceding American entry into World War I, they had created what actually signified "an economic alliance with Britain and her partners."[102] The European estimate of the 1937 act bears out this interpretation. Early in 1937, Secretary of the Treasury Henry Morgenthau, Jr., had written British Chancellor of the Exchequer Neville Chamberlain asking him his opinion on how the United States and Britain could halt the world-wide armament race. In late March, before the adoption of the 1937 act, Chamberlain had replied: "The greatest single contribution which the United States could make at the present moment to the preservation of world peace would be the amendment of the existing neutrality legislation." He then went on to point out how the mandatory arms embargo aided a potential aggressor and suggested that it be left to the discretion of the President.[103] Though the administration could not satisfy Chamberlain's request,[104] the new legislation drew a favorable response

[101] "A Non-committal Neutrality Act," *Current History*, XLVI (June, 1937), 16–17; *Peace Action*, III (May, 1937), 1; "To Stay Out of War," *New Republic*, XCI (May 12, 1937), 4–5.

[102] Walter Lippmann, "Rough-Hew Them How We Will," *Foreign Affairs*, XV (July, 1937), 587.

[103] John Morton Blum, *From the Morgenthau Diaries* (Boston, 1959), pp. 458–59; *FR: 1937*, I, 100.

[104] In early June, Secretary of State Hull replied to Chamberlain by affirming American hopes for peace and pointing out the discretionary nature of the cash-and-carry provisions of the 1937 act. Roosevelt approved this message, telling Sumner Welles that Hull's statement was "completely pious—I can think of no other characteristic." *FR: 1937*, I, 102–6; Roosevelt to Welles, May 28, 1937, 740.00/184.

from both the British and the French. In reporting a discussion with the French Foreign Minister and the British ambassador in Paris on April 30, William C. Bullitt, American ambassador to France, told Hull that they "expressed themselves as extremely satisfied by our neutrality legislation."[105] The German press reacted adversely—a Berlin paper claimed that cash-and-carry "amounts in practice to an Anglo-American alliance."[106] Yet when advocates of international co-operation turned to the Far East, they must have been disappointed at its probable effect on China. Certainly the Chinese were unhappy. The Shanghai *China Press* stated that the American legislation would favor the well-armed country and "for this reason it is much to be regretted."[107]

The third group interested in neutrality legislation—defenders of freedom of the seas—found little to please them in the 1937 act. Though grateful that Congress did not impose more severe restrictions on American trade, they condemned cash-and-carry as an unwarranted surrender of neutral rights. Henry Cabot Lodge, Jr., writing in the *Saturday Evening Post*, voiced a common complaint. "The cash-and-carry policy would reduce our foreign trade materially and would thus throw out of employment American citizens whose living depends on it," he charged.[108] Among international lawyers, there was little respect for the new scheme. Edwin Borchard condemned it as a futile abandonment of historic rights, claiming it would not prevent involvement in war. Other experts warned of the danger of invoking restrictions on trade while a war was in progress—such measures would affect belligerents unequally and thus invite reprisals. James Garner summed up the general opinion of international lawyers when he called

[105] Bullitt to Hull, April 30, 1937, 740.00/156.

[106] William E. Dodd to Hull, March 9, 1937, 811.04418/242.

[107] C. E. Gauss to Hull, March 25, 1937, 811.04418/258.

[108] Henry Cabot Lodge, Jr., "Cutting the Cables," *Saturday Evening Post*, CCIX (May 1, 1937), 23, 64–66.

cash-and-carry "a policy of scuttle and run to the storm cellar on the part of the United States."[109]

There is no evidence available to indicate Roosevelt's estimate of the permanent legislation enacted by Congress. Given the strong isolationist temper of Congress and his own dwindling influence over that body, he was undoubtedly relieved to be given the modest degree of discretion embodied in the 1937 act. By keeping aloof from the debate and working quietly to support flexible provisions in the House, Roosevelt had salvaged a part of his discretionary program. But viewed in the perspective of his desire for a broad, permissive neutrality policy, the act must be judged a serious setback for the President. On almost all vital matters—arms, embargoes, loans, passenger travel—he was compelled to follow ironclad rules laid down in advance by Congress. Only in the area of trade restrictions did he possess the flexible authority he deemed essential. Here he could invoke restrictions that would not interfere seriously with exports to England and France in case of war in Europe, while he was free to withhold these limitations in a conflict between China and Japan. To this extent, he could still exercise some degree of control over American policy in the event of war abroad. For a man who had originally sponsored neutrality legislation in order to be free from economic pressures and past precedents, this was at best a small consolation.

In the last analysis, the neutrality act of 1937 was a haphazard compromise which failed to establish a clear-cut neutrality policy for the nation. The overwhelming majority of the American people favored legislation that would guarantee abstention from war. Yet Congress, torn by the conflicting arguments for mandatory and for discretionary controls, and fearful of endangering the country's economic well-being, was unable to agree on how to fulfill this national goal. By fusing together the Nye thesis and the cash-and-carry scheme, it produced legislation which failed to define America's role in world affairs. The United States would abstain

[109] *Proceedings of the American Society of International Law, 1937* (Washington, 1937), pp. 109–14, 173–74, 176–77, 178–79.

from the arms trade and refuse to finance foreign wars, but at the same time it would supply the basic sinews of modern warfare to any nation able to buy and ship the goods itself. The result was a policy which encouraged aggression overseas, favored sea powers such as Britain and Japan, lessened the chances for the United States to prevent war abroad, and did not guarantee American abstention from foreign conflicts. Neutrality legislation, aimed at the simple goal of peace, had led only to hopeless confusion.

CHAPTER SEVEN

CRACKS IN THE NEUTRALITY WALL, 1937–38

Congress wrote a neutrality law; the administration has made it a scrap of paper.

NEW REPUBLIC, June 22, 1938

After two years of intense debate, the neutrality bloc had succeeded in embodying its isolationist principles in permanent legislation designed to prevent American entry into a major world war. This triumph was destined to be short-lived. In the year following the passage of the 1937 act, the open intervention of German and Italian forces in the Spanish Civil War and the outbreak of an undeclared conflict in China called into question the basic premise of the neutrality bloc. The American people discovered that they were concerned about the march of aggression overseas, and they learned with dismay that neutrality legislation could lead them into a silent partnership with totalitarian states. These unpleasant realities began to destroy confidence in mandatory neutrality legislation and led to a growing realization that the United States could not sever the moral, economic, and political ties that bound it to the world community. As this new understanding slowly developed, the administration searched for ways to bring American influence to bear on the course of events abroad without risking involvement in war.

I

The first real test of the new neutrality act came in the Far East. On July 7, 1937, Japanese troops stationed in North China under the Boxer protocol of 1900 were engaging in maneuvers near the Marco Polo Bridge, eighteen miles west of Peking. During the evening, the Japanese units clashed with elements of the Chinese Twenty-ninth Army. Apparently unpremeditated, the fighting continued intermittently for three days before a truce was arranged. For two weeks, while protracted negotiations took place, Japan rushed reinforcements into North China. In late July the fighting erupted again, and by the end of the month the Japanese had occupied Peking. What had begun as a minor incident now assumed ominous proportions. On August 9, Chinese troops in Shanghai shot and killed a Japanese naval officer and a seaman. Several days later, the main units of the Japanese fleet anchored off Shanghai and the Japanese launched a full-scale attack on the Chinese city by air, land, and sea.[1] Though neither side declared war—or even broke off diplomatic relations—a major conflict had broken out which proved to be the beginning of the Pacific phase of World War II.

The outbreak of undeclared war in China created serious and complex problems for American foreign policy. Under the neutrality act of 1937, the President was to invoke the arms embargo and the other automatic restrictions when he found a state of war to exist. Thus, until a formal state of war was declared, President Roosevelt could exercise his own discretionary authority on the matter of applying the neutrality legislation. In the confused situation that existed in North China from July 7 to mid-August, the administration refrained from issuing any specific statements in regard to either American attitudes toward the Japanese invasion or to the possible application of the neutrality act. Both Roosevelt and Hull, hoping that the hostilities signified only a minor clash and not the beginning of a major Japanese thrust, waited for further developments. Yet as they watched the events unfold, they were aware of the probable effect of the neutrality act on the two belligerents. The Chinese, who depended almost

[1] Whitney H. Shepardson and William D. Scroggs, *The United States in World Affairs, 1937* (New York, 1938), pp. 192–94.

entirely on imports for their arms supply, would be badly hurt by an American munitions embargo, while the Japanese, largely self-sufficient in regard to armaments, would be relatively untouched. Japan did import many strategic items from the United States, notably petroleum products and scrap iron, but this trade would not be affected by the arms embargo. If the President chose to invoke the further restrictions embodied in the cash-and-carry provisions, again Japan, with its large merchant marine and control of the sea, would not be seriously injured, though China would suffer additional hardships, since it lacked the shipping to transport supplies from the United States.[2]

In essence, Roosevelt was faced with a choice of neutral policy which ruled out any possibility of genuine impartiality. If he decided to invoke the neutrality legislation, Japan would benefit, and if he did not apply the legislation, China would gain. Until mid-August, when the Japanese assault on Shanghai indicated that Japan was bent on waging full-scale war in China, the administration remained silent on the question of neutrality. However, Senator Key Pittman touched off a spirited debate when he released a statement to the press on July 29 criticizing those who "impatiently and unreasonably" urged the invocation of the neutrality act against China and Japan. Defending Roosevelt's exercise of discretionary power, Pittman contended that a neutrality proclamation would prevent the United States from using its influence to end the hostilities in the Orient.[3] Congressional supporters of mandatory neutrality quickly challenged Pittman's statement. Hamilton Fish deplored the steady flow of American arms to the belligerents "for sake of blood money and for sake of war profits," while Representative O'Malley of Wisconsin stated bluntly, "All Asia is arming and this country must not be connected with the conflict in any way."[4]

When the Japanese began their all-out assault on Shanghai on

[2] *The Memoirs of Cordell Hull* (2 vols.; New York, 1948), I, 556–57.

[3] *Congressional Record*, July 30, 1937, p. 7862.

[4] *Ibid.*, August 2, 1937, p. 8058; *ibid.*, August 3, 1937, p. 8156.

August 13, 1937, the administration gave serious consideration to the possibility of invoking the legislation. On August 16 a series of conferences took place in the State Department and at the White House. The President's advisers finally agreed that the neutrality act should not be applied to the war in China "unless and until absolutely necessary."[5] The next day President Roosevelt told the press that the invocation of neutrality legislation was on "a 24-hour basis."[6] This phrase, designed to placate the congressional demands for prompt action, revealed the uncertainty which prevailed in the administration. At a cabinet meeting three days later, the President warned Hull that he could not postpone action indefinitely. The Secretary replied that he hoped to be able to reach a clear-cut decision within two or three days.[7] Yet, whether realizing it or not, the administration had made its choice—the "24-hour" statement gradually hardened into the official stand on applying the neutrality law to the war in China. The government had decided not to invoke the arms embargo until either a formal declaration of war or an obvious threat of American involvement made such a step imperative.

As it gradually became clear that the administration did not intend to apply the neutrality legislation, isolationists in Congress, in the peace movement, and in the press launched vigorous criticisms. Senators Nye and Clark issued a public statement on August 18 reminding the President that the purpose of the neutrality act was not to favor one side or another, but rather to insure American abstention from war. In a radio interview two days later, Nye repeated this assertion, and then went on to argue that the law, if put into effect, would hurt Japan as well as China by preventing the issuance of loans to finance Japanese purchases of raw materials.[8] In the House, twenty-five Representatives signed a joint

[5] *New York Times*, August 17, 1937, p. 1; Moffat Diary, August 16, 1937.

[6] Press Conference No. 392, August 17, 1937, FDR Papers, PPF 1-P, X, 162.

[7] *The Secret Diary of Harold Ickes* (3 vols.; New York, 1953–54), II, 199.

[8] *Congressional Record*, August 19, 1937, Appendix, p. 2187; *ibid.*, August 21, 1937, Appendix, p. 2257.

statement demanding the immediate application of the arms embargo in order to "stop feeding the war which means destruction of thousands of lives in the Orient and the danger of war to all the world."[9] Outside of Congress, which adjourned for the summer on August 21, the NCPW issued a series of press releases and public letters to Roosevelt urging an immediate proclamation of neutrality.[10] The editors of the *Christian Century* and the *New Republic* voiced similar demands, warning that any attempt to choose sides by not invoking the law would lead to disaster for the nation.[11]

The advocates of collective security, on the other hand, strongly endorsed the administration's policy. The *New York Times* praised Roosevelt, arguing that a formal neutrality proclamation would injure the chances for a peaceful settlement of the crisis in China; the *Nation* stressed the need to uphold the Open Door against Japanese aggression. "The logical way to deal with the dilemma in which the United States finds itself," the editors suggested, "is to repeal the Neutrality Act."[12] Charging that the legislation was unneutral, a writer in *Amerasia* urged Congress to add strategic raw materials such as scrap iron and oil to the embargo list.[13] Business journals agreed with these comments—both the *Commercial and Financial Chronicle* and *Business Week* cited the war in China as proof of the folly of neutrality legislation.[14] Most Americans gave tacit support to the administration's policy of inaction. Aside

[9] *Peace Action*, IV (September, 1935), 7.

[10] *Ibid.*, p. 1; *New York Times*, August 18, 1937, p. 4; Frederick J. Libby to Roosevelt, August 19, 1937, HCP, File 75A-D13.

[11] "Apply the Neutrality Law," *Christian Century*, LIV (August 11, 1937), 989–91; "Scuttle or Bluster," *New Republic*, XCII (September 15, 1937), 144–45.

[12] *New York Times*, August 19, 1937, p. 18; "Neutrality in the Far East," *Nation*, CXLV (August 7, 1937), 144–45.

[13] "Washington and the Sino-Japanese Crisis," *Amerasia*, I (August, 1937), 243–44.

[14] "The Costs and Risks of Neutrality," *Commercial and Financial Chronicle*, CXLV (August 28, 1937), 1317, 1329–30; "To Keep Out of War," *Business Week*, September 4, 1937, p. 60.

from the traditional isolationist sources, there was no vociferous cry for application of the neutrality act. A Gallup poll in early August revealed the reason for this apparent indifference. Asked which side they favored in the Far Eastern conflict, 55 per cent replied neither, 43 per cent named China, and only 2 per cent listed Japan.[15] As long as there was no immediate threat of American involvement, the strong sympathy of many Americans for China tended to uphold the administration's decision to avoid invoking legislation that favored Japan.

The warfare in China became more menacing for the United States in late August. During the fighting in Shanghai, three American citizens died from aerial bombing. On August 20, 1937, a shell accidentally struck the American cruiser "Augusta," killing one sailor and injuring seventeen others. Hull and Roosevelt, alarmed by this loss of life, urged American citizens to leave China while at the same time the President sent additional marines to Shanghai to protect American interests there.[16] An even more serious problem developed on August 25 when the Japanese proclaimed a blockade of the China coast extending for 800 miles southward from Shanghai. Though Japan announced that this measure was aimed solely at Chinese shipping, it warned that the Japanese navy would stop other ships to determine their nationality. Four days later, a jittery American public learned that the S.S. "Wichita," a government-owned freighter operated by the American Pioneer Line, had sailed from Baltimore with a cargo of nineteen airplanes destined for the Chinese government via Hong Kong. This disclosure led to a widely expressed fear that the Japanese would halt the ship, confiscate the planes, and thus create a dangerous incident that could lead to war.[17]

[15] Hadley Cantril and Mildred Strunk (eds.), *Public Opinion, 1935–1946* (Princeton, 1951), p. 1081.

[16] *New York Times*, August 22, 1937, IV, 3; Shepardson and Scroggs, *U.S. in World Affairs, 1937*, pp. 195–97.

[17] *Ibid.*, pp. 197–98; *New York Times*, August 26, 1937, p. 1; *ibid.*, August 29, 1937, p. 31; *ibid.*, September 2, 1937, p. 2. The nineteen airplanes, produced by the Bellanca Aircraft Company, were single-engine, two-seater planes

A group of six peace societies, led by the NCPW, seized upon the sailing of the "Wichita" to renew their demand for application of the arms embargo. Beginning September 1, these pacifist groups issued a series of daily press releases warning of the danger of war if the "Wichita" was allowed to complete its voyage. On September 2, in an open letter to Roosevelt, the pacifists asked the President "to stop the *Wichita* and any other American vessels carrying such cargoes to the war zones." In a public appeal a few days later, the six peace societies drew a parallel with the events that led to entry into World War I. "The business interests which will profit from war shipments are pushing the boats out," they charged.[18] Ridiculing the administration's contention that the fighting in China did not constitute a war, these critics charged Roosevelt with a deliberate repudiation of the neutrality statute. "I feel that the President is practicing nullification of the law in not invoking the Neutrality Act, for a state of war exists," Frederick Libby told a Quaker audience.[19] Though a few spokesmen of internationally minded peace groups publicly endorsed Roosevelt's policy, the pacifist campaign to stop the "Wichita" and invoke the arms embargo proved highly embarrassing to the administration.[20]

The mounting public concern over the danger of involvement in the Far Eastern war caused the administration to reconsider its

---

originally designed for sale to the United States government to carry air mail. When the government rejected the planes as unsafe for long flights, they were sold to the Hanover Sales Corporation, which intended to ship them to the Spanish Loyalists via France. The State Department, however, refused to issue an export license because of the Spanish arms embargo, and the Hanover Sales Corporation finally sold the planes to the Chinese government. Memorandum by Joseph C. Green, August 30, 1937, *FR: 1937*, IV, 522.

[18] *New York Times*, September 1, 1937, p. 3; *ibid.*, September 3, 1937, p. 3; *ibid.*, September 5, 1937, p. 19. The peace societies involved in this effort, in addition to the NCPW, were World Peaceways, Emergency Peace Campaign, Women's International League, Fellowship of Reconciliation, and Committee on Militarism in Education.

[19] *Ibid.*, September 7, 1937, p. 11.

[20] *Ibid.*, September 5, 1937, p. 19. Among those supporting the administration's stand were James T. Shotwell and Carrie Chapman Catt.

stand. Before leaving Washington on August 27 for a two-week vacation, the President conferred with his cabinet and then told reporters that American policy remained on a twenty-four hour basis.[21] Inside the State Department, however, strong sentiment developed in favor of invoking the neutrality act.[22] On September 6, Secretary Hull, torn by conflicting advice, sent an urgent request to the American ambassadors in China and Japan, Nelson T. Johnson and Joseph C. Grew, asking them for their views on the neutrality issue. Johnson, who had reported in August that China considered the neutrality act discriminatory in its effect, warned that its application would cause great resentment and would "react dangerously for Americans in China." Ambassador Grew, however, strongly urged invocation of the act. He believed that Japan would accept it as a guaranty of absolute impartiality by the United States. Pointing out that Japan might interfere with American ships carrying arms to China, Grew held that it was "advisable" to apply the neutrality act in order "to reduce the chances of the United States becoming involved in the present hostilities."[23]

With his advisers at home and abroad so sharply divided, Hull decided to wait for the President's return to Washington before taking any action. On September 10 the State Department did issue a press release warning that the conflict in the Far East had created a danger zone along the coast of China, but the government did not apply any restraints on American shipping at this time.[24] Meanwhile, the "Wichita" had stopped at San Pedro, California, for refueling before proceeding across the Pacific. Hull conferred with Joseph P. Kennedy, chairman of the Maritime Commission, on September 13, and late in the day Kennedy ordered the American Pioneer Line to detain the ship until further notice.[25] When Roosevelt arrived in Washington the following

[21] *Ibid.*, August 27, 1937, p. 1; *ibid.*, August 28, 1937, p. 2.

[22] Moffat Diary, August 31, 1937.

[23] *FR: 1937*, III, 514–17.

[24] State Department, *Press Releases*, XVII (September 11, 1937), 223–24.

[25] Memorandum by Joseph C. Green, September 13, 1937, *FR: 1937*, IV, 527.

morning, he held a long conference with Hull and Kennedy and then released a statement announcing that government-owned ships would not be permitted to carry arms to either China or Japan. "Any other merchant vessels, flying the American flag," Roosevelt added, "which attempt to transport any . . . [arms] to China and Japan will, until further notice, do so at their own risk." The President then stated that the question of applying the neutrality act remained "on a 24-hour basis."[26]

Roosevelt's action, though it directly affected only thirteen government-owned ships engaged in the Pacific carrying trade, was deeply resented by the Chinese. On September 15, when Stanley K. Hornbeck, Hull's adviser on Far Eastern affairs, explained the new policy to C. T. Wang, the Chinese ambassador, Wang angrily commented that the United States was "forgetting its moral obligations."[27] Two days later Wang called on Hull to express his government's "disappointment" over the new American policy. "The Ambassador," according to Hornbeck's memorandum of this interview, "said that when a friend suddenly pursues a course which injures his friend, the injured party cannot but feel that there is some deliberate intent."[28] Ambassador Johnson reported similar disappointment and resentment among Chinese officials in Nanking. In Japan, on the other hand, government spokesmen hailed the new policy as a sign of American willingness to respect the Japanese blockade of China.[29]

Roosevelt's statement had a surprisingly slight effect on the American people. A few extreme advocates of collective security condemned the ship order. "The United States has in effect taken sides in the Far Eastern conflict and aligned herself with the

[26] *New York Times*, September 15, 1937, p. 1; Department of State, *Peace and War: United States Foreign Policy, 1931–1941* (Washington, 1943), p. 380. On September 16, the "Wichita" unloaded the nineteen airplanes and a small quantity of arms and ammunition before sailing to Hong Kong. Memorandum by Green, September 16, 1937, *FR: 1937*, IV, 533.

[27] *Ibid.*, IV, 530.

[28] *Ibid.*, III, 531–32.

[29] *Ibid.*, IV, 535; *New York Times*, September 16, 1937, p. 2.

aggressors," wrote the editors of the *Nation*.[30] The peace societies were partly mollified, but they continued to demand invocation of the neutrality act.[31] Business groups did not protest against the ship order, and indeed it seems to have had little influence on American exporters. Unlike the moral embargo against Italy in 1935, the government did not try to pressure American businessmen into abandoning their trade with China. In fact, when the Du Pont Company informed the government that it would not accept any additional orders from either of the Far Eastern belligerents, the State Department repeatedly pointed out that it had no objections to such sales. But the Du Pont Company, still resentful over the treatment it had received from the Nye committee, continued its private embargo, announcing that it would not sell munitions to China or Japan unless specifically directed to do so by Secretary Hull.[32] Other American exporters, impressed by the government's trade-at-your-own-risk policy, conducted their business with China on a purely cash-and-carry basis. However, despite these handicaps, American trade in munitions to China continued to flourish as arms flowed across the Atlantic in American ships to England, and then were reloaded on British ships for eventual delivery to China via Hong Kong. In the last three months of 1937, the State Department granted licenses for the export of over 2.5 million dollars worth of munitions to China.[33]

Despite the Chinese indignation, the ship order was a policy which in the long run favored China. Faced with the growing pressure of the peace societies, and the strong case they had in the "Wichita" incident, Roosevelt had issued his statement in order to head off an overwhelming public demand for invocation

[30] "Embargo against China," *Nation*, CXLV (September 25, 1937), 309.

[31] *New York Times*, September 16, 1937, p. 2.

[32] Memorandums by Green, September 20, 1937, September 30, 1937, and October 5, 1937, *FR: 1937*, IV, 536, 540, 541–43.

[33] *Export Trade and Shipper*, XXXVI (September 20, 1937), 15; note by Roosevelt in Samuel Rosenman (ed.), *The Public Papers and Addresses of Franklin D. Roosevelt* (13 vols.; New York, 1938–50), VI, 355; State Department, *Press Releases*, XVII (July–December, 1937), *passim*.

of the neutrality act. Knowing that the arms embargo and the loan ban would have a crippling material and psychological impact on the Chinese, the President chose the less severe limitations involved in the restraint on American shipping. His policy met the immediate need—avoidance of provocative incidents with Japan—while at the same time it allowed Americans to continue their trade with China. Relying on the widespread American sympathy for the Chinese, Roosevelt was continuing to exercise his discretionary authority to avoid aligning the United States on the side of Japan.[34] This policy was legal; it was popular with the American people; but it was a total denial of the ideal of impartiality which the neutrality bloc championed. Roosevelt, by indirection, had challenged the isolationist assumptions which underlay the neutrality legislation.

II

Throughout the early stages of the China incident, the United States had pursued a cautious, circumspect policy. Restrained by the isolationist mood of the people, the administration had withheld any condemnation of Japanese aggression in China, despite the obvious Japanese disregard for the Nine-Power Treaty signed at the Washington Conference in 1922 which pledged both Japan and the United States to uphold the territorial integrity of China. In July, 1937, Hull had reaffirmed American adherence to basic principles of international morality, including proper respect for the sanctity of treaties and the avoidance of force as an instrument of policy. However, Hull did not specifically mention Japan in this statement.[35] When China called upon the United States and the other major powers to act against Japan's violation of the

[34] In a Gallup poll taken on October 4, 1937, 59 per cent of those interviewed expressed sympathy for China, 1 per cent for Japan, and 40 per cent for neither country. This marked a sharp increase in pro-Chinese sentiment over a previous poll taken in August, when only 43 per cent favored China. Cantril and Strunk, *Public Opinion*, p. 1081.

[35] *Peace and War, 1931–1941*, pp. 370–71.

Nine-Power Treaty, Hull did consult with Great Britain, but he refused to institute any efforts to condemn the Japanese advance. In September, China finally appealed to the League of Nations for help, and when the League Council began considering this issue later in the month, the United States permitted the American minister to Switzerland, Leland Harrison, to take part in the deliberations as an informal observer. Thus by the end of September, 1937, the United States, though cautiously co-operating with the League, had failed to adopt a forthright stand in opposition to the Japanese invasion of China.[36]

In early October the administration suddenly and dramatically ended its silence on the Far Eastern crisis. President Roosevelt, engaged in a speaking tour of the West, decided to give a major address on foreign affairs in Chicago on October 5. In biting, forceful words, the President described the breakdown of peace in the world. "The present reign of terror and international lawlessness began a few years ago," he declared. Blaming 10 per cent of the population of the world for "the epidemic of world lawlessness," the President observed, "When an epidemic of physical disease starts to spread, the community approves and joins in a quarantine of the patients in order to protect the health of the community against the spread of the disease." Though Roosevelt failed to spell out the measures he favored for the quarantine of aggressors, he did call for "a concerted effort" to restrain those "creating a state of international anarchy and instability from which there is no escape through mere isolation or neutrality." "There must be," the President affirmed, "positive efforts for peace."[37]

The quarantine speech, as the press quickly labeled the address, marked a radical shift in Roosevelt's outlook on world affairs. In his last important speech on foreign policy, at Chautauqua over a year earlier, he had expressed isolationist, even pacifist, sentiments. Now, though he failed to single out any specific country,

[36] Shepardson and Scroggs, *U.S. in World Affairs, 1937*, pp. 209–16.

[37] State Department, *Press Releases*, XVII (October 9, 1937), 276–79.

he spoke as an internationalist, concerned over the rising threat of aggression and determined to find a means of preventing war. The isolationists quickly condemned the President, charging him with warmongering, while enthusiastic advocates of collective security warmly embraced the new presidential line. Both groups were aware that Roosevelt's speech directly contradicted the neutrality legislation.[38] Yet Roosevelt proceeded to confound both his critics and his admirers by denying that his words in any way signified a repudiation of the neutrality act. At a press conference on October 6, the President refused to state what specific steps he had in mind to implement his quarantine speech, but he amazed reporters by claiming that his new policy, instead of reversing American neutrality policy, might expand it. In the face of persistent questions, Roosevelt declared, "We are looking for some way to peace; and by no means is it necessary that that way be contrary to the exercise of neutrality."[39]

Roosevelt's intentions in delivering his Chicago address remain as mysterious today as they were to contemporary observers in 1937. He may have had no specific plan in mind beyond testing out the strength of isolationist sentiment, hoping to launch a more active policy if the public seemed receptive. There is a possibility that he had a vague scheme of forming a neutral bloc with other democratic nations to use moral and legal pressure against aggressors.[40] Certainly there are no indications that Roosevelt in-

[38] *Hull Memoirs*, I, 545; Shepardson and Scroggs, *U.S. in World Affairs, 1937*, pp. 221–23.

[39] Rosenman, *Public Papers of FDR*, VI, 422–24.

[40] Dorothy Borg, "Notes on Roosevelt's Quarantine Speech," *Political Science Quarterly*, LXXII (September, 1957), 405–33. Miss Borg, challenging the traditional view, argues that "the quarantine speech was not a vital landmark in Mr. Roosevelt's foreign policy but part of a groping attempt to find some means of forestalling war. . . ." *Ibid.*, p. 420. In his book *Seven Decisions That Shaped History* (New York, 1950), Sumner Welles states that when Roosevelt returned to Washington after delivering the quarantine speech, Welles suggested a plan whereby the President would deliver an address on Armistice Day to the diplomatic corps in Washington in which he would ask all governments to enter into an exchange of views in order to end the armaments race and achieve a peaceful world. To implement this proposal, Welles

tended to embark on any radical program of economic sanctions, either alone or in co-operation with other nations. Whether he had a concrete program in mind or not, Roosevelt undoubtedly was trying to rally public opinion against what he privately termed "a psychology which comes very close to saying, 'Peace at any price.' "[41] In a letter to Colonel Edward M. House on October 19 Roosevelt stated, "I verily believe that as time goes on we can slowly but surely make people realize that war will be a greater danger to us if we close all the doors and windows than if we go out in the street and use our influence to curb the riot."[42] If this was his purpose at Chicago, the speech was a failure, for the angry isolationist reaction caused Roosevelt to retreat into silence on the vital issues of world affairs.

Though Roosevelt did not mention Japan in the quarantine speech, there was little doubt that the aggression in China was uppermost in his mind. The next day, when the League of Nations condemned Japan for violating both the Kellogg-Briand Pact and the Nine-Power Treaty by its warfare in China, the State Department immediately issued a statement concurring in this judgment.[43] The League suggested that the signatories of the Nine-Power Treaty consult together on the proper measures to be taken, and President Roosevelt quickly accepted an invitation to send American delegates to a conference in Brussels. His appointment of Norman H. Davis to head the American delegation encouraged the sponsors of collective action, but Roosevelt, both in press conferences and in public statements, firmly announced that the

---

suggested that Roosevelt invite nine small nations to join with the United States in serving as an executive committee to draw up an agenda for action by all the governments of the world. Though Welles apparently convinced the President of the wisdom of this plan, Cordell Hull strongly opposed it, and by the end of October Roosevelt decided to drop the project. Welles, *Seven Decisions*, pp. 13–14.

[41] Roosevelt to Endicott Peabody, October 16, 1937, *F.D.R.: His Personal Letters*, I, 716–17.

[42] *Ibid.*, p. 719.

[43] *New York Times*, October 7, 1937, p. 1.

United States had no intention of participating in any joint efforts to coerce Japan. Davis went to Brussels, as Roosevelt stated, "without any commitments on the part of this government to other governments."[44]

The Brussels Conference opened on November 3, 1937, but the refusal of the Japanese to attend destroyed any chance for a peaceful solution to the war in China. Nevertheless, Davis tried to work out a program with the other delegates to restrain Japan. In a cable to Hull on November 10, he pointed out that the neutrality act "tends to negative our affirmation of high moral principles and advocacy of a moral pressure upon Japan," and then he suggested that the Secretary recommend to Congress repeal or at least a suspension of the neutrality legislation as far as the war in China was concerned. "This would startle and worry Japan, encourage the Chinese and have a dynamic effect upon world opinion," Davis argued.[45] His plea met with a cold reception in the State Department. R. Walton Moore, in a note to Roosevelt, pointed out that while a number of isolationist senators, including William E. Borah, supported the non-application of the neutrality act to the Sino-Japanese conflict, they would oppose either suspension or repeal of the legislation.[46] On November 16, Hull informed Davis that there was "no present prospect" of any modification of the neutrality act and that he "should proceed on the assumption that no such action will occur."[47] A week later the Brussels Conference adjourned without achieving any progress on the settlement of the Far Eastern war. The sudden hope for effective international action against Japan, raised by Roosevelt's quarantine speech and the American willingness to consult with other nations, died as quickly as it had sprung up.

The Roosevelt administration, restrained by the isolationist fear of involvement in collective measures for peace, nevertheless con-

[44] Shepardson and Scroggs, *U.S. in World Affairs, 1937*, p. 226.

[45] *FR: 1937*, IV, 177.

[46] Moore to Roosevelt, November 12, 1937, FDR Papers, PSF, Box 24.

[47] *FR: 1937*, IV, 193.

tinued to avoid invoking the neutrality legislation. When Congress convened in November, Republican members, led by Representative Hamilton Fish, savagely attacked the President for his failure to proclaim American neutrality toward the war in China. Claiming that the neutrality act clearly directed the President to apply it to all wars, whether declared or not, Fish described Roosevelt's disregard for the mandate of Congress as "a step toward Fascism."[48] Representative Everett M. Dirksen of Illinois charged that an unneutral sympathy for China had influenced the President. The fate of democracy overseas was no concern of the United States, Dirksen asserted. "I am willing to confine my thinking and my solicitude to the democracy that exists between the Atlantic and the Pacific ocean," he concluded.[49] Other Republicans tried to embarrass the administration by introducing resolutions demanding the immediate application of the neutrality act to the war in China. The Democratic leadership, fearful of an open debate that would reveal rifts within the President's own party, succeeded in tabling these motions.[50]

On November 30, 1937, while the administration was riding out the storm in Congress, Ambassador Grew warned the State Department that the Japanese government planned to declare war on China within the next few days. Hull immediately informed Roosevelt, who was cruising in the Caribbean on the yacht "Potomac," and suggested that the President sign a blank neutrality proclamation to be issued as soon as Japan declared war.[51] Roosevelt quickly agreed to this procedure and then asked Hull to study the possibility of adding raw materials to the list of embargoed materials. "I think we should seek in every way possible to avoid helping one side and not the other," the President added. In a letter to his wife, Roosevelt voiced his concern over the new situa-

[48] *Congressional Record*, November 17, 1937, p. 92.

[49] *Ibid.*, November 18, 1937, pp. 144–45.

[50] *Ibid.*, November 17, 1937, p. 88; *ibid.*, November 24, 1937, pp. 365–66; *ibid.*, December 6, 1937, pp. 935–36.

[51] Grew to Hull, November 30, 1937, *FR: 1937*, III, 735; Hull to Roosevelt, November 30, 1937, *ibid.*

tion and expressed his regret that a neutrality proclamation "will actually favor Japan."[52] On December 1, Hull sent the President a draft neutrality proclamation by seaplane, along with a note pointing out that the 1937 act specifically prohibited the inclusion of raw materials under the arms embargo.[53] Though Roosevelt signed the proclamation, it never went into effect. Grew's information proved faulty, and Japan continued its invasion of China without declaring war.

The brutal Japanese bombing of the American gunboat "Panay" on the Yangtze River in mid-December shifted the focus of attention away from the neutrality issue. Despite an almost immediate Japanese apology and offer of indemnity, strong evidence indicating that this assault had been intentionally carried out by the Japanese navy severely strained relations with Japan. The United States finally accepted the Japanese explanation and apology, but the "Panay" incident reinforced the prevailing public sympathy for China and the animus against Japan.[54] Even isolationists halted their demands for invocation of the neutrality act and, in March, Hull felt that it was safe for the administration to affirm publicly the policy it had been following for nearly nine months. In a speech on March 17, the Secretary stated that because of the peculiar circumstances in China, "application of the [neutrality] law would be most likely to endanger the very objectives which the law was designed to promote. Accordingly, exercising the discretion vested in him by the law itself, the President has refrained from putting the provisions of that law into effect."[55] This statement was hardly news to anyone, but it did signify that the administration had officially abandoned the "24-hour basis" subterfuge for a forthright declaration of its intention of withholding the neutrality legislation from the Sino-Japanese war.

[52] Roosevelt to Hull, November 30, 1937, *ibid.*, p. 736; Roosevelt to Eleanor Roosevelt, November 30, 1937, *F.D.R.: His Personal Letters*, I, 730.

[53] Hull to Roosevelt, December 1, 1937, *FR: 1937*, III, 740–41.

[54] Shepardson and Scroggs, *U.S. in World Affairs, 1937*, pp. 231–34; *New York Times*, December 17, 1937, p. 4.

[55] *Peace and War, 1931–1941*, p. 413.

In mid-1938, Hull took one further step in the direction of partiality toward China. In a press conference on June 11, the Secretary, obviously referring to Japanese air attacks on Chinese cities, condemned the bombing of civilian populations. In response to a reporter's question, Hull added that he was speaking "to the American public and especially to the manufacturers of bombing planes."[56] The hint was unmistakable. Three weeks later, Joseph C. Green, who was in charge of issuing licenses for arms exports, sent a circular letter to all airplane manufacturers calling their attention to Hull's denunciation of the bombing of civilians; ". . . it should be clear to all concerned," Green wrote, "that the Government of the United States is strongly opposed to the sale of airplanes or aeronautical equipment which would materially aid or encourage that practice in any countries in any part of the world." Green then stated that licenses for the export of airplanes to nations guilty of bombing civilians would be issued only "with great regret."[57] The aircraft industry, which was heavily dependent on government contracts, complied with the new policy, and after December, 1938, with only minor exceptions, no further licenses for the export of aircraft to Japan were issued.[58]

In commenting upon this final step in the administration's neutrality policy toward the Sino-Japanese conflict, the *New Republic* charged, "Congress wrote a neutrality law; the administration has made it a scrap of paper."[59] The accusation cannot be denied; the Roosevelt administration, fearing the unfavorable impact of the arms embargo on the Chinese resistance to Japanese aggression, intentionally pursued a course partial to China. Roosevelt, in an off-the-record press conference with the American Society of Newspaper Editors in April, 1938, frankly argued that the neu-

[56] *Ibid.*, p. 421.

[57] "Third Annual Report of the National Munitions Control Board," *House Document No.* 92, 76th Cong., 1st sess. (Washington, 1939), p. 80.

[58] *Ibid.*; Elton Atwater, *American Regulation of Arms Exports* (Washington, 1941), p. 218.

[59] "Mr. Hull's Economic Sanction," *New Republic*, XCV (June 22, 1938), 172.

trality act would have an unequal impact, denying China arms but permitting a continued flow of vital raw materials to Japan. "Therefore," Roosevelt stated, "by virtue of this excuse that they are not at war—it is only an excuse—we are maintaining, in fact, a neutral position."[60] Yet it is by no means certain that the administration policy was as favorable to China as Roosevelt evidently believed. In the last six months of 1937, the State Department granted export licenses for arms, munitions, and implements of war totaling slightly over $7 million to China as opposed to licenses for slightly under $2 million to Japan. But in 1938 heavy Japanese purchases of aircraft, negotiated prior to Hull's moral embargo on airplanes, led to almost equal export of implements of war to the two Far Eastern belligerents.[61] Moreover, some critics argued that if Roosevelt had invoked the full neutrality provisions, including the cash-and-carry clause, Japan would quickly have run out of funds with which to buy raw materials as well as airplanes in the United States. While such a policy would have hurt China, it could have had disastrous results for Japan, with its heavy reliance on the United States for scrap iron and petroleum products.[62]

Whatever the effect of this policy on the Far Eastern belligerents, it had a great impact on the attitude of the American people toward the neutrality legislation. Roosevelt, with the support of the majority of the American public, had revealed the way in which discretionary authority could be used to throw American weight behind one side in a foreign war. The refusal to invoke the neutrality act, coupled with the moral embargo on the export of

[60] Rosenman, *Public Papers of FDR*, VII, 287.

[61] Statistics compiled from monthly list of export licenses in the State Department's *Press Releases*. The actual figures are as follows:

	China	*Japan*
1937 (July–Dec.)	$7,009,565.02	$1,802,865.52
1938 (Jan.–Dec.)	8,892,618.28	9,092,999.86

[62] "Apply the Neutrality Law," *Christian Century*, LIV (August 11, 1937), 989–91; *Amerasia*, I (November, 1937), 423; *Congressional Record*, August 19, 1937, Appendix, p. 2187.

aircraft to Japan, had destroyed any illusion of impartiality toward the Far Eastern belligerents. This policy heartened the supporters of collective security, who realized that presidential discretion could overcome the basic intent of the neutrality legislation, while at the same time it confirmed the fears of isolationists who had always fought against discretionary authority. Most of all, the war in China caused many Americans to realize that they did have a genuine interest in the course of events overseas. For the first time since 1935, the powerful drive for mandatory neutrality began to lose strength.

III

Although the conflict in the Far East brought to light the first cracks in the neutrality wall, the nation remained strongly isolationist in its outlook. Since 1935, Representative Louis Ludlow, an Indiana Democrat, had been sponsoring a constitutional amendment which would require a nationwide referendum before Congress could declare war. This measure, which would not apply in cases of foreign invasion, had been bottled up in the House Judiciary Committee. For several years, Ludlow had been trying to get a majority in Congress to sign a discharge petition to permit his measure to reach the floor. In the spring of 1937 the advocates of strict neutrality, both in Congress and in the peace movement, announced their support for Ludlow's bill. Senator Nye introduced a companion measure in the Senate, while the NCPW began a steady propaganda campaign in behalf of the war referendum idea. Though Ludlow picked up a great many signatures before Congress adjourned in August, he still was far short of the 218 needed to discharge his resolution from the Judiciary Committee. But when Congress met in special session in November, 1937, an ever growing stream of representatives, worried over the increasing possibility of American involvement in war, joined Ludlow's crusade. In early December he had 205 signatures. Then, the Japanese attack on the "Panay" provided the final impetus—by December 14, thirteen more representatives had signed the discharge petition. Congress would now have to consider Ludlow's motion to compel the Rules Committee to permit a floor debate on the war referendum.[63]

The congressional decision to act on the Ludlow referendum was a serious challenge to President Roosevelt's leadership in foreign affairs. By placing the decision for war in the hands of the people, isolationists hoped to insure that no President could ever lead the nation into war against its will. The war referendum, with its clear implication of distrust for the President, would thus undermine administration efforts to halt the spread of aggression abroad. Fully aware of these dangers, Roosevelt did not hesitate to answer with a flat no when a reporter asked him if the war referendum was consistent with representative government. Though prominent Republicans, including Henry L. Stimson and Alfred M. Landon of Kansas, Roosevelt's opponent in 1936, publicly backed the President's stand, the administration knew that the issue would be extremely close in Congress, since nearly half of the Democrats in the House had signed the Ludlow discharge petition.[64] The President now used his full political influence to win back as many Democrats as he could. When Congress took up Ludlow's motion on January 10, 1938, Speaker William Bankhead of Alabama read a letter from Roosevelt condemning the referendum as likely to "cripple any President in his conduct of our foreign relations" and "encourage other nations to believe that they could violate American rights with impunity."[65] After a brief debate, limited by the parliamentary situation, the House rejected Ludlow's motion by a vote of 209 to 188.

Though the administration succeeded in beating down Ludlow's challenge, the margin of victory revealed the continuing strength of the isolationist forces in Congress and in the nation at large. One hundred and eleven Democrats had joined with sixty-

[63] Garry L. Nall, "The Ludlow War Referendum" (Master's thesis, University of Texas, 1959), pp. 47–60; Shepardson and Scroggs, *U.S. in World Affairs, 1937*, pp. 235–37.

[64] Nall, "Ludlow Referendum," pp. 65–66.

[65] *Peace and War, 1931–1941*, pp. 400–401.

four Republicans in voting to strip Congress of the constitutional power to declare war—here was a clear and unmistakable sign that the nation was not yet ready for a more active and responsible foreign policy.[66] If Roosevelt, as some suspected, had been planning to implement his quarantine speech by asking Congress to repeal or modify the 1937 neutrality act, such a course no longer appeared feasible.[67] Though the President moved later in January for a great increase in naval construction, he carefully refrained from making any further provocative statements on foreign policy, and he showed no intention of challenging the existing neutrality act.

Though isolationism seemed stronger than ever by early 1938, a vigorous attack on rigid neutrality legislation began in the winter and spring. Congressmen and senators introduced over twenty bills ranging from outright repeal of the 1937 act to drastic amendments which would permit discriminatory embargoes against aggressors. The internationalist wing of the peace movement renewed its demands for a more flexible policy. The National Conference on the Cause and Cure of War, representing eleven national women's organizations, urged that the President be given power to remove embargoes against nations "agreed to be victims of aggression"; the Committee for Peace through World Co-operation, organized by Protestant and Jewish clergymen who opposed the spread of fascism, demanded immediate revision of the arms embargo so that it applied solely to aggressors.[68] Even former President Herbert Hoover, usually classified as an isolationist, spoke out vigorously against the neutrality act. "If enforced," he told the Women's National Republican Club, "it will sometimes place us in practical economic alliance with the aggressor."[69] The strongest impulse for revision, however, came from left-wing groups. Two

[66] *New York Times*, January 11, 1938, p. 1. Eight members of the Progressive party and five Farmer-Laborites also voted for the referendum.

[67] *Ibid.*, January 16, 1938, IV, 6.

[68] *Ibid.*, January 22, 1938, p. 4; *ibid.*, April 5, 1938, p. 11.

[69] *Ibid.*, January 16, 1938, pp. 1, 4.

Communist-front organizations, the National Lawyers Guild and the American League for Peace and Freedom, led the agitation for a new neutrality policy that would place a total economic and financial embargo on nations violating the Kellogg pact.[70]

The administration, while it probably sympathized with the movement to revise the neutrality legislation, offered no public encouragement. When Senator Pittman asked Hull for his opinion on a bill to repeal the 1937 act, the Secretary refused to endorse it. Stating that he approved of the cash-and-carry provisions, the ban on loans, and, "under certain circumstances," the arms embargo, Hull recommended only that there should be greater discretion for the President in applying these restrictions.[71] On March 20, 1938, the *New York Times* reported that a bipartisan drive was under way in Congress with the unofficial blessing of Hull and Roosevelt to revise the 1937 neutrality act and thus "permit a reversal of the Administration's foreign policy."[72] Yet two days later, when the House Foreign Affairs Committee met to consider the wide variety of bills proposing revision of the 1937 act, Chairman McReynolds firmly announced his opposition to any hearings or committee action. Warning that it would be dangerous to reopen the debate on neutrality policy in view of the threatening world situation, McReynolds asked the committee to postpone this issue until the next session of Congress. Then, by a unanimous vote, the committee agreed not to hold hearings.[73] Several weeks later, in a letter to Joseph P. Kennedy, now American ambassador to Britain, McReynolds revealed another reason for his opposition, saying that he was being bombarded with letters favoring neutrality revision from "the Communistic crowd in New York."[74]

[70] David Barr, Secretary, National Lawyers Guild, to Senator Key Pittman, May 28, 1938, SCP, File 75A-F9.1; memorandum by Carlton Savage, March 18, 1938, 811.04418/303.

[71] Hull to Pittman, February 24, 1938, SCP, File 75A-E2.

[72] *New York Times*, March 20, 1938, p. 1.

[73] Memorandum by George S. Messersmith, March 23, 1938, 811.04418/304.

[74] McReynolds to Kennedy, April 14, 1938, HCP, File 75A-F16.1.

The adamant refusal of the House Foreign Affairs Committee to reopen the subject of general neutrality legislation finally led those favoring revision to concentrate on one issue—the Spanish arms embargo. Though Congress had voted overwhelmingly for the embargo on Spain in January, 1937, the course of the Civil War created growing doubts about the wisdom and fairness of this policy. Increasing evidence that Germany and Italy were supplying guns, planes, and even troops to Franco's forces indicated that the British and French efforts at limiting the war had failed. Since the American embargo was based largely on the idea of co-operating with the non-intervention policy of the European democracies, many Americans now felt that the United States should abandon the embargo and revert to its traditional policy of selling arms to the established government, in this case the Spanish Loyalists.[75] The first sign of the growing dissatisfaction with the embargo came in March, 1937, when Senator Nye introduced a resolution suggesting that the Spanish arms embargo be extended to include other nations participating in the civil war.[76] Secretary Hull, who feared that any open American recognition of German and Italian aid to Franco would undermine the British and French efforts at non-intervention, strongly opposed this measure, and his views prevailed. On June 2, 1937, following an announcement by President Roosevelt that the American policy toward the Spanish Civil War remained unchanged, the Senate Foreign Relations Committee tabled the Nye resolution.[77] A few weeks later the President asked Hull to question American ambassadors in Europe on the extent of German and Italian participation in the Spanish war, but when the replies from Europe advised against any extension of the embargo, Roosevelt allowed his earlier decision to stand.[78]

[75] F. Jay Taylor, *The United States and the Spanish Civil War* (New York, 1956), pp. 88–89.

[76] *Congressional Record*, March 25, 1937, p. 2737; *ibid.*, April 9, 1937, p. 3315.

[77] *Hull Memoirs*, I, 510–11; *New York Times*, June 3, 1937, p. 2.

[78] Roosevelt to Hull, June 29, 1937, FDR Papers, OF 1561, Box 1; *FR: 1937*, I, 344–47, 354–55.

The demand for applying the arms embargo to Italy and Germany gave way in the spring of 1938 to a new attempt to repeal the embargo on Spain. Liberal groups, passionately sympathetic to the Loyalists, pointed to the injustice in denying arms to the established government of Spain and charged that the American policy aided the Fascist cause; ". . . failure to act," wrote the editors of the *Nation*, "so encourages the fascist powers that it constitutes a clear challenge not only to peace but to the philosophy on which all decent international relations must rest." Even the *New Republic*, which staunchly defended the neutrality act, favored an exception for Spain.[79] A wide variety of prominent Americans, from Henry L. Stimson to Norman Thomas, backed the drive for repeal of the embargo. College faculties, left-wing popular front organizations, Protestant clergymen, and the international wing of the peace movement all added their voices to the cause.[80] The crusade for repeal reached substantial proportions when Senator Nye introduced a resolution proposing that the United States lift the embargo on the Loyalists, as the established government, but continue to deny the export of arms to the Rebels. To guard against provocative incidents, Nye included a cash-and-carry provision for all arms exports to the Spanish Loyalists.[81] With the most outspoken champion of neutrality legislation now leading the demand for repeal, the prospects for a change in policy suddenly appeared favorable.

The Nye resolution placed the Roosevelt administration in a serious dilemma. Though public opinion polls showed that most Americans were indifferent to the outcome of the Spanish Civil War, the conflict had created intense partisanship among small but vocal sections of the population.[82] In general, liberal groups,

[79] "End the Embargo against Spain," *Nation*, CXLVI (March 26, 1938), 344; "Hull Muddling," *New Republic*, XCIV (April 6, 1938), 259.

[80] Taylor, *U.S. and the Spanish Civil War*, pp. 169–71.

[81] *Congressional Record*, May 2, 1938, p. 6030; text of Senate Joint Resolution 288, SCP, File 75A-E2.

[82] A Gallup poll, taken in January, 1937, showed that 66 per cent of the people interviewed sympathized with neither side in the Spanish Civil War,

which strongly supported the New Deal, sided with the Loyalists, while the Catholic hierarchy, as well as many Catholic laymen of Irish and Italian descent, favored Franco's Rebels. Both groups represented important segments of the political coalition on which Roosevelt had risen to power. Confronted with a choice which inevitably would alienate some of his political supporters, Roosevelt hesitated. In a private press conference with newspaper editors in April, he defended the embargo on the grounds that any change would aid the Rebels, who Roosevelt claimed now controlled the seaports of Spain. In a private conversation with Secretary of the Interior Harold L. Ickes on May 1, Roosevelt repeated this defense of his policy, but Ickes scoffed at it, feeling that Roosevelt was trying to evade the issue.[83] The next week, Roosevelt departed on a Caribbean fishing cruise, leaving the difficult Spanish problem for the State Department to study.[84]

Though the discussions inside the State Department remain shrouded in mystery, there is substantial evidence that Hull and his advisers reached a tentative decision to support repeal of the embargo for both belligerents in the Spanish war. In their syndicated newspaper column, Drew Pearson and Robert S. Allen reported that the top officials of the State Department reached this conclusion at a conference on May 3, 1938.[85] Two days later, the *New York Times* published a front-page story asserting that the administration had not only decided to support the Nye resolution, but that it had lined up sufficient votes to assure passage of the measure in both houses of Congress.[86] This report alarmed the pro-Franco elements in the United States, and when Roosevelt returned to Washington on May 9, a great controversy was

22 per cent with the Loyalists, and 12 per cent with the Rebels. A *Fortune* poll taken three months later gave almost identical results. Cantril and Strunk, *Public Opinion*, p. 807.

[83] Rosenman, *Public Papers of FDR*, VII, 284–86; *Ickes Diary*, II, 380.

[84] *New York Times*, May 6, 1937, p. 5.

[85] Taylor, *U.S. and the Spanish Civil War*, p. 174.

[86] *New York Times*, May 5, 1938, p. 1.

raging. The President conferred with Secretary Hull, and then met with a number of congressional leaders, including McReynolds and Sam Rayburn, House majority leader, who both indicated their opposition to the Nye resolution.[87] When the Senate Foreign Relations Committee met on May 13, Senator Pittman read a letter from Hull firmly opposing repeal of the Spanish arms embargo. Stating that the embargo had been enacted by Congress to prevent incidents that might involve the United States in the Spanish Civil War, Hull declared that repeal "would still subject us to unnecessary risks we have so far avoided. We do not know what lies ahead in the Spanish situation. The original danger still exists." Hull then suggested that instead of dealing with questions of neutrality revision piecemeal, the committee should undertake a broad study of the whole problem. "It is evident," Hull concluded, "that there is not sufficient time to give study to such questions in the closing days of this Congress."[88]

The Senate Foreign Relations Committee immediately followed the administration's recommendation and tabled the Nye resolution by a vote of 17 to 1.[89] This action effectively killed the hopes of liberals for repeal of the Spanish arms embargo. In bitter editorials, the *Nation* and the *New Republic* denounced the administration. Calling Hull's letter to Pittman "one of the most reactionary state papers in history," the liberal journals accused Roosevelt and Hull of submitting to pressure from both the Catholic hierarchy in the United States and the appeasers in the British Foreign Office.[90] Both charges contain some substance, but there were other considerations that influenced Roosevelt's decision. The State Department, and especially Cordell Hull, hoped to establish closer relations with England and France by uphold-

[87] *Ibid.*, May 10, 1938, p. 1.

[88] State Department, *Press Releases*, XVIII (May 14, 1938), 578–79.

[89] *New York Times*, May 14, 1938, p. 1.

[90] "The Spanish Embargo Remains," *New Republic*, XCV (May 25, 1938), 60–61; "Hull of Downing Street," *Nation*, CXLVI (May 21, 1938), 576; Max Lerner, "Behind Hull's Embargo," *ibid.*, CXLVI (May 28, 1938), 607–10.

ing their non-intervention policy. Hull also feared that a determined effort to alter neutrality legislation would create a dangerous controversy in Congress.[91] Probably the dominant consideration related to the domestic political scene. With the New Deal coalition disintegrating after the Supreme Court fight, Roosevelt did not dare endanger the large Catholic vote that was vital to the Democratic political machine. By retaining the embargo, he only antagonized liberals who would continue to support his domestic reform program, not on the basis of personal loyalty, but out of conviction and principle.

Though the drive for repeal of the Spanish arms embargo ended in frustration for its sponsors, once again the wisdom of the neutrality legislation was brought into question. Though probably only a minority of the American people were deeply stirred by this issue, the way in which the neutrality act aided a Fascist group in Europe reinforced the doubts raised by the Sino-Japanese war. The fact that ardent advocates of rigid neutrality like Senator Nye and the editors of the *New Republic* openly opposed the application of their own program in a specific case undoubtedly weakened the neutrality bloc. For more lukewarm supporters of neutrality like Senator Pittman, who tended to align himself with the isolationists, the flaws in the legislation became more apparent. In June, 1938, Pittman, taking his cue from Hull's letter in May, announced that his committee would begin a thorough re-examination of the entire subject of neutrality in the next session of Congress.[92] A month later, Pittman revealed the direction this revision might take when he stated his belief that the President should have greater discretion in administering the neutrality act. Admitting that the 1937 act had been drafted primarily with Europe in mind, Pittman acknowledged its inadequacy for the Far East and implied that he would lead a movement to make the legislation more flexible.[93] Thus the author of the 1937 act revealed his misgivings over mandatory neutrality.

[91] *Hull Memoirs,* I, 514–16.

[92] *New York Times,* June 19, 1938, p. 1.

[93] *Ibid.,* July 10, 1938, p. 21.

President Roosevelt must have drastically revised his own personal estimate of the neutrality legislation on the basis of the experience in China and Spain, but the evidence is slim on this point. The quarantine speech, whatever its purpose, was a clear sign that the President, watching the world move inexorably toward general war, realized the impossibility of American isolation. Sometime in the late 1930's, Roosevelt had finally ended his own vacillations between isolation and a more active world policy. In the Sino-Japanese war, he severely strained the letter of the 1937 act to avoid action harmful to China, and though in Spain he refused to aid the Loyalists because of domestic considerations, he later acknowledged that the Spanish embargo had been "a grave mistake."[94] But even as Roosevelt began to develop this new outlook, he faced the difficult problem of reversing a congressional policy that he had originally fostered. He would find it far easier to overcome his own isolationist tendencies than to transform the deeply rooted convictions of the American people. Always supple and flexible, Roosevelt had learned quickly from the shifting pattern of world events, but he would find the public, and especially Congress, far less resilient. In order to translate his new internationalist convictions into specific policies, he would have to move cautiously, frequently disguising his true objective. In terms of neutrality legislation, this would require a continued public endorsement of the basic objective—avoidance of war—while actually moving in the direction of a very different goal—preventing the outbreak of war.

[94] *Ickes' Diary*, II, 569. Ickes reports Roosevelt making this remark at a cabinet meeting on January 27, 1939.

CHAPTER EIGHT

NEUTRALITY REVISION: FAILURE

The neutrality situation seems to be going from bad to worse.

J. PIERREPONT MOFFAT, May 3, 1939

In September, 1938, the world crisis which had been developing since the Manchuria incident in 1931 moved into its final stage. Adolf Hitler, emboldened by his bloodless seizure of Austria in March, now threatened war in Europe with his demands on the Sudeten area of Czechoslovakia. During the last two weeks in September, American newspapers and radio networks reported in detail the British and French offers for a compromise solution of the Czech crisis. When Hitler finally issued an ultimatum on September 22, demanding Czech withdrawal from the disputed area by October 1, the outbreak of war seemed certain. Then an eleventh-hour appeal by Mussolini brought about the conference at Munich, where Neville Chamberlain and Edouard Daladier, the British and French prime ministers, surrendered the Sudetenland in return for Hitler's promise to end his expansionist policies. Though many Americans rejoiced at the news that the dreaded conflict had been averted, the weeks of crisis produced a new awareness of the explosive state of world affairs. Both isolationists and internationalists realized the imminence of war in Europe and intensified their efforts to shape the course of American diplomacy.[1]

[1] Whitney H. Shepardson and William O. Scroggs, *The United States in World Affairs, 1938* (New York, 1939), pp. 21–24, 66–87; William L. Langer

The quickening tempo of the world crisis confronted Franklin Roosevelt with a serious dilemma. Since his overwhelming re-election in 1936, the President had met with a series of defeats which had greatly weakened his prestige. After the bitter Supreme Court fight in 1937, which created a serious split inside the Democratic party, the nation's economy suffered a sudden setback which threatened to undermine the New Deal's recovery effort. Though a resumption of previously curtailed government spending programs finally overcame the recession, Roosevelt found his hold on Congress slipping. A group of conservative Democrats joined with Republican congressmen to block any further domestic reform legislation. In an effort to strengthen the liberal wing of the party, and also to gain personal revenge, the President decided to intervene in a number of the primary elections in the summer and early fall of 1938. The results were disastrous for Roosevelt. All but two of his candidates lost to the conservative incumbents, the most spectacular defeats coming in Georgia, Maryland, and Iowa, where Walter F. George, Millard E. Tydings, and Guy M. Gillette easily thwarted the President's efforts to oust them from the Senate. This internal strife weakened the Democratic party, and in the November elections the Republicans made a striking resurgence, gaining eighty-one seats in the House and eight more in the Senate.[2] Thus at the very moment when the world situation imperiled American security, the President had lost the confidence of broad sections of the electorate.

In the weeks following the Munich conference, President Roosevelt embarked on a new phase of his political career. Quietly abandoning his New Deal reforms, which had become the primary source of internal dissension, he set out to unite both conservatives and liberals behind a program of national preparedness designed to meet the dangers facing the United States in the inter-

---

and S. Everett Gleason, *The Challenge to Isolation, 1937–1940* (New York, 1952), pp. 35–36.

[2] *Ibid.*, p. 39; Basil Rauch, *Roosevelt from Munich to Pearl Harbor* (New York, 1950), pp. 71–72.

national arena. Though his basic aim was to employ American strength to bolster the efforts of England and France to resist the threat of German aggression, he carefully masked this objective, emphasizing instead the need to strengthen the armed forces in order to defend the Western Hemisphere. On October 11, 1938, when the President announced an increase of $300 million for national defense, the public response was overwhelmingly favorable.[3] But military preparedness alone would not fulfill Roosevelt's basic policy of standing firmly behind the Western democracies. He needed to secure repeal of the restrictive features of the neutrality legislation in order to warn Hitler that in case of war the United States would once again open its productive facilities to England and France. Yet Roosevelt was hesitant to advocate openly either repeal or revision of the 1937 neutrality act since public opinion polls taken in the fall of 1938 revealed that over two-thirds of the people preferred mandatory neutrality legislation to a flexible policy of presidential discretion.[4] Fearful that isolationists would join with the enemies he had created on domestic issues, the President decided to follow an indirect course, raising the issue of neutrality revision in only the most general terms and then relying on internationalists in Congress to carry through the specific changes he desired. Thus, throughout the neutrality debate of 1939 the President stood aside, permitting the State Department and congressional spokesmen to lead the fight for revision.

I

The drive for revision of the neutrality legislation began in the State Department in the fall of 1938. On September 22, three

[3] *Ibid.*, pp. 80–91; Langer and Gleason, *Challenge to Isolation*, pp. 36–39.

[4] In a Gallup poll taken on September 23, 1938, 73 per cent of those who were asked which plan for keeping out of war they had more faith in chose stricter neutrality legislation by Congress, compared to 31 per cent who favored "leaving the job up to the President." When the same question was asked on October 2, 69 per cent indicated stricter legislation, 31 per cent presidential discretion. Hadley Cantril and Mildred Strunk (eds.), *Public Opinion, 1935–1946* (Princeton, 1951), p. 966.

months before the new Congress was due to meet, R. Walton Moore wrote Senator Pittman "confidentially" to suggest possible changes in the neutrality act. Moore's recommendations were quite mild. He favored re-enactment of the cash-and-carry provisions, due to expire in May, and two new provisions, one empowering the President to prohibit American ships from entering designated combat zones and another giving the President discretion to invoke the arms embargo only when he decided "it is in the interest of the United States for him to do so. . . ."[5] Pittman replied to Moore on October 13. Although stating that he shared the administration's view that the totalitarian governments of Europe threatened American security, Pittman warned that "extreme and foolish pacifist sentiment" in Congress would block any effort to grant the President any further discretionary authority. Then he suggested a different approach. "There would be a better chance," he wrote Moore, "of repealing the embargo provision with regard to arms, ammunition, and implements of war and retaining the other provisions of the act. Congress might agree that any materials might be exported to belligerents, including arms, ammunition, and implements of war, if title was divested before export and exportation was carried in foreign bottoms." Pittman closed by urging caution. "When Congress is assembled, we can feel out and determine how far we can go."[6]

Pittman's suggestions for the repeal of the arms embargo and the extension of cash-and-carry to all trade with belligerents touched off a lively debate inside the State Department. On October 18, Moore held a long conference with a dozen top-ranking department officials. Those primarily concerned with the threat of aggression in Europe, led by J. Pierrepont Moffat, chief of the Division of European Affairs, strongly endorsed Pittman's plan on the grounds that it would enable the United States to help England and France in a war with Germany. However, Stanley K. Hornbeck voiced the objections of the Far Eastern experts, point-

[5] Moore to Pittman, September 22, 1939, SCP, File 75A-F9.1.

[6] Pittman to Moore, October 13, 1939, SCP, File 75A-F9.1.

ing out that such a policy would aid Japan in its conquest of China. "The only thing we all agreed on," Moffat observed, "was the impossibility of working out any formula that would meet our needs in all circumstances."[7] On November 7, after a three-man subcommittee conducted an intensive study of the possible alternatives, the State Department experts met again in Moore's office. After a long discussion, they agreed to recommend repeal of the arms embargo and the adoption of the cash-and-carry formula for all exports to belligerents. If this program proved politically unwise, they suggested that the invocation of the arms embargo be made discretionary, so that the President would not be compelled to put it into effect automatically upon declaration of war.[8]

Though Secretary Hull undoubtedly passed these recommendations on to the President, there is no evidence of Roosevelt's reaction to them. The administration kept silent on its neutrality plans throughout the fall of 1938, and when the United Press published a report indicating that Roosevelt planned to ask Congress for authority to levy discriminatory embargoes against aggressors, Undersecretary Sumner Welles branded this rumor as utterly false, claiming that the State Department had not drawn up any proposals for legislative action.[9] By December there was widespread speculation in the press over the administration's probable line of action, with most observers expecting the President to state his views in his annual message to Congress in January.[10]

When Congress assembled on January 4, 1939, both isolationists and internationalists eagerly awaited the President's opening address. In calm, measured tones, Roosevelt described the menacing march of aggression overseas and spelled out its implica-

[7] Moffat Diary, October 18, 1939. Moffat, who had served as chief of the Division of Western European Affairs from 1932 to 1935, had returned to Washington in 1937 after two years as consul general in Australia.

[8] Memorandum by Green H. Hackworth, Joseph C. Green, and Carleton Savage, October 28, 1938, 811.04418/325½; Moffat Diary, November 7, 1938.

[9] *New York Times*, November 29, 1938, p. 15; memorandum by Joseph C. Green, December 1, 1938, 811.04418/386½.

[10] *New York Times*, December 18, 1938, p. 1.

tions for American security in the Western Hemisphere. "We know," he declared, "what might happen to us of the United States if the new philosophies of force were to encompass the other continents and invade our own." Though he urged the continued strengthening of the armed forces, Roosevelt warned that national defense alone was not enough to stem aggression. "Words may be futile, but war is not the only means of commanding a decent respect for the opinions of mankind. There are many methods short of war, but stronger and more effective than mere words, of bringing home to aggressor governments the aggregate sentiments of our own people." Then the President dealt directly with the neutrality issue:

> At the very least, we can and should avoid any action, or any lack of action, which will encourage, assist, or build up an aggressor. We have learned that when we deliberately try to legislate neutrality, our neutrality laws may operate unevenly and unfairly—may actually give aid to an aggressor and deny it to the victim. The instinct of self-preservation should warn us that we ought not to let that happen any more.[11]

The President's "measures short of war" speech provoked intense reactions from Congress and the nation's press. Supporters of collective security generally praised Roosevelt. The *New York Times* called his statement "a turning point" in American foreign policy, though the editors noted that the President failed to offer any specific proposals for revising neutrality legislation. Senator Pittman was more graphic in his comments. Interpreting Roosevelt's remarks as advocating "moral, commercial, and financial sanctions," Pittman exclaimed, "Why shoot a man when you can starve him to death?"[12] In contrast, isolationist spokesmen bitterly denounced the President's address. The *New Republic* warned that only those who "want to free the President to lead us into

[11] Samuel Rosenman (ed.), *The Public Papers and Addresses of Franklin D. Roosevelt* (13 vols.; New York, 1938–50), VIII, 1–3.

[12] *New York Times*, January 5, 1939, pp. 1, 22.

war" advocated revision of the neutrality act, while Frederick J. Libby, leader of the National Council for the Prevention of War, issued a call for an arms embargo "on all countries at all times."[13] Senator Robert A. Taft spoke for most Republicans when he stated, "The logical conclusion is another war with American troops again sent across the ocean." The most extreme criticism came from a southern Democrat, Representative John Rankin of Mississippi, who charged that Roosevelt's new policy was the product of "insidious alien influences," which he defined as Communist agitators and greedy munitions makers.[14]

These responses revealed the deep division both in Congress and in the nation at large on the issue of neutrality revision. Roosevelt, treading gingerly, was probably alarmed by the prospect of an all-out fight in Congress which could well end in disaster. Stung by the criticism of the general recommendations he had offered in his annual message, he was reluctant to engage openly in the fight for revision by putting forth a specific program. As the President wrestled with this problem of tactics, Senator Pittman offered a tempting solution. In a long memorandum on January 11, Pittman urged Roosevelt to allow the Senate Foreign Relations Committee, rather than the State Department, to frame new neutrality legislation. Pointing out that he expected a large number of neutrality bills to come before Congress, he suggested that his committee hold a series of lengthy hearings in order to air the various viewpoints and feel out the sentiments of the people. "After this process is ended," Pittman continued, "I may be able to bring about a satisfactory compromise in the Committee. My position as a compromiser would be weakened if I presented bills and resolutions at this time setting forth my present opinions as to the character of legislation that should be adopted." Pittman concluded by urging the President to remain

[13] "Yes and No to the President," *New Republic*, XCVII (January 18, 1939), 299–300; Frederick J. Libby, "President Says Peace but Policies Say War," *Peace Action*, V (January, 1939), 1–2.

[14] *New York Times*, January 5, 1939, p. 13; *ibid.*, January 11, 1939, p. 13.

silent on neutrality revision until the committee had completed its task.[15]

After conferring with Hull, the President allowed Pittman to take charge of the movement for neutrality revision in Congress.[16] This strategy, based on Pittman's belief that forceful presidential leadership would jeopardize the chances for successful revision, meant that the administration would voluntarily surrender its control over the neutrality issue at a time when decisive action was vital to the nation's foreign policy. The risks in this course must have been apparent to both Roosevelt and Hull. Ever since his failure to gain acceptance of a discriminatory arms embargo in his committee in 1933, Senator Pittman had shown a total inability to serve as an effective leader for the administration on neutrality issues in Congress. Indeed, the record indicated that Pittman's own views were more nearly akin to those of the Nye neutrality bloc. In both 1935 and 1937 he had sponsored the very legislative provisions which the administration now wished to see removed. Nevertheless, the President, fearful that a strong stand by the administration would antagonize an already rebellious Congress, decided to gamble on the questionable leadership of the Nevada senator.

II

Senator Pittman began the effort for neutrality revision on January 11, 1939, when he declared that the Senate Foreign Relations Committee would begin hearings on various neutrality proposals toward the end of the month. Eight days later, Pittman suddenly announced the indefinite postponement of the hearings, explaining that the members of his committee were busy on other legislative matters.[17] The real reason for the delay was not sena-

[15] Memorandum from Pittman to Roosevelt, January 11, 1939, FDR Papers, PPF 745.

[16] *The Memoirs of Cordell Hull* (2 vols.; New York, 1948), I, 613; Joseph Alsop and Robert Kintner, *American White Paper* (New York, 1940), pp. 39–40.

[17] *New York Times*, January 12, 1939, p. 7; *ibid.*, January 20, 1939, p. 1.

torial overwork—rather it was the re-emergence of the politically explosive issue of the Spanish arms embargo. In early January, with Franco's armies nearing a complete victory in Spain, pro-Loyalist groups in the United States began a desperate last effort to permit the shipment of American arms to the Spanish government. On January 9, J. Pierrepont Moffat reported that Loyalist supporters were "pouring into Washington from all over the country" to begin the first day of "Lift the Embargo Week."[18] Left-wing groups, led by the editors of the *Nation*, urged all opponents of fascism to join in writing their congressmen and senators, "The embargo must go."[19] Catholic spokesmen immediately organized a counter-campaign of their own, celebrating a "Keep the Embargo Week" and adding to the deluge of letters to Congress.[20] As a result, intense political pressure began to build up on the Senate Foreign Relations Committee. In the third week of January this group received over 35,000 letters on the Spanish arms embargo issue—on one morning, 3,000 telegrams arrived.[21] It was this pressure which caused the committee to vote unanimously on January 19 to postpone all consideration of neutrality revision until the agitation over the Spanish embargo died down. In explaining this vote to Moffat, Key Pittman stated that "the conflicting avalanche of telegrams from both sides had convinced individual Senators that they were in too hot a spot to sit with ease and that the sooner they could get off it by avoiding the issue, the happier they would be."[22]

For the rest of the month, the State Department officials tried to decide whether or not to press for neutrality revision in the midst of the agitation over the Spanish arms embargo. Though in November the President had seriously considered a message to

[18] Moffat Diary, January 9, 1939.

[19] "Lift the Embargo," *Nation*, CXLVIII (January 21, 1939), 77–79.

[20] *Commonweal*, XXIX (February 3, 1939), 407; Moffat Diary, January 9, 1939.

[21] *New York Times*, January 26, 1939, p. 4.

[22] Moffat Diary, January 19, 1939.

Congress advocating repeal of the embargo on Spain, by January the administration, realizing that a Franco victory was imminent, ruled out this possibility.[23] The major fear was that the bitterness stirred up over the Spanish issue would be transferred to the congressional debates on general neutrality revision. Though Norman H. Davis argued for "a frontal attack" on the existing neutrality act, the majority shared Moffat's view "that while people's thoughts were entirely centered on Spain . . . any discussion of the Neutrality Act would be considered by both the Congress and the people in relation to that particular struggle and not in relation to the broad European field." The State Department officers finally agreed to ask Pittman to press for general repeal of the arms embargo and the extension of cash-and-carry to all belligerent trade, the program they had agreed on in November, but to wait for the Spanish issue to subside before bringing the matter before Congress.[24]

During the debate over the Spanish arms embargo, a new controversy developed which further delayed consideration of neutrality revision. On January 23 a new, experimental American bomber crashed in California, killing several American crew members and an official of the French Air Ministry. As a result, the nation learned that the administration was encouraging the sale of military aircraft to England and France and was even allowing foreign personnel to fly United States Army planes.[25] When this sensational disclosure provoked a violent outcry by isolationists in Congress, President Roosevelt invited the members of the Senate Military Affairs Committee to the White House in order to explain the administration's policy. Though the senators were sworn to secrecy, on February 1 newspapers reported that the President had told the group that the administration planned to aid the democracies in every way possible short of war. According to the press accounts, Roosevelt then stated that the frontier of American de-

[23] Moffat Diary, November 19, 1938, January 23, 1939.

[24] Moffat Diary, January 23, 25, and 26, 1939.

[25] Langer and Gleason, *Challenge to Isolation*, p. 48.

fense lay on the Rhine. Though the President later branded this statement a "deliberate lie," isolationists in the Senate seized upon it to charge that Roosevelt was determined to lead the nation into war.[26] Frightened by this furor in Congress, Senator Pittman, with Hull's reluctant consent, decided to postpone the drive for neutrality revision until a more propitious moment.[27]

While Pittman stalled the administration's effort to amend the neutrality act, internationalists came forth with a sweeping proposal to reorient American policy along collective security lines. On February 13, Senator Elbert D. Thomas of Utah introduced Senate Joint Resolution 67, which proposed to grant the President authority to forbid the export to belligerents of all war supplies, raw materials as well as arms, and with the approval of Congress, to lift such embargoes against victims of aggression.[28] This measure, which defined an aggressor as a nation which went to war in violation of its treaty obligations, was intended to permit the United States to aid the democracies while denying any material assistance to totalitarian nations. Though Senator Thomas formally sponsored the bill, it was actually drawn up by the Committee for Concerted Peace Efforts, composed of fifteen national organizations including the League of Nations Association, the American Association of University Women, the General Federation of Women's Clubs, the American Youth Congress, and the World Alliance of International Friendship through the Churches.[29] Thus the Thomas amendment represented a determined effort by internationalist peace societies, women's clubs, and religious bodies to reverse the mandatory neutrality policy and align the United States with England, France, and China against the threat of aggression by Germany, Italy, and Japan.

The Thomas amendment quickly won enthusiastic support

[26] *Ibid.*, p. 49; Rauch, *Roosevelt*, p. 113; *New York Times*, February 1, 1939, p. 1; *ibid.*, February 2, 1939, p. 1.

[27] Moffat Diary, February 17, 1939.

[28] *Congressional Record*, February 13, 1939, p. 1347.

[29] *New York Times*, December 3, 1938, p. 10; *ibid.*, January 28, 1939, p. 5.

from advocates of collective security. The *New York Times* praised it as a way "to abandon, in clear-cut cases, that indifference to the moral issue of aggression which is implicit in the present law and which is in reality a counsel of cowardice and a bankruptcy of American idealism."[30] An even stronger endorsement came from former Secretary of State Henry L. Stimson in a letter to the *New York Times* on March 7. Though Stimson did not refer specifically to the Thomas amendment, he warned that the only way the United States could prevent the outbreak of war in Europe would be to stand firmly behind the democracies. ". . . I am unalterably opposed," Stimson stated, "to the doctrine preached in many quarters that our Government and our people must treat the nations on both sides of this great issue [freedom versus dictatorship] with perfect impartiality; that, for example, we must sell to a nation that has violated its treaties with us . . . the very instruments with which to continue its wrongdoing as freely as we sell to its victim the instruments for its self-defense."[31]

The same day the Stimson letter appeared, Franklin Roosevelt spoke out on neutrality revision for the first time since his annual message to Congress. In response to a reporter's question whether or not the neutrality act had helped preserve peace, the President stated, "We might have been stronger if we had not had it." Despite further questions, Roosevelt refused to indicate when the administration would press for revision of the legislation. His silence was tantamount to rejection of the Thomas amendment.[32] Nevertheless, the President's remarks helped rekindle congressional interest in the neutrality issue. Later the same day, Alben W. Barkley, the Senate majority leader, denounced the existing law and hinted that the administration was at last ready to move. On March 8 Pittman announced that his committee would begin consideration of various neutrality proposals within the next

[30] *Ibid.*, February 15, 1939, p. 22.

[31] *Ibid.*, March 7, 1939, p. 16.

[32] Rosenman, *Public Papers of FDR*, VIII, 154–55; *New York Times*, March 8, 1939, pp. 1, 11.

ten days.[33] This statement led to a counter-blast from Senator Nye, who warned that his followers would filibuster to block administration attempts to change the existing legislation. "Any effort to repeal or emasculate the Neutrality Act," he declared, "will keep the Senate here all summer."[34] Nye's threat evidently impressed Pittman, for despite his earlier announcement, he failed to bring the subject of neutrality revision before the Senate Foreign Relations Committee at its meeting on March 15. When questioned about this by reporters, Pittman stated that so far the Senate had shown no interest in neutrality revision. He said that none of his colleagues had even talked to him about this subject.[35] Thus despite the introduction of the Thomas amendment and the administration's obvious desire for action, Pittman continued to avoid initiating congressional consideration of the most pressing issue of foreign policy confronting the nation.

It was Adolf Hitler who finally forced Congress and the administration to act on neutrality legislation. At 6 o'clock on the morning of March 15, 1939, the German army marched into Czechoslovakia and in a short time completely occupied that country in direct violation of the pledge Hitler had given at the Munich conference. This flagrant act of aggression thoroughly angered the American people and their leaders. William C. Bullitt, the American ambassador to France, sent the President a telegram on March 15 pleading for retaliatory action by the United States. "I believe you should recommend immediate elimination of section one [the arms embargo] of the neutrality act," Bullitt wired Roosevelt.[36] Sumner Welles, Acting Secretary of State in Hull's absence from Washington, favored a more moderate course, stating that he believed Congress would now act on neutrality revision without further urging by the President.[37] Roosevelt himself was more deter-

[33] *Ibid.*, March 8, 1939, p. 1; *ibid.*, March 9, 1939, pp. 1, 8.

[34] *Ibid.*, March 10, 1939, p. 1.

[35] *Ibid.*, March 16, 1939, p. 8.

[36] Bullitt to Roosevelt, March 15, 1939, 811.04418/358.

[37] Memorandum of transatlantic telephone conversation between Bullitt and Welles, March 15, 1939, *FR: 1939*, I, 41.

mined than ever to have the arms embargo removed. "If Germany invades a country and declares war," he told Senator Tom Connally of Texas on March 16, "we'll be on the side of Hitler by invoking the act. If we could get rid of the arms embargo, it wouldn't be so bad."[38]

On March 17 the administration publicly responded to the German seizure of Czechoslovakia. In a formal statement to the press, Sumner Welles condemned "the temporary extinguishment of the liberties of [the] free and independent people" of Czechoslovakia. "It is manifest," Welles continued, "that acts of wanton lawlessness and of arbitrary force are threatening world peace and the very structure of modern civilization."[39] Later the same day, President Roosevelt spoke out again on neutrality revision at his press conference, affirming the necessity for prompt action by Congress.[40] Senator Pittman needed no further encouragement. While the President spoke to the press, Pittman met with R. Walton Moore at the State Department and began drafting a comprehensive neutrality bill.[41] The resulting measure, finished the next day, embodied the basic position that the State Department had been urging since November—repeal of the arms embargo section and adoption of cash-and-carry for all trade with belligerent nations. The cash-and-carry section forbade any American ship to enter a belligerent port and required that American citizens transfer title to all exports to nations at war before the goods left the United States. In addition, the Pittman bill, labeled the Peace Act of 1939, continued the other provisions of the 1937 statute, including the prohibition of loans to belligerents, travel on belligerent ships, and the arming of American merchantmen. There were two further changes. The President was required to put the

[38] Tom Connally and Alfred Steinberg, *My Name Is Tom Connally* (New York, 1954), p. 226.

[39] Department of State, *Peace and War: United States Foreign Policy, 1931–1941* (Washington, 1943), pp. 454–55.

[40] Press Conference No. 530A, March 17, 1939, FDR Papers, PPF 1-P, XIII, 204; *New York Times*, March 18, 1939, p. 3.

[41] Moore to Roosevelt, March 18, 1939, 811.04418/375A.

law into effect within thirty days after the outbreak of either a declared or an undeclared war and he was given discretionary authority to proclaim combat zones from which he could ban all American ships and travelers, even if they were en route to a neutral port.[42] The result was a compromise bill which would enable the United States to export arms as well as raw materials to England and France while at the same time guarding against the loss of American lives and property on the high seas.

On Sunday evening, March 19, Senator Pittman described his new proposal in a nationwide radio broadcast. Stating that the sole cause of American entry into the First World War was a futile defense of neutral rights, Pittman asserted that the cash-and-carry features he proposed would prevent a repetition of this experience. He stressed the danger for the United States from the spread of totalitarian governments abroad and the need to help bolster the democracies through the shipment of arms. "We are interested in seeing that there is maintained in Europe a substantial balance of power," he concluded, "because if any one group obtains absolute power over Europe and Asia then we are faced with the defense of the Monroe Doctrine in Latin America."[43] The next day, Pittman formally introduced his bill in Congress, carefully pointing out that it represented his own views and not those of either the State Department or President Roosevelt.[44]

The congressional reaction to Pittman's bill revealed the difficult struggle facing the administration. The isolationists, led by Senator Borah, strongly condemned the proposed repeal of the arms embargo. In a statement to the press on March 19, Borah urged that the arms embargo not only be retained, but that it be extended to include all war supplies. Instead of selling war materials, Borah wanted the United States to proclaim to the world, "We will not contribute in any way to mass murder."[45] Senators

[42] The text of the Pittman bill (Senate Joint Resolution 97) is printed in the *Congressional Record*, March 20, 1939, p. 2923.

[43] *Ibid.*, March 20, 1939, p. 2925.

[44] *Ibid.*, p. 2923; *New York Times*, March 20, 1939, p. 1.

[45] *Congressional Record*, March 20, 1939, p. 2926.

Nye, Clark, and Bone responded to the Pittman bill by introducing a measure of their own to retain the 1937 act and strengthen it by adding a mandatory cash-and-carry section for all exports other than arms.[46] At the other extreme, Senators Thomas of Utah and Claude Pepper of Florida advocated the policy embodied in the Thomas amendment of discriminating against aggressors. A poll of the Senate Foreign Relations Committee conducted by the *New York Times* revealed that still another group of senators favored the total repeal of all neutrality legislation, while a majority had not yet decided which alternative they would support.[47] In this confused picture, only one fact stood out clearly—the failure of the administration to put forward its own neutrality program had created a hopeless tangle of conflicting proposals which ruled out any chance for a prompt decision by Congress.

The severest criticism of the Pittman bill came from the Chinese government. On March 27 the American embassy in Chungking informed Hull that the Chinese foreign office was "very unhappy" with the proposed legislation. In particular, the Chinese objected to the clause requiring the President to invoke the law in the case of undeclared wars. They pointed out that if the measure were passed by Congress, all trade between the United States and Far Eastern belligerents would have to be conducted on a cash-and-carry basis, which would give Japan, with its control of the sea, an enormous advantage.[48] Two days later, the Chinese ambassador in Washington handed Hull a personal letter of protest from Chiang Kai-shek to the President. When the ambassador expressed his own "apprehension" over the cash-and-carry clause of the Pittman bill, Hull tried to reassure him. "I replied that of course he knew where the personal sympathies of Senator Pittman and mostly all others here lie," the Secretary noted.[49]

[46] *New York Times*, March 29, 1939, p. 9.

[47] *Ibid.*, March 26, 1939, p. 1.

[48] Telegram from Willys R. Peck, Chargé d'Affaires at Chungking, to Hull, March 27, 1939, 811.04418/362.

[49] Memorandum of conversation with Dr. Hu Shih by Hull, March 29, 1939, 811.04418/372.

Nevertheless, the Chinese protests continued. Newspapers in China bitterly denounced the cash-and-carry proposal, pleading for the United States to draw a distinction between aggressors and their victims. On April 9, Dr. H. H. Kung, president of the Executive Yuan, appealed directly to Senator Pittman. "We are painfully surprised to find that it [the Pittman bill] fails to distinguish between the aggressor and victim, thereby tending to penalize China in face of Japan's aggression," Kung wrote.[50]

When the State Department brought these protests to the attention of President Roosevelt, he immediately revealed his sympathy for China's position. In a letter to Hull on March 28, the President stated that the cash-and-carry plan "works all wrong in the Pacific. The more I think the problem through, the more I am convinced that the existing Neutrality Act should be repealed *in toto* without any substitute. I do not mind if you pass this word to Senator Pittman and the leaders."[51] The State Department then proceeded to inform Pittman of the weakness of his bill in regard to the Far East, sending him paraphrases of dispatches from Chungking and a critical analysis of his measure's probable effect on China.[52] After a two-and-a-half hour conference with the State Department experts on April 25, Pittman drew up a separate resolution to accompany his neutrality bill. This new proposal, introduced in Congress on April 27, empowered the President to embargo both imports and exports to any country guilty of violating the Nine-Power Treaty.[53] Since the United States had already accused Japan of violating this agreement, the Pittman resolution would have in effect permitted Roosevelt to prevent Japan from taking advantage of the cash-and-carry provisions in the Peace Act of 1939.

[50] *New York Times*, March 28, 1939, p. 10; *ibid.*, April 2, 1939, p. 36; Kung to Pittman, April 9, 1939, SCP, File 76A-F9.

[51] Elliott Roosevelt (ed.), *F.D.R.: His Personal Letters, 1928–1945* (2 vols.; New York, 1950), II, 873.

[52] Memorandums by Department of State, March and April, 1939, SCP, File 76A-E2; memorandum by Stanley K. Hornbeck, April 10, 1939, SCP, File 76A-E2.

[53] *New York Times*, April 26, 1939, p. 12; *ibid.*, April 28, 1939, p. 4.

The Pittman resolution pleased the Chinese government and met with a favorable reception from the American people. In a Gallup poll taken on May 18, 72 per cent of the persons interviewed expressed their approval of a ban on the sale of war materials to Japan.[54] Yet at the same time, the new resolution highlighted the inconsistency in the American approach to neutrality legislation. The administration's main goal was to revise the existing act so as to guarantee aid to nations resisting aggression. But Roosevelt and Hull dared not challenge the strong public feeling that the United States should avoid any risk of involvement in European or Asian conflicts. The result was the cash-and-carry formula, which preserved the superficial appearance of impartial neutrality but which in reality was designed to aid the European democracies in the approaching war with Germany. When it became apparent that this formula did not fit the Far Eastern situation, the State Department, instead of abandoning all pretense of neutrality as Roosevelt evidently preferred, chose to press for a special policy of discrimination against Japan. The administration, by rejecting the Thomas amendment—the only legislative proposal clearly embodying the basic objectives of Roosevelt's foreign policy—had undermined its entire effort to revise the 1937 neutrality act.

III

Formal congressional consideration of the neutrality issue finally began on April 5, 1939, when the Senate Foreign Relations Committee opened public hearings on the various proposals to revise the 1937 act. Senator Pittman had hoped to avoid the ordeal of a lengthy committee discussion, but his colleagues voted 11 to 8 to hold the hearings and then rejected a motion to limit the proceedings to a two-week period.[55] This decision virtually doomed any chance for legislative action before May 1, the date on which

[54] Willys R. Peck (Chungking) to Hull, May 9, 1939, 811.04418/440; Cantril and Strunk, *Public Opinion*, p. 1157.

[55] *New York Times,* March 30, 1939, p. 8.

the temporary cash-and-carry provisions were due to expire. Shortly after the Senate hearings commenced, the House Committee on Foreign Affairs decided to conduct its own public session. As a result, throughout April and most of May the two committees heard a wide variety of testimony on all aspects of the neutrality issue. Though designed to acquaint the legislators with all sides of the issue, the hearings tended only to heighten the confusion in Congress on the complex neutrality problem.

On the morning of April 5, an overflow crowd gathered in the large caucus room of the Senate Office Building to hear the first witness, former Secretary of State Henry L. Stimson, give the Senate committee his views on neutrality legislation. All but one of the committee members were present when Senator Pittman called the session to order. The entire Washington press corps was in attendance, and the spectators included Senator Nye, conspicuously jotting down notes during the proceedings, and J. Pierrepont Moffat, sent by Hull to record his "personal impressions" of the reactions of individual senators to the various witnesses. As the hearings continued for the next six weeks, a series of prominent men, including Bernard M. Baruch, General Hugh S. Johnson, and Bainbridge Colby, Secretary of State in Wilson's administration, aired their views before the committee. In addition, the senators heard from representatives of pacifist groups, veterans' organizations, labor unions, patriotic societies, women's clubs, and ethnic bodies.[56] Meanwhile, the House hearings got under way. Despite invitations to such well-known Americans as Charles A. Lindbergh, Herbert Hoover, John Bassett Moore, Charles A. Beard, and Colonel Robert R. McCormick, the Foreign Affairs Committee was unable to attract any prominent witnesses. Instead, a half-dozen congressmen, along with the spokes-

[56] "Neutrality, Peace Legislation, and Our Foreign Policy," *Hearings before the Senate Committee on Foreign Relations*, 76th Cong., 1st sess. (Washington, 1939); *New York Times*, April 6, 1939, p. 11; Moffat Diary, April 4, 1939.

men for pressure groups, gave most of the testimony.[57] As these two sets of hearings dragged on into May, the original interest in them withered before the seemingly endless stream of warnings, impassioned pleas, and trite arguments. Newspapers and periodicals, which had reported fully on the opening sessions, turned to more lively subjects; the ranks of spectators in the caucus rooms thinned each day; and even the committee members began to absent themselves more and more frequently.

In the course of the hearings, four distinct viewpoints emerged. Surprisingly, the largest number of witnesses supported the Thomas amendment, advocating a policy which would permit the United States to co-operate with the other nations to oppose aggression. Stimson stated this position most clearly. Warning that the world was facing its greatest crisis in history, he declared that the threat of aggression overseas directly imperiled American security in the Western Hemisphere. He pleaded for broad discretionary power so that the President could take "economic action" to restrain aggressor nations. Throughout his remarks, Stimson avoided moral arguments, stressing the need to protect American security rather than aid democracy abroad. "Should a general war come in Europe this spring," he contended, "this Neutrality Act might put us in the position of facilitating a result of that war which would make the United States the next victim of attack."[58] Other witnesses, especially international lawyers and spokesmen for internationalist peace groups, took the same position. "We cannot live peacefully in a lawless world," declared Charles Fenwick, a college professor from Bryn Mawr. "We are not crusading to make the world safe for democracy, we are trying to protect our own right to live at peace in the world." Adopting as their slogan, "No trade with treaty-breakers," the collective security enthusiasts claimed that the Thomas amendment provided the only feasible way to use

57 "American Neutrality Policy," *Hearings before the House Committee on Foreign Affairs*, 76th Cong., 1st sess. (Washington, 1939); letter files, April, 1939, HCP, File 76A-F17.3.

58 "Neutrality," Senate *Hearings*, 76th Cong., 1st sess., pp. 3–4, 7, 10–12, 24.

American influence to prevent the outbreak of war, and thus guarantee peace for the United States.[59]

Representatives of labor unions, veterans' groups, and the isolationist peace societies appeared in large numbers to defend mandatory neutrality legislation. Warning that war was inevitable in Europe, they praised the 1937 act as an effective and proven safeguard for the United States. "This is no time for experimentation," declared a spokesman for the AF of L, while Dr. Thomas Healy, dean of the School of Foreign Service at Georgetown University, argued that the "sole purpose" of the 1937 act "was to keep America out of foreign wars, and it has done that."[60] Isolationists sharply challenged the view that aggression abroad endangered American security. Ridiculing the possibility of foreign attack, a Dartmouth professor asserted, "Whatever happens in Europe or Asia, the United States is safe as a kitten in its basket—entirely safe."[61] Dismissing the Thomas amendment as an obvious invitation to war, the neutrality bloc concentrated its attack on the Pittman bill. Left-wing spokesmen condemned cash-and-carry as an insidious device to wring profits from foreign wars. "You cannot have the profit system and have peace—take your choice," a Socialist told the House committee.[62] Other isolationists hammered away at the unneutral objective of the Pittman bill. A representative of the National Council for the Prevention of War opposed cash-and-carry "because it is a deliberate and calculated attempt to put us in a position to take sides with Great Britain and France." A Pennsylvania congressman stated more forcefully, "The design of the [Pittman] bill is just as peaceful as a dynamite bomb." In rejecting both the Thomas amendment and the Pittman bill, the neutrality bloc called instead for an extension of the arms embargo

[59] *Ibid.*, pp. 168, 181, 555; "American Neutrality Policy," House *Hearings*, 76th Cong., 1st sess., pp. 177–78, 186, 537–38.

[60] *Ibid.*, pp. 70–72; "Neutrality," Senate *Hearings*, 76th Cong., 1st sess., p. 321.

[61] *Ibid.*, p. 562; "American Neutrality Policy," House *Hearings*, 76th Cong., 1st sess., p. 156.

[62] *Ibid.*, pp. 139, 296, 418–19.

to include all war materials. They warned that only a policy of absolute insulation from foreign wars could insure American neutrality in the coming world conflict.[63]

A third group of witnesses at the hearings urged the repeal of the 1937 act and a return to the traditional principles of international law. The majority taking this position presented themselves as isolationists. Using arguments popularized by Edwin Borchard and John Bassett Moore, they claimed that international law provided "the safest guide and surest foundation for national policy and legislation in so unsettled a time as the present." They denied that traditional neutrality had caused American entry into war in 1917. "We were dragged into the World War, not because of our original neutrality policy," asserted Congressman Maas of Minnesota, "but because we failed to enforce and defend that policy."[64] In particular, they condemned the cash-and-carry policy as a cowardly surrender of American rights on the high seas. "It has always been our impression," stated a representative of the CIO Maritime Committee, "that the Navy was built for the purpose of protecting our foreign trade routes and therefore it was built to protect the merchant marine." Another witness declared, "American commerce should be allowed to engage in perfectly legitimate trade at all times."[65] A few of those advocating total repeal attacked the existing legislation for its support of aggression. "It strikes me," stated a Republican congressman from New York, "that this thing is brutally unneutral in its effect: it penalizes the little fellow, and does it deliberately." Dorothy Thompson, the prominent newspaper columnist, agreed, urging a flexible policy of presidential discretion.[66] Yet most of the advocates of international law were nationalists, unconcerned over aggression abroad but determined

[63] *Ibid.*, pp. 62–64, 448–50; "Neutrality," Senate *Hearings*, 76th Cong., 1st sess., pp. 528, 538, 543.

[64] *Ibid.*, pp. 68, 510–12; "American Neutrality Policy," House *Hearings*, 76th Cong., 1st sess., pp. 10–12, 27.

[65] *Ibid.*, pp. 23, 37, 210, 492.

[66] *Ibid.*, pp. 31–32; "Neutrality," Senate *Hearings*, 76th Cong., 1st sess., pp. 322–26.

to assert American rights and defend American interests at all costs.

The supporters of cash-and-carry and the Pittman bill formed the last, and the smallest, category of witnesses. Bernard M. Baruch was the most effective proponent of this position. Pointing out that there was no valid distinction between arms and raw materials in modern warfare, Baruch championed cash-and-carry as the only sensible compromise between the two extremes of total embargo, which would disrupt the economy, and economic sanctions, which would lead to war. General Hugh S. Johnson and Breckenridge Long, who had served as ambassador to Italy during the Ethiopian crisis, strongly endorsed Baruch's argument. Both warned against any attempt to punish aggressors, with Johnson ridiculing the idea that "you can fight an economic war and starve women and children and yet avoid military war."[67] Only one witness, Raymond L. Buell of the Foreign Policy Association, openly advocated cash-and-carry as a means of aiding England and France. Stating that the United States had nothing to fear from the European democracies, he warned that if the Axis powers were victorious in Europe, "their next objective will be the rich resources of the Western Hemisphere."[68]

By the time the hearings came to an end in May, no consensus on neutrality legislation had emerged in Congress. Indeed, there was not even a clear-cut alignment between isolationists and supporters of collective security. The isolationists were divided; some, led by Nye, still favored rigid neutrality legislation and others, notably Hiram Johnson and William E. Borah, leaned toward total repeal. Among those favoring revision, there was a similar split. The more active internationalists championed the Thomas amendment, while Pittman continued to press for his compromise cash-and-carry measure. In late April, Pittman tried hard to win over the supporters of the Thomas amendment. He explained in a letter to Baruch on April 26 that he could count on ten senators

[67] *Ibid.*, pp. 53–56, 74, 215–16, 277–78.

[68] *Ibid.*, pp. 235–37.

of the twenty-three on his committee to support cash-and-carry. "I am sure," he added, "that two more will come to me after the Thomas amendment is defeated."[69] Four days later, he wrote to Henry L. Stimson, asking him to urge backers of the Thomas amendment to shift their support to his cash-and-carry proposal. "I fear that the divisions of opinion among the leading peace societies in the country will tend to prevent any legislation at all," he warned.[70] Yet despite these appeals, Pittman was unable to rally a majority of the committee behind his bill. With the President maintaining his silence on neutrality revision, the Democrats in Congress continued to divide their support between the Thomas and Pittman proposals. Thus, four months after Roosevelt's original plea for revision of the neutrality legislation, Congress had not taken a single concrete step toward this goal.

During this protracted period of legislative procrastination, the debate over revision had spread from Congress to the nation at large. Newspapers, magazines, pressure groups, and civic bodies all discussed the relevant issues and attempted to reach intelligent conclusions. But the result paralleled that in Congress—growing confusion and uncertainty over the wide range of alternatives. The public opinion polls for this period reveal a trend in favor of removing the arms embargo. In a poll taken on February 16, 1939, 52 per cent of those interviewed said that they favored selling military equipment to England and France if war broke out. The number approving the export of arms rose to 66 per cent immediately after the German seizure of Czechoslovakia, and then leveled off at 57 per cent at the end of the month.[71] Though there was probably a slim majority in favor of ending the arms embargo, as the polls suggest, the over-all difference of opinion on neutrality legislation was more accurately reflected in newspaper editorials. The State Department, which was carefully taking the

[69] Pittman to Baruch, April 26, 1939, SCP, File 76A-F9.

[70] Pittman to Stimson, April 30, 1939, SCP, File 76A-F9.

[71] Cantril and Strunk, *Public Opinion*, pp. 1156–57.

public pulse, arrived at the following breakdown of editorial opinion in the spring of 1939:[72]

Editorial Stand	March (Per Cent)	April (Per Cent)	May 1-15 (Per Cent)
Cash-and-carry	10	12	32.2
Rigid neutrality	30	33	24.7
Flexible neutrality	18	12	4.0
Repeal of 1937 act	20	6	15.8
No definite opinion	22	37	23.3

The evident trend toward cash-and-carry and the rapid decline in popularity of flexible neutrality, including the Thomas amendment, indicated that the public was gravitating toward the Pittman bill. Yet the continued support for rigid neutrality and the high percentage of indecisive editorials reflected the still uncertain temper of public opinion.

The wide divergence in viewpoint on revision also ran through the pressure groups interested in neutrality legislation. Most businessmen favored the repeal of the arms embargo, but there was little agreement beyond this point. Exporters favored traditional neutral rights; a former president of the United States Chamber of Commerce backed the Thomas amendment; several business journals supported Baruch's plan for a cash-and-carry policy.[73] Labor was similarly split, with the AF of L favoring the arms embargo while the CIO called for its repeal.[74] Among religious bodies, the division which had been evident throughout the 1930's grew even deeper. The Federal Council of Churches, representing the major Protestant denominations, was divided evenly between

[72] Memorandums from Joseph C. Green to James C. Dunn, April 12, 1939, 811.04418/390; April 26, 1939, 811.04418/411; May 13, 1939, 811.04418/417; May 29, 1939, 811.04418/431.

[73] *Report of the Twenty-fifth National Foreign Trade Convention, 1938* (New York, 1939), p. xxii; *New York Times*, May 17, 1939, p. 12; "How To Be Neutral," *Magazine of Wall Street*, LXIV (July 14, 1939), 318; "Sound Sense," *Commercial and Financial Chronicle*, CXLVIII (April 8, 1939), 2009.

[74] *New York Times*, May 20, 1939, p. 12; "Neutrality," Senate *Hearings*, 76th Cong., 1st sess., p. 321; "American Neutrality Policy," House *Hearings*, 76th Cong., 1st sess., p. 492.

mandatory neutrality and the Thomas amendment. When the Senate Foreign Relations Committee asked the leader of this organization to testify at the hearings, he declined, stating, "I do not feel sufficient unanimity in church circles at present time to justify statement."[75] There was greater agreement among Catholics, with the two leading Catholic journals of opinion, as well as most of the faculty at Georgetown University, staunchly defending the 1937 act.[76]

The most clearly defined polarity occurred within the ranks of the peace movement. The internationalist peace societies, led by the League of Nations Association, the National Conference on the Cause and Cure of War, and the Carnegie Endowment for World Peace, had formed the Committee for Concerted Peace Efforts in the fall of 1938 and had subsequently directed the campaign for the Thomas amendment. This committee co-ordinated the efforts of some fourteen major peace and women's societies, held mass meetings in various cities, and celebrated "Peace and Security Week" in late April, 1937.[77] On the other side, the National Council for the Prevention of War, the Women's International League, World Peaceways, and the Fellowship of Reconciliation spearheaded the fight to retain the arms embargo. In *Peace Action*, Frederick J. Libby constantly questioned Roosevelt's motive in calling for neutrality revision and warned that repeal of the arms embargo "would give the Executive the power to choose sides and involve the United States in a foreign war."[78] This dissension among the pacifists even disrupted the college antiwar strikes in the spring of 1939. A majority of the campus

[75] "Neutrality," Senate *Hearings*, 76th Cong., 1st sess., p. 130; Samuel H. Cavert to Pittman, April 5, 1939, SCP, File 76A-F9.

[76] "Our Views on Neutrality," *Commonweal*, XXIX (February 17, 1939), 452–53; "The Carry Clause," *America*, LXI (June 24, 1939), 254.

[77] "Neutrality," Senate *Hearings*, 76th Cong., 1st sess., p. 127; William H. Hinckley to Pittman, February 14, 1939, SCP, File 76A-E2; *New York Times*, March 26, 1939, II, 5; *ibid.*, April 28, 1939, p. 4.

[78] "Neutrality," Senate *Hearings*, 76th Cong., 1st sess., p. 125; *Peace Action*, V (December, 1938), 4–5; *ibid.*, V (Summer, 1939), 1–3.

youth, led by the American Student Union, renounced the Oxford oath and demonstrated in favor of Roosevelt's policy of co-operation against aggressors, while a minority, headed by the Youth Committee against War, doggedly maintained their pacifist ideals and agitated for mandatory neutrality legislation. At New York University, the two factions compromised and held a joint rally at which three speakers for each viewpoint spoke to a "united front" audience.[79]

The disagreement on neutrality revision even cut across party lines. In the Gallup polls, the breakdown of choices by political preference revealed that voters of both parties favored repeal of the arms embargo by almost identical margins.[80] Among political leaders, the majority of Democrats backed the administration's call for revision, but there was a strong minority, led by Bennett C. Clark in the Senate and Louis Ludlow in the House, who announced their firm opposition to any change in the 1937 act.[81] The Republican leaders of the neutrality bloc, Senator Gerald P. Nye and Congressman Hamilton Fish, represented the dominant view of their party. In April, in an effort to rally the supporters of mandatory legislation, Fish organized the National Committee to Keep America Out of Foreign Wars. Fish had the support of fifty other Republican members of Congress, and he announced that their purpose was to combat "the inspired and dangerous White House war propaganda."[82] Other Republican leaders, though opposing Roosevelt's program of measures short of war to halt aggression, favored repealing the arms embargo and returning to traditional international law. Former President Herbert Hoover took this position in a widely reported speech in February. "The arms embargo," Hoover charged, "compels us to take sides rather

[79] *New York Times*, April 20, 1939, p. 9; *ibid.*, April 21, 1939, p. 10.

[80] Cantril and Strunk, *Public Opinion*, p. 1156; *New York Times*, April 14, 1939, p. 5.

[81] "American Neutrality Policy," House *Hearings*, 76th Cong., 1st sess., pp. 418–19; *New York Times*, March 29, 1939, p. 91.

[82] *Congressional Record*, April 11, 1939, Appendix, p. 1396; *New York Times*, April 14, 1939, p. 12.

than be neutral."[83] This broad difference in viewpoint inside the party finally led the House minority leader, Joseph W. Martin, Jr., to announce in April that the Republicans would not make neutrality revision a partisan issue. "There are too many varieties of opinion on our own side of the House," Martin declared. "Every man will have to speak for himself."[84] The political confusion also carried over to the left-wing groups. Norman Thomas firmly announced the support of the Socialist party for the existing neutrality act at the House hearings, but the American League for Peace and Democracy, the main instrument for Communist agitation on foreign policy issues, demanded the adoption of the Thomas amendment to halt aggressors. "It will help make it possible," the secretary of this organization wrote Cordell Hull, "for the United States to aid those victims of aggression who are in the front line trenches in defense of democracy."[85]

The wide divergence in views expressed in the spring of 1939 indicates both the complexity of the neutrality issue and the uncertainty of the American people. Though nearly everyone agreed on the imminence of war abroad, there was no clear support for any single policy that would keep the United States out of danger. This fact in itself is significant, for it marked the decline of the once-popular belief that rigid neutrality legislation would safeguard America in time of war. The experience in China and Spain, coupled with a growing awareness of Hitler's menace to the entire world, had destroyed for many the illusion that a simple withdrawal from the world could insure peace and security at home. The majority of Americans, however, still distrusted the opposing concept that the nation could best defend itself by co-operating against aggression abroad. The result was a stalemate in which a large number of perplexed and undecided people held the balance between the conflicting concepts of rigid and discretionary neu-

[83] *Ibid.*, February 2, 1939, p. 6.

[84] *Ibid.*, April 8, 1939, p. 6.

[85] "American Neutrality Policy," House *Hearings*, 76th Cong., 1st sess., pp. 133–35; *New York Times*, January 7, 1939, p. 3; Leona Poliner to Hull, April 14, 1939, 811.04418/388.

trality. A nation torn by doubt and indecision needed more than ever before a clear-cut call to action from the White House. Roosevelt's request in January for measures short of war and a revision of the neutrality legislation had touched a responsive chord in the American people. Now the times demanded that he abandon his cautious maneuvering and give the firm, incisive leadership which alone could forge a majority in Congress and in the nation for the neutrality revision which he felt was so essential in the unfolding world crisis.

IV

Throughout April and May the administration struggled to define a coherent program of neutrality revision. On April 6, the day after the Senate hearings opened, Cordell Hull called in his eight leading advisers on neutrality and began to discuss with them the statement he would make when he appeared before the Senate Foreign Relations Committee at the close of the hearings. These meetings, held two or three times a week for the next two months, progressed very slowly. Hull would throw out an issue and then sit back and listen while his aides talked back and forth. After several sessions, the group agreed on the general theme that Hull would present to the senators, but the process of deciding on specific proposals was time-consuming. "Obviously," noted J. Pierrepont Moffat, "nine or ten people cannot agree on details or shading of meanings, with the result that a great deal of time is lost in discussing nonessentials." Finally, on April 24, Moffat reported that the group had reached the point "where we are discussing draft statements rather than general principles." Hull had decided to advocate the main provisions of the Pittman bill, but he intended to limit cash-and-carry to clearly defined combat areas in order to preserve the American shipping industry. In addition, the Secretary favored making the bill apply only to future conflicts so that the existing war in China could be exempted. As a defense against hostile questioning by isolationists, especially

Hiram Johnson, Hull's advisers urged the Secretary to be vague in his statement to the committee, "a procedure," noted Moffat, "at which he is a past master."[86]

While the State Department worked out its stand on neutrality legislation, the administration did not state its views publicly. In a speech at the University of Virginia on April 13, however, Undersecretary of State Sumner Welles indicated the government's basic viewpoint. Stating that he was speaking only as a private citizen, Welles declared that the United States could best advance the cause of peace "by permitting nations which suffer attack to obtain such supplies, including munitions, as they may require for their self-defense. . . ."[87] A week later, President Roosevelt held a special press conference for the nation's newspaper editors in which he touched on the issue of neutrality. Stating that "we have to try to do everything we can to prevent messes in the war zone," Roosevelt advocated legislation to keep American ships out of combat areas. On cash-and-carry, the President expressed his general agreement, but he pointed out that it would aid the Japanese in the Pacific. ". . . it is a terribly difficult thing," Roosevelt concluded, "to write down a hard and fast law that will apply with equal justice everywhere in the world." Beyond these mild words of caution, the President offered no ringing appeal for action and indeed he seemed content to let the question of neutrality revision drift along.[88]

The expiration of the cash-and-carry provisions of the 1937 act on May 1 produced a new awareness of the need for decision. In a public statement on April 29, Senator Pittman warned that, without cash-and-carry, the United States would be forced to rely on traditional international law, with all the dangers this involved for American shipping on the high seas. Senator George W. Norris of Nebraska, who had voted against war in 1917, now came out in favor of Pittman's cash-and-carry proposal. Declaring his sym-

[86] Moffat Diary, April 4, 7, 10, 12, 17, 18, and 24, 1939.

[87] *New York Times*, April 14, 1939, p. 5.

[88] Press conference No. 540A, American Society of Newspaper Editors, April 20, 1939, FDR Papers, PPF 1-P, XIII, 319.

pathy for England and France, Norris stated, "If we can pass a law that will rebound to their benefit, without violating the principles of neutrality, that is the kind of law I want to pass."[89] The neutrality bloc was divided in its response to the expiration of cash-and-carry. Senator Nye said he would not press for continuation of the 1937 cash-and-carry provisions because they gave the President excessive discretion, but Senator Vandenberg countered with a resolution to continue the provisions of the 1937 act indefinitely. The Michigan senator then recommended that the Senate abandon any further effort at revision of the neutrality statute, warning that the world situation was too explosive to permit further experimentation on this issue.[90] Vandenberg's suggestion strongly appealed to a growing number of senators, led by minority leader Charles L. McNary of Oregon and John H. Bankhead, an Alabama Democrat, who had been proposing an early adjournment of the Senate. This group proposed that the House and Senate committees study the neutrality question at greater length and make their recommendations when Congress met again in 1940.[91]

By May 3 the situation had become critical. Moffat reported that in the Senate he had heard "everything from a rumor that the Administration wants complete repeal to the rumor that the Administration wants nothing done." He observed that Pittman's leadership had disintegrated, that Hull was "looking harassed," and that Roosevelt was "afraid to enter the picture for fear of the reaction against his personal wishes."[92] Though the State Department experts still could not agree on many points, Hull held daily sessions in his office to prepare his statement to the Senate committee. And the process had become even more tedious. "I sat in for an hour and saw one paragraph approved," Moffat noted in his diary. "I was out of the room for an hour and a half and came

[89] *New York Times*, April 30, 1939, p. 32.

[90] *Ibid.*, May 1, 1939, p. 17; *ibid.*, May 5, 1939, p. 9.

[91] *Ibid.*, April 27, 1939, p. 10; *ibid.*, May 3, 1939, p. 10.

[92] Moffat Diary, May 3, 1939.

back to find the group still working on the second paragraph."[93] Then, on May 8, Senator Pittman came down to the State Department, read the Secretary's proposed statement, and "remarked acidly that that sort of presentation would do no good." Stating that the committee demanded that Hull appear at a public session, Pittman warned that Senators Borah and Johnson wished to question Hull on the relationship of neutrality revision to American policy toward England, France, and China. Fearful of the effect of this isolationist onslaught on public opinion, Hull reluctantly decided to cancel his appearance before the Senate Foreign Relations Committee. "Ten days' work on the part of eight high officials of the Department has gone into the wastepaper basket," Moffat commented.[94]

The sudden change in the administration's strategy greatly alarmed the British and the French, who had been carefully observing the course of the neutrality debate. In March and April the French ambassador had frequently asked State Department officials about the possibility of revising the 1937 act, expressing his concern over the repeated delay.[95] On May 10, Moffat explained to him the reasons for Hull's decision not to appear before the Senate committee and tried to assure this worried diplomat that the administration would still press for new legislation.[96] The same day Ambassador William C. Bullitt reported on a conversation he had held with the British ambassador in Paris. "The British Government . . . considered it of highest importance that the modification of the Neutrality Act should if possible be brought about in the near future," he cabled. "Such a modification of the Neutrality Act would end all chance that Ribbentrop [Ger-

[93] *Ibid.*, May 4, 5, and 6, 1939.

[94] *Ibid.*, May 8, 1939; *Hull Memoirs*, I, 642.

[95] Memorandums of conversations with French ambassador by Joseph C. Green, March 21, 1939, 811.04418/371, and May 5, 1939, 811.04418/424; memorandum of conversation with French ambassador by J. Pierrepont Moffat, April 12, 1939, *FR: 1939*, I, 126–27.

[96] Memorandum of conversation with French ambassador by Moffat, May 10, 1939, 811.04418/425.

man Foreign Minister] might persuade Hitler to risk immediate war. Bonnet [French Foreign Minister] said the same thing to me tonight."[97] In a memorandum to Roosevelt two days later, R. Walton Moore cited Bullitt's telegram in urging the President to use his influence to break the log jam in Congress on neutrality revision.[98]

The failure of Senator Pittman's leadership in the Senate, the growing movement in Congress for postponement of the neutrality issue, and the insistent pressure from the British and French governments finally led the administration to begin exploring the possibility of initiating its legislative program in the House of Representatives. In March the House committee had expressed a desire to report out its own neutrality bill, but the State Department had discouraged this move because it lacked confidence in the acting chairman of the House committee, Representative Sol Bloom of New York.[99] Bloom, who had taken charge of the Foreign Affairs Committee when Congressman McReynolds suffered a crippling heart attack in the fall of 1938, was a colorful and flamboyant figure who had little knowledge of the complex neutrality issue. Born in Illinois, Bloom had built up a fortune first as a sheet-music publisher and then later as a real estate dealer in New York City. He had been elected to Congress in 1923 and had won a reputation as a bouncy, smiling extrovert whose amusing antics made him an easy target for ridicule by his political opponents.[100] Throughout the spring of 1939, Bloom repeatedly asked the State Department to let him lead the administration's drive for neutrality revision in Congress. After Pittman discouraged Hull's appearance before his committee, the State Department finally began to consider this alternative. On May 10, Joseph C. Green attended an executive meeting of the House

[97] Bullitt to Hull, May 10, 1939, *FR: 1939*, I, 185.

[98] Moore to Roosevelt, May 12, 1939, FDR Papers, PSF, Box 33.

[99] Memorandum from Joseph C. Green to Sumner Welles, March 21, 1939, 811.04418/365; Welles to Green, March 23, 1939, 811.04418/366.

[100] "Bloom's Rise," *Newsweek*, XIV (July 17, 1939), 15–16.

Foreign Affairs Committee and handed Bloom a draft bill for his group to study.[101] Two days later, Bloom conferred with the President. Though the New York congressman denied that he discussed the neutrality issue with Roosevelt, a memorandum by Moore, sent to Roosevelt prior to the meeting with Bloom, indicates that this was their major topic of conversation. Moore, expressing strong reservations about Bloom's leadership abilities, warned that "he has in mind legislation vesting practically unlimited discretion in the Executive which, while very desirable, is hardly within the range of possibility. I have thought that you may believe it wise to urge Bloom to talk with Pittman at once."[102]

There is no record of Bloom's conversation with the President, but Roosevelt evidently did not consent to shifting the neutrality battle to the House. Then, on May 16, Pittman dealt the administration another staggering blow. In a letter to Hull, he calmly announced that he planned to postpone any further consideration of neutrality revision for several weeks. "The situation in Europe," Pittman wrote, "does not seem to induce any urgent action on neutrality legislation."[103] The next day, Hull, thoroughly angered by Pittman's procrastination, became irate when the House Foreign Affairs Committee invited him to testify at a public hearing. Announcing that he would not subject himself to cross-examination by Hamilton Fish, the Secretary criticized Bloom for failure to control his committee.[104] But despite this outburst Hull finally decided to allow Bloom to go ahead with neutrality revision. In a meeting at the State Department on May 18, Hull approved a draft bill which would repeal the arms embargo and bar American shipping from entering combat zones, but which would not include any cash-and-carry provisions.[105]

[101] *New York Times*, May 4, 1939, p. 7; memorandum by Joseph C. Green, May 10, 1939, 811.04418/423.

[102] *New York Times*, May 13, 1939, p. 6; Moore to Roosevelt, May 12, 1939, FDR Papers, PSF, Box 33.

[103] Pittman to Hull, May 16, 1939, SCP, File 76A-F9; Moffat Diary, May 16, 1939.

[104] Moffat Diary, May 17, 1939; *New York Times*, May 17, 1939, p. 12.

[105] Moffat Diary, May 18, 1939.

The final decision on administration strategy came at a White House conference on May 19, attended by Hull, Bloom, Speaker William B. Bankhead, and House Majority Leader Sam Rayburn. Using a memorandum prepared by R. Walton Moore which warned that the existing legislation would cripple British and French resistance to Germany in case of war, Roosevelt made a vigorous plea for repeal of the arms embargo. According to Hull, the President stated that "this would actually prevent the outbreak of war in Europe, or, if it did not, it would make less likely a victory for the powers unfriendly to the United States." Stressing the overriding importance of the arms embargo, Roosevelt indicated that he cared less about the other provisions of the legislation, though he expressed approval of a combat zone clause and "saw no objection" to the cash-and-carry formula. When Bankhead and Rayburn voiced their fears that the House might not accept this program, Roosevelt made clear his determination to press the issue regardless of the opposition it would create. Urging prompt action, the President expressed his hope that the House could act favorably before the forthcoming visit of the king and queen of England, who were due to arrive in the United States on June 12.[106]

The White House conference marked a significant turning point in the long struggle for revision. At last, Roosevelt had decided to commit the administration to an all-out effort to repeal the arms embargo. After more than four months of delay and confusion, the government had adopted a clear-cut program and was prepared to risk defeat in a concerted effort to reshape the nation's foreign policy. In the State Department, the high officials resumed their meetings with a new sense of purpose. In daily sessions, they reshaped the draft of Hull's statement to the Senate committee into a public letter to Representative Bloom and Sena-

[106] Moore to Roosevelt, May 19, 1939, FDR Papers, PSF, Box 33; *Hull Memoirs*, I, 643; memorandum by Carleton Savage, May 19, 1939, quoted in Langer and Gleason, *Challenge to Isolation*, pp. 138–39. At a cabinet meeting the same day, Roosevelt announced his determination to have Congress repeal the arms embargo. *The Secret Diary of Harold Ickes* (3 vols.; New York, 1953–54), II, 637.

tor Pittman which would clearly delineate the administration's position on neutrality legislation.[107] Meanwhile, Hull held a series of conferences with the Democratic members of both the House and Senate committees at his apartment in the Carleton Hotel. In this way, he was able to impress upon friendly congressmen and senators the administration's desire for revision without undergoing the ordeal of cross-examination by isolationist Republicans. This procedure enraged Hamilton Fish, who denounced Hull's secret meetings as "undemocratic and un-American."[108]

On May 26 the State Department experts completed the letter to Bloom and Pittman amid an atmosphere of growing uncertainty. Moffat reported that the congressional leaders had told Hull that "no one knows what would happen if the measure came on the floor." "In fact," Moffat commented, "the feeling is so fluid that the Legislature has been likened to a flock of sheep in a pen where if one sheep jumped out in a given direction all the rest would immediately follow after. The only trouble is no one could calculate just which side of the pen the first sheep would jump out." The great fear of the administration was a Senate filibuster that would doom the legislation even if the House acted favorably.[109] Nevertheless, Hull sent his letter to Roosevelt on the evening of May 26 for the President's approval. The letter came back with the notation:

CH

Excellent!

FDR[110]

The next afternoon, May 27, Hull sent his message to Bloom and Pittman, simultaneously releasing the text to the press. It was

[107] Moffat Diary, May 23, 25, and 26, 1939.

[108] *Ibid.*, May 17, 1939; *New York Times*, May 25, 1939, p. 14; *ibid.*, May 27, 1937, pp. 1, 4.

[109] Moffat Diary, May 23, 25, 26, and 27, 1939.

[110] Memorandum by Carleton Savage, May 27, 1939, 811.04418/434A. Savage stated that the letter to Bloom and Pittman was written by Sumner Welles, R. Walton Moore, Francis Sayre, Adolf Berle, Green H. Hackworth, James Dunn, Stanley K. Hornbeck, Herbert Feis, J. Pierrepont Moffat, Joseph C. Green, and Secretary Hull.

a calm, judicious statement which cautiously advocated a policy of preserving American neutrality while striving at the same time "to foster that state of relations among nations which will maintain the fabric of world peace." Hull warned against rigid, inflexible legislative restrictions. "The course of world affairs is unpredictable," he declared. "What we should try to do for the purpose of keeping this country out of war is to enact measures adapted to the safeguarding of our interests in all situations of which we can conceive and at the same time imposing a minimum of abnormal and unnecessary burdens upon our nationals. . . ." Pointing out that in modern warfare there was no valid distinction between munitions and raw materials, Hull called for a return to traditional international law through repeal of the arms embargo. The great danger of involvement in war, Hull maintained, came not from exports but from the movement of American ships and citizens into war zones. Therefore, Hull suggested a six-point neutrality program which would remove the arms embargo, ban American ships and travelers from combat areas, provide for the transfer of title on all exports to belligerents, and continue both the existing prohibitions on loans and credits and the licensing of arms exports by the National Munitions Control Board. These provisions, Hull concluded, "would make easier our twofold task of keeping this nation at peace and avoiding imposition of unnecessary and abnormal burdens upon our citizens."[111]

This letter represented the culmination of the long debate on neutrality revision which had gone on inside the administration since the fall of 1938. The ultimate goals had never been in question—as early as the preceding November the State Department experts had agreed on the necessity of repealing the arms embargo in favor of a modified cash-and-carry formula. The great disagreement had been on tactics and timing. Fearful of provoking an overwhelming reaction from isolationists in Congress, Roosevelt had tried to achieve his objective by indirect means. By allowing Senator Pittman to take charge of revision, the President had hoped to stay in the background while Congress took the initiative

[111] State Department, *Peace and War*, pp. 461–64.

in amending the neutrality legislation. Only in May, when the complete breakdown of Pittman's leadership became obvious, did Roosevelt finally decide to risk the administration's prestige in an all-out drive for revision. And even then, the President deliberately kept himself aloof from the battle, letting Cordell Hull state the administration's position. As a result, five months after the opening of Congress, the question of revision still resided on the lowest rung of the congressional ladder, awaiting action before the foreign affairs committees of the two Houses. Ahead lay the slow process of committee approval, floor debate, and final passage during the hectic and often unpredictable closing months of the congressional session. Given the complexity of the neutrality issue and the evident indecision of many congressmen, there seems to be little basis for Hull's confident statement to the French ambassador on May 27 that "in the end Congress would support our views as we were presenting them."[112]

V

With the publication of Hull's letter, the administration began a concerted effort to force congressional action on neutrality legislation. On May 29, Sol Bloom introduced a new neutrality resolution which embodied Hull's six-point program. The Bloom bill provided for repeal of the arms embargo and the adoption of a modified cash-and-carry formula—title to all exports to belligerents would have to be transferred before the goods left American ports, but American ships would be permitted to carry these cargoes to any area except combat zones designated by the President.[113] With the introduction of this resolution, the administration leaders began exerting intense pressure on Congress. Cordell Hull concentrated on Democratic congressmen, conferring with them by telephone and in person at his hotel apartment. "I gave the legis-

[112] Memorandum of conversation with the French ambassador by Hull, May 27, 1939, 811.04418/437.

[113] *New York Times*, May 29, 1939, p. 32; *ibid.*, May 30, 1939, p. 6.

lation top priority on my schedule," Hull later recorded, "since I considered it crucial in our foreign relations."[114] On May 30, Roosevelt added his voice to Hull's. In a press conference in the morning, he stressed the necessity for prompt action on the Bloom resolution. The following day he met with the Democratic leaders in Congress and impressed upon them his determination to enact neutrality revision before adjournment regardless of any effort by the isolationists to conduct a filibuster. In a note a few days later to R. Walton Moore, Roosevelt wrote, "I am pushing the Neutrality matter and hope you will see as many people in the House and Senate as you can."[115]

The House Foreign Affairs Committee began considering the Bloom bill on June 5. Two State Department officials, Hackworth and Moore, attended the executive sessions in an advisory capacity. Though Hull expressed himself as "delighted" with the first day's proceedings, he was startled the next day when the committee voted to repeal the arms embargo by the narrow margin of 11 to 9.[116] On June 7 the committee rejected a series of restrictive amendments put forward by Hamilton Fish but the smooth progress suddenly ended late in the day when a majority voted to suspend further discussion of the Bloom bill during the visit of the king and queen of England to the United States.[117] Finally, after nearly a week's delay, the House committee reported favorably on the Bloom bill on June 13. The vote followed party lines—twelve Democrats supported the measure while eight Republicans opposed it.[118]

As finally adopted by the House committee, the Bloom bill proposed four significant changes in the existing neutrality act. It

[114] *Hull Memoirs*, I, 645.

[115] *New York Times*, May 31, 1939, p. 1; *ibid.*, June 1, 1939, p. 2; Roosevelt to Moore, June 7, 1939, FDR Papers, PSF, Box 33.

[116] Moffat Diary, June 5 and 6, 1939; *New York Times*, June 6, 1939, p. 2.

[117] *Ibid.*, June 8, 1939, p. 10; *Commercial and Financial Chronicle*, CXLVIII (June 17, 1939), 3617.

[118] *New York Times*, June 14, 1939, p. 1.

repealed the arms embargo, granted the President discretion to invoke the act only when "it is necessary to promote the security or preserve the peace of the United States," allowed the President to decide when to apply the transfer of title provision as well as to select the types of exports to be covered by this clause, and authorized the President to designate combat zones which would be closed to both American ships and American travelers. In essence, this was an extremely flexible bill which proposed a very high degree of presidential discretion. In the majority report, Bloom argued that the wide latitude granted the President would "serve the double purpose of discouraging war and preventing this country from being involved in any foreign war that may possibly occur."[119] The Republican members, in their minority report, charged that the flexible provisions would enable the President to act unneutrally in behalf of a belligerent nation that he favored. Attacking the combat zone clause as especially dangerous, the Republicans asserted, "We should not evade our responsibility by granting the President additional power and conferring upon him additional responsibilities."[120]

The administration was pleased with the favorable committee action, but the strong Republican opposition led to renewed efforts to solidify Democratic support for the Bloom bill. Hull asked seven high-ranking State Department officials to prepare speeches on neutrality revision "to be used by his friends in the Senate or House in case of need." The Secretary also sent every congressman a copy of his May 27 letter. In an effort to sway wavering legislators, Hull sent three of his aides to a meeting of the Democratic steering committee on June 19. Despite these pressures, reporters noted that a considerable number of Democrats, including several congressmen representing Irish districts in New York City, were likely to vote against the Bloom bill.[121] At his press confer-

[119] "Neutrality Act of 1939," *House Report No. 856*, 76th Cong., 1st sess. (Washington, 1939), pp. 2–4.

[120] *Ibid.*, pp. 21–24.

[121] Moffat Diary, June 5, 1939; memorandum to Hull from Carleton Savage, June 14, 1939, 811.04418/434C; memorandum by Carleton Savage, June 19,

ence on June 20, Roosevelt again made a plea for the Bloom bill, stating that "it would help our influence for peace." The President stressed the need for an immediate decision. If Congress failed to act on neutrality and a war then broke out, "we would find it very difficult to change legislation to create neutrality without having it said that we were favoring one side or the other," Roosevelt warned.[122] In a final attempt to win support for the administration, Democratic leaders in the House announced on June 26 that they would drop the combat zone provision from the Bloom bill because it offered the President excessive discretionary power.[123]

The debate began on the floor of the House on June 27. The State Department, concerned over Bloom's inexperience on neutrality and his tendency toward ill-advised humor, persuaded the New York congressman to allow Representative Luther Johnson of Texas to take charge of his bill during the debate.[124] Johnson performed his task skillfully, choosing speakers who stressed the need for greater flexibility in neutrality policy in order to safeguard American interests in a changing and unpredictable world situation. In attacking the arms embargo, Johnson claimed that it was illogical to ban the shipment of arms to belligerents while permitting the export of war materials such as oil, steel, and cotton. Repeal of the embargo, Johnson declared, would bring American policy back in line with traditional international law. Bloom joined Johnson in this moderate approach, stating that the sole purpose of his bill was to keep the United States out of war. The administration's spokesmen repeatedly denied any intention of altering the neutrality act in order to aid England and France. A

1939, 811.04418/444; *New York Times*, June 22, 1939, p. 8; *ibid.*, June 24, 1939, p. 5.

[122] Press conference No. 555, June 20, 1939, FDR Papers, PPF 1-P, XIII, 426; *New York Times*, June 21, 1939, p. 10.

[123] *Ibid.*, June 27, 1939, p. 9.

[124] Moffat Diary, June 10, 1939; *Congressional Record*, June 27, 1939, p. 7988.

North Carolina congressman summed up this approach when he announced, "We are seeking not alliance, but peace; we are not endeavoring to help any country or hurt any country, but to encourage peace, to discourage war, and to maintain our own position in the world."[125]

Despite these efforts to minimize the effect of revision on the European balance of power, a number of congressmen frankly stated that they opposed the arms embargo because it favored Germany, Italy, and Japan. Calling the embargo "unneutral" and "a green light to aggressors," the supporters of collective security warned that failure to repeal it would lead to rejoicing "on the streets of Berlin." Representative Robert G. Allen of Pennsylvania, admitting that the Bloom bill would favor England and France, bluntly asserted, "I prefer indirectly to aid those nations which have demonstrated a friendly attitude toward us than to abet the onward march of the totalitarian powers." Representative John A. Martin of Colorado voiced the most outspoken condemnation of the 1937 act. "First, last, and all the time, I am for the democracies and against the dictators; and I am for them, Neutrality Act or no Neutrality Act," he declared.[126]

The advocates of mandatory neutrality, led by Hamilton Fish, replied by attacking the discretionary features of the Bloom bill. Republicans, conditioned by their previous efforts to deny the President broad executive power in domestic legislation, expressed their horror at the flexible provisions of the proposed bill. Attacking the "vast discretionary powers" given the President in the Bloom measure, a Minnesota congressman declared, "The people of the United States do not want one-man government. They do not want the discretion of life and death of their children lodged in the ambitious hands of one man." Speaker after speaker warned against surrendering the power to declare war to the President. "If this bill is passed in its present form," asserted a Democratic

[125] *Ibid.*, June 27, 1939, pp. 7988–90, 7991, 7998, 8013.

[126] *Ibid.*, June 27, 1939, pp. 8004, 8008–10; *ibid.*, June 28, 1939, pp. 8171–72; *ibid.*, June 29, 1939, pp. 8245–46, 8277–78.

congressman, "we will fight any nation that the President designates."[127] Many congressmen, responding to the arguments of the collective security proponents, warned that the administration would use discretionary powers to align the United States with England and France. Calling the Bloom measure "an un-American, 10 Downing Street bill," extreme isolationists attacked England and France as "so-called democracies" and declared, "We will defend [their] stolen colonies with the blood of our youth."[128] Other opponents of the Bloom bill, recalling the Nye committee hearings, condemned the effort to repeal the arms embargo as an "immoral and un-Christian" campaign sponsored by munitions makers. "It is a brazen attempt of interventionists to involve us into the international racket of finance and munitions manufacturing," declared a midwestern Democrat, while Louis Ludlow announced, "If we are going to be the world's arsenal, let us burn our Bibles and our churches." Hammering away at the administration's pleas for the sale of arms to preserve peace, a Montana Democrat charged, "You cannot extinguish a blaze by contributing gasoline instead of water to the firefighters. . . . We must either be for peace," he continued, "or for the gold accruing from the sales of implements of war."[129]

While this emotional and frequently hysterical exchange of views continued, a number of congressmen indicated they would prefer a return to traditional international law. When the House began considering amendments on June 29, Representative Robert G. Allen, a Pennsylvania Democrat, put forward a motion to repeal all existing neutrality legislation. "The security of our nation," he declared, "is better assured in the vault of international law than behind the barriers of any neutrality legislation we may write here today." Though Allen's proposal won strong support

[127] *Ibid.*, June 27, 1939, pp. 7995–96, 8005, 8011–12; *ibid.*, June 28, 1939, pp. 8164, 8175–76; *ibid.*, June 29, 1939, pp. 8240, 8260, 8265, 8268.

[128] *Ibid.*, June 27, 1939, pp. 7984, 8017; *ibid.*, June 28, 1939, p. 8168; *ibid.*, June 29, 1939, p. 8244.

[129] *Ibid.*, June 27, 1939, pp. 8007, 8017; *ibid.*, June 28, 1939, pp. 8151–52, 8154; *ibid.*, June 29, 1939, p. 8249.

from members of both parties, it created a temporary bond between the advocates of flexible and mandatory neutrality. Thus both Hamilton Fish and Luther Johnson spoke out against this amendment, warning that it would lead to the loss of American lives on the high seas and eventual American involvement in war. This argument prevailed—after a lengthy debate, the House rejected Allen's amendment by a vote of 195 to 68.[130] Then another series of amendments offered by isolationists to tighten up the Bloom bill were defeated by decisive majorities. As the debate continued, the House accepted only the committee change put forward by Sol Bloom to strike out the combat zone clause.[131]

Late in the evening of June 29, when it appeared that the administration leaders were moving toward certain passage of the Bloom bill, Representative John M. Vorys of Ohio, a Republican, offered a crucial amendment. Warning that the United States must not become "the potential slaughterhouse of the world," Vorys proposed the enactment of a limited embargo covering arms and ammunition but excluding implements of war. Explaining that the latter category, which would include aircraft, contained items that were also used for peaceful purposes, he argued that his proposal would be a reasonable compromise that would prevent the United States from selling belligerents lethal weapons that contributed to mass murder. After a brief debate, the House rejected this amendment on a show of hands. But Hamilton Fish demanded an accurate count by tellers. To the astonishment of the congressional leaders, the House then voted 159 to 157 in favor of the Vorys amendment.[132] This stunning vote suddenly changed the complexion of the entire debate. Now that the Bloom bill included a modified arms embargo it virtually nullified the administration's revision program.

When the House met on June 30, the Democratic leaders made a determined effort to strike the arms embargo from the Bloom

[130] *Ibid.*, June 29, 1939, pp. 8288–8311.

[131] *Ibid.*, June 29, 1939, p. 8333.

[132] *Ibid.*, June 29, 1939, pp. 8320–25.

bill. In a complicated parliamentary maneuver, Luther Johnson offered a substitute resolution which simply embodied the original Bloom measure without the Vorys amendment. Although Majority Leader Sam Rayburn and Speaker William B. Bankhead appealed to their Democratic colleagues to support the administration's stand, the House rejected the Johnson substitute by the margin of four votes, 180 to 176.[133] This tally, taken while the House was meeting as a Committee on the State of the Union, was made secretly, without an open roll call of the members. When the House came out of committee, the Democratic leaders called for a record vote on the Vorys amendment. With many legislators fearful of being recorded as opposed to the arms embargo, the House defeated this final effort to remove the Vorys amendment by the decisive vote of 214 to 173. Then the congressmen proceeded to pass the amended Bloom resolution by a margin of fourteen votes, with the advocates of mandatory neutrality voting against it.[134] Though the members of the neutrality bloc would have preferred to continue the 1937 act, they rejoiced in their successful effort to retain a modified arms embargo.

An analysis of the vote on the Vorys amendment indicates that the administration's defeat was very largely the result of partisan political pressures. The Republicans displayed a surprising unity in support of the arms embargo—only seven Republican congressmen voted against the Vorys amendment. However, the Democrats were unable to hold their ranks firm. Sixty-one Democratic congressmen joined with their Republican colleagues to sustain the arms embargo.[135] Sectionally, only the South voted for the administration's position. Though six of the seven Republicans

[133] *Ibid.*, June 30, 1939, pp. 8502–11.

[134] *Ibid.*, June 30, 1939, pp. 8511, 8513.

[135] The vote by parties on the question of adopting the Vorys amendment was as follows:

	Yes	*No*
Republican	150	7
Democractic	61	165
Other	3	1

who opposed the Vorys amendment came from the East, the Democratic supporters of the arms embargo came almost equally from all sections of the nation, with the largest single bloc from the Middle West.[136] Anglophobia probably influenced the outcome, for the list of sixty-one Democrats who bolted their party is sprinkled with surnames of Irish, Italian, and German origin. Given the welter of conflicting interests represented in the House and the complexity of the neutrality issue, it is impossible to single out any one reason for the administration's defeat. But the vote can be interpreted as a rebellion against Roosevelt's leadership. Frustrated by years of failure on domestic legislation, Republicans gleefully exploited the growing rift inside the Democratic party to block a policy which they knew the President ardently desired. A combination of partisan animosities, isolationist yearnings, and growing resentment at strong presidential leadership converged to destroy Roosevelt's cautious attempt to reorient American foreign policy.

The administration leaders did not disguise their anguish over the retention of the arms embargo. In a statement to the press on July 1, Cordell Hull called the action of the House "a matter of regret and disappointment from the standpoint of peace." Though President Roosevelt avoided any immediate public comment, the *New York Times* reported that he had taken a "no surrender" stand on the arms embargo issue.[137] In a letter on July 1 to Congresswoman Caroline O'Day, a New York Democrat who had supported the Vorys amendment, Roosevelt wrote, "I honest-

[136] The vote by sections on the question of adopting the Vorys amendment was as follows:

	Yes	No
Middle West	97	32
Northeast	74	42
South	20	83
Far West	23	16

Of the 61 Democrats who voted for the Vorys amendment, 13 came from the Northeast, 17 from the South, 19 from the Middle West, and 12 from the Far West.

[137] *New York Times*, July 2, 1939, pp. 1, 2.

ly believe that the vote last night was a stimulus to war and that if the result had been different it would have been a definite encouragement to peace." The same day, following a suggestion made by Harold L. Ickes at a cabinet meeting on June 30, the President asked the Attorney-General how far he could go "in ignoring the existing act."[138]

The administration's concern was heightened by reports from American diplomats abroad. On July 1, William C. Bullitt cabled Hull that the French were asking him "if the House of Representatives desires to precipitate war at this moment, and also if the House really desires the defeat of Great Britain, France and Poland and the triumph of Hitler and Mussolini."[139] On July 2, Hull sent a circular telegram to the American embassies in Western Europe asking for further reports on European reactions to the vote in Congress. The replies were very discouraging. The Dutch, Belgians, and French felt war was now imminent; Italians were rejoicing at what they felt was a blow against England and France; the Germans remained silent; and the British Foreign Office, according to Ambassador Joseph P. Kennedy, was worried but still confident of eventual American support "if there is trouble."[140] These reports intensified the administration's fears that the retention of the arms embargo would encourage Hitler and Mussolini to speed up their preparations for war.[141] To avoid this possibility, President Roosevelt decided to continue the fight for repeal. In an informal press conference held at Hyde Park on July 4, 1939, the President called on the Senate to reverse the decision of the House of Representatives, announcing that he intended to keep Congress in session until the arms embargo was repealed, even if this meant delaying adjournment until September.[142] Certain that American neutrality legislation had a vital

[138] E. Roosevelt, *F.D.R.: His Personal Letters*, II, 899–900; *Ickes Diary*, II, 676.

[139] Bullitt to Hull, July 1, 1939, 811.04418/454.

[140] *FR: 1939*, I, 281–83, 662–67.

[141] *Hull Memoirs*, I, 646–48.

[142] *New York Times*, July 5, 1939, p. 5.

bearing on the coming of war in Europe, Roosevelt had decided to risk his prestige in an all-out battle with his congressional opponents.

VI

In early July, the debate shifted to the Senate. Throughout the previous month, Senator Pittman had continued to mark time, stating that his committee would wait until the House had acted before it began its own final deliberations on neutrality legislation. When the House finally passed the amended Bloom bill, Pittman promised that the Senate Foreign Relations Committee would take up this subject at its regularly scheduled meeting on Wednesday, July 5.[143] The committee met as planned, but it did not act on neutrality legislation. Instead Pittman deferred final consideration until Saturday, July 8, explaining that several members of the committee were deeply involved in a floor fight over domestic legislation. Later in the week, Pittman decided to postpone the committee deliberation until Tuesday, July 11. Several members of the group would be out of town over the weekend, he explained, and he wanted to insure full attendance for this critical meeting.[144]

While Pittman procrastinated, both the administration leaders and the members of the neutrality bloc exerted intense pressure upon the Senate Foreign Relations Committee. Secretary Hull and other cabinet officers conferred with Democratic members of the committee, pleading for repeal of the arms embargo.[145] President Roosevelt threw his personal influence into the balance. Hearing that Senator Pat Harrison of Mississippi was preparing to leave Washington, Roosevelt wrote him on July 6, urging him to stay and participate in "the next big thing on the calendar—the Neutrality bill."[146] Admiral Richard Byrd, the famed Antarctic ex-

[143] *Ibid.*, July 5, 1939, p. 5.

[144] *Ibid.*, July 6, 1939, p. 8; *ibid.*, July 8, 1939, pp. 1, 3.

[145] *Ibid.*, July 9, 1939, p. 1.

[146] Roosevelt to Harrison, July 6, 1939, FDR Papers, PSF, Box 33.

plorer, offered his aid to Roosevelt, writing that he would spend the weekend of July 9–10 visiting "some Senator friends." On July 11, Byrd told the President, "I have been going like a steam engine on the Neutrality Bill, and will keep at it."[147] At the same time, isolationist leaders, notably Gerald P. Nye, Hiram Johnson, and Bennett C. Clark, began organizing a solid bloc of senators to support the arms embargo. On July 7 thirty-four senators gathered in Johnson's office in the Capitol to announce that they were "unalterably opposed to repeal or modification of the present Neutrality Law." Explaining that they would maintain their position "by every honorable means at our command," this isolationist bloc threatened to filibuster if the Senate committee reported favorably on the administration's proposals. Reporters were quick to note the symbolic parallels with the great debate of 1919—the isolationists' manifesto was reminiscent of the Republican Round Robin while their meeting place was the very office that had served as headquarters for the irreconcilables' campaign against the Treaty of Versailles.[148]

When the Senate Foreign Relations Committee met on the morning of July 11, the administration had eleven certain votes, the isolationists ten. Two Democratic senators, Walter F. George of Georgia and Guy M. Gillette of Iowa, would determine the outcome. Both were known to favor repeal of all neutrality legislation, but both were also bitter political foes of the President. In 1938, Roosevelt had unsuccessfully tried to purge George and Gillette in the Democratic primaries. Hull had held frequent meetings with these two men, but they were still wavering.[149] Then, on the evening of July 10, Bennett C. Clark, the leading Democratic supporter of mandatory neutrality, conferred with George and Gillette. Knowing that they were sympathetic to

[147] Byrd to Roosevelt, undated, and Byrd to Roosevelt, July 11, 1939, FDR Papers, PPF 201.

[148] *New York Times*, July 8, 1939, p. 1; "34 in a Lair," *Time*, XXXIV (July 17, 1939), 13.

[149] *New York Times*, July 9, 1939, p. 1; "Neutrality Bill," *Newsweek*, XIV (July 17, 1939), 17–18.

flexible legislation, Clark shrewdly refrained from asking them to vote against the Bloom bill, but instead he urged them to vote for postponement of the entire issue until the next session of Congress. This strategy proved effective. When Senator Pittman gaveled his committee to order, Senator Clark immediately made a motion to postpone consideration of neutrality legislation until 1940. The administration supporters, caught unprepared by this parliamentary maneuver, voted against Clark's proposal, but Senators George and Gillette joined the isolationist minority and the motion carried by a vote of 12 to 11. The committee then adjourned. The meeting had lasted only fifteen minutes, but it was long enough to undo six months of intense effort by the administration.[150]

President Roosevelt's immediate reaction was pure anger. He quickly began to prepare a message to Congress denouncing his isolationist opponents. In this statement, the President planned to declare, "Those who scream from the housetops that this nation is being led into a world war, that American armies will soon be headed overseas to the East or to the West, that this government is being tricked into the support of any group of foreign nations, deserve only the utmost contempt and pity of the American

[150] T. R. B., "Politics at the Water's Edge," *New Republic*, XCIX (August 2, 1939), 360; *New York Times*, July 12, 1939, p. 1. In his autobiography, Senator Tom Connally, who was a member of the Senate Foreign Relations Committee, claimed that at the beginning of the July 11 meeting he offered a motion to consider the Bloom bill. According to Connally, no one seconded this motion. Then Clark offered his proposal for postponement. It is difficult to believe that not one of the other ten Democrats on the committee who voted against the Clark motion would agree to second the motion Connally claims he offered. A search of the Connally Papers in the Library of Congress turned up no written evidence to support the senator's assertion. Thus, I have followed the more logical account offered by the Washington correspondent of the *New Republic*. See Tom Connally and Alfred Steinberg, *My Name Is Tom Connally* (New York, 1954), p. 227. In the crucial vote, five Democrats, George, Gillette, Van Nuys, Reynolds, and Clark, joined five Republicans and one Progressive (La Follette) and one Farmer-Laborite (Shipstead) in supporting postponement. The eleven negative votes were all cast by Democrats. Thus even though the Democrats held 16 of the 23 seats on the committee, the administration was unable to command a majority. *New York Times*, July 12, 1939, p. 9.

people." These allegations, Roosevelt believed, were "unspeakable and unsupported charges" stemming from "personal and partisan" motives.[151] This message was never sent to Congress. Sometime after it was drafted, Cordell Hull conferred with Roosevelt and warned that such an attack could only lead to further defeats in Congress. The President finally accepted Hull's advice, though there evidently was a stormy debate between the two men. White House aides had told newsmen that Roosevelt was ready to "erupt" at Congress, and when the reporters learned that Hull favored a milder statement, they sent out a story about a rift between the President and his Secretary of State. On July 13, Roosevelt angrily denied this report, labeling it "wholly false." The President then went on to say that the administration had not yet decided whether or not to send a message to Congress on neutrality revision.[152] The evidence is not at all clear, but it seems reasonable to conclude that Roosevelt, after an initial release of his feelings, finaly realized the wisdom of Hull's advice and decided to follow a more moderate course.[153]

On July 14, Roosevelt sent a message to Congress on neutrality revision, and its mild and formal tone indicated that Hull's views had prevailed. The statement was in the form of a summation by Cordell Hull of the administration's recommendations on neutrality legislation, accompanied by a brief covering letter from the President. In very restrained language, Roosevelt simply reminded the legislators that he had long felt that it was "highly advisable" for Congress to revise the nation's neutrality policy "at this session." "In the light of present world conditions, I see no reason to change that opinion," the President concluded. In his lengthy

[151] Unused draft of a message to Congress, dated July 14, 1939, FDR Papers, PSF, Box 33.

[152] Rosenman, *Public Papers of FDR*, VIII, 380–81; *Newsweek*, XIV (July 24, 1939), 15–16; *New York Times*, July 16, 1939, p. 1.

[153] In his account of his association with Roosevelt, Samuel Rosenman states that the President and Hull saw "eye-to-eye" on the message of July 14. However, the heated nature of Roosevelt's denial of any split with Hull on this issue suggests a very different situation. Samuel I. Rosenman, *Working with Roosevelt* (New York, 1952), p. 185.

statement, Hull repeated the arguments he had put forward in his May 27 letter to Bloom and Pittman. He attacked the arms embargo as unneutral and illogical, championed cash-and-carry and combat zone restrictions as effective and necessary safeguards, and then reiterated his six-point program for new legislation. In his final paragraphs, Hull warned that the arms embargo, because it favored aggressors, "encourages a general state of war, both in Europe and Asia. Since the present embargo has this effect," Hull continued, "its results are directly prejudicial to the highest interests and to the peace and security of the United States."[154]

This message marked the beginning of a final effort to secure neutrality revision in the waning weeks of the congressional session. Defeated in the House of Representatives and in the Senate Foreign Relations Committee, Roosevelt and Hull were asking the Senate to override its own committee and institute legislative proceedings by floor action. In an effort to carry out this procedure, Roosevelt invited Hull, Vice-President John Nance Garner, and a half-dozen Senate leaders, Republican and Democratic, to an informal conference at the White House on the evening of July 18. The meeting took place in the President's second-floor study, and after Roosevelt used his famous charm to establish a cordial atmosphere, he suddenly became serious. "Our decision," he began, "might well affect not only the people of our own country, but also the peoples of the world." Roosevelt then stated his deep concern over the imminence of war in Europe and his conviction that repeal of the arms embargo would help prevent a conflict. When Senator Borah challenged Roosevelt's assertion that war was likely to break out during the summer, the President asked Hull to explain the ominous reports the State Department was receiving daily from American diplomats in Europe. Hull described the situation as it appeared to him, and then he invited Borah to come to the State Department and examine the evidence. In disdainful tones, the old Idaho warrior replied, "So far as the reports in your Department are concerned, I wouldn't be

[154] *Congressional Record*, July 14, 1939, pp. 9127–28.

bound by them. I have my own sources of information which I have provided for myself, and on several occasions I've found them more reliable than the State Department." Close to tears, Hull restrained himself from making any further comments. Garner quietly canvassed the assembled senators, and then he bluntly told Roosevelt, "You haven't got the votes, and that's all there is to it." Roosevelt hid his disappointment gracefully, and the meeting "broke up in laughter."[155] The administration's drive for neutrality revision had ended in absolute failure.

The next morning the White House issued a press release summarizing the negative results of this conference. In an effort to place the responsibility for retention of the arms embargo squarely on Congress, the statement reported that both the majority and minority leaders of the Senate, Alben W. Barkley and Charles L. McNary, agreed that the senators present at the conference had informed Roosevelt that "no action on neutrality legislation can be obtained in the Senate at the present session and that a majority of the Senate would concur in this view." The statement also made clear the administration's fundamental disagreement over the wisdom of this decision. "The President and the Secretary of State maintained the definite position that failure by the Senate to take action now would weaken the leadership of the United States in exercising its potent influence in the cause of preserving peace among other nations in the event of a new crisis in Europe between now and next January."[156] In a press conference on July 21 the President reiterated his belief that the Senate's decision for postponement, which he attributed to partisan Republican opposition, made the outbreak of war more likely in Europe. Announcing that the neutrality issue was now dead until Congress met again in 1940, Roosevelt took one last shot at his opponents by suggesting that the failure of the Senate to act would damage the

[155] This White House conference has been described in many accounts. The fullest description is in Joseph Alsop and Robert Kintner, *American White Paper* (New York, 1940), pp. 58–59. See also *Hull Memoirs*, I, 649–50, and Langer and Gleason, *Challenge to Isolation*, pp. 143–44.

[156] Rosenman, *Public Papers of FDR*, VIII, 387–88.

American economy. "We are concerned, rightly, to a certain extent, with the prosperity picture . . . ," the President asserted, "and the failure of the Senate to take action, deferring everything until January, is, without any question, going to slow up the wheels of industry in this country."[157]

VII

The reaction of the American people to the congressional refusal to repeal the arms embargo revealed a deep uncertainty over the nation's role in the world crisis. The isolationist and internationalist extremes responded in predictable fashion. The *New York Times* called the Senate's action "an invitation to aggressor nations to use war to achieve their conquests"; the *Christian Century* praised the congressional retention of the arms embargo as a firm denial of "Mr. Roosevelt's effort to place American support behind Great Britain and France."[158] But the mass of the people stood indecisively between these extremes. A Gallup poll taken on July 8 showed that 60 per cent still favored the sale of arms to England and France in a general European war. Yet a month later, 51 per cent of those questioned indicated that they thought Congress was right in retaining the arms embargo, with 37 per cent disagreeing and 12 per cent expressing no opinion.[159] The nation was in a period of transition which fostered this confusion. A people who only a few years before had believed that withdrawal from the world was not only wise but possible was gradually learning that the United States could not escape from the march of events abroad. Ever since Munich, there had been a growing revulsion over Hitler's aggressive and brutal policies, both in his open seizure of Czechoslovakia and his renewed persecu-

[157] *Ibid.*, pp. 390–93, 395.

[158] *New York Times*, July 20, 1939, p. 18; *Christian Century*, LVI (July 12, 1939), 870–71.

[159] Cantril and Strunk, *Public Opinion*, p. 1157.

tion of Jews inside Germany. As Americans began to feel personally involved in the world crisis, they began to question the older assumptions that had grown out of the disillusion over World War I. Yet they still were filled with a fear of American involvement in another great war. Oscillating between these conflicting emotions, the people were reluctant to commit themselves to any positive course of action. When this vacillation came face to face with the complexity of the neutrality problem, the result was indecision and hesitation. In this sense, the congressional stalemate was probably a fairly accurate reflection of popular sentiment.

Confronted with this shifting and unstable public mood, the administration had failed to offer clear-cut, vigorous, and effective leadership on neutrality revision. Roosevelt had raised the issue in his January message to Congress, but then he had maintained a long and perplexing silence while Senator Pittman fumbled the issue in Congress. Only late in the session, when the best opportunities for effective action had passed, did the administration show any vigor in pressing for a change in neutrality policy. And even then, Roosevelt remained in the background, issuing bland recommendations in his press conferences but allowing Cordell Hull to carry the main burden. As a result, the many disparate groups which favored a reorientation of American foreign policy found themselves involved in a losing struggle. There were many individuals, both in organized pressure groups and in the public at large, who favored a repeal of the arms embargo, but the President failed to rally these potential allies and give them the leadership and encouragement they so desperately needed.

In fairness to Roosevelt, it must be admitted that there were powerful reasons behind his calculated policy of disengagement from the neutrality debate. Aware of the rifts he had created inside his own party during the court fight and in the unsuccessful purge, he feared that his personal intervention would alienate potential supporters in Congress. Moreover, there were many Republicans who were not isolationists, yet who might allow their hatred of Roosevelt to overcome their opposition to mandatory neutrality legislation. By remaining aloof, the President evidently believed that he could prevent the personal animosities he had aroused in Congress from influencing the outcome. This proved to be a fundamental miscalculation. Roosevelt's opponents in Congress knew that he favored a flexible, discretionary policy and they were determined to deny him this triumph. Two astute political commentators who wrote from very different perspectives, Arthur Krock of the *New York Times* and Freda Kirchwey of the *Nation*, agreed that the overriding issue in the congressional defeat of neutrality revision was a fundamental distrust of Roosevelt.[160] His opponents, who already believed that he had usurped enormous power on domestic issues, were determined to restrict his control of foreign policy. His refusal to state his political ambitions for 1940 was probably the greatest unknown factor in the entire debate. While it could never be proved, it is likely that many congressmen and senators, fearful that Roosevelt would run for a third term in 1940, decided to postpone the final decision on neutrality revision until they knew whether or not Roosevelt would control American destinies for another four years. "Fear of increasing the power of the Executive, general opposition to the New Deal, above all, the imminence of the 1940 election," commented Freda Kirchwey, "these were the decisive weights in the small balance recorded against the President's foreign policy."[161]

Roosevelt's strategy backfired—he was unable to prevent his political enemies from blocking his neutrality program, while at the same time he failed to win the support of potential allies in Congress and among the people. Bold and precise executive leadership might have won over many wavering congressmen and stimulated a public ground swell in behalf of arms embargo repeal. It is difficult to see how a forthright appeal could have cost him appreciable strength—his Democratic and Republican opponents fought

[160] *New York Times*, July 12, 1939, p. 18; *ibid.*, July 20, 1939, p. 18; Freda Kirchwey, "Two Foreign Policies," *Nation*, CXLIX (July 29, 1939), 116–17.

[161] *Ibid.*, p. 116.

against him despite his silence. Yet even if Roosevelt had openly championed the fight for neutrality revision, he might still have lost. The thirty-four senators pledged to a summer-long filibuster against revision could have blocked the administration's program even if it had won approval in the House and in the Senate Foreign Relations Committee. But at least the President could have had the satisfaction of knowing he had made the supreme effort to reorient American foreign policy before war began in Europe. And he might have won.

CHAPTER NINE

NEUTRALITY REVISION: SUCCESS

The repeal of the Neutrality Act of the United States is a momentous event, for, while it affords America the means of maintaining her neutrality, it reopens for the Allies the doors of the greatest storehouse of supplies in the world.

NEVILLE CHAMBERLAIN, November 9, 1939

A few minutes before three o'clock on Friday morning, September 1, 1939, the strident ring of the bedside phone aroused President Roosevelt. Ambassador William C. Bullitt, calling from Paris, somberly informed the President that a few hours earlier the German army had marched across the frontiers of Poland. Roosevelt quickly relayed this news to Cordell Hull and then went back to sleep. At 6:30 Bullitt telephoned again to report that the French Premier, Edouard Daladier, had stated flatly that England and France would come to Poland's aid. A few minutes later, Ambassador Joseph P. Kennedy called from London to confirm this report.[1] The long-developing European crisis, which had reached a critical stage on August 23 when Germany and Russia signed their non-aggression pact, had finally culminated in world war.

At 10:30 in the morning, the President held a special press con-

[1] Joseph Alsop and Robert Kintner, *American White Paper* (New York, 1940), pp. 58–59.

ference at which he told the assembled reporters that he believed the United States could and would remain at peace. Then he conferred with Hull and, with the Secretary's concurrence, decided to call Congress into special session within a short time to revise the neutrality act.[2] In a cabinet meeting that afternoon, the President confirmed this decision and then indicated that he would wait for a formal declaration of war before putting the arms embargo into effect. "This would make it possible for the countries opposing Germany to export war materials from us," he explained to his colleagues.[3] The next day Roosevelt asked the State Department to prepare drafts of a fireside chat which he planned to deliver to the nation when England and France declared war. Meanwhile, Chamberlain and Daladier made last-minute efforts to preserve peace, calling on Hitler to withdraw his armies from Polish territory. He ignored these appeals, and on Sunday morning the Allied governments sent ultimatums to Germany, stating that unless the Nazi armies retreated from Poland within five hours, a state of war would exist. When the time limit expired on the afternoon of September 3, England and France formally declared war on Germany.[4]

On Sunday evening, President Roosevelt delivered his radio address to the American people. In a plea for national unity, he dedicated himself to the single goal of preserving peace in the Western Hemisphere. Yet at the same time, Roosevelt warned that the war would inevitably affect America. "You must master at the outset a simple but unalterable fact in modern foreign relations," he declared. "When peace has been broken anywhere, peace of all countries everywhere is in danger." Though he went on to promise that he would issue a formal proclamation of neutrality, he did not demand that the American people be impartial.

[2] *The Memoirs of Cordell Hull* (2 vols.; New York, 1948), I, 672–73.

[3] *Ibid.*, p. 675; *The Secret Diary of Harold Ickes* (3 vols.; New York, 1953–54), II, 709–10.

[4] Alsop and Kintner, *American White Paper*, p. 66; Whitney H. Shepardson and William O. Scroggs, *The United States in World Affairs, 1939* (New York, 1940), p. 153.

"This nation must remain a neutral nation," he announced, "but I cannot ask that every American remain neutral in thought as well. . . . Even a neutral cannot be asked to close his mind or his conscience." The President reiterated his oft-stated hatred of war, and he concluded by promising that there would be "no blackout of peace in the United States."[5]

Two days later, on September 5, the State Department issued two presidential proclamations of neutrality. The first was nearly identical with Wilson's proclamation in 1914—it adhered to traditional international law and warned American citizens not to give illegal aid to any of the belligerent powers. A few hours later, the second proclamation was made public. Based on the 1937 neutrality act, this document applied the arms embargo to all belligerents.[6] In an accompanying statement, the State Department explained that the second proclamation was issued separately because proposals were pending before Congress to modify the existing neutrality statute. On the same day, the government also imposed restrictions on American travel on belligerent ships, which applied only to the North Atlantic area, and on September 6, exercising his discretionary authority, the President exempted "ordinary commercial credits and short-time obligations" from the ban on loans to nations at war.[7]

The proclamation of September 5 completed the initial response of the Roosevelt administration to the European war in regard to neutrality. Though every step reflected a correct regard for the existing law, the President had deliberately displayed strong antagonism to a rigid neutrality policy. His brief delay in issuing the proclamations, his obvious refusal to call for impartiality in

[5] Samuel Rosenman (ed.), *The Public Papers and Addresses of Franklin D. Roosevelt* (13 vols.; New York, 1938–50), VIII, 460–63.

[6] State Department, *Bulletin*, I (September 9, 1939), 203–11. The belligerents listed were France, Germany, Poland, the United Kingdom, India, Australia, and New Zealand. Supplementary proclamations were issued on September 8 and 11 to include the Union of South Africa and Canada when they entered the war. *Ibid.*, pp. 211, 246–49.

[7] *Ibid.*, pp. 203, 219–20, 221.

thought, and his careful distinction between neutral duties imposed by international law and those made mandatory by domestic legislation were all moves designed to lay the basis for a congressional modification of American neutrality policy. In his *Memoirs*, Cordell Hull states unequivocally that both he and the President "saw clearly that it would be to our own national interest to assist England and France, first in the effort to keep the war from coming, and second, to win the war if it came."[8] Roosevelt himself never stated his personal beliefs so frankly, but all his actions on neutrality are in harmony with this viewpoint. Though he had originally favored neutrality legislation, the deterioration of world affairs in the late 1930's convinced him that the United States had to support democratic nations against the totalitarian powers in order to safeguard American security in a shrinking world.

All the reports which the President received from Europe in the first few weeks of the war reinforced this concept of America's role in the world struggle. Ambassador Kennedy reported on September 15 that Prime Minister Neville Chamberlain believed that repeal of the arms embargo "would be the greatest psychological lift that England could have at this time and failure to pass it would be 'sheer disaster' for England and France."[9] From Paris, Ambassador Bullitt was even more pessimistic. He stated that his military and naval attachés advised him that a continuation of the arms embargo "will mean inevitably the defeat of England and France." Bullitt then warned, "I am entirely certain that if France and England should be unable to defeat Hitler in Europe, American soldiers will have to fight him in America."[10]

Roosevelt's own evaluation of America's position on the world scene, reinforced by these dire predictions from his European ambassadors, led him to the inescapable conclusion that the United States must repeal the arms embargo in order to aid England and France. On September 11 he wrote Neville Chamberlain, "I hope

[8] *Hull Memoirs*, I, 684.

[9] *FR: 1939*, I, 440.

[10] *Ibid.*, p. 673.

and believe that we shall repeal the embargo next month and this is definitely a part of the Administration's policy."[11] Yet, having made his decision, Roosevelt knew that he could never present it to the American people as a measure to aid the Allies. The setback in Congress in the spring had made him more wary of isolationist strength than ever before. And he knew that a Gallup poll taken just after the outbreak of war revealed that public opinion was now evenly divided on the arms embargo question.[12] The President thus faced a momentous challenge—he had to convince the people and their representatives in Congress that the arms embargo endangered American security without openly advocating American support for England and France. To accomplish such a task, he would have to use all of his political skill, directing and commanding the administration's policy personally. In short, he would have to abandon the aloof stance that had undermined the drive for repeal in the spring. The risks were grave—if he failed he would destroy his own political stature and sacrifice whatever hope England and France still had for eventual American support. But if he triumphed, it would be a vital turning point in his struggle to free American foreign policy from the grip of isolationism.

I

President Roosevelt's first step in his campaign to secure revision of the neutrality act was to call a special session of Congress. Though he had reached this decision on September 1, he decided to sound out congressional opinion before making it public. During the first week of September, he consulted with administration leaders in Congress, asking them to poll their colleagues on neutrality revision. These congressional leaders conducted a telephone check of the Senate and reported to the President that approxi-

[11] Elliott Roosevelt (ed.), *F.D.R.: His Personal Letters, 1928–1945* (2 vols.; New York, 1950), II, 919.

[12] *New York Times*, September 3, 1939, p. 12. In this poll, 50 per cent favored repeal of the arms embargo, 50 per cent opposed. In the spring, the ratio was 57 per cent to 43 per cent in favor of repeal.

mately sixty Senators would vote for repeal of the arms embargo. Roosevelt's own staff arrived at a similar estimate on September 7, and the next day at his news conference the President told the press that he would call Congress into session in the near future. He refused to set a specific date, but he did announce that he would ask for the repeal of the arms embargo.[13] When R. Walton Moore wrote on September 8 that the outbreak of war had caused many congressmen to reconsider their previous opposition to revision, Roosevelt revealed his growing optimism. "My own personal opinion," the President told Moore on September 11, "is that we can get the votes in the House and the Senate but that the principal difficulty will be to prevent a filibuster in the latter."[14]

Encouraged by these favorable signs, the President and his aides renewed their efforts to insure substantial majorities in Congress. Typewritten lists of Democratic congressmen who had supported the Vorys amendment in June circulated through the executive offices, indicating an intense effort to win back these straying members of the party.[15] Some significant gains were made. On September 15, Representative Ross Collins, a Mississippi Democrat who had voted against the Bloom bill, called the White House to announce his return to the fold; five days later Assistant Secretary of State Adolf A. Berle reported the conversion of Representative Jerry Voorhis of California.[16] With the drive for repeal

[13] *New York Times*, September 8, 1939, p. 1; *ibid.*, September 9, 1939, p. 1; *ibid.*, September 15, 1939, p. 13; Porter Sargent, *Getting Us into War* (Boston, 1941), p. 130; Stephen Early to Roosevelt, September 7, 1939, E. Roosevelt, *F.D.R.: His Personal Letters*, II, 918; Rosenman, *Public Papers of FDR*, VIII, 480–81.

[14] Moore to Roosevelt, September 8, 1939, FDR Papers, PPF 1820; Roosevelt to Moore, September 11, 1939, E. Roosevelt, *F.D.R.: His Personal Letters*, II, 919.

[15] FDR Papers, OF 1561, Boxes 2 and 3. One of these lists bears the notation by Roosevelt, "To put in middle drawer of my desk in office."

[16] Edward Watson to Roosevelt, September 15, 1939, FDR Papers, OF 1561, Box 2; Berle to Roosevelt, September 20, 1939, FDR Papers, OF 1561, Box 2.

gathering momentum, Roosevelt called Congress to meet in special session on September 21. At the same time, he invited eleven congressional leaders, including several Republicans, to meet with him at the White House on September 20, the day before the new session began.[17]

The inclusion of Republican leaders in the invitation to this conference was the beginning of a new attempt by the President to smother his opposition in a spirit of bipartisan co-operation. In order to align majorities in both houses of Congress, Roosevelt needed the votes of the anti–New Deal coalition, made up of both Democratic and Republican congressmen who had been alienated by his domestic reforms, the Supreme Court fight, and the unsuccessful purge of 1938. In particular, the President concentrated on winning back the support of dissident Democrats. In early September he asked Tom Connally of Texas and James Byrnes of South Carolina to assist Pittman in leading the repeal drive in the Senate. Connally was to take charge of debate on the floor while Byrnes, who excelled at subtle political maneuvering, was to use his talents in winning over conservative senators.[18] The President revealed his eagerness to smooth over old political feuds when Senator Guy M. Gillette, whom Roosevelt had opposed for re-election in 1938, sent a telegram on September 3 pledging his support on neutrality revision. Thanking Gillette for his wire, Roosevelt told him of his plan to call Congress into special session

[17] *New York Times*, September 14, 1939, p. 1. The invitations were sent to Vice-President Garner, Speaker Bankhead, Democratic Senators Barkley, Pittman, Minton, and Byrnes, Democratic Representatives Rayburn and Bloom, Republican Senators McNary and Austin, and Republican Representative Martin. Telegram from Roosevelt, September 13, 1939, FDR Papers, OF 1561, Box 2.

[18] James F. Byrnes, *All in One Lifetime* (New York, 1958), p. 111; "The Great Fugue," *Time*, XXXIV (September 25, 1939), 12–13; T. R. B., "Ordeal by Lung Power," *New Republic*, C (October 18, 1939), 294. In his memoirs, Connally states that Key Pittman, rather than Roosevelt, asked him to guide the revision effort on the floor of the Senate. Tom Connally and Alfred Steinberg, *My Name Is Tom Connally* (New York, 1954), p. 228.

and then added, "I am limiting the heads of the Executive Branch to more action and less words. I know you will understand."[19]

Roosevelt received unexpected and welcome support from prominent business leaders. Thomas W. Lamont, a partner in J. P. Morgan and Company, called the White House on September 2 to offer his services in the fight for repeal of the arms embargo. The President subsequently conferred with Lamont, who became a staunch advocate of the administration's foreign policy. On September 16, Lamont wrote encouragingly, "I cannot think but that the country—and Congress—will respond to your appeal that we must keep out of war but that we must do away with these boycotts against nations with whose difficulties 95 per cent of our citizens sympathize."[20] Another prominent businessman, Myron Taylor, former chairman of the board of U.S. Steel, called Roosevelt's press secretary, Stephen Early, on September 7 to request the names of important congressmen who opposed repeal of the arms embargo, saying that such a list would be "quite helpful." Early quickly sent him a breakdown of the House vote on the Vorys amendment. Another prominent Republican businessman, identified only by his initial, reported to Edward Watson, one of Roosevelt's personal aides, that many Republican senators favored repeal of the embargo if it were replaced by cash-and-carry restrictions. Encouraged by this support, Roosevelt decided to strengthen his bipartisan approach in mid-September by asking Alfred M. Landon and Colonel Frank Knox, the unsuccessful Republican candidates in the presidential election of 1939, to attend the conference with congressional leaders on September 20.[21]

[19] Gillette to Roosevelt, September 6, 1939, and Roosevelt to Gillette, September 7, 1939, FDR Papers, PPF 6176. In July, Gillette had voted for postponement of neutrality revision until the next session of Congress.

[20] Memorandum by Edward Watson, September 2, 1939, and Lamont to Roosevelt, September 16, 1939, FDR Papers, PPF 70.

[21] Taylor to Early, September 7, 1939, Early to Taylor, September 9, 1939, memorandum by Watson, September 13, 1939, FDR Papers, OF 1561, Box 2; *New York Times*, September 19, 1939, p. 1.

While Roosevelt personally supervised the campaign to gain support in Congress, the State Department began building up the administration's case for repeal. Hull asked Carleton Savage, James C. Dunn, and J. Pierrepont Moffat to gather material for the President. On September 18 the Division of Controls submitted a memorandum to this trio urging the administration to replace the arms embargo with legislation banning American ships from entry into European war zones. The report pointed out that the submarine problem from 1914 to 1917 arose not from munitions exports, which made up only 10 per cent of American trade with the Allied powers in that period, but from the export of war supplies and raw materials. In addition, this report suggested that the continuation of the arms embargo would amount not to neutrality but rather to taking sides with Germany against England and France—an act clearly against American national interests.[22] This memorandum, along with other reports and written advice, was sent on to Assistant Secretary Berle, who was charged with drafting the speech the President planned to deliver to Congress when it convened on September 21. By the nineteenth, Berle had completed the President's speech. Secretary Hull did not approve it, however, and soon he had several other members of the Department preparing new drafts. The next day Judge Samuel I. Rosenman arrived at the White House and began combining drafts of the speech prepared by Tom Corcoran, Ben Cohen, Berle, and Roosevelt himself. After an evening session with Berle, Hull, and Roosevelt, Rosenman finally finished the speech in the early hours of the morning and then met with the President later in the day to make a few minor stylistic revisions.[23]

While the final drafting went on, Roosevelt and Hull met with the congressional leaders and the Republican spokesmen, Landon

[22] Moffat Diary, September 12 and 15, 1939; memorandum by Charles W. Yost, September 18, 1939, 811.04418/584.

[23] Moffat Diary, September 18 and 19, 1939; Samuel I. Rosenman, *Working with Roosevelt* (New York, 1952), p. 189. Hull favored a long message which rebutted all possible arguments against repeal of the arms embargo while Roosevelt wanted a briefer statement emphasizing the positive reasons for change. Moffat Diary, September 19, 1939.

and Knox, at the White House on the afternoon of September 20. Roosevelt opened the conference by affirming his determination to keep the nation at peace, and then he stated his belief that this goal could best be accomplished by repealing all the neutrality legislation enacted since 1935 and returning to traditional international law. He particularly stressed the penalties the arms embargo placed on England and France: ". . . automatically, as has been well said, we are handing a navy to Germany." The congressional leaders, while agreeing on the repeal of the arms embargo, insisted that it would have to be replaced by cash-and-carry restrictions to prevent the sinking of American ships and the loss of American property in the North Atlantic. Roosevelt quickly accepted this qualification, commenting, "We are all for cash-and-carry neutrality." After two hours of desultory discussion, the meeting broke up, with the Republicans thoroughly disillusioned. They had come expecting to take part in momentous decisions—they found themselves instead listening to Democrats discuss legislative strategy.[24]

Shortly after noon the next day, September 21, the President drove to the Capitol to deliver his address to Congress. The senators and representatives filled the floor of the House chamber; the galleries were crowded with spectators fortunate enough to gain admittance—several hundred who arrived too late waited outside. In the sections reserved for foreign governments, Allied diplomats waited expectantly for the President's words, though German, Italian, and Japanese representatives were conspicuously absent. When the President entered and walked slowly to the reading desk, there was a polite ripple of applause. His features were grim; there was no friendly wave to old colleagues, no trace of his familiar smile.[25]

[24] Transcript of the White House conference, September 20, 1939, FDR Papers, OF 1561, Box 2; Alsop and Kintner, *American White Paper*, pp. 75–76; *New York Times*, September 21, 1939, pp. 1, 16.

[25] *Ibid.*, September 22, 1939, pp. 1, 14, 18; Alsop and Kintner, *American White Paper*, pp. 76–77; "Opening Gun," *Time*, XXXIV (October 2, 1939), 11.

In slow, measured tones, the President began to speak. He reviewed the slow disintegration of peace in the world since 1931 and the development of neutrality legislation by Congress. He dwelt for a moment on the 1935 act. "I regret that Congress passed that act. I regret equally that I signed the act." Then he came to the theme of his appeal—a return to international law. He asked Congress to repeal the arms embargo, which he termed "wholly inconsistent with ancient precepts of the law of nations." Briefly he summarized traditional American neutrality, noting that the only previous departure came with Jefferson's unsuccessful embargo. "I seek reenactment of the historic and traditional American policy which, except for the disastrous interlude of the Embargo and Nonintercourse Acts, has served us well for nearly a century and a half." Though he did not specifically recommend replacing the embargo with a cash-and-carry plan, he stated his belief that the government should keep American citizens and ships away from combat zones, forbid the extension of loans and credits to belligerents, and demand the transfer of title on all exports to nations at war. He asserted that such a program offered "far greater safeguards than we now possess or have ever possessed to protect American lives and property from danger." Then he concluded with a ringing appeal to the overwhelming American desire to remain aloof from the war:

> Destiny first made us, with our sister nations on this hemisphere, joint heirs of European culture. Fate now seems to compel us to assume the task of helping to maintain in the western world a citadel wherein that civilization may be kept alive. The peace, the integrity, and the safety of the Americas—these must be kept firm and serene.[26]

It was a brilliant political speech. With unerring skill, Roosevelt had laid the case for repeal of the embargo on the altar of international law. Always stressing his desire to return to traditional American practice, he made the embargo appear as a dangerous and unwise experiment. He hammered away at the need to protect the United States from involvement in war, and his audience ap-

[26] *Congressional Record,* September 21, 1939, pp. 10–12.

plauded vigorously every time he announced his determination to keep the nation firmly on the path of peace.[27] Yet it was an inconsistent and contradictory statement. In only one regard did Roosevelt actually propose a return to international law—by repeal of the arms embargo. His other proposals—loan ban, combat zones, transfer of title—were all innovations which ran directly counter to the traditional American concept of freedom of the seas. Most significant, Roosevelt was something less than honest with his listeners. Not once did he reveal his deep concern for the fortunes of England and France. Fearful of arousing the isolationists, he disguised his true motive. In doing this, he set the tone for the ensuing debate—for the next six weeks, the administration carried on the elaborate pretense that the sale of arms to the Allies was but the accidental by-product of a program designed solely to keep the United States clear of war.

II

Roosevelt's address placed the issue squarely before Congress and the nation—the administration was asking for the repeal of the arms embargo and the adoption of cash-and-carry restrictions to prevent American involvement in the European war. Congress would have to make the final decision, but to a very large extent the public response would determine the outcome of the struggle. The isolationists, fully aware that they were in a minority in Congress, began an intense effort to persuade the American people to reject the President's program. They launched their appeal in mid-September, a week before the President spoke to Congress, and for the next month they used every available technique of mass communication on behalf of the arms embargo. They arranged for a series of radio speeches by prominent Americans; they directed a massive mailing barrage aimed at individual members of Congress; they held mass rallies in major cities; and they even

[27] Moffat Diary, September 21, 1939.

resorted to dramatic aerial gymnastics, arranging for a woman aviator to drop propaganda leaflets on the White House.[28]

Senator Borah opened this campaign on September 14 with a nationwide radio broadcast. In this speech, which had been planned at a meeting of Republican senators on September 11, Borah charged that the administration's drive for repeal was motivated solely by the desire to aid England and France. "Is not this laying the foundation for intervention—in fact, is it not intervention—in the present European war?" Borah asked his audience.[29] The next evening, the isolationist group, now labeling itself "the peace bloc," presented Charles A. Lindbergh, the great hero of the 1920's, who spoke to the nation over all three major networks. This speech, the first public address Lindbergh had made since 1931, commanded as large an audience as Roosevelt's fireside chat earlier in the month. "I speak tonight," Lindbergh began, "to those people in the United States of America who feel that the destiny of this country does not call for our involvement in European wars." He then forcefully stated his belief that isolation was the only sane policy for the nation to pursue. Although he made no direct mention of the embargo issue, he touched on it obliquely. "We cannot count on victory merely by shipping abroad several thousand airplanes and cannons. We are likely to lose a million men, possibly several million—the best of American youth."[30]

These isolationist appeals had an immediate impact. On September 19 a deluge of mail demanding the retention of the arms

[28] The flyer, Laura Ingalls, used pamphlets prepared by the Women's National Committee To Keep the United States Out of War. *New York Times*, September 27, 1939, p. 27; *Newsweek*, XIV (October 9, 1939), 27–28.

[29] *New York Times*, September 12, 1939, p. 1; *ibid.*, September 15, 1939, p. 1; William Borah, "Retain the Arms Embargo," *Vital Speeches*, V (October 1, 1939), 741–43.

[30] Charles Lindbergh, "Appeal for Isolation," *ibid.*, V, 751–52; *New York Times*, September 16, 1939, p. 1. This speech was arranged by the conservative radio commentator Fulton Lewis, Jr., who met Lindbergh at a Washington dinner party in July. Kenneth S. Davis, *The Hero: Charles A. Lindbergh and the American Dream* (New York, 1959), pp. 386–87.

embargo flowed into Washington. For the next two weeks, individual congressmen and senators found themselves overwhelmed with letters, postcards, and telegrams opposing the administration's program. In three days, a million pieces of mail arrived, with some senators receiving as many as four thousand communications a day. On September 21 the telegraph companies were forced to add new lines to their Capitol offices to handle the huge volume of messages. The ratio in favor of the arms embargo varied from 10 to 1 to as high as 1,000 to 1.[31] Much of the mail was spontaneous—an analysis of the letters received by two members of Congress reveals that only about 15 per cent consisted of form letters. The heaviest concentration came from the Middle West, where Father Coughlin, the Detroit priest, had been issuing pleas to his radio listeners to petition congressmen with letters demanding, "No cash-or-carry, no foreign entanglements and no blood business!"[32] German-American groups also actively stimulated the letter-writing campaign. A breakdown of mail received by a New York congressman showed that German and Irish names were disproportionately large among those protesting against repeal, while English and Jewish names predominated in the messages favoring the administration's program. As the deluge continued through the remainder of the month, only Southern congressmen escaped the pressure. One Southern member of the House received only twenty-five letters on this subject during the entire debate.[33]

There can be no doubt that this flood of mail had a great impact. On September 25 Representative William J. Miller, a Connecticut Republican who had advocated total repeal of all neutrality legislation in the spring, told a State Department official that

[31] *New York Times*, September 21, 1939, p. 16; *ibid.*, September 22, 1939, p. 15; *ibid.*, September 29, 1939, p. 24; "Peace Blizzard," *Newsweek*, XIV (October 2, 1939), 29.

[32] L. E. Gleeck, "96 Congressmen Make Up Their Minds," *Public Opinion Quarterly*, IV (March, 1940), 14–15; text of radio speech by Father Charles E. Coughlin, September 10, 1939, SCP, File 76A-E9.

[33] Gleeck, "96 Congressmen," pp. 15–16; "Peace Blizzard," *Newsweek*, p. 29; Dr. William Knipe to Stephen Early, September 27, 1939, 811.04418/595.

he now favored retaining the arms embargo. Miller then disclosed that he had received nearly 1,800 letters and telegrams, with only 76 favoring the administration's program. Two New Jersey Republicans who leaned toward repeal, Congressman Robert W. Kean and Senator W. Warren Barbour, confided to State Department officers that their mail was running heavily in favor of the arms embargo. Kean stated that he still intended to support repeal, but Barbour said that he was now uncertain how he would vote. The over-all effect is difficult to judge, but at the time political observers felt that the mail had caused the odds favoring a quick administration victory to drop to even money.[34]

The "peace bloc," delighted with this initial response, quickly formulated plans to intensify the campaign. On September 21, following the President's speech to Congress, twenty-four senators gathered in Hiram Johnson's office in the Capitol. When the meeting broke up, Senator Robert La Follette, Jr., Wisconsin Progressive, announced that this group would fight "from hell to breakfast" to prevent repeal of the arms embargo.[35]

During the next three weeks, the isolationists made a supreme effort to win further public support. On September 29 a group of isolationist peace organizations began an "Anti-War Mobilization" in Washington. During the day, delegates called on individual congressmen, and then in the evening they attended a mass rally at the Washington Theatre to hear speeches by Gerald P. Nye, Bennett C. Clark, and Norman Thomas. Two weeks later, the Citizens' National Keep America Out of Foreign War Committee, organized by Hamilton Fish the preceding spring, held another mass meeting at Carnegie Hall in New York City. Senator Nye delivered the featured address, which was carried over the NBC radio network. Ardently defending the arms embargo, Nye

[34] Memorandum of conversation with Representative Miller by Stewart, September 25, 1939, 811.04418/698; memorandum of telephone conversation with Representative Kean by Joseph C. Green, September 22, 1939, 811.04418/585; Moffat Diary, September 22, 1939; *Time*, XXXIV (October 2, 1939), 16.

[35] *New York Times*, September 22, 1939, p. 15; *ibid.*, September 23, 1939, p. 1; *ibid.*, September 24, 1939, p. 27.

declared, "Stark tragedy is the American lot if we permit this repeal to be accomplished. Repeal can be counted definitely the first step in that tramp, tramp of American sons in Europe's war."[36] On October 10 the neutrality bloc gained powerful support from Herbert Hoover, who had favored repeal in the spring. In a nationwide radio broadcast, Hoover offered a compromise proposal. He suggested that Congress enact a modified embargo forbidding the sale of offensive weapons such as bombing planes, poison gas, and submarines, but permitting the export of pursuit planes, anti-aircraft guns, and depth charges. "We would not be throwing the weight of our arms manufacture into European power politics; we would be throwing it toward greater humanity in the world and less destructive war," Hoover declared.[37] Three days later, Lindbergh spoke out again to support Hoover's plan to exempt "defensive arms" from the embargo. But he made clear his fundamental opposition to the sale of munitions, announcing, "I would as soon see our country traffic in opium as in bombs."[38]

By mid-October, despite the strenuous efforts of the neutrality bloc, the campaign to elicit public support was losing its effectiveness. The flow of mail reached its peak in late September, but within two weeks it had dwindled to a trickle.[39] The greatest handicap facing Borah, Nye, and their associates was the lack of financial backing. On September 20, Borah had asked former Republican Senator George Wharton Pepper of Pennsylvania to help raise money. A few days later, Senators Nye and Clark met with Captain Eddie Rickenbacker, president of Eastern Airlines, and J. C. Hormel, the midwestern meat-packer, to discuss raising funds to finance speeches, rallies, and anti-repeal literature. When Henry

[36] *Ibid.*, September 29, 1939, p. 12; *ibid.*, September 30, 1939, p. 7; *ibid.*, October 12, 1939, p. 16; Gerald P. Nye, "Neutrality," *Reference Shelf*, XIV (New York, 1940), 57.

[37] *New York Times*, October 11, 1939, pp. 1, 16.

[38] Charles Lindbergh, "What Our Decision Should Be," *Vital Speeches*, VI (November 1, 1939), 58.

[39] *New York Times*, September 29, 1939, p. 24; Gleeck, "96 Congressmen," p. 15.

Ford issued a strong statement on September 20 calling the existing neutrality act "foolproof" and charging that the munitions makers were behind the repeal effort, a report circulated that the auto-maker would underwrite the cost of the isolationist crusade.[40] However, money from these varied sources was not forthcoming. In early October, Borah told a Chicago supporter that his group's effort to "raise some funds to pay some necessary expenses connected with presenting the cause to the people" had been unsuccessful.[41] Yet even though the isolationists failed to raise the money necessary to continue their campaign, they had been able to reach a broad segment of the American public and thus focus strong pressure on their colleagues in Congress.

III

When President Roosevelt first learned that the neutrality bloc planned to stir up public opinion against his program, he instructed his staff to line up support for repeal among prominent Americans outside the administration. By September 14, Stephen Early reported substantial progress—Alfred M. Landon, Colonel Henry Knox, and Henry L. Stimson all agreed to speak out for the President's program. In addition, Early told Roosevelt that James B. Conant and Karl T. Compton, the presidents of Harvard and the Massachusetts Institute of Technology, would enlist the support of the nation's leading educators. When Borah opened the isolationist campaign with his radio speech on September 14, Roosevelt had already arranged for Colonel Knox to issue a statement in rebuttal. Knox also printed a front-page editorial in the *Chicago News* taking issue with Borah, as did Roy Roberts in the *Kansas City Star*.[42] These statements and editorials by prominent Republicans greatly lessened the impact of Borah's speech.

[40] Borah to Pepper, September 20, 1939, William E. Borah Papers, Library of Congress, Box 427; *New York Times*, September 24, 1939, p. 27; *Commercial and Financial Chronicle*, CXLIX (September 23, 1939), 1850; "War or Peace for America," *Newsweek*, XIV (October 2, 1939), 26.

[41] Borah to Edgar J. Cook, October 4, 1939, Borah Papers, Box 426.

[42] Early to Roosevelt, September 14, 1939, E. Roosevelt, *F.D.R.: His Personal Letters*, II, 921; *Ickes Diary*, III, 7–8.

When the isolationist onslaught began to gain momentum after the opening of Congress, Roosevelt decided to rely entirely on spokesmen outside the administration to carry on the debate. Following his speech on September 21, the President maintained an absolute silence on the whole subject of neutrality. In a letter to Lord Tweedsmuir, the governor-general of Canada, on October 5, Roosevelt wrote, ". . . I am almost literally walking on eggs and, . . . I am at the moment saying nothing, seeing nothing, and hearing nothing."[43] The President also instructed all members of his official family to be equally circumspect, asking them neither to mention the neutrality issue publicly nor to engage in any political discussion. When Harold L. Ickes asked Roosevelt for permission to recommend him for a third term in a radio speech, the President replied, "Wait until we get this neutrality legislation before we discuss any political subject."[44] In late October, Henry A. Wallace violated this instruction at a news conference in San Francisco by stating that the war in Europe compelled Roosevelt to run for the Presidency again in 1940. The next day Roosevelt had Stephen Early publicly rebuke Wallace for this indiscretion.[45]

Yet while the administration remained silent on the neutrality debate, behind the scenes Roosevelt directed a concerted effort to win popular support for his program. When the avalanche of mail began to flow into Congress on September 19, the President had the State Department call in Clark Eichelberger, director of the American Union for Concerted Peace Efforts. Eichelberger, who was a highly effective leader of the collective security wing in the peace movement, had been waging a fight against the embargo since 1938 without any presidential encouragement. When war broke out, he had immediately sent a telegram to Roosevelt pledging the services of his organization in the cause of repeal, but there was no response until the isolationist campaign began to worry the administration. In a conference with Joseph C. Green on Sep-

[43] E. Roosevelt, *F.D.R.: His Personal Letters*, II, 934.

[44] *Ickes Diary*, III, 21–22.

[45] *New York Times*, October 26, 1939, p. 1; *ibid.*, October 27, 1939, p. 12.

tember 19, Eichelberger recommended the formation of a committee to organize and direct an intensive effort to lay the case for repeal before the American people.[46] With the endorsement of the State Department, Eichelberger began working on plans to create such an organization. On September 26, acting on Hull's recommendation, he asked William Allen White, the well-known Republican newspaper editor from Kansas, to lead a group entitled the Non-Partisan Committee for Peace through Revision of the Neutrality Act. White, who had originally supported mandatory neutrality legislation, was at first reluctant, but finally he agreed to assume this responsibility.[47]

The new organization began its activities on October 2 when White disclosed that he had invited several hundred American writers, educators, clergymen, and business leaders to join him in forming a committee to fight for the repeal of the arms embargo. Five days later, White announced that over two hundred prominent Americans had agreed to serve on his committee.[48] For the next few weeks, the White committee conducted an extremely effective publicity campaign. With Frederick McKee, a Pittsburgh industrialist, and Henry Luce, publisher of *Life* and *Time*, providing financial support, this group set up local units in thirty states to win grass-roots backing for repeal.[49] The national office, with Eichelberger in charge, issued a series of press releases to bolster support for neutrality revision. A release on October 9 reported that 90 per cent of college presidents and deans polled by the White committee favored repeal of the arms embargo. Three weeks later, Eichelberger published a statement by thirty well-known Jewish, Catholic, and Protestant religious leaders. "We

[46] Eichelberger to Edward Watson, September 3, 1939, FDR Papers, OF 1561, Box 2; John Masland, "The 'Peace' Groups Join Battle," *Public Opinion Quarterly*, IV (December, 1940), 668–70; Green to Walton Moore, September 19, 1939, 811.04418/696.

[47] Walter Johnson, *William Allen White's America* (New York, 1947), pp. 512, 516–17.

[48] *New York Times*, October 3, 1939, p. 12; *ibid.*, October 8, 1939, p. 38.

[49] Johnson, *White's America*, p. 518.

support revision," the statement read, "because we believe its safeguards are not only best calculated to keep us out of war but will throw the vast moral and material weight of this country on the side of liberty, in which alone religious institutions can flourish."[50]

The White committee particularly concentrated on sponsoring radio broadcasts by prominent Americans to rebut the arguments advanced by Nye, Hoover, and Lindbergh. On October 15, White delivered a speech over a national network in which he frankly urged Americans to stand behind the democracies in their fight against dictator nations. The committee also arranged for a broadcast by Henry L. Stimson on October 5.[51] Two days earlier, Stimson telephoned Hull and read him parts of this speech in which he bluntly argued that repeal of the embargo was necessary in order to help England and France win the war. Hull, who was aghast at this directness, asked Stimson to tone down his remarks, but Stimson refused, saying he would not speak unless he could say what he pleased. After a hurried conference, the State Department decided to let Stimson go ahead. The speech proved so successful that the White committee printed up copies of the text for nationwide distribution.[52] The committee also sponsored an address by Alfred E. Smith designed to appeal to Catholics, many of whom were opposing repeal out of anti-British prejudice. Introduced to his audience as "a prominent Catholic layman," Smith urged all Americans to "stand solidly" behind Roosevelt on neutrality revision.[53]

Although the administration relied primarily on the White committee to influence public opinion, Roosevelt himself took an active, though hidden, role in applying pressure in certain crucial areas. Continually worried over Catholic opposition to repeal, the President arranged with Cardinal Mundelein, the Catholic leader in the Middle West, for Bishop Bernard J. Sheil to deliver a ma-

[50] *New York Times*, October 11, 1939, p. 1; *ibid.*, October 30, 1939, p. 7.

[51] Johnson, *White's America*, p. 517.

[52] Moffat Diary, October 3, 1939; *New York Times*, October 6, 1939, p. 15; printed text of Stimson's speech, HCP, File 76A-F17.3.

[53] *New York Times*, October 2, 1939, p. 1.

jor speech in favor of neutrality revision. Roosevelt sent one of his ablest speech-writers, Tom Corcoran, to Chicago to help Sheil prepare his address, scheduled for October 2. Though Cardinal Mundelein died that morning, Sheil went ahead and delivered the speech, which had a very favorable impact on Catholic opinion.[54] The President also took steps to prevent the American Legion from going on record in favor of retaining the arms embargo, a position championed by National Commander Stephen Chadwick. Assistant Secretary of War Louis Johnson and Federal Security Administrator Paul V. McNutt, both former national commanders, lobbied at the Legion's annual convention in Chicago in behalf of repeal. Colonel Frank Knox also used his influence, and as a result the Legion adopted a noncommittal resolution on the neutrality issue.[55] Finally, at the suggestion of Senator Joseph F. Guffey of Pennsylvania, Roosevelt had Ickes ask John L. Lewis to speak out in favor of repeal at the CIO convention in San Francisco in early October. Lewis agreed, and in his opening address to the meeting he strongly affirmed the President's neutrality program.[56]

At the same time Roosevelt did not neglect his problems in Congress. He held a series of conferences with individual senators and representatives and kept in close touch with Republican legislators.[57] By the end of September, the President was becoming more optimistic. When Vice-President Garner reported at a cabinet meeting on September 29 that "things looked good" in Congress, Roosevelt remarked, according to Ickes, "that he hadn't had

[54] *Ickes Diary*, III, 28–29; *New York Times*, October 3, 1939, p. 15; Frank Knox to Roosevelt, October 4, 1939, FDR Papers, OF 1561, Box 3.

[55] *New York Times*, September 25, 1939, pp. 1, 11; *ibid.*, September 27, 1939, p. 14; *Ickes Diary*, III, 65; Roosevelt to Knox, October 4, 1939, E. Roosevelt, *F.D.R.: His Personal Letters*, II.

[56] *Ickes Diary*, III, 32; *New York Times*, October 11, 1939, p. 20.

[57] Matthew F. McGuire to Roosevelt, September 21, 1939, FDR Papers, PSF, Box 33; press conference No. 583, September 26, 1939, FDR Papers, PPF 1-P, XIV, 195; Edward Watson to Roosevelt, September 27, 1939, FDR Papers, OF 1516, Box 2; Watson to Roosevelt, October 18, 1939, FDR Papers, PSF, Box 33.

to buy a Senator yet." He was highly pleased that his conciliatory tactics had won over a number of conservative Democratic senators, including Carter Glass and Harry F. Byrd of Virginia and Josiah W. Bailey of North Carolina.[58] This optimism was well founded. The White committee had offset the initial success of the isolationist bloc; the nation was slowly rallying behind the President's cautious but skillful leadership. By avoiding the mistakes he had made in the spring, Roosevelt had put the drive for repeal into motion with genuine prospects for a successful outcome in Congress.

IV

The American people, beset by pressures from both the isolationist bloc and the supporters of neutrality revision, slowly began to align themselves behind the President's program. In September, public opinion polls revealed a pronounced shift in sentiment against the arms embargo. When the war broke out in Europe, the people were evenly divided on the question of exporting arms and munitions to the belligerents. However, in a Gallup poll taken in mid-September, 57 per cent of those questioned favored repealing the arms embargo. After the President's speech to Congress, this majority rose to 62 per cent, then leveled off at 60 per cent in early October. Though there was a gradual downward trend until the end of the debate, at no time did sentiment supporting repeal drop below 56 per cent. Regional breakdowns indicated that every section favored repeal, with the strongest backing coming from the South. In the East and Far West, the ratio reflected the national trend, but in the Middle West, only a bare majority—in one poll, 50.5 per cent—supported repeal. In regard to cash-and-carry restrictions, there was very nearly unanimous approval throughout the nation. The Gallup poll in mid-September revealed that 90 per cent of the people wanted belligerents to pay cash for all goods purchased in the United States, while 94 per

[58] *Ickes Diary*, III, 27.

cent wished to ban American ships from carrying cargoes to nations at war.[59]

The nation's newspaper and magazine editors backed the administration's program even more strongly than the general public. In a survey of 50 newspaper executives in early September, *Newsweek* reported that 32 favored immediate repeal of the arms embargo, 13 were undecided, and only 5 were definitely opposed. A *Christian Science Monitor* poll of 120 newspapers showed that 88, with a combined circulation of over eleven million, favored the President's plans for neutrality revision.[60] Among periodicals, only one major magazine, the *Saturday Evening Post*, urged retention of the arms embargo. Even the *New Republic*, which had consistently upheld mandatory neutrality legislation, reversed its stand. In an editorial written just before the outbreak of war, the editors urged the repeal of the arms embargo and the enactment of a comprehensive cash-and-carry law.[61]

Despite the national trend in favor of neutrality revision, sharp divisions of opinion continued to characterize the attitude of pressure groups on this issue. In the economic sector, businessmen displayed an overwhelming sentiment for repeal. The major journals of business opinion attacked the arms embargo, arguing for a return to traditional international law.[62] Labor was more neutral. Though both John L. Lewis and William Green, presidents of the CIO and the AF of L, spoke out strongly in behalf of the administration's program, neither leader was able to secure resolutions for repeal of the arms embargo at the annual conventions

[59] *Public Opinion Quarterly*, IV (March, 1940), 105–8; *New York Times*, September 24, 1939, p. 30.

[60] *Newsweek*, XIV (September 4, 1939), 10; *Christian Science Monitor* clipping, HCP, File 76A-F17.3.

[61] "Phantasy of a Bloodless Sword," *Saturday Evening Post*, CCXII (October 14, 1939), 30, 154; "America's Role in the War," *New Republic*, C (September 6, 1939), 116–17.

[62] "We Are Not Neutral," *Magazine of Wall Street*, LXIV (September 23, 1939), 594; "The Neutrality Embargo," *Barron's*, XIX (September 11, 1939), 10; *Commercial and Financial Chronicle*, CXLIX (September 16, 1939), 1652–53.

of their organizations.[63] Farm interests were hostile to neutrality revision, with only one major farm group, the American Farm Bureau Federation, openly backing the administration's position. In a poll of midwestern farmers conducted by the *Kansas City Star,* 66 per cent registered their support for continuation of the arms embargo.[64] The tight lines of division in the peace movement continued to hold firm throughout the fall of 1939. The isolationist groups, led by the National Council for the Prevention of War, campaigned against neutrality revision, while the internationalist wing joined with the White committee in pressing for repeal of the embargo.[65] The most consistent opposition to revision came from religious groups. The *Christian Century* warned that the sale of arms to England and France would create a vast war boom which would inevitably lead to American involvement in the European conflict. Officials of the Methodist church took a similar position in letters to Senator Pittman.[66] Catholic opinion was equally strong—three leading Catholic periodicals spoke out against repeal, countering with a demand for a total embargo on all trade with belligerents.[67]

As the debate continued, the administration won valuable support from international lawyers. During the effort to repeal the embargo in the spring, Senator Pittman had argued for immediate revision on the grounds that once war broke out, it would be unneutral to alter the legislation.[68] Worried that this argument would

63 *New York Times,* October 3, 1939, p. 1; *ibid.,* October 12, 1939, p. 20.

64 List of organizations supporting repeal of the arms embargo, HCP, File 76A-F17.3; *New York Times,* October 1, 1939, III, 2.

65 Masland, "Peace Groups," p. 670; Frederick J. Libby to Pittman, September 27, 1939, SCP, File 76A-E6.

66 "Keep the Arms Embargo," *Christian Century,* LVI (September 20, 1939), 1126–27; N. C. McPherson to Pittman, September 16, 1939, Charles F. Boss, Jr., to Pittman, September 28, 1939, SCP, File 76A-F9.

67 "Spot Cash," *America,* LXI (October 7, 1939), 613–14; James W. Gillis, "Neutrality?" *Catholic World,* CL (November, 1939), 129–37; "How Will the Neutrality Issue Be Decided?" *Commonweal,* XXX (September 15, 1939), 485–86.

68 "Neutrality," Senate *Hearings,* 76th Cong., 1st sess., p. 1.

be used against repeal, Cordell Hull had asked Roosevelt to refute it in his message to Congress. When the President declined to do so, Hull issued a special statement in which he declared, "This nation, or any neutral nation, has a right during a war to change its national policies whenever experience shows the necessity for such change for the protection of its interests and safety."[69] In a letter to the *New York Times* on September 21, two international lawyers, Charles Cheney Hyde and Philip C. Jessup, challenged Hull's view, charging that repeal of the embargo after the outbreak of war would "in fact and law amount to governmental participation in the conflict." In October the *New York Herald-Tribune* published the results of a poll of international lawyers on this question. Of the thirteen who responded, only three, Hyde, Jessup, and Edwin Borchard, declared that repeal would be a violation of neutral obligations. The other ten sided with Hull, thus strongly bolstering the case for revision.[70]

The most significant gains the administration made during the public debate came from the Republican party. Though Republican leaders had stated in the spring that their party would take no stand on neutrality, the great majority of Republican congressmen had voted against the Bloom bill, and in the crucial vote in the Senate Foreign Relations Committee in July, Republican senators had voted unanimously for postponement of the neutrality issue. After the outbreak of war, Roosevelt's attempts to woo support from his political opponents began to achieve substantial results. In September, Senators Robert A. Taft of Ohio and Wallace H. White of Maine announced their intention of voting for repeal of the arms embargo. On September 26, the National Republican Club, whose members included many prominent industrialists and financiers, voted 46 to 6 to back the administration's neutrality program.[71] A week later, Senator George W.

[69] Stephen Early to R. Walton Moore, September 21, 1939, FDR Papers, OF 1561, Box 2; State Department, *Bulletin*, I (September 23, 1939), 280.

[70] *New York Times*, September 21, 1939, p. 17; *New York Herald-Tribune*, October 25, 1939, p. 1.

[71] "U.S. Is Made Rigidly Neutral," *Newsweek*, XIV (September 18, 1939), 28; *New York Times*, September 27, 1939, p. 16.

Norris of Nebraska, who had voted against war in 1917, delivered a powerful plea for revision on a national radio broadcast. Frankly stating that his sympathies lay with England and France, he stated that repeal "puts us on the side of humanity and civilization."[72] Norris' speech greatly encouraged the administration, for though Norris had left the Republican party in 1936 to become an independent, his views carried great weight among western, progressive Republicans who had traditionally supported rigid neutrality legislation.

These various indexes of American attitudes—the public opinion polls, newspaper editorials, the stands taken by pressure groups, international lawyers, and prominent Republicans—all point to substantial support for the administration's neutrality program throughout the nation. This shift, with its inevitable impact on the congressional decision, cannot be traced to any one factor. The intensive publicity campaign waged by the White committee and the constant efforts of the administration to influence significant segments of the American public undoubtedly contributed to the favorable trend. But probably the course of events in Europe played the decisive role. Germany's invasion of Poland, coming as the culmination of an aggressive campaign to gain mastery over Europe, made a profound impression on the American people. Though their desire to remain aloof from the war was intense, at the same time they could not hide their sympathy for England and France.[73] Few yet saw Hitler as an ultimate threat to American security, but the great majority of Americans were appalled by Germany's totalitarian disregard for human freedom and dignity. Americans were thus torn between two incompatible emotions—their fear of war and their desire for a German defeat.[74] Aware

[72] George W. Norris, "American Neutrality," *Vital Speeches*, V (November 1, 1939), 62–64.

[73] A Gallup poll taken on October 22, 1939 asked the question, "Which side do you want to see win the war?" 84 per cent replied the Allies, 2 per cent Germany, and 14 per cent said neither. Shepardson and Scroggs, *U.S. in World Affairs, 1939*, p. 338.

[74] Raymond Clapper, "America and Neutrality," *Current History*, LI (October, 1939), 39–42.

of this emotional conflict, the administration offered a program tailored to appeal to the American people. By removing the arms embargo, the United States could render aid to England and France; yet by restricting American shipping in the North Atlantic, the nation could avoid the specific risks that led to war in 1917. "What a majority of the American people want," wrote Freda Kirchwey in the *Nation*, "is to be as unneutral as possible without getting into war."[75] Though Roosevelt presented his policy as a return to international law, the American people supported it because it enabled them to aid England and France in a cautious yet significant way.

V

While the neutrality bloc and the administration engaged in their intensive efforts to influence American public opinion, the legislative struggle to repeal the arms embargo began in Congress. At the White House conference on September 20, the Democratic congressional leaders laid out their strategy, agreeing to work in the Senate first. In order to avoid the legislative delay that would face a new bill, the administration decided to have the Senate Foreign Relations Committee draft a substitute to the Bloom bill, which had passed the House with the Vorys amendment the previous June.[76] Then when the Senate acted, the House could agree to the new legislation simply by instructing conferees to accept the Senate substitute. In effect, the Bloom bill would be the vehicle for arms embargo repeal, but it would be entirely rewritten by the Senate committee.

After the President delivered his message to Congress on September 21, Key Pittman met with Senators Tom Connally of Texas and Elbert Thomas of Utah to prepare a preliminary draft bill. They completed this task in two days, relying on technical advice from the State Department's legal adviser, Green H. Hack-

[75] "What Americans Want," *Nation*, CXLIX (September 23, 1939), 307–8.

[76] State Department, *Bulletin*, I (September 23, 1939), 281; *Hull Memoirs*, I, 693.

worth. Then Pittman and Connally decided on an unusual procedure to avoid obstruction by Republican members of the Foreign Relations Committee. Instead of calling the full committee together, Pittman invited eleven Democratic members to meet informally with Connally, Thomas, and himself to revise the first draft. These meetings began on Saturday, September 23, and two days later the Democratic members had agreed on a final revision. Pittman immediately called the White House, telling one of Roosevelt's aides, ". . . we had to make some compromises in the Committee. We got as much as we could."[77]

On September 26, Senator Pittman presented the bill to the full committee. After some discussion and a few minor changes, the committee reported out the measure on September 28 by a vote of 16 to 7. Fifteen Democrats, including four who had voted for postponement in July, supported the bill, along with Republican Wallace H. White of Maine. The seven dissenters included one Democrat (Bennett C. Clark), four Republicans (Borah, Hiram Johnson, Arthur H. Vandenberg, and Arthur Capper), one Progressive (Robert M. La Follette, Jr.), and one Farmer-Laborite (Henrik Shipstead). The margin was impressive, but three members who voted for the bill in committee announced that they reserved the right to reverse their position on the floor of the Senate.[78]

The bill which the Senate committee approved repealed the arms embargo, but in every other respect it embodied the philosophy of mandatory neutrality. In the words of the report, ". . . the committee has written into the proposed substitute definite and mandatory legislation wherever discretion could be eliminated." Its chief feature was a sweeping application of the cash-and-carry

[77] *New York Times*, September 24, 1939, pp. 1, 27; Connally and Steinberg, *Tom Connally*, p. 229; *Congressional Record*, October 2, 1939, p. 50; Edward M. Watson to Roosevelt, September 25, 1939, FDR Papers, PSF, Box 33.

[78] *New York Times*, September 29, 1939, p. 1; *Commercial and Financial Chronicle*, CXLIX (September 30, 1939), 2009. The three senators who indicated that they might vote against the bill were Guy Gillette of Iowa, Robert Reynolds of North Carolina, both Democrats, and Wallace White, the Maine Republican.

formula. All American exports to belligerent ports throughout the world would have to be carried in foreign ships and title would have to be transferred before the goods left the United States. Aside from Western Hemisphere trade south of 30° north latitude and inland commerce with Canada, there were no exemptions for cargoes destined for belligerent territory outside the European war zone—shipments to such areas as Hong Kong, Australia, and South Africa were treated in exactly the same manner as exports to England and France. The President was given authority to ban the entry of American ships, aircraft, or citizens into any area which he designated as a combat zone, but he had no power to make any exceptions to the cash-and-carry provisions. The measure continued the ban on loans and sharply defined the President's authority to permit short-term commercial credits, limiting such arrangements to a ninety-day period. In addition, the bill maintained the ban on American travel on belligerent ships, forbade the arming of American merchant vessels, and preserved the lesser restrictions of the 1937 act. In a further attempt to limit executive discretion, the act could be invoked by Congress as well as by the President whenever either one found a state of war to exist between foreign nations.[79]

The Senate bill was one of the most stringent neutrality measures ever to emerge from the Foreign Relations Committee. In an obvious effort to conciliate isolationists, Senator Pittman had limited executive authority to an irreducible minimum. Only in the matter of proclaiming combat zones was the President given wide latitude. The measure imposed severe restrictions on the American merchant marine, denying it the possibility of trade with English and French colonies in the Pacific, Indian, and South Atlantic Oceans. Nevertheless, the bill did embody the administration's major objective—the repeal of the arms embargo. In the committee report, Senator Pittman echoed Roosevelt's words to Congress in justifying this change in policy. "It is contrary to the accepted precepts of international law which prescribe that any

[79] "Neutrality Act of 1939," *Senate Report No. 1155*, 76th Cong., 2d sess. (Washington, 1939), pp. 1–14.

belligerent may purchase any articles or materials in any neutral country," the report stated. Thus the committee ruled that in order to return to international law in regard to the sale of arms, the United States would have to place ironclad restraints on all trade with belligerent nations.

The Senate, which had adjourned following Roosevelt's speech on September 21, began consideration of the new neutrality measure on October 2. There was an air of tense expectancy in the Senate chamber. Almost every senator was present and the galleries were filled with spectators, the great majority of them isolationists who had come to cheer on Borah, Nye, and Vandenberg.[80] Senator Pittman presented his committee's bill and then delivered the opening speech. He began by affirming the administration's ardent desire to keep the nation at peace, declaring that this goal could be achieved "so long as we conform to the admitted precepts of international law and prevent our citizens from subjecting themselves to destruction in the mad war raging in Europe." He dealt briefly with the arms embargo, labeling it a serious departure from international law which "helps Germany while injuring Great Britain and France." But his great emphasis was on the necessity to enact restrictions on American trade with belligerents. He vigorously denounced the Nye thesis, stating that German attacks on American shipping, not imaginary intrigues by munitions makers and bankers, had led to war in 1917. Only by adopting a rigid system of cash-and-carry control could the United States avoid the loss of life and property which would inevitably result in American involvement in the European conflict. Admitting that his bill would impose serious handicaps on American trade, and especially on the American merchant marine, Pittman maintained that such sacrifice was the price that had to be paid to keep the United States at peace.[81]

When Pittman finished, Senator Borah arose to state the isolationist case. Old and feeble, his once-powerful voice barely audible, Borah leaned on his desk as he read from a manuscript which

[80] *New York Times*, October 3, 1939, pp. 1, 15.

[81] *Congressional Record*, October 2, 1939, pp. 49–55.

Edwin Borchard and Dean Thomas Healey of Georgetown University had helped him prepare.[82] He immediately challenged Pittman's contention that the arms embargo was a departure from the law of nations. "I know of no rule of international law," Borah proclaimed, ". . . which in any way denies the right of a nation to prohibit the sale of arms and munitions." The United States had pledged itself not to export arms to belligerents long before the war began, he continued, and to depart suddenly from that firm position was a flagrant breach of neutrality. The demand for repeal, Borah asserted, "came from the war hounds of Europe." Claiming that the true motive of the administration was to aid England and France, he called repeal "an act of intervention." Turning to the cash-and-carry provisions, he denounced them as a clever subterfuge designed to stimulate a vast war boom in the United States. When the Allies ran out of money, the administration would induce Congress to end the ban on loans, and once again the United States would find itself drawn into a bloody European conflict. To avoid this catastrophe, Borah concluded, the nation had to honor its long-standing commitment to deny the sale of arms and munitions to all belligerents.[83]

These opening speeches set the pattern the two sides would follow for the next four weeks. The administration's spokesmen, following the curt advice of Vice-President Garner "to keep their mouths shut," allowed the isolationists to dominate the debate.[84] In their briefer speeches, advocates of repeal continually affirmed their desire to avoid involvement in the war by restricting American commerce. "We are trying to keep out of war—not get closer to it," exclaimed Tom Connally in a reply to Borah. Senator Sherman Minton of Indiana joined Connally in attacking the isolationists' contention that the export of arms caused American in-

[82] *New York Times*, October 3, 1939, p. 15; memorandum by Healey, September 23, 1939, Borchard to Borah, September 29, 1939, Borah Papers, Box 544.

[83] *Congressional Record*, October 2, 1939, pp. 66–73.

[84] Memorandum by White House staff to Roosevelt, September 21, 1939, F. Roosevelt, *F.D.R.: His Personal Letters*, II, 924.

volvement in the First World War. "Never in the history of our country," Minton declared, "or in the history of any other country did the sale of munitions ever drag a country into war." In 1917, Connally asserted, "we were dragged in by repeated insults and repeated outrages, and repeated murder of American citizens." The only way to avoid a repetition of this experience, these speakers warned, was to replace the arms embargo with the stringent cash-and-carry and combat zone provisions embodied in the Pittman bill.[85]

Throughout the debate, the administration's spokesmen carefully avoided any implication that the purpose of their measure was to enable England and France to buy munitions from the United States. However, a number of Democratic and Republican senators revealed that their support for repeal was based precisely on this consideration. Senator Edward R. Burke of Nebraska, an anti–New Deal Democrat, delivered the frankest speech of the entire debate. Pointing out that the arms embargo gave Germany an advantage over the Allies, Burke declared, "I see no justification on any ground for permitting a law to stand that favors Hitlerism." He then went on to state that American security depended on British and French dominance in Europe and announced that he would vote for the Pittman bill because it would "go far toward insuring victory for the European democracies." Senator Robert A. Taft expressed a similar attitude when he declared that the arms embargo "favors the aggressor against the peaceful nation." A southern Democrat, Kenneth McKellar of Tennessee, was more outspoken. "I shall vote for repeal of the embargo," he announced, "because it operates to injure two of the great democracies of the world, France and England."[86] Though these sentiments undoubtedly were shared by virtually all proponents of the Pittman bill, the majority of speakers advocating repeal refrained from disclosing their views. As a result, the de-

[85] *Congressional Record,* October 4, 1939, pp. 83, 92; *ibid.,* October 14, 1939, pp. 435–36; *ibid.,* October 23, 1939, p. 745.

[86] *Ibid.,* October 11, 1939, pp. 285–91; *ibid.,* October 13, 1939, p. 358; *ibid.,* October 29, 1939, p. 653.

bate had an artificial quality, with the real issue at stake being carefully hidden by profuse oratory portraying the Pittman bill as a measure designed solely to keep the nation out of war.

The opponents of revision, frustrated by the administration's refusal to reveal its sympathy for England and France, responded by hammering away at one basic argument—repeal was an unneutral act which would lead directly to American entry into the war. Senator Vandenberg delivered the most cogent and effective speech on this theme. "We are guided by the one, single, hard-headed thought that to repeal the arms embargo is to strike down a great, indispensable, insulating defense against our involvement in this war," he declared. "In the long run, I do not believe we can become an arsenal for one belligerent without becoming a target for another." Almost every senator who spoke against the Pittman bill echoed this assertion, calling repeal "the first step toward war," "a definite move toward intervention," and "a proposition to enter the war by the left hand, to become the neutral ally of England and France." Once the arms embargo was lifted, the succeeding stages in American involvement in the conflict "will follow with the inevitability of Greek tragedy," declared Senator Henry Cabot Lodge, Jr.[87] Other speakers, recalling the original arguments for the adoption of the arms embargo, denounced the sale of munitions as "immoral," "inhumane," and "un-Christian." "We want to sell guns to make a profit, even if it bathes the earth in mothers' tears," asserted a South Dakota Republican, while Rush Holt, a West Virginia Democrat, declared, "The issue, in plain language, is, Shall the United States of America become a merchant of death?"[88]

As the debate continued, the isolationists indignantly charged that their opponents were distorting the issue when they stated that the choice lay between the arms embargo and the cash-and-carry restrictions. Senators Nye, Clark, and Vandenberg repeat-

[87] *Ibid.*, October 4, 1939, pp. 96, 98; *ibid.*, October 10, 1939, pp. 250–51; *ibid.*, October 12, 1939, p. 325; *ibid.*, October 13, 1939, p. 382; *ibid.*, October 19, 1939, p. 592.

[88] *Ibid.*, October 12, 1939, p. 310; *ibid.*, October 18, 1939, p. 541.

edly announced their wholehearted support of the cash-and-carry system, which they wished to see adopted in addition to, not in place of, the arms embargo. Clark reminded the Senate that he had supported the cash-and-carry concept since 1935, while Nye declared, "I hope to see both the arms embargo and the cash-and-carry plan made the law of the land."[89] In an effort to sustain this position, Senator Charles W. Tobey of New Hampshire proposed a motion to adopt the cash-and-carry formula immediately, postponing the question of repealing the arms embargo until the regular session of Congress in January. On October 10 the Senate defeated this motion by the overwhelming vote of 65 to 26.[90]

The decisive rejection of Tobey's motion was a clear sign that the administration had more than enough votes to carry through its program in the Senate. After a week of debate, the isolationists were in a futile position. Public interest had quickly vanished—the galleries were no longer filled and the flow of mail to Congress had subsided. Each day fewer senators entered the chamber, and many appeared only after repeated calls for a quorum. Day after day, isolationists read long speeches from prepared manuscripts while the dozen or so senators quietly dozed in their chairs. Nevertheless, the opponents of repeal continued to speak in the hope of enlisting support in the House of Representatives.[91]

While the Senate moved slowly toward repeal of the arms embargo, American commercial interests began an intensive lobbying campaign against the cash-and-carry restrictions in the Pittman bill. Export associations, representatives of the shipping industry, and local chambers of commerce adopted resolutions of protest, sent a stream of telegrams and letters to the White House, the State Department, and the Senate Foreign Relations

[89] *Ibid.*, October 4, 1939, p. 101; *ibid.*, October 5, 1939, p. 113; *ibid.*, October 11, 1939, pp. 269–70.

[90] *Ibid.*, October 4, 1939, p. 106; *ibid.*, October 10, 1939, p. 237.

[91] *New York Times*, October 7, 1939, p. 1; *ibid.*, October 17, 1939, p. 1; *ibid.*, October 22, 1939, IV, 6; "History in the Making," *Current History*, LI (November, 1939), 6–7; Kenneth G. Crawford, "Shadowboxing in Congress," *Nation*, CXLIX (October 14, 1939), 403–6.

Committee, and met in person with individual congressmen and senators. The National Foreign Trade Council, holding its annual convention in New York in early October, passed a strongly worded resolution condemning both the transfer of title and the shipping provisions of the proposed legislation. "It is the considered opinion of this Convention," the resolution stated, "that the peace and security of the United States will not be safeguarded by drastic restrictions on American trade and shipping." On October 13 the Maritime Association of the Port of New York sent President Roosevelt a resolution denouncing the cash-and-carry proposals and warning that they would have a "calamitous" impact on the American economy.[92] Exporting groups from the West Coast sent William L. Montgomery, manager of the San Francisco Chamber of Commerce, to Washington to express their views to the administration. Montgomery conferred with Senator Pittman, officials of both the State Department and the United States Maritime Commission, and individual congressmen and senators from the West Coast, telling them that the application of cash-and-carry restrictions on American shipping to Hong Kong, Singapore, and other British possessions in the Far East would cripple American commerce in the Pacific. The State Department also received strong resolutions of protest from American chambers of commerce in Johannesburg, Manila, and Shanghai which Hull passed along to Congress.[93]

This powerful pressure from American business groups stimulated a movement in the Senate to liberalize the cash-and-carry provisions. On October 7, Senator Josiah W. Bailey, chairman of the Senate Commerce Committee, invited several Democratic

[92] *Report of the Twenty-sixth National Trade Convention* (New York, 1940), pp. xvi–xvii; P. B. Blanchard to Roosevelt, October 13, 1939, 811.04418/677.

[93] Memorandum of conversation with William L. Montgomery by Maxwell M. Hamilton, October 6, 1939, 811.04418/679; resolution of Pacific Coast Chambers of Commerce, October 3, 1939, SCP, File 76A-E6; resolutions of American Chambers of Commerce, Johannesburg, Manila, and Shanghai, October 6, 12, and 13, 1939, HCP, File 76A-D14.

members of the Foreign Relations Committee to meet with Rear Admiral Emory S. Land, chairman of the United States Maritime Commission. Admiral Land pointed out the potentially disastrous effects of the neutrality bill on American shipping, but Senator Pittman remained adamant, announcing his opposition to any changes in the cash-and-carry provisions. Three days later, Bailey brought the issue before the Senate. Using material prepared by the Maritime Commission, Bailey showed that the restrictions would force the withdrawal of at least 130 American vessels from service and deprive 9,000 American seamen of their jobs. The next day, Senator Wallace White of Maine took up the same theme. Calling cash-and-carry a "surrender of American rights," he warned that it would have a disruptive effect on the entire American economy. "In this proposed legislation," White declared, "we are depriving American business and agriculture of their export market."[94] These appeals won widespread support from isolationists as well as advocates of repeal. On October 12, Senator Hiram Johnson, one of the staunchest backers of the arms embargo, handed Pittman a proposed amendment to permit American vessels to trade with belligerent ports in the Pacific.[95]

In the face of this pressure, Pittman began to reconsider his earlier stand. He invited both White and Bailey to submit draft amendments to the cash-and-carry sections of the bill and he agreed to call a meeting of the Democratic members of the Foreign Relations Committee to consider these proposals. On October 13, Senator Bailey handed Pittman a draft of an amendment which would permit American vessels to enter belligerent ports in the Indian and Pacific oceans and along the Atlantic coast of the Western Hemisphere. "I cannot see that we run any risk by this amendment," Bailey told Pittman. "The principle we follow is the principle of avoiding danger. . . ." Bailey also sent this amendment

[94] *New York Times*, October 8, 1939, p. 39; *Congressional Record*, October 10, 1939, pp. 248–49; *ibid.*, October 11, 1939, p. 294.

[95] Pittman to Walter George, October 12, 1939, SCP, File 76A-E6.

to the White House, asking Roosevelt to use his influence in winning Pittman's approval.[96]

The State Department also entered into the discussions on cash-and-carry restrictions. On October 14, Hull called for a series of staff meetings at which Herbert Feis, the economic adviser, warned that the restrictions in the Pittman bill would greatly injure the American economy. Feis told Hull that officials of the Maritime Commission and the War and Navy Departments were asking the State Department to take "the initiative" in asking Congress to modify the shipping limitations. The next day, Sunday, October 15, Hull's aides drew up a sweeping amendment limiting the ban on shipping to the North Atlantic. Hull took this draft to Roosevelt that afternoon, and though the President sent it on to Pittman, the Nevada senator refused to accept it.[97]

The pressures from American business interests continued to mount. On October 16, Eugene P. Thomas and Cresswell M. Micou, officials of the National Foreign Trade Council, called at the State Department, and Assistant Secretary George S. Messersmith made appointments for them to see Senators Pittman and Bailey. "I told them," Messersmith recorded, "that it was much better to take up this matter with them than with us." Thomas and Micou met with Pittman later that day and endorsed the State Department proposal to limit the shipping ban to the combat area in the Atlantic.[98] Finally, on October 18, Pittman met with Democratic members of his committee and they worked out a compromise amendment. Under this proposal, American ships would be permitted to travel to belligerent ports in the Indian and Pacific oceans and in Latin America provided that they did not carry any arms, ammunition, or implements of war. The next

[96] Pittman to White, October 12, 1939, Pittman to Bailey, October 12, 1939, Pittman to Walter George, October 12, 1939, and Bailey to Pittman, October 13, 1939, SCP, File 76A-E6; Bailey to Roosevelt, October 14, 1939, FDR Papers, PSF, Box 33.

[97] Moffat Diary, October 14 and 15, 1939; Feis to Hull, October 14, 1939, 811.04418/698; *Hull Memoirs*, I, 694.

[98] Messersmith to Green H. Hackworth, October 16, 1939, 811.04418/749; telegram from Thomas to Pittman, October 18, 1939, SCP, File 76A-E6.

day Pittman and Senator Tom Connally jointly introduced this amendment in the Senate.[99]

The Pittman-Connally amendment failed to satisfy American commercial interests. Soon after it was made public, American shipping companies engaging in trade with British and French possessions on the Atlantic coast of Africa bombarded Pittman with protests. They pointed out that the amendment failed to permit American vessels to trade with this area and that as a result, they would have to suspend their operations. These complaints were reinforced by protests to the State Department from the Union of South Africa. On October 24, Hull forwarded the South African protests to Pittman and asked him to broaden his amendment to include the Atlantic coast of Africa south of 30° north latitude.[100] At the same time, the National Foreign Trade Council urged Pittman to remove the transfer of title restrictions on all American exports to belligerent ports in the Indian, Pacific, and South Atlantic Oceans. In a series of letters to Pittman, Eugene Thomas argued that the transfer of title clause worked a great hardship on American exporters, preventing them from shipping goods to belligerent ports on a consignment basis. "Our exporters," he wrote, "feel that there is no reasonable justification for discriminating against American owned commercial cargoes, and that they should be permitted to go wherever American vessels are permitted."[101]

Though Pittman refused to sponsor any further changes, he finally agreed to allow Senator Connally to offer additional amendments to permit American ships to trade at belligerent ports in West Africa south of 30° north latitude and to waive the transfer of title provision for cargoes destined for all belligerent ports

[99] *New York Times,* October 19, 1939, p. 1; undated memorandum from Connally to Pittman, SCP, File 76A-E6; *Congressional Record,* October 19, 1939, pp. 602–3.

[100] SCP, File 76A-E6; memorandums of conversations with Ralph W. Close by Hull, October 18 and 23, 1939, 811.04418/700 and 706; Hull to Pittman, October 24, 1939, *FR: 1939,* I, 679–80.

[101] Thomas to Pittman, October 20 and 21, 1939, SCP, File 76A-E6.

where American ships were permitted to trade. On October 24, the Senate accepted the Pittman and Connally amendments, which in effect confined the cash-and-carry restrictions solely to the North Atlantic area.[102] Thus American commercial interests succeeded in removing the stringent limitations that Pittman had originally written into his bill. The administration had objected to these provisions, but it dared not make them an issue for fear of jeopardizing the chances for repeal of the arms embargo. There is no evidence that the executive branch solicited the protests from shipping and export groups, but Roosevelt and Hull used the spontaneous outcry from the business community as a lever to overcome Pittman's insistence on rigid cash-and-carry restrictions.

While the struggle to liberalize the cash-and-carry sections was taking place, the neutrality bloc continued to voice its opposition to repeal of the embargo from the floor of the Senate. On October 24, after several unsuccessful efforts, Senator Alben W. Barkley, the Democratic majority leader, was finally able to secure a unanimous consent agreement to begin consideration of amendments to the Pittman bill. After agreeing to liberalize the cash-and-carry provisions, the Senate accepted an amendment by Pittman to strike out the clause permitting the President to grant short-term commercial credits for periods up to ninety days. This provision had been bitterly attacked by many senators, and Pittman made this concession in hopes of speeding up final passage of his bill.[103] For the next three days, the isolationists offered a series of amendments which were defeated by heavy majorities. The most intensive debate came on a proposal by Senator Robert M. La Follette, Jr., to establish trade quotas limiting exports of every commodity to the average exported to each belligerent nation in the four years prior to the war. The Senate rejected this proposal by a vote of 67 to 22.[104]

The debate finally reached an end on October 27. Senator Bennett C. Clark offered the last amendment—a proposal to restore

[102] Memorandum of conversation with Ralph W. Close by Hull, October 23, 1939, 811.04418/706; *Congressional Record*, October 24, 1939, pp. 780–90.

[103] *Ibid.*, p. 776.

[104] *Ibid.*, October 25, 1939, pp. 841–56.

the arms embargo. It was defeated by a vote of 60 to 33. Then shortly before nine in the evening, the Senate passed the Pittman bill, 63 to 30. After almost four weeks of debate, in which seventy senators joined in a chorus of more than one million words, the administration had achieved its cherished goal. An analysis of the vote reveals that eight Republicans crossed party lines to support the Pittman bill, while twelve Democrats opposed it. Regionally, the administration won its greatest support in the Northeast and the South. The western senators were more evenly divided, approving the bill by a margin of only four votes.[105]

This substantial victory in the Senate was a tribute to President Roosevelt's skillful leadership. By working quietly behind the scenes, he won the support of conservative Democrats who had consistently opposed him on domestic issues. In asking Byrnes and Connally to take charge of the debate in the Senate, he had insured the strong support from the South which transformed a close issue into a clear-cut triumph. The appeal to the symbol of international law, the careful avoidance of all political activity, and the willingness to accept limitations on American commerce with the belligerent powers in Europe all contributed to the final outcome. But the most important factor was the powerful public backing which the administration had been able to arouse through the efforts of the White committee. The American people did not want to retain an embargo on arms which favored Hitler and penalized England and France.

VI

Final passage of the new neutrality bill now rested with the House of Representatives, which had been marking time while the lengthy Senate debate took place. Administration leaders,

[105] *Ibid.*, October 27, 1939, pp. 1022–24; *New York Times*, October 28, 1939, p. 1. The sectional and party breakdowns are as follows:

Section	*Yes*	*No*
Northeast	15	7
South	23	2
Middle West	14	12
Far West	11	9

Party	*Yes*	*No*
Democratic	54	12
Republican	8	15
Other	1	3

who had been concentrating their attention on the Senate since early September, became concerned with the problem of favorable action in the House in mid-October. At a cabinet meeting on October 13, Postmaster-General James A. Farley reported that he had checked with House leaders and they were certain of a strong majority. However, Vice-President Garner disagreed, pointing out that both Speaker Bankhead and Majority Leader Rayburn were out of town and that "nobody knew just how the situation stood in the House." Roosevelt, remembering the fate of the Bloom bill in the spring, ordered Farley "to get after the House situation." At the next cabinet meeting, held on October 19, Farley had alarming news, announcing that Irish Catholic representatives were leading a revolt against the neutrality bill.[106]

During the next week, the administration began using every possible means of influencing the outcome in the House. While Farley worked on Democratic congressmen, Roosevelt called on Republicans for help. The President told Gifford Pinchot, former Republican governor of Pennsylvania, that the House was "kicking up its heels." "Do what you can with such Members of Congress as you can work on," Roosevelt wrote. Frank Knox again offered his aid, sending every Republican congressman an editorial from the *Chicago Daily News* urging repeal of the arms embargo. William Allen White appealed to Joseph Martin, the House minority leader, to persuade Republican congressmen to vote for the Pittman bill. "Personally," White told Martin, "I would hate to have my party put itself in a posture where it can be charged that we played Mr. Hitler's game in the matter of the embargo."[107] These tactics proved effective. When the cabinet met again on October 28, Garner expressed his belief that the neutrality bill would pass the House "with some twenty to forty votes to spare." Two days later, Senator Josh Lee of Oklahoma reported that he had talked to the Oklahoma congressional delegation as Roose-

[106] *Ickes Diary*, III, 38, 43.

[107] Roosevelt to Pinchot, October 26, 1939, E. Roosevelt, *F.D.R.: His Personal Letters*, II, 946; Knox to Roosevelt, October 30, 1939, FDR Papers, PPF 4083; White to Martin, October 23, 1939, in Walter Johnson (ed.), *Selected Letters of William Allen White* (New York, 1947), p. 399.

velt had requested and had persuaded the entire group to agree to vote for the Pittman bill.[108] Yet despite these encouraging reports, the administration leaders had reason to fear that the House, larger and more difficult to handle than the Senate, might still reject their program.

The House began its consideration of the neutrality issue on October 31 when the Rules Committee reported a motion to disagree with the Senate amendments to the Bloom bill and call for a conference. This maneuver was designed to prevent a long debate. If the rule was accepted, the House would then proceed to decide whether or not to instruct the conferees to insist on any amendments to the Pittman bill. This debate would be limited to ten hours, with each side given equal time. The Republicans bitterly assailed the action of the Rules Committee, demanding the right to a full and free debate. Hamilton Fish denounced the motion as "one of the most vicious gag rules ever written in the history of the House." However, the House quickly voted to accept the recommendation of the Rules Committee by a vote of 237 to 177.[109]

For the next three days, the House engaged in a fierce debate marked by brief, sharply worded speeches, frequent emotional outbursts, and a brutal frankness that laid bare the central issues. The question before the House was a motion by Representative James A. Shanley, a Connecticut Democrat, to instruct the conferees to insist on the retention of the arms embargo when they met with representatives of the Senate in the conference committee. Shanley, who had voted for repeal in the spring, took the position that it was unneutral for the United States to alter its neutrality policy after the outbreak of war. He cited Edwin Borchard, who was one of his constituents, in maintaining that repeal at this time would be a flagrant denial of "the historic traditions and precepts of the founding fathers of the country."[110] The administration leaders, carefully keeping Sol Bloom out of the debate,

[108] *Ickes Diary*, III, 51; memorandum of telephone conversation with Lee by Henry M. Kannee, October 31, 1939, FDR Papers, OF 1561, Box 3.

[109] *Congressional Record*, October 31, 1939, pp. 1092–1103.

[110] *Ibid.*, October 31, 1939, pp. 1104, 1116–17; *ibid.*, November 2, 1939, pp. 1337–39.

had two southern congressmen, Luther A. Johnson of Texas and James P. Richards of South Carolina, reply to Shanley. They portrayed the arms embargo as a measure designed to discourage nations from engaging in war. Now that a major conflict had broken out, they said it was time for the United States to abandon the old policy and adopt a new one to meet the present crisis—the threat to American ships and American lives on the high seas. By replacing the arms embargo with the cash-and-carry safeguards, declared Johnson, the United States would be doing "what we think is for the best interests of our country." National security, not the technicalities of international law, should be the touchstone of American policy.[111]

As the debate progressed, the advocates of repeal frankly expressed their desire to aid England and France. They pictured the conflict in Europe as a struggle between democracy and dictatorship which the United States could not ignore. "If you really love American institutions, which are the outgrowth of English ideals," declared an Oregon congressman, "you simply cannot be indifferent to the struggle in Europe. I want those fighting in Europe on our side to share our stores." Representative John McCormack of Massachusetts, who had supported the embargo in the spring, now attacked it because it aided atheistic dictators. "As Americans we should put our country in a position where the results of our law do not help the anti-God forces of the world and do not penalize those that stand for the existence and the permanence of religion, of Christianity, and of democracy."[112] Other speakers argued that American security as well as American ideals were at stake in the European war. "I feel that our self-interest requires that England and France not be crushed in the war," declared Representative John R. Murdoch of Arizona, while Congressman William I. Sirovich of New York called England and France "our first line of defense" and claimed that the United States held "a vested interest in an Allied victory."[113]

[111] *Ibid.*, November 2, 1939, pp. 1284–86, 1301.

[112] *Ibid.*, November 1, 1939, pp. 1168–70; *ibid.*, November 2, 1939, p. 1300.

[113] *Ibid.*, October 31, 1939, pp. 1150–51; *ibid.*, November 1, 1939, p. 1244.

The neutrality bloc met these arguments head on. First, they reiterated the familiar assertion that repeal of the embargo would involve the United States in the European conflict. "There are just three steps which will lead us inevitably into war," declared Representative Dewey Short, a Missouri Republican. "First, we furnish munitions; second, we furnish money; and, finally, we furnish men."[114] The isolationists also condemned their opponents' willingness to sponsor the sale of weapons of destruction and thereby contribute to the "diabolical, unChristian, brutal murder" of millions of Europeans. "I submit that there is a distinction between those things which destroy life and those things which preserve life," asserted a Michigan congressman. "This bill makes it easier to ship bombs and bullets and harder to ship bread and butter."[115] Finally, the opponents of repeal ridiculed the argument that the European war was a struggle between democracy and dictatorship which imperiled American security. Representative Martin L. Sweeney of Ohio condemned England and France as "synthetic democracies" which "hold in subjection in their colonies today millions and millions of black men, yellow men, and white men." A New York congressman denied that democracy was at stake in the European war, declaring, "It is but another page in the bloody history of Europe's continuous fight for the balance of power." And Representative Dewey Short emphatically proclaimed, "For our own sake, for humanity's sake, for God's sake, let us save democracy in America and not again send our sons to foreign fields to die for democracy where it is already dead."[116]

The debate reached its climax on November 2. Before voting on the Shanley motion, the House considered a compromise proposal by Representative John M. Vorys of Ohio to instruct the conferees to insist on a limited embargo which would forbid the sale of arms and ammunitions but permit the export of implements of war. This proposal was identical to the amendment which Vorys

[114] *Ibid.*, November 1, 1939, p. 1167.

[115] *Ibid.*, November 2, 1939, pp. 1309, 1312–13.

[116] *Ibid.*, November 1, 1939, pp. 1169, 1227; *ibid.*, November 2, 1939, pp. 1314–15.

had succeeded in attaching to the Bloom bill in the spring. But now the administration's lines held firm. The House voted down the Vorys proposal and then rejected the Shanley motion by a vote of 243 to 181, a margin of 62 votes, some 30 more than the administration had expected.[117] In this crucial division, congressmen hewed closely to party lines—37 Democrats voted for the arms embargo while 24 Republicans declared for repeal. The sectional breakdown reveals the key to the administration's victory. A majority of the representatives from the Northeast and the Midwest supported the Shanley motion, but Southern congressmen voted 110 to 8 against it.[118] The solid Democratic South, won over by Roosevelt's conciliatory tactics, had delivered the decisive votes to repeal the arms embargo.

The next morning, November 3, a conference committee composed of five representatives and six senators met to agree on the final form of the legislation. The House conferees, unencumbered by any binding instructions, quickly accepted the Pittman bill as amended by the Senate, and after a few technical refinements, the committee reported out this measure. Though four Republicans, Senators Borah and Johnson and Representatives Fish and Charles A. Eaton, refused to sign the report, both Houses accepted it after very brief debates. The final vote was 55 to 24 in the Senate and 243 to 172 in the House.[119] With this action, Congress had completed its task—the arms embargo was repealed.

The President was delighted with this news. When reporters asked him for his reaction, he grinned broadly and commented, "The most terse way of putting it is that I am very glad that the

[117] *Ibid.*, November 2, 1939, pp. 1343–45; Moffat Diary, November 2, 1939.

[118] The sectional and party division on the Shanley motion was as follows:

Section	*Yes*	*No*
Northeast	65	59
South	8	110
Middle West	94	46
Far West	14	28

Party	*Yes*	*No*
Democratic	37	217
Republican	142	24
Other	2	2

[119] "Neutrality Act of 1939," *House Report No. 1475*, 76th Cong., 2d sess. (Washington, 1939); *Congressional Record*, November 3, 1939, pp. 1352–56, 1381–88.

bill has restored the historic position of the neutrality of the United States." He then announced that he was inviting a dozen congressional leaders, including four Republicans, to witness his signing of the legislation the next day.[120] At noon on November 4, Secretary of State Hull, Vice-President Garner, Speaker Bankhead, Senators Pittman, Barkley, Byrnes, and McNary, and Congressmen Rayburn, Bloom, and Boland gathered at the White House. With newsreel cameras recording the ceremony, Roosevelt signed the bill using two pens, which he presented to Pittman and Bloom.[121] The President then issued a proclamation defining a war zone which encompassed the Bay of Biscay, all waters adjacent to Great Britain and Ireland, the English Channel, the North Sea, and the Baltic. No American ship could enter this area even if destined for a neutral port. The Mediterranean and Black Seas were not included, but American vessels could not call at any belligerent ports in these waters.[122] The restrictions on loans and passenger travel in the 1937 act were continued under the new legislation. American ships and American-owned cargoes were permitted to go to all belligerent ports in the Indian, Pacific, and South Atlantic oceans. However, American vessels were not allowed to carry arms, ammunition, or implements of war to belligerent ports in these areas. Thus, in essence, the new legislation made only two vital changes in American neutrality policy. From this time forward, American exporters could ship arms, ammunition, and implements of war to belligerents, but all trade with the nations at war in Europe would be conducted in foreign ships, with title to the cargoes passing out of American hands before the goods left the United States.

VII

The repeal of the arms embargo and the adoption of the limited cash-and-carry formula gave England and France a tremendous

[120] *New York Times*, November 4, 1939, p. 8.

[121] *Ibid.*, November 5, 1939, p. 1.

[122] State Department, *Bulletin*, I (November 4, 1939), 455.

boost. When the Senate acted favorably on October 27, there was great rejoicing in London. Though government officials refused to comment, the English press printed headlines proclaiming "Allied Victory in the United States" and "A Smashing Blow to Germany."[123] On November 8, Prime Minister Chamberlain wrote a warm letter of appreciation to Roosevelt, stating that the measure was "a profound moral encouragement to us in the struggle upon which we are engaged." In a public speech the next day, Chamberlain declared, "The repeal of the Neutrality Act of the United States is a momentous event, for, while it affords America the means of maintaining her neutrality, it reopens for the Allies the doors of the greatest storehouse of supplies in the world."[124] Though France placed substantial orders for munitions and war supplies, England did not take immediate advantage of her new opportunity. Fearful of depleting their dollar reserves, the British did not begin large-scale purchasing of war material in the United States until the German invasion of France in 1940.[125] Nonetheless, the fact that the United States was abandoning its former attitude of aloofness toward the European struggle gave Britain new hope that the United States would take more active steps in the future to insure an Allied victory. Above all else, the repeal of the arms embargo was a symbol of American sympathy for the European democracies in their struggle against Nazi Germany.

For isolationists in the United States, the revision of the neutrality act came as an emotional shock. Many had become firm believers in the Nye thesis—they were convinced that the sale of munitions was inherently evil and could only lead to national disaster. Many liberal Democrats, eager to follow Roosevelt's leadership, found themselves unable to accept his reasoning on the arms embargo. In a letter to President Roosevelt on November 3, Representative Jerry Voorhis of California explained why he felt compelled to vote for the Shanley motion. "All my life," he wrote,

[123] *New York Times*, October 28, 1939, p. 1.

[124] *FR: 1939*, I, 681; *New York Times*, November 10, 1939, p. 6.

[125] *Hull Memoirs*, I, 700.

"I have believed the munitions traffic to be wrong and in the face of the tragic situation of today, I am compelled to cling to certain fundamentals of belief or lose my moorings."[126] To other isolationists, whose views were conditioned more by fear of European entanglement than distaste over the sale of arms, the new neutrality law was an act of hypocrisy. Senator Borah, in a letter to an Idaho constituent, termed the cash-and-carry plan "the most sordid and cowardly piece of legislation ever written upon the statute books of this country." "Lying back of all this maneuvering," Borah believed, "is the desire to break down the traditional foreign policy of the United States and to associate ourselves in practically everything of importance that comes up in Europe in which Great Britain is deeply interested."[127]

The administration leaders, though deeply pleased with the congressional decision, found it difficult to rejoice. "I could not help feeling," wrote Hull in his *Memoirs*, "that our victory would have been far more effective for the cause of the peace-loving nations if it could have been gained in the spring and summer of 1939 rather than in the autumn."[128] Roosevelt, too, must have felt remorseful at the failure of the United States to act until the war had brought home the need for a new policy. From the beginning of the neutrality struggle, he had played an equivocal role. Failing to realize the strength of the isolationist forces, he had first encouraged the Nye committee to enter into the subject of neutrality legislation. When he belatedly discovered the overpowering desire of the American people to avoid war at all costs in 1935, he shrank from an open contest, contenting himself with a cryptic warning that neutrality legislation might encourage rather than deter war. Working toward the goal of executive discretion, he had tried to moderate the isolationist impulse in 1936 and 1937 with little success. As his own realization of American responsibility for European stability gradually developed, he attempted to educate

[126] Voorhis to Roosevelt, November 3, 1939, 811.04418/806.

[127] Borah to Jess Hawley, October 31, 1939, Borah Papers, Box 426.

[128] *Hull Memoirs*, I, 697.

Congress in his new understanding. But his efforts, both in the quarantine speech and in the more concrete attempt to repeal the arms embargo early in 1939, were handicapped by his domestic political reverses and his resultant unwillingness to state his views forthrightly. Only when the reality of war finally began transforming public opinion did he move effectively to revise the neutrality legislation. And even then he had to compromise, accepting the cash-and-carry restrictions as the necessary price for repeal of the arms embargo.

Yet the responsibility for neutrality legislation does not rest solely, or even primarily, on Roosevelt. It was the small but highly effective neutrality bloc in Congress—Gerald P. Nye, Bennett C. Clark, and Hamilton Fish in particular—who developed the concept of legislating against war and fought with grim determination to force it upon a reluctant administration. And the weakness of Key Pittman, who failed to exercise his authority as chairman of the Senate Foreign Relations Committee, also contributed heavily. But in the last analysis, the ultimate responsibility lies with the American people. They accepted the glib historical doctrine that munitions makers and bankers led the nation into war in 1917; they applauded the single-track investigation of the Nye committee; they affirmed the arms embargo, the ban on loans, and the curb on passenger travel as a panacea that would prevent American involvement in world conflict. It was also the American people, however, who dictated at least the partial abandonment of mandatory neutrality when it failed to accord with the realities of the world situation. As Americans watched Hitler's career of aggression in Europe, they discovered that they did believe in the high ideals Cordell Hull so often set forth. Repelled by the seizure of Czechoslovakia and sickened by the invasion of Poland, they found themselves unable to maintain a posture of aloof impartiality toward the European war.

The neutrality act of 1939 was a perfect expression of the contradictory mood of the American people. They strongly favored the cause of England and France, yet they did not want to risk American involvement in the European conflict. Unwilling to resolve this dilemma, they backed a policy whereby they could render aid to the Allies without directly committing themselves to intervention in the war. Cash-and-carry neutrality was an illogical policy, yet it was exactly what the nation wanted. In the course of the next two years, the American people, reacting to the succession of German triumphs in the battlefield, moved closer and closer to war, but they still maintained their fierce determination to avoid the final plunge. In November, 1941, Congress finally enacted a further revision of the neutrality act, allowing American merchant ships to cross the Atlantic, enter a war zone where German submarines were taking a daily toll of shipping, and travel to British ports. Yet, even in remnant form, the neutrality act continued until the Japanese assault on Pearl Harbor resolved the contradiction in American policy and put an end to an experiment that had long since failed.

BIBLIOGRAPHICAL ESSAY

The historical literature on American foreign policy in the 1930's suffers from two critical weaknesses. The intense interest in American entry into World War II has led American historians to neglect diplomatic developments in the years prior to 1939. In addition, the continuing controversy between revisionist writers and authors sympathetic to Franklin D. Roosevelt's foreign policy has distorted much of the work that has been done on the earlier period. Seeking to find evidence to substantiate their theses on American entry into the war, many writers have failed to evaluate the administration's diplomatic efforts in the context of the mid-1930's. As a result, the literature has a theological quality which obscures rather than illuminates the diplomatic history of the New Deal years.

On the specific subject of neutrality legislation, there have been two periods of intense output. In the late 1930's, a number of scholars interested in current American foreign policy attempted to trace the major outlines of the neutrality struggle and evaluate the resulting legislation. Then, immediately after the war, several doctoral dissertations were written on this subject which relied largely on the printed sources available at that time. After 1950, many manuscript materials became available for scholarly research. It is the purpose of this essay to discuss and evaluate both the sources and the literature upon which this study is based.

General

BIBLIOGRAPHICAL AIDS

The most thorough bibliographical guides for this period are the volumes published by the Council on Foreign Relations, R. G. Woolbert, *Foreign Affairs Bibliography, 1932–1942* (New York, 1945), and William L. Langer, *Foreign Affairs Bibliography, 1919–1932* (New York, 1933). Library of Congress, *Recent References on Neutrality* (Washington, 1941), and Carnegie Endowment for International Peace, *Neutrality* (New York, 1938), provide more detailed lists for this specific subject. Oscar Handlin *et al.*, *Harvard Guide to American History* (Cambridge, 1954), contains an excellent selection of books on foreign policy published before 1952. More recent works can be found in the book review sections and the lists of articles in the *American Historical Review* and the *Mississippi Valley Historical Review*. Wayne S. Cole has written a very penetrating historiographical article on the period of the 1930's, "American Entry into World War II: A Historiographical Appraisal," *Mississippi Valley Historical Review*, XLIII (March, 1957), 595–617.

MANUSCRIPT SOURCES

Archives.—The fundamental sources for a study of any aspect of American foreign policy in the 1930's are the files of the Department of State in the National Archives. These materials are open to qualified researchers without restriction for the years prior to 1930. For the period from 1930 to 1942, permission must be secured from the Office of the Historical Adviser, and all notes taken must be submitted to this office for review. The policy is very liberal, and, at least in my case, there was very little editing of the notes. The State Department files are arranged by a decimal system according to countries and subjects, and there is an excellent cross-reference system which greatly simplifies their use. In general, the Department's files are most useful for correspondence between the State Department and American diplomats abroad. There is less material on the development of policy inside the Department. Memorandums indicating final decisions reached are common, but there are few papers which reveal the clash of opinion between Department officials and the various alternatives which were considered on each issue. In the area of neutrality legislation, the bulk of the significant papers is located in files 811.113 and 811.04418.

Congressional manuscript materials are also located in the National Archives in Washington. The papers of the two congressional committees concerned with foreign policy—the Senate Foreign Relations

Committee and the House Foreign Affairs Committee—contain a wide variety of material, including printed copies of bills, letters from constituents and pressure groups, petitions and memorials, and occasionally copies of letters from the committee chairman to individuals and to the Secretary of State. This last category is by far the most significant, for it often reveals the actual sentiments of key congressional leaders. Access to the Senate committee materials is unrestricted; permission to use the House committee papers must be secured from the Clerk of the House, and no direct quotations are permitted from these files. For neutrality legislation, the papers of the Special Senate Committee Investigating the Munitions Industry proved valuable. Most of the material consists of the documentary evidence collected by the committee's staff in the course of the investigation and which was subsequently published in the committee hearings. The letter files, especially those of the committee's secretary, Stephen Raushenbush, contain a great deal of information on the role of the committee in sponsoring neutrality legislation. There is no file of Senator Nye's letters in this collection.

Personal Papers and Diaries.—The Franklin D. Roosevelt Papers, located in the Roosevelt Library at Hyde Park, New York, are an indispensable source for a study of neutrality legislation. The bulk of the material on this subject is in Official File 1561. In addition, there is correspondence relating to neutrality in the President's Personal Files and the President's Secretary's File. In particular, Roosevelt's correspondence with R. Walton Moore in PPF 1820 and with Key Pittman in PPF 745 is extremely helpful. The stenographic record of the President's press conferences is also useful.

The J. Pierrepont Moffat Papers in the Houghton Library at Harvard University are a vital collection for neutrality legislation. Moffat, who served in the State Department from 1933 to 1935, and again from 1937 to 1940, kept a very full diary which gives information on the internal developments in the Department of State which are not recorded in the Department's files. There are also files of Moffat's correspondence, which contain a few letters dealing with neutrality matters.

The Norman H. Davis Papers in the Library of Congress are very useful for the period from 1933 to 1935. Davis' correspondence with

Joseph C. Green in the summer of 1935 provides a wealth of information on the events behind the passage of the first neutrality act.

The William E. Borah Papers in the Library of Congress form a vast collection, but are very disappointing on neutrality. There are only a few scattered references to this subject in the letter files.

The Key Pittman Papers and the Tom Connally Papers in the Library of Congress are totally devoid of any material on the neutrality legislation. This is most surprising in the case of Pittman, since he played a primary role in this development.

PRINTED SOURCES

Governmental.—The published congressional materials form a major source for the study of neutrality legislation. The *Congressional Record* contains the record of speeches and debate on this subject from 1928 to 1939. The various *Hearings* of the two congressional committees concerned with foreign affairs provide a full record of the views of individuals and pressure groups which were interested in neutrality. Finally, the many *Reports* of the congressional committees provide the text of the bills sent to the floor of Congress and also the arguments for and against their passage.

The State Department publication of diplomatic papers, *Foreign Relations of the United States,* contains many of the most noteworthy documents in the Department files for the years from 1933 to 1939. Other significant documents are printed in Department of State, *Peace and War: United States Foreign Policy, 1931–1941* (Washington, 1943), State Department, *Press Releases,* until June 30, 1939, and State Department, *Bulletin,* from July 1, 1939, on. The administration of the arms embargo is summarized in "Second Annual Report of the National Munitions Control Board," *House Document No. 465,* 75th Congress, 3d session (Washington, 1938), and "Third Annual Report of the National Munitions Control Board," *House Document No.* 92, 76th Congress, 1st session (Washington, 1939).

Aspects of British policy which bear on the neutrality legislation are contained in E. L. Woodward and Rohan Butler (eds.), *Documents on British Foreign Policy, 1919–1939,* Ser. 2 (London, 1940 ——).

Private.—Samuel Rosenman (ed.), *The Public Papers and Addresses of Franklin D. Roosevelt* (13 vols.; New York, 1938–50), provides a full, but not complete, record of the President's public statements. Many of the speeches contain only excerpts, and there is only a small selection of the stenographic record of Roosevelt's press conferences. These volumes also contain notes by President Roosevelt, though there is evidence which indicates that these notes were drafted by Rosenman and merely revised by Roosevelt himself. Elliott Roosevelt (ed.), *F.D.R.: His Personal Letters, 1928–1945* (2 vols.; New York, 1950), is a selection of the President's correspondence from the files of the Roosevelt Papers.

A small sampling of the vast amount of material in the Moffat Diary is provided in Nancy Harvison Hooker (ed.), *The Moffat Papers* (Cambridge, Mass., 1956).

NEWSPAPERS AND PERIODICALS

Newspapers.—The files of the *New York Times* provide an indispensable public record of the neutrality legislation. The Washington staff of the *Times* consistently reported the major developments in neutrality throughout the 1930's, and the manuscript materials now available reveal the astonishing accuracy of these newsmen. The *Times* is also valuable for revealing the statements and views of pressure groups on this subject. Editorially, the *Times* was bitterly critical of neutrality legislation.

Periodicals.—For general developments in American foreign policy in the 1930's, *Foreign Affairs*, *American Journal of International Law*, and *Proceedings of the American Society of International Law* are excellent. The volumes of the *Proceedings* for 1933 and 1935 contain valuable articles reflecting the intense division of opinion among international lawyers on the problem of neutrality.

General news magazines helpful toward providing understanding of the neutrality issue are *Literary Digest* and *Today* down through 1936, and *Newsweek*, *Time*, and *Current History* for the later period. *Vital Speeches* prints the full text of many significant speeches on neutrality in 1939.

The *Nation* and *New Republic* were both vitally concerned with the neutrality issue throughout the 1930's. The *Nation* consistently opposed mandatory legislation and advocated collective security measures; *New Republic* championed rigid neutrality until the fall of 1939.

The views of Protestant isolationists and pacifists are expressed in *Christian Century*. The divergent trends in Protestant attitudes toward neutrality are revealed in Federal Council of the Churches of Christ in America, *Annual Report* and *Federal Council Bulletin*. *Commonweal* and *America* gave Catholic views on neutrality, which were strongly isolationist.

The organ of the National Council for the Prevention of War, *Peace Action*, is a prime source for the isolationist wing of the peace movement. The views of the internationalist wing can be found in *International Conciliation*, published by the Carnegie Endowment for International Peace.

Business opinion can be sampled in the editorial pages of *Business Week*, *Commercial and Financial Chronicle*, *Barron's*, and *Magazine of Wall Street*. For exporting groups, the most valuable publications are *Export Trade and Shipper*, *American Exporter*, *Reports* of the National Foreign Trade Conventions (New York, 1935–39), and Chamber of Commerce of the State of New York, *Monthly Bulletin*.

MEMOIRS

There is a vast literature of memoirs and personal reminiscences by individuals active in the Roosevelt administration, but most of these books deal exclusively with the domestic aspect of the New Deal. The one great exception is *The Memoirs of Cordell Hull* (2 vols.; New York, 1948). Though Hull tends to overplay his opposition to neutrality legislation, especially in the drive for revision in 1939, this is a reasonably accurate and full account of his role as Secretary of State. *The Secret Diary of Harold L. Ickes* (3 vols.; New York, 1953–54) deals largely with domestic matters, but there are a number of important entries, especially on cabinet meetings, relating to neutrality. Tom Connally and Alfred Steinberg, *My Name Is Tom Connally* (New York, 1954), and Samuel I. Rosenman, *Working with Roosevelt* (New York, 1952), are less useful on this subject. There is some interesting material on Henry Morgenthau's correspondence with Neville Chamberlain in regard to neutrality legislation in John Blum, *From the Morgenthau Diaries: Years of Crisis, 1928–1938* (Boston, 1959). Henry L. Stimson's views on neutrality are briefly summarized in Henry L. Stimson and McGeorge Bundy, *On Active Service in Peace and War* (New York, 1947). Raymond Moley, *After Seven Years* (New York, 1939), gives valuable insight into the economic nationalism of one of Roosevelt's early advisers who strongly supported the development of mandatory neutrality. Dorothy Detzer gives an illuminating account of her role as a lobbyist for the peace movement in Dorothy Detzer, *Appointment on the Hill* (New York, 1948).

GENERAL WORKS

Two volumes of the *Chronicles of America* series by Allan Nevins, *The United States in a Chaotic World, 1920–1933* (New Haven, 1950), and *The New Deal and World Affairs, 1933–1945* (New Haven, 1950), provide a broad survey of American foreign policy on the interwar years. In *American Foreign Policy in the Making, 1932–1940* (New Haven, 1946), Charles A. Beard expounds the thesis that Roosevelt followed an isolationist policy throughout the early 1930's and misled the American people when he shifted to an internationalist policy near the end of the decade. A more virulent attack on Roosevelt is made by Charles C. Tansill in his *Back Door to War* (Chicago, 1952). Using mainly State Department files, Tansill is extremely inconsistent and haphazard in his emphasis, neglecting almost completely the whole issue of neutrality legislation. Basil Rauch, *Roosevelt from Munich to Pearl Harbor* (New York, 1950), written as a rebuttal to Beard, is a highly uncritical account of Roosevelt's foreign policy based on the questionable assumption that the President was a strong internationalist throughout the 1930's. Donald Drummond, *The Passing of American Neutrality* (Ann Arbor, 1955), is an excellent survey of American foreign policy after 1939 which contains a good summary of the neutrality issue of the 1930's in the first chapter. The most thorough treatment of America's foreign policy in the late 1930's is William L. Langer and S. Everett Gleason, *The Challenge to Isolation, 1937–1940* (New York, 1952). The sections on the drive for revision of the neutrality legislation in 1939 are very comprehensive and illuminating.

Three accounts by journalists which give insight into American foreign policy in the late 1920's and early 1930's are Frank Simonds, *American Foreign Policy in the Post-war Years* (Baltimore, 1935),

Drew Pearson and Constantine Brown, *The American Diplomatic Game* (New York, 1935), and Ernest K. Lindley, *Half-way with Roosevelt* (New York, 1937). Denna F. Fleming, *The United States and World Organization, 1920–1933* (New York, 1938), is a full account of American relations with the League written from an internationalist viewpoint. Richard N. Current gives a more critical analysis of the concept of collective security in "The United States and 'Collective Security': Notes on the History of an Idea," in Alexander DeConde (ed.), *Isolation and Security* (Durham, N.C., 1957), pp. 33–55. Aspects of isolationism in the 1930's are developed in Selig Adler, *The Isolationist Impulse* (New York, 1957), George L. Grassmuck, *Sectional Biases in Congress on Foreign Policy* (Baltimore, 1951), and Alexander DeConde, "On Twentieth-Century Isolationism," in DeConde, *Isolation and Security*, pp. 3–32. Albert C. F. Westphal, *The House Committee on Foreign Affairs* (New York, 1942), is an institutional analysis which sheds some light on the committee's role in neutrality legislation.

The most thorough accounts of the development of neutrality legislation appear in the annual surveys of American foreign policy prepared by the Council on Foreign Relations, *The United States in World Affairs*, written by Walter Lippmann in 1933, and by Whitney H. Shepardson and W. O. Scroggs for the years from 1933 to 1939. Briefer accounts appear in the Royal Institute's annual *Survey of International Affairs*, edited by Arnold J. Toynbee. Elton Atwater, *American Regulation of Arms Exports* (Washington, 1941), provides an excellent study of the evolution of arms embargo legislation, though it is based primarily on published sources. Contemporary accounts by critics of mandatory neutrality include Charles G. Fenwick, *American Neutrality, Trial and Failure* (New York, 1940), and Allen W. Dulles and Hamilton Fish Armstrong, *Can America Stay Neutral?* (New York, 1939), while Edwin Borchard and W. P. Lage, *Neutrality for the United States* (New Haven, 1937), written from the viewpoint of traditional international law, is sharply critical of the effort to enact discriminatory embargoes. Another contemporary account, Philip C. Jessup and Francis Deak, *Neutrality: Its History, Economics, and Law* (4 vols.; New York, 1936), argues for a policy of co-operation among neutrals. James M. Seavey, *Neutrality Legislation in the United States* (Washington, 1939), is a brief summary of American neutrality statutes since 1794.

Three unpublished doctoral dissertations dealing with neutrality legislation in the late 1930's are C. Richard Cleary, "Congress, the Executive, and Neutrality: 1935–1940" (Ph.D. diss., Fordham University, 1953), Earl R. Cain, "Analysis of the Neutrality Debates, 1935–1941" (Ph.D. diss., Northwestern University, 1950), and John C. Donovan, "Congress and the Making of Neutrality Legislation, 1935–1939" (Ph.D. diss., Harvard University, 1949). Donovan has written an article, "Congressional Isolationists and the Roosevelt Foreign Policy," *World Politics*, III (April, 1951), 299–316, in which he develops the thesis that Roosevelt had little choice but to accept the program forced on him by isolationists in Congress who supported his domestic reforms.

The standard history of the peace movement, Merle Curti, *Peace or War: The American Struggle, 1636–1936* (New York, 1936), has a brief account of pacifist attitudes toward neutrality. Robert H. Ferrell, "The Peace Movement," in DeConde, *Isolation and Security*, pp. 82–106, and Robert Bowers, "The American Peace Movement, 1933–1941" (Ph.D. diss., University of Wisconsin, 1950), provide a more thorough analysis of the peace movement in the 1930's and its relationship to neutrality legislation. The attitudes of two important pressure groups are developed in Roscoe Baker, *The American Legion and American Foreign Policy* (New York, 1954), and Roland N. Stromberg, "American Business and the Approach of War, 1935–1941," *Journal of Economic History*, XIII (Winter, 1953), 58–78. Hadley Cantril and Mildred Strunk (eds.), *Public Opinion, 1935–1946* (Princeton, 1951), is a compilation of public opinion polls that is extremely useful for gauging popular attitudes.

There are a large number of biographies of Franklin D. Roosevelt. The most penetrating, and certainly the fullest on the neutrality issue, is James MacGregor Burns, *Roosevelt: The Lion and the Fox* (New York, 1956). Edgar E. Robinson, *The Roosevelt Leadership, 1933–1945* (Philadelphia, 1955), is less satisfactory, but it does contain an excellent commentary on the Roosevelt literature. Harold B. Hinton, *Cordell Hull* (New York, 1942), is a journalistic account of Hull's career which has been superseded by the Secretary's *Memoirs*. Two conflicting interpretations of Henry L. Stimson's public service are given in Richard Current, *Secretary Stimson: A Study in Statecraft* (New Brunswick, N.J., 1954), which is highly critical, and in Elting E. Morison, *Turmoil and Tradition* (Boston, 1960), which is warmly sympathetic. Neither deals very fully with Stimson's views on neutrality.

Wayne S. Cole evaluates Key Pittman as a moderate isolationist in "Senator Key Pittman and American Neutrality Policies, 1933–1940," *Mississippi Valley Historical Review*, XLVI (March, 1960), 644–62.

The New Neutrality, 1927–33

GOVERNMENTAL SOURCES

The reaction to the Burton resolution is given in "Exportation of Arms, Munitions, or Implements of War to Belligerent Nations," *Hearings before the House Committee on Foreign Affairs*, 70th Congress, 1st session (Washington, 1929). The committee views are disclosed in "To Prohibit the Exportation of Arms, Munitions, or Implements of War to Belligerent Nations," *House Report No. 492*, 70th Congress, 1st session (Washington, 1928). "Prohibiting the Exportation of Arms or Munitions of War from the United States to Certain Countries," *Hearing before the House Committee on Foreign Affairs*, 70th Congress, 2d session (Washington, 1929), consists of Secretary of State Kellogg's views on the question of arms embargoes. "Exportation of Arms or Munitions of War," *Hearings before the House Committee on Foreign Affairs*, 72d Congress, 2d session (Washington, 1933), and "Prohibit the Exportation of Arms or Munitions of War from the United States under Certain Circumstances," *House Report No. 2040*, 72d Congress, 2d session (Washington, 1933), deal with the Hoover administration's attempt to enact a discretionary arms embargo in early 1933. The unsuccessful effort of the Roosevelt administration to achieve this same objective can be traced in "Exportation of Arms or Munitions of War," *Hearings before the House Committee on Foreign Affairs*, 73d Congress, 1st session (Washington, 1933), "Prohibit the Exportation of Arms or Munitions of War from the United States under Certain Conditions," *House Report No. 22*, 73d Congress, 1st session (Washington, 1933), and "Prohibiting the Exportation of Arms or Munitions of War," *Senate Report No. 101*, 73d Congress, 1st session (Washington, 1933).

CONTEMPORARY ARTICLES AND BOOKS

The fullest account of the Burton and Capper resolutions is Joseph P. Chamberlain, "The Embargo Resolutions and Neutrality," *Interna-*

tional Conciliation, No. 251 (June, 1929), pp. 259–342. Other significant aspects of the new neutrality are developed in *Annals of the American Academy of Political and Social Science*, CXLIV (July, 1929), a symposium on ways of strengthening the Kellogg pact, Philip C. Jessup, "American Neutrality and International Policies," *World Peace Foundation Pamphlets*, XI, No. 3 (Boston, 1928), and "American Neutrality and League Wars," *Foreign Policy Reports*, IV (March 30, 1928), 19–34. James T. Shotwell, *On the Rim of the Abyss* (New York, 1936), and Evans Clark (ed.), *Boycotts and Peace* (New York, 1932), argue for a policy of sanctions against aggressors. The clearest statement of the new neutrality is Henry L. Stimson's speech before the Council on Foreign Relations in 1932, "The Pact of Paris: Three Years of Development," *Foreign Affairs*, XI (Special Supplement, October, 1932), i–ix. John Bassett Moore, "An Appeal to Reason," *Foreign Affairs*, XI (July, 1933), 547–88, is a powerful isolationist reply to Stimson by an eminent international lawyer.

SPECIAL STUDIES

The best study of the evolution of the Kellogg pact is Robert H. Ferrell, *Peace in Their Time* (New Haven, 1952). Among the many accounts of the Manchurian incident, the most useful are Sara R. Smith, *The Manchurian Crisis, 1931–1932* (New York, 1948), and Robert H. Ferrell, *American Diplomacy in the Great Depression* (New Haven, 1957). Ferrell's book also contains a good summary of the contributions of the Hoover administration to the Geneva Disarmament Conference. Merze Tate, *The United States and Armaments* (Cambridge, Mass., 1948), is illuminating on this conference, while Benjamin Williams, *The United States and Disarmament* (New York, 1931), deals with earlier disarmament efforts of the 1920's.

The Nye Committee and the First Neutrality Act, 1934–35

GOVERNMENTAL SOURCES

The text of the Chaco arms embargo is given in "Prohibit the Sale of Arms or Munitions of War," *Senate Report No. 1153*, 73d Congress,

2d session (Washington, 1934) and "Prohibit Sale of Arms or Munitions of War in the United States under Certain Conditions," *House Report No. 1727*, 73d Congress, 2d session (Washington, 1934). "Investigation of the Munitions Industry," *Hearings before the Special Senate Committee Investigating the Munitions Industry*, 73d and 74th Congresses (39 parts; Washington, 1934–36), contains the voluminous record of the proceedings and exhibits of the Nye committee. The conclusions and legislative recommendations which resulted from this investigation are presented in detail in "Munitions Industry," *Senate Report No. 944*, 74th Congress, 2d session (7 parts; Washington, 1936). Parts 5 and 6 of this report deal extensively with the neutrality issue. The prevailing views on neutrality in 1935 are expressed in "American Neutrality Policy," *Hearings before the House Committee on Foreign Affairs*, 74th Congress, 1st session (Washington, 1935). "Prohibition of Export of Arms and War Munitions," *Senate Report No. 1419*, 74th Congress, 1st session (Washington, 1935), gives the text of the compromise neutrality bill which was finally passed by Congress.

CONTEMPORARY ARTICLES AND BOOKS

"Arms and Men," *Fortune*, IX (March, 1934), 52–57, 113–26, Helmuth C. Engelbrecht and F. C. Hanighen, *Merchants of Death* (New York, 1934), and Gilbert Seldes, *Iron, Blood, and Profits: An Exposure of the World-wide Munitions Racket* (New York, 1934), are the most influential exposés of the munitions industry of the 1930's. More objective accounts of the nature and significance of the arms trade are William T. Stone, *International Traffic in Arms* (New York, 1933), and "Arms Manufacturers and the Public," *Foreign Affairs*, XII (July, 1934), 639–53. William T. Stone, "The Munitions Industry," *Foreign Policy Reports*, X (December 5, 1934), 250–68, is an excellent summary of the first series of hearings held by the Nye committee.

The development of revisionist interpretation in regard to American entry into World War I is fully treated in Richard Leopold, "The Problems of American Intervention, 1917: An Historical Retrospect," *World Politics*, II (April, 1950), 405–25. The most influential revisionist account to appear in 1935 is Walter Millis, *Road to War: America, 1914–1917* (Boston, 1935).

Charles Warren, the first writer to suggest a policy of limiting neutral rights by domestic legislation, sets forth his views fully in "Troubles of a Neutral," *Foreign Affairs*, XII (April, 1934), 377–94, and "Prepare for Neutrality," *Yale Review*, XXIV (March, 1935), 467–78. Allen W. Dulles, "The Cost of Peace," *Foreign Affairs*, XII (July, 1934), 567–78, is a reply to Warren by an advocate of collective security. The views of Warren and other international lawyers are discussed at length in a symposium on neutrality printed in *Proceedings of the Academy of Political Science*, XVI (January, 1935).

SPECIAL STUDIES

The best account of the final defeat of the World Court is Denna F. Fleming, *The United States and the World Court* (New York, 1945).

The Trade Issue, 1936–37

GOVERNMENTAL SOURCES

The administration's effort to establish a trade quota system to govern the export of raw materials to belligerents, and the controversy this proposal evoked, are revealed in "American Neutrality Policy," *Hearings before the House Committee on Foreign Affairs*, 74th Congress, 2d session (Washington, 1936), and "Neutrality," *Hearings before the Senate Committee on Foreign Relations*, 74th Congress, 2d session (Washington, 1936). "Extending and Amending the Joint Resolution Approved August 31, 1935," *House Report No. 2001*, 74th Congress, 2d session (Washington, 1936), and "Report Accompanying Senate Joint Resolution 198," *Senate Report No. 1557*, 74th Congress, 2d session (Washington, 1936), record the congressional decision to extend the 1935 act for another year. The fight over cash-and-carry and the conflict between the House and the Senate over the limits of presidential discretion in 1937 can be traced in "American Neutrality Policy," *Hearings before the House Committee on Foreign Affairs*, 75th Congress, 1st session (Washington, 1937), "Neutrality," *Hearing before the Senate Committee on Foreign Relations*, 75th Congress, 1st session (Washington, 1937), "Neutrality Act of 1937," *House Report No. 363*, 75th Congress, 1st session (Washington, 1937), and "Amendments to the Neutrality Act," *Senate Report No. 118*, 75th Congress, 1st session (Washington, 1937).

CONTEMPORARY ARTICLES AND BOOKS

Charles Warren gave an incisive analysis of the competing concepts of neutrality in 1936 in "Congress and Neutrality," in Quincy Wright (ed.), *Neutrality and Collective Security* (Chicago, 1936). Warren developed his own belief in the need to restrict the export of raw materials in "Safeguards to Neutrality," *Foreign Affairs,* XIV (January, 1936), 199–215. Charles A. Beard provided the most reasoned arguments for mandatory neutrality in a series of articles in the *New Republic,* "Peace for America: The Devil Theory of History and War," LXXXVI (March 4, 1936), 100–102; "Solving Domestic Crises by War," LXXXVI (March 11, 1936), 127–29; and "In Time of Peace Prepare for War," LXXXVI (March 18, 1936), 156–59. Bernard M. Baruch put forth the idea for cash-and-carry in three articles, "Cash and Carry," *Today,* V (November 2, 1935), 6–7; "Neutrality," *Current History,* XLIV (June, 1936), 32–44; and "Neutrality and Common Sense," *Atlantic Monthly,* CLIX (March, 1937), 368–72. "A Study of Neutrality Legislation," *International Conciliation,* No. 316 (January, 1936), pp. 1–61, is a detailed description of the proposals of the collective security wing of the peace movement for discriminatory embargoes against aggressors. Walter Lippmann analyzed the inconsistencies in the 1937 neutrality act in "Rough-hew Them How We Will," *Foreign Affairs,* XV (July, 1937), 587–94.

SPECIAL STUDIES

American policy toward Italy in the Ethiopian crisis is described in Herbert Feis, *Seen from E.A.* (New York, 1947). John Norman gives an excellent account of the attitude of Italian-Americans toward neutrality legislation during the Ethiopian War in "Influence of Pro-Fascist Propaganda on American Neutrality, 1935–1936," in Dwight E. Lee and George E. McReynolds (eds.), *Essays in History and International Relations* (Worcester, Mass., 1949), pp. 193–214. The second volume of F. P. Walters, *A History of the League of Nations* (2 vols.; London, 1952), provides a full account of the League's effort to apply sanctions against Italy.

The Drive for Revision, 1938–39

GOVERNMENTAL SOURCES

The many conflicting views on American neutrality policy in the spring of 1939 are revealed in "Neutrality, Peace Legislation, and Our Foreign Policy," *Hearings before the Senate Committee on Foreign Relations*, 76th Congress, 1st session (Washington, 1939), and "American Neutrality Legislation," *Hearings before the House Committee on Foreign Affairs*, 76th Congress, 1st session (Washington, 1939). The text of the Bloom bill is given in "Neutrality Act of 1939," *House Report No. 856*, 76th Congress, 1st session (Washington, 1939). The proposals for repeal in the fall of 1939 are described in "Neutrality Act of 1939," *Senate Report No. 1155*, 76th Congress, 2d session (Washington, 1939), and "Neutrality Act of 1939," *House Report No. 1475*, 76th Congress, 2d session (Washington, 1939).

CONTEMPORARY ARTICLES AND BOOKS

The issues of *Amerasia* for the latter half of 1937 contain many items on American policy toward Japan's invasion of China. An article by Francis O. Wilcox, "The Neutrality Fight in Congress, 1939," *American Political Science Review*, XXXIII (October, 1939), 811–25, analyzes the unsuccessful effort to repeal the arms embargo in the spring of 1939. Joseph Alsop and Robert Kintner, *American White Paper* (New York, 1940), gives a breezy, but substantially accurate, account of the fight for repeal. Porter Sargent, *Getting Us into War* (Boston, 1941), contains some interesting material relating the activities of the collective security wing of the peace movement to business interests.

SPECIAL STUDIES

F. Jay Taylor, *The United States and the Spanish Civil War* (New York, 1956), is a thorough account which stresses the significance of the Spanish arms embargo. The impact of the Far Eastern war on American commercial interests is developed in W. C. Johnstone, *The United States and Japan's New Order* (New York, 1941), and John W. Masland, "Commercial Influence upon American Far Eastern

Policy, 1937–1941," *Pacific Historical Review,* XI (September, 1942), 281–99. Dorothy Borg views Roosevelt's quarantine speech as a sincere effort to find a new basis for American co-operation with other neutrals against aggressors in her article, "Notes on Roosevelt's 'Quarantine' Speech," *Political Science Quarterly,* LXXII (September, 1957), 405–33.

The role of William Allen White and his committee in the drive for repeal in the fall of 1939 is fully developed in Walter Johnson, *William Allen White's America* (New York, 1947). Kenneth S. Davis, *The Hero: Charles A. Lindbergh and the American Dream* (New York, 1959), traces Lindbergh's contributions to the isolationist campaign against repeal. John Masland, "The 'Peace' Groups Join Battle," *Public Opinion Quarterly,* IV (December, 1940), 664–73, and L. E. Gleeck, "96 Congressmen Make Up Their Minds," *Public Opinion Quarterly,* IV (March, 1940), 3–24, are both very useful studies of the pressure techniques employed in the embargo fight in the fall of 1939.

INDEX

PRINTED IN U.S.A.